ATTENTION
MAILROOM
FROM: THE PUBLISHER

The objective of THE PRISON MANUAL is to educate prisoners on how to do their time productively and in a positive manner. We encourage reflection, education, and rehabilitation. It is our hope that THE PRISON MANUAL will show and encourage prisoners to use their time as a tool for positive growth so they can get out of prison and become productive members of society.

THE PRISON MANUAL does **NOT** contain:

The promotion of gangs or violence
The promotion of being non-compliant with prison officials
Information on making weapons or pruno
Information about drugs, escaping or smuggling contraband
Nudity or sexual acts

If you have any questions or concerns, please feel free to contact us at 888.950.8253; thecellblock.net@mail.com

Thank you,

TCB staff

THE CELL BLOCK PRESENTS...

THE PRISON MANUAL

The Guide to Surviving the American Prison System

Published by: THE CELL BLOCK™

THE CELL BLOCK
P.O. Box 1025
Rancho Cordova, CA 95741

Corrinks: info@thecellblock.net
Instagram: @mikeenemigo
Facebook.com/thecellblock.net

Cover design by Mike Enemigo

Send comments, reviews, or other business inquiries:
info@thecellblock.net
Visit our website: thecellblock.net

CONTENTS

FOREWORD

I was arrested February 23, 1999 and sentenced to life without the possibility of parole at the end of 2002. Since that time, with the exception of drug abuse, homosexuality and snitchin', I've participated in just about every aspect of the prison lifestyle and experience one can. I won't get into too many details because that would likely make this book too controversial and difficult to get into the prisons, which is counterproductive. This book is not about prison shenanigans or the promotion of them. This is a book of jewels – how to do your time as comfortable as possible and avoid some of the pitfalls and mistakes I and other contributors have learned over the years, and often the hard way. With this book, I hope to educate and guide you through the treacherous terrains of the American prison system and point out the wisest way to travel, so that you can get to the finish line successfully, should you be lucky enough to have one. May you get through your time safely, learn all that you can, get out and never come back. Fuck prison.

Without further ado, let's get to it.

Sincerely,

M.

CHAPTER 1
USE YOUR TIME WISLEY

I understand that you are probably in prison for something that you did not do. Or, maybe you did *something*, but *not* what "they" said you did. Maybe you did do a crime, but the prosecutor railroaded you and you were given way too much time for what it is you actually did. Or, maybe you did everything "they" said you did *plus* some, and you just got caught. Whatever your situation is, I get it. But what I also get is that you are here (in prison), and this is where you're going to stay unless your appeal gets granted or your release date arrives (*if* you're lucky enough to have one).

That is the reality of your situation *today*, so it's time to *accept* your reality and deal with it as it is *today*, and as it is *today* you've got time to do. With that said, your best play is to figure out how to benefit from said time; turn your *negative* into a *positive*. Here's how...

Don't waste time

I see so many prisoners just sitting around and doing absolutely nothing. All they do is let time (life) pass by without doing anything to benefit themselves, improve their lifestyle, prepare for the future, etc. They have no drive or ambition. They just walk around looking defeated; straight schmuckery.

Many guys come to prison and do 5, 6, 7 years, and leave no better of a man than they came. I recently met a 30 year old who came to prison and could not read or write. He's been in prison for the last 6 years and he goes home in 3 months. Guess what? He still cannot read or write. He talks about how he's going to learn when he "goes home." He asked me what type of advice I have for him; I told him he needed my advice during his first

3 months, not his last 3 months. He asked me why that was; I asked him if he can learn to read and write in 3 months. He stated "no." My response? "Exactly" (followed by my turning around and walking away).

The guy I'm talking about is an absolute schmuck. His waste of 6 years, disgusting. As much as I want people to win, and as much as I try to assist people in doing so, I realized that there was/is nothing I can do for him. Sad, but true.

Not only did the guy waste 6 years of his life, but, as much as I hate to say it, he will be wasting more time soon. He will be back; probably before I get out of the SHU for my last hit....

I have life in prison. Unless something happens with my appeal, I will die in a cell. What I wouldn't give for another shot at life now that I'm older and wiser, now that I get it and my perspective is clear. However, despite what my situation is, my reality; I'm pushing daily. I'm trying to get it; understand? Every day I am on beast mode. Like 50 Cent said: get rich or die tryin'.

With that out the way, nothing is more disgusting to me than someone who comes to prison and *will* be out someday, as he has a date, but does *nothing* with his time except jack off and God know what else, gets out no better of a man than he entered, and ends up coming right back.

Do not waste time (life). Turn your "negative" into a positive and *benefit* from your situation. Figure out (early on!) what you want to do during your stay in prison, what it's going to take to do it, and get down to business.

So, what do you want to do?

Now that we understand that it is our wisest move to turn our negative into a positive and we must figure out how we can get the most out of our time, it's time to figure out exactly what you want to do.

The first question is, what are you into that at least some aspect of can be mastered while you are in prison, and that is realistic considering the amount of prison time that you have?

For example, maybe you want to be an artist of some kind. If so, then during your stay in prison you should study, learn, and practice drawing as much as you can each day. If your goal is to be a professional artist and you have 5-6 years in prison, imagine how good you can be by the time you get out if you dedicate every second of your time learning and practicing it.

And let's say you want to get out and paint murals on cars or do graphic design. Maybe in prison you will not be able to practice those specific crafts, but you can master at least one aspect of them: Drawing. Yes; if you want to paint murals on cars or do graphic design, then become the best that you can at drawing while you're in prison because both of those jobs demand the trained eye of an artist who can draw; the better you are at drawing, the better you will be as a muralist or graphic designer.

Drawing is a good passion to have for a man in prison. It's something that can realistically be mastered right from your prison cell. You will almost always have access to a pen and/or pencil and a piece of paper to practice your craft. And, even if you're not going to get out of prison, drawing is one of the best skills you can have while in prison; there's always a demand for it. From your fellow prisoners to guards, from pen pals to people online, great drawings will always be in demand, and there is even a market specifically for prison art/drawings.

Writing is another good passion to have. It's very realistic to become a master writer from a prison cell. You will almost always have a pen and some paper to write what it is that you want to write/create.

3

For example, maybe you want to write and publish your own books. Well, you can always get books on how to write properly and self-publish. Get the books relevant to those subjects and learn the *entire* business inside *and* out. Then, write as many books as you can so that when you get out you can publish them. Or, if you're not getting out, publishing books from prison is a realistic goal. It *can* be done; especially with today's technology. Today's technology, especially the internet, has levelled the playing field a bit. I have life in prison, and you are reading a book that I wrote in my prison cell, sent out, and self-published.

Regardless of what your passion is, whether it's to write articles for a magazine, or launch your own magazine when you get out, whether it's to write books or movie scripts, all of these things require you to be a great writer. So, become a great writer if what you want to do has *something* to do with writing.

Again, both writing and drawing are great crafts to master even if you aren't getting out of prison because they can always be done from a prison cell. However, if you are getting out, your options greatly increase.

Now, let's say you have a passion for cars and you want to start your own mechanic shop when you get out. Maybe you will not have a lot of hands-on opportunities in most prisons, but you can still get books and learn *everything* there is to know about the mechanics of a car. Don't wait until you get out to go to school, use your prison time to learn what it is that you need to know so that you're ready as soon as you get out.

Real estate is another good business (usually). If you have a passion for it, get books relevant to real estate and learn every aspect possible about it. That way, when you get out of prison, you're ready to go.

There are *many* things you can study, learn, and master from/in a prison cell. Whether you are able to

4

study the exact craft that you are interested in, or something related to it, there is always something you can do to turn your negative into a positive and benefit from your prison time.

And it doesn't necessarily have to be a business, either. Making money just happens to be my passion, so I used those things as examples. If you don't know how to spell or add that well and you wish to improve upon it, *do* it. If you want to get your GED, *do* it. Just don't sit there and wait until you get out to start. Start now and *use* your prison time.

Be realistic

When deciding what it is that you want to do/get-into, make sure that you pick something realistic. For example, if your passion is basketball, you're good at it and you want to be in the NBA when you get out, but when you get out you'll be 32 years old, that's not too realistic. So, instead you should study something that has to do with basketball, like coaching or managing players, and study *those* aspects of the business.

Another example is if you rap well and you want to be a rapper when you get out but when you get out you'll be 48; in that case, maybe you should study other aspects of the music/hip-hop business. Breaking out as a rap star at age 48 might be a bit difficult, but starting your own label and producing is very realistic.

Whatever it is that you decide you want to study, learn, and do with your time, whatever your passion is and whatever goals you have set, fantastic; make it happen. Just make sure that it's realistic (even if you have to make a few tweaks and adjustments), and that you use all of your prison time mastering it. Do not wait until you "get out" to learn, study, etc.

Ways to study and learn your craft

Once you have decided exactly what it is that you want to do, you will need to figure out the best way to learn and master it. Don't forget, when creating your game plan, keep in mind the resources you have available to you. For example, money for books, courses, supplies, etc.

What's available at your prison?

The first thing you should do is see if your prison offers a trade or something that is relevant to whatever it is that you want to do. For example, some prisons have welding classes. If what you want to do involves welding, you should obviously do what you can to get into that class. Or, for example, there are prisons that offer such things as a mechanics class, a shop print class, or bakery jobs. If your plan even consists of working on cars, printing, or cooking, you should do what you can to get assigned to the relevant class or job.

Use your prison for whatever you can get from it. If it offers something that relates to/furthers *your* goal, take advantage of it.

College courses

Many prisoners take college courses through the mail. If what you want to do is available via correspondence course, or if you are getting out and having a certificate will be beneficial to your end goal (for example, if your goal is to work for a company and having certificates showing your credentials will help you land the job), then taking college courses may be a good idea for you.

Keep in mind that correspondence courses can be rather costly, so in order to take them you will need to have the financial resource. However, if you can afford it and it will benefit you, do it *while* you are in prison. Don't wait until you "get out."

Buy and read books

If what you want to do is not available via correspondence course, if you cannot afford to pay for a correspondence course, or if you plan to start your own business and do not need/care-about a certificate, then I suggest you purchase books relevant to what you want to do, and use them to study, learn, and teach yourself everything you want and need to know.

For example, I choose not to take correspondence courses. Instead, I prefer to purchase books relevant to what I want to do, and learn *all* that I can about the specific subject(s). Not only does this route allow me to pinpoint exactly what it is I want to learn about, it is also much more affordable. But then again, I have life in prison and I own my own business, so I have no need for a credential-proving certificate. If I only had 10 years to do, I'm sure I'd still create my own business upon release; however, I might want the credential-proving certificate(s) because they can really come in handy on the outside. Sometimes, even when you own your own business, you still occasionally work for others.

If you find your interests similar to mine and you think the book route is the best one for you, and you want to learn about, say... the music business, you can buy the book "Everything there is to know about the music business" by Donald S. Passman. From there, depending on exactly what it is you want to do, you can get books relevant to that specific part of the music business – producing, managing, starting a record label, etc., and master the subject by studying everything you can about it, or, say, for example, if you want to learn about drawing, you can get *Drawing for Dummies* by Brenda Hoddinott and Jamie Combs study and learn all the information it teaches, and once you've got that down buy some books that are a bit more advanced in the subject until you are a fucking *master*.

In conclusion

I can go on and on giving you examples of how to use your time wisely, and ideas of specific ways you can accomplish you goals; however, my main points are:

Turn you negative into a positive. Don't just sit around and waste time (life!) while you are in prison. Instead, dedicate every second of your time to doing something that is going to benefit you. And, no matter what your goal is, there is always something you can do to move towards it. Even if you can't afford correspondence classes, etc., don't let that discourage you; instead, purchase books relevant to what you're into and learn everything you can about it. Buying and studying books specifically aimed at your interest(s) will give you a great education at an affordable price.

True Story!

My original passion/craft is making hip-hop. I've been rapping since 1993 and really learning about the business since 1997. Everything I do rap-wise is on point. My concepts are dope; I'm creative as fuck; I'm a lyrical beast; and my flow is liquid.

I got locked up in February of 1999, and at the end of 2004 I decided I was going to record my vocals in my prison cell, smuggle them out, have my songs produced in the form of mixtapes, and still release my music. Guess what? I recorded my lyrics in my prison cell, smuggled them out, had several songs produced, and then ran into a wall; not a wall in here where *I* have the ability to get creative and find a way to do things, but a wall out there. It was too difficult for people to get things done to my standards without me being there and I wouldn't release my music without it being done right. Therefore, getting songs produced correctly – to my standards – became a very long and difficult process.

Then, Lil Wayne raised the bar extremely high by releasing so much material in such a short amount of time. It changed the pace of the game – even for underground artists – to a speed I could never keep up with from a prison cell; it became popular for artists to release weekly freestyles and remixes, etc.

And my trouble didn't stop there. People stopped buying CDs. Everybody just downloads everything for free now, so there's really no money in CD sales. In order to make money, you have to be able to do live shows; something I obviously cannot do from a prison cell.

At first it was hard for me to accept but I had to recognize reality, and the reality of the situation is, if I was to get out of prison at a young enough age, I am sure I could do very well in the hip-hop business. However, as my reality is today, I have life in prison and I will not be able to compete in today's market, and I will not be able to make the kind of money I want to make by doing music. And when it all boils down, my passion for getting money is stronger than my passion to use all my time and resources making hip-hop. So, I had to adjust my sights.

And I did. I had always planned to eventually write books – something much more realistic to do from a prison cell. I just had to jump into the game sooner than I had originally planned.

I've always been creative and crafty, but my technical writing skills weren't up to par. So, I bought "English Grammar for Dummies" and stepped my grammar-game up. I also bought a MacMillan Dictionary to make sure my word game is on point.

My plans to write urban books – basically the same stories that are in my rhymes, just without the need for a beat or an engineer (my wall) – so I bought about 15 of the damn things and read every single one of them from the beginning to the end. I dissected the entire format of my urban book collection – what the prices are, how many pages they usually have, roughly how many words are in these kinds of books, how well these guys are writing, etc. I broke it all down into math; something I understand.

Then I looked at all the information I'd gathered and compared it to what I *know* (the underground game of the hip-hop music business, specifically the mixtape hustle), and I realized that it's basically the same game – entertainment in the form of urban stories, but sold in the format of a book instead of a CD.

From there I created my game plan; I would write and publish urban books using the same strategy and formula I'd use for my music had my circumstance been different. Writing and publishing books is much more realistic for me. I write and create everything myself; I don't need a beat, an engineer, a dope mix, *nothing*.

Once I re-directed my focus, it was over. I created the The Cell Block publishing. And from that, my good man, even from my prison cell I'm gettin' *money*. However, it all stems from my original passion: the-business-of/making hip-hop.

So, you see? The reason I can tell you about turning a negative into a positive is because it's what *I* do. The reason I can tell you to benefit from your time and use it wisely is because it's what *I* do. I pimp the shit out of prison time. As a matter of fact, I just recently completed a 15-month SHU term for a slashing. However, right when I was supposed to get out of the SHU, they hit me with another 6 months because of *past* "disciplinary history." Therefore, I am still in the SHU, even right now as I write this. I am obviously not too happy about the additional 6 months; I have a lot of things to do and need to get out of the SHU to conduct certain business. However, since I have no choice but to do these 6 months, I made a commitment to myself to write two books during this time – this one and another. Well, each book sells for $15.00+ a copy, so just selling 1,000 copies of each book is 30 stacks. Again, I pimp my time. I *always* turn a negative into a positive and so should *you...*

For information on how to write urban books while incarcerated, order our book *How to Write Urban Books for Money & Fame: Prisoner's Edition*. To learn how to make lots of money LEGALLY when you get out of prison, order our book *Get Out, Get Rich: How to Get Paid Legally When You Get Out of Prison*! If you want to start your own business, order our book *The CEO Manual: How to Start Your Own Business When You Get Out of Prison*! All these books are available from The Cell Block Bookshop at the end of this book.

CHAPTER 2

BACK TO SCHOOL: EDUCATION OPPORTUNITES FOR INMATES

Pursuing an education while you are incarcerated or upon release is highly recommended and shown to drastically reduce the risk of recidivism. If you've been putting it off, now is the time to do your homework. No matter what level of education you currently possess, advancing your education can improve the quality of life both in and out of prison. Anyone can pursue an education, even an inmate or ex-con. Research shows that continued education helps keep inmates from returning to prison. Studies show that inmates who took college courses while incarcerated were four times more likely to stay out of trouble upon release.

While Incarcerated

While you are still incarcerated, here are some steps you can take:

1. First and foremost, check with your local prison's education department. Ask what level of education they offer and see if it meets your needs. Many prisons offer only the most basic of classes, such as a high school diploma or General Educational Development (GED) certificate equivalent. This should be your first step if you haven't already completed this. Types of classes to look for:

- Basic Literacy
- High School Equivalency/GED
- Vocational Training
- College Classes
- Correspondence Courses (see below)

2. Many prisons also offer vocational schools. These are hands on classes that help you develop a trade. Unfortunately, space can often be limited in these classes. Talk to the appropriate official at your prison to see about adding your name to a list if space is short. Be sure to keep your disciplinary record clean while awaiting class. As you're undoubtedly aware, this can have an impact on your status at the prison and your likelihood of being accepted into a vocational program.

3. Once you are familiar with the educational opportunities your prison offers, make the most of them.

Paying for your education can be a challenge. Since 1994 the government no longer awards Pell Grants to inmates. Inmates or their families pay the bulk of the tuition fees. Perkins Grants are available for vocational or technical courses, but these typically do not cover the full cost. Grant applications can be requested through the school to which you are applying. Private foundations and social organizations (e.g., Rotary, Lions) also provide funding. You may need someone on the outside to help you locate these organizations and their contact information. Work closely with the school to help secure funding for your classes. It is also possible that student loans will be available.

Correspondence courses are an excellent way for inmates to pursue a degree in higher education. However, with the easy access of the Internet, many universities have switched to offering online courses instead of the traditional paper and pencil courses that could be sent through the mail. Internet access is not available to inmates; therefore, correspondence courses are not as readily available. Below is a list of schools that continue to reach out to inmates to provide higher education. (Note: If you are aware of a college or university that provides courses specifically for inmates, please contact us so that we can update our information.)

Correspondence Schools for Inmates

Adams State University
208 Edgemont Boulevard
Alamosa, Colorado

Agape Life Ministries
P O Box 2052
Harrisonburg, VA 22801
Cost: No charge for inmates

American Bible Academy
PO Box 1627
Joplin MO 64802

Argosy University
333 City Blvd W
#18 10
Orange, CA 92868

Believers Behind Bars
P.O. Box 62
New Trenton, IN 4703 5-0062

Cost: No Cost to Inmates

Blackstone School of Law
Blackstone Career Institute

218 Main Street, PO Box 899
Emmaus, PA 18049-0899

Offers a well-known accredited paralegal program.

Christ Truth Ministry
PO Box 610
Upland, CA 91785
Cost: No cost to Inmates

Christian Bible College Seminary
10106 East Truman Road
Independence, MO 64052

Cost: No Cost to
Inmates

**CLEP (College
Level Exam
Program)**
PO Box 6600
Princeton, NJ
08541-6600

College credits for
self-taught
knowledge.

**Coastline
Community
College**
Attn: Incarcerated
Student Support
Services 11460
Warner Avenue
Fountain Valley,
CA 92708-2597

**Crossroad Bible
Institute**
PO Box 900
Grand Rapids, MI
49509-0900

Cost: No Cost to
Inmates

**Emmaus
Correspondence
School**
2570 Asbury Road

Dubuque IA 52001

**Feather River
College**
570 Golden Eagle
Avenue
Quincy, California
95971

Global University
1211 S. Glenstone
Avenue
Springfield,
Missouri 65804

**Good News Jail
and Prison
Ministry**
PO Box 9760
Richmond, VA
23228-0760

There are 184
lessons available
covering 13 books
of the New
Testament and the
book of Genesis,
all keyed to the
King James Bible,
on a basic to
intermediate level.
Cost: No Cost to
Inmates

**Grace Unlimited
Ministries**

7259 Jonquil Drive
Orlando, FL 32818

Lassen Community College District
PO Box 3000
Susanville, California 96130-3000

LOOPS Ministries
Correspondence Course
PO Box 14953
Odessa, TX 79768

Cost: All correspondence courses are available to the inmate free.

Louisiana State University
Baton Rouge, Louisiana 70803

Loved Ones of Prisoners
(LOOPS)
P. O. Box 14953
Odessa, TX 79768

Cost: No Cost to Inmates

Mount Hope Prison Ministry
25 Summit Avenue
Hagerstown, MD 21740

Cost: No Cost to Inmates

Mount Zion Bible Institute
2603 W Wright Street
Pensacola, FL 32505

Cost: No Cost to Inmates

Northwestern University
633 Clark Street
Evanston, IL 60208

Ohio University College Program for the Incarcerated
Haning Hall 222
Athens, OH 45701

Palo Verde College
1 College Drive
Blythe, CA 92225

**Rio Salado
College**
2323 W 14th Street
Tempe, AZ 85281

**Ron Thompson
Jail and Prison
Ministry**
P.O. BOX 618477
Orlando, FL 32861

**Thomas Edison
College**
101 W State Street
Trenton, NJ 08608

University of Iowa
Iowa City
1-800-272-6430

**University of No
Iowa**
Cedar Falls
1-800-772-1766

University of North
Carolina-Chapel Hill
Associate Director
for Correctional
Education
100 Friday Center
Drive,
Campus Box 1020
Chapel Hill, NC
27599

Once you are released, take immediate steps to continue your education, even if it is just taking one class at a time at your local community college. Community colleges offer a wide array of courses you will need if you plan to go on for your bachelor's degree, and they are reasonably priced. If you already have your associate's degree, consider applying at a state university. These, too, are more reasonably priced. Also, once you are out of prison you can sign up for online courses as long as you have access to a computer and the Internet. This can save considerable expense in traveling to and from classes and provide scheduling flexibility so you can hold down a job while going to school. A word of warning: online courses do require you to be well organized and self-starting. Schedule time for your studies! And choose friends that will offer encouragement.

Some people do not realize that they CAN pursue an education that has been interrupted. If you have dropped out of high school, or even elementary school, no matter how old you are right now, you can pick up where you left off and take your education as far as you want. Here is the order of a traditional education:

- High School Diploma or Equivalency (GED)
- Associate's Degree (usually from a community college)
- Degree (from a four-year college or university)
- Master's Degree (from a college or university with a graduate program)
- Doctorate Degree (from a college or university with a doctoral program)

There will be an application process that usually includes placement tests or other qualifying exams. Don't be afraid of these! If you don't do well at first, the school can recommend a tutoring program. Most schools have these types of resources available right there on campus. There will also be an application fee. The financial aid office will guide you through the process of applying for financial aid and determining your eligibility for grants. Do not let the fear of paying for college stop you. College schedules are extremely flexible today so that students can be employed full-time even while attending school. There are also more "non-traditional" students than ever before – students that are far older than the typical college student. Some colleges have programs designed to help with re-entry, such as:

Prisoner Reentry Institute John Jay College/CUNY
555 W. 57th Street, 6th Floor
New York, NY 10019
Phone: 212484-1399

Ask friends and family members to inquire on your behalf before you are released to the college or university you are most interested in attending. Plan ahead!

REMEMBER:

The Bureau of Prisons conducted research on inmates who participated in programs inside the prison, such as vocational training and mock job fairs. Their studies showed that these programs that teach marketable skills to prisoners help to reduce recidivism and/or repetition of criminal behavior patterns.

Access to education can change an inmate's life, lower taxes for taxpayers, and provide skilled labor for the workforce. Education uplifts the human spirit, promotes understanding and empathy, and improves the quality of lives for families.

Take charge of YOUR education. Do not just sit inside your cell counting off the days. Get busy. Do some research. Find out what courses are available. Volunteer to help teach others – it will help you in your own studies. Begin applying to colleges before you are released. Ask your friends and family on the outside to make calls to schools where you have an interest. There are more opportunities than you realize, but you have to take the initiative.

CHAPTER 3
LETTER WRITING LIKE A PRO!

Writing (especially letter writing) skills are extremely beneficial to have when doing time in prison. After all, writing will probably be your main source of communication with the outside world. At times you may have access to a phone, or you may even get a visit, but both of those can easily be taken from you for various reasons. Letter writing, however, is pretty much something you'll always be able to do even on lockdowns or from the hole.

Being able to write well is an extremely powerful tool; the better you learn to write, the more powerful you will become. Most of my communication, including the stuff pertaining to my business, is all accomplished through letter/instruction writing. My ability to write well is a major part of my ability to pull off the things I do, which is how I make money, and which is a big part of how I survive prison.

However, I was not born a great writer; it is something that I had to take the time out to learn to do. When strategizing how I was going to become successful from a prison cell, I quickly figured out that being a great writer was going to be a huge ingredient in my recipe for success. Whether it's articulating my idea, or convincing people to see things my way; whether it's writing out a long, detailed business plan, or the instructions on how to pull off each part of my plan; it all starts with being able to not only write, but write well.

A bit of perspective

Now, before we go on, let's think about what writing actually is and what it's used for.

Writing is a form of communication; it's used to communicate a message – information, thoughts, ideas, etc. With that in mind, if you wish to communicate your message clearly, you must be able to write it clearly and correctly.

If you do not learn how to write properly and convey your message clearly, the person/people you are communicating it to may *mis*understand the message rather than understand the message. Now, I understand that what I just wrote may seem like common sense, but what isn't common sense are all the rules to how to write (communicate) properly. And yes, the rules are important, because something as "minor" as a misplaced comma, the failure to put a comma, or the misspelling of a word can actually change the meaning of the sentence (statement, command, question, or exclamation).

If the meaning of your sentence is not what you intend it to be then your point might be missed. And when your point is missed, you've failed to communicate; and communication, my friend, is key.

So, since I am stressing the importance of writing for communication purposes, feel free to make the following word associations when reading this chapter.

Write	= Communicate
Writing	= Communicating
Written	= Communicated
Writer	= Communicator

Study and Learn

Being able to write (communicate) well has increased my power immensely. However, as I mentioned earlier, it is something I had to teach myself to do.

A lot of prisoners have their own way of writing (typically a "prison" style), but I strongly recommend

22

that you learn the *proper* way of constructing and punctuating sentences. The majority of people, even on the outside, don't actually write all that well. Learning how to construct and punctuate sentences properly – just those 2 things! – will put you on another level, so be sure to make it a *point* to learn and master these 2 aspects of writing.

There are many different ways you can improve your writing. If you have someone who will purchase you books, I suggest that you get/read/study "English Grammar for Dummies" by Geraldine Woods. I've read and studied "English Grammar for Dummies" and it really helped my dumb ass out a lot. In fact, it is one of the must-haves in my book collection, I keep a copy.

If you don't have someone who'll purchase books for you, you can get a *free* book from Pen American Center titled "Handbook for Writers in Prison." It's a writer's/resource handbook that will benefit you greatly. In fact, since it's free to prisoners anyway, I suggest you get this book even if you *do* have the ability to get other books. The more information, the better, all it can do is help you.

To request a free copy of "Handbook for Writers in Prison," write to:

Pen American Center
588 Broadway, Suite 303
New York, NY 10012

Note: There are many programs that send books to prisoners for free. They might not be able to get you a specific title, but if you tell them you'd like a book on English grammar, they will likely send you one.

Another way prisoners can learn to write well is by reading books (or magazines) and paying close attention to how they are written – how the writer constructs sentences, uses punctuation, etc. It's not a bad idea to pick up your favourite writers' books and study their style, their flow. Just make sure it's a writer whose books/articles are professionally edited.

Get and use a Dictionary

A good dictionary is a must-have tool for anyone wishing to write well, as proper spelling/use-of-the-word is critical when communicating.

There are many great dictionaries. However, I'd have to say that my favourite is the "MacMillan." Not only does it have a large selection of works (probably any-and-everything you'd ever want/need to use), but it also gives examples of how many of the words are used in a sentence, as well as common phrases, etc. Get the best dictionary you have the ability to get – even if you have to pay a prisoner to steal you one from education, as they often have a bunch of collegiate dictionaries which are also very good – and *use* it. Do not be lazy. If you are unsure of how a word is to be spelled or exactly what it means, look it up so that what you end up writing is absolutely correct. Doing so will really improve the quality of your work and your communication.

Letter Writing Tips

OK, so we now know that writing is basically communicating, and that to write well (communicate well) we must learn how to write properly – learn proper grammar, use a dictionary, etc. Now let's get into a few other kinds of tips.

The art of writing (a bit of perspective):

Think of writing as an art – because it is. When you write, imagine that you are writing a picture; you want your words to form a visual picture in your readers' minds.

Sketch:

Just as an artist wishing to draw a picture will first grab a pencil and a piece of paper and sketch, erase, adjust, shade, etc., until the picture finally relays the message he/she wishes to express, and to his/her satisfaction, a writer (who is *also* an artist) must use his/her tools the same way: you grab your pen and paper and you write, edit, erase, adjust, etc., until you have expressed your message to *your* satisfaction.

Note: When writing an informal letter, if you have a lot to write about, I suggest you write a list of everything you want to touch on, put it in an order to where it makes the most sense, and then write your letter. When writing a formal letter (a business letter; long, detailed instructions; etc.), I suggest you always start with an outline and then write a rough draft. That way you can go back, reread it, make the necessary adjustments and then rewrite it correctly, nice and neat. Sure, its extra work, but it will allow you to produce a better-quality letter.

Stay on topic/theme:

A lot of people's – especially in this day and age – minds are going 100 miles a minute. Therefore, they often jump back and forth from topic to topic, and by doing so, it can confuse the reader.

When you write your letters, *stay on topic*. Write about one subject at a time until everything you want to communicate has been communicated. It will not only make the experience of reading one of your letters easier and much more enjoyable, but easier to understand, too.

Paint a clear picture:

Never assume people know what you mean (intend to communicate). You need to be very thorough and paint a clear picture.

Develop your own style:

Just as any great artist works towards developing his/her own drawing/painting style and perfecting it, you should do the same with your writing. Sure, it's OK to mimic someone else's style/flow while learning – just as an artist often learns how to draw/paint by drawing/painting others' works – but over time, as you get more comfortable, try to come into your own.

Now that we've went over a few basic tips that pertain to anything you write, let's get into a few *specific* category of writing.

Informal Letter Writing

Informal letter writing is how you'd write a letter to your mom, dad, grandma, wife, sister, brother, pen pal, etc. Now while it's best to use proper grammar no matter what you're writing or who you're writing to as it will help you express your message clearly, it's OK to use a little bit of slang that the person you're writing to will understand. For example, if your sister or brother is from the internet/social-networking/texting generation, it's OK to use abbreviations like LMAO, LOL, OMG, etc.

Why? Because those are familiar terms to them, so your message will still clearly be conveyed. However, if your dad or grandma often complains that they are computer and technology illiterate, then you probably don't want to use those kinds of terms with them as they may not understand what you're trying to communicate.

The best thing for you to do in order to convey your message clearly is to write your message in a language that the person you're writing to uses – what they understand. This means that you should customize each letter you write to the specifications of each person you write to. And, of course, when in doubt, always use proper grammar.

Informal Response

There is a proper way to respond to an informal letter that you have received; doing so will make your letter (communication) more thorough, detailed, and organized, which will make it easier to read and understand.

When responding to an informal letter, do so in these 3 steps:

1) The first thing you should do is give a brief, upbeat greeting "Hello, how are you? Absolutely fantastic, I hope. I received your most welcomed letter yesterday, so I've decided to spend today with you." Or, "I received your letter and I am extremely excited to hear from you. Thank you so much for taking the time out to write me." Stick to something like that; simple and basic.

Whatever you do, don't do the ol' cliché, half-page "prisoner-style" greeting: "Esteemed salutations. I send my upmost respects to you. Please excuse me for this brief interruption as I sprinkle these words upon you..."

etc., etc., etc. That's 1970s shit – when the world/people was/were much slower. It's now Y2K+ and ain't nobody trying to read all that nonsense. Furthermore, it's corny.

2) The second thing you should do is respond to everything they wrote about in their letter; in the order it was written, one paragraph at a time. The only exception to this is if the person who wrote you is a bit scatter-brained and they jump back and forth between subjects in their letter. In that case, you will have to take control of the communication; you should put a mark be each "related" paragraph and respond to one *subject* at a time.

Note: Communicating via snail mail takes a while because you have to wait for it to go back and forth with that said; sometimes people forget exactly what it was they wrote about (mentioned, asked, etc.) by the time they get your response. When this is the case, it is a good idea to write what your "pen pal" stated or asked first, then respond to it. For example: In your letter you asked me what I think about the pictures you recently sent me – the ones where you're in a white thong. Well, in my opinion, your body is absolutely beautiful; your booty is the definition of perfection.... etc.

3) The third and final thing you should do is write all of the things *you* want to write about – discuss, mention, etc.

Formal Letter Writing

Sometimes while in prison you may need to write a more formal type of letter. In such a case, the rules are a bit different than when writing an informal letter.

When writing a formal letter or document – a letter in regards to business of something else you want to be taken seriously about – you *never* want to use slang, and you want to be as clear and to the point as possible. As lot of times, if you are writing a formal letter, the person you are writing to well be one who is often busy and pressed for time. You don't want to annoy them with a whole bunch of unnecessary script. Respect their time by choosing works that will convey your message clearly, without the possibility of confusion or misunderstanding, while still keeping it as short and simple as possible. Doing so is more likely to get you the results you're looking for.

Instruction writing tips

In order to get anything even semi-major done from a prison cell, you are going to have to learn how to write very organized and detailed instructions. That way, whomever it is that's helping you on the outside knows exactly what it is they are to do, and with the *least* amount of chance for confusion/error as possible.

Writing very detailed and organised instructions is usually a bit of work. It usually always calls for you to:

1. Write an outline of the points you want to make and put them in an order they make the best sense.
2. Write a rough draft from your outline.
3. Edit your rough draft by reading and re-reading it over and over again until it clearly expresses all of your points.

Type your final draft; or, if you don't have access to a typewriter, print your instructions nice and neat and in an organized fashion.

Hopefully the information I have given you will help you improve your writing ability. However, you should remember that I have only given you the very basics, and it is in your best interest to take your writing studies much deeper. I cannot stress enough how important and powerful the ability to write great can be for a man in prison; although, as you improve on your ability, I expect that you will *see* how it will improve your lifestyle and make your stay in prison much more comfortable.

CHAPTER 4
PEN PAL WEBSITES: THE SECRETS

There are many pen pal services available on the internet that is specifically designed to connect prisoners with free-world pen pals. Many of the services charge a fee; however, there are some free services as well.

Online prisoner-based pen-pal services are kind of like our version of Instgram and Facebook; they're our way of making friends and socially networking with people on the outside, all around the world. Sure, Instgram and Facebook are much bigger networks (and there are companies who build those for prisoners as well), but to utilize them properly they have to be maintained, and that's something that's hard to do if you don't have internet access yourself.

Some of the benefits of being on a pen pal service that specializes in connecting prisoners with people on the outside, however, are:

1. They are maintained, updated, adjusted, etc., by the service provider.
2. The people on the outside who review these services are specifically looking to write, befriend, connect with, etc., a prisoner.

These services come in handy if you're looking to make friends on the other side of the wall. Whether your objective is to find romance, spiritual guidance, legal assistance, help with your projects, a drug runner, a sugar mama, or just get mail, if you use these sites correctly, you can usually find what you're looking for.

Contrary to what some may believe, there are many women (and even men; however, I'm going to write this from the perspective you're looking to write a woman) out there who go to these websites in order to befriend prisoners. In fact, some of these sites have hundreds of women a day reviewing them and searching for that special someone with whom they can share their time with for one reason or another. Some of the women are looking to minister, and some of the women are in school and want to learn about a prisoner's experience. Some of the women are looking for love, and some of the women simply want sex letters.

There are prisoners who try these websites and have no luck. However, there are also prisoners who use these websites and find exactly what they're looking for – whatever that may be.

There is a way to use these services properly, and if you do, you will increase your chances of success. There is an art to pen-palling – strategy, if you will.

Now, before I go on; I tend to look at things from a business perspective. So, with that said, I'm going to make a lot of comparisons between pen-palling and business to help explain the following strategies.

Choosing your service(s)

The first thing you must do is decide what service(s) you'd like to use. The determining factor(s) in your decision may vary. Do you have money to pay for a service, or are you looking for a free service? What specifically are you looking for in a pen pal, and are there services or options that specifically target your objective(s)? What service has the most to offer? What service is said to provide the best results?

You can usually send a SASE (Self Addressed Stamped Envelope) to these services and they will send you one of their brochures/applications, and if you have any specific questions that will not be covered in their brochure, they will usually answer those as well. Once you gather the necessary information, you can review each one and then decide which of them you think best suites your needs. For a complete listing, order my book *The Best Resource Directory for Prisoners*, and also *Pretty Girls Love Bad Boys: The Prisoner's Guide to Getting Girls*.

Choosing a photo (graphics for your ad)

Choosing a photo to put on your profile is a critical part of the process. It will be your first impression. Your potential pen pal will first see your photo, then, if she likes what she sees, she will take the time out to read your intro.

The best type of photo to use is a photo where you're smiling. You want to show that you are friendly and approachable. You don't want to look too menacing and scare off your potential pen pal(s). So even if you're a tough guy with tattoos all over, if you want to be successful with this, use a photo that doesn't make you look like an angry serial-killer.

Intro (Sales-pitch/ad-synopsis)

The next thing you will need to do is write your intro. You will want to be sure that you do it within the allowed word count of your service, as going over the limit will usually cost an additional fee.

Writing a proper intro is a very important part of this process. It is pretty much the second part of your first impression – the first part being your photo. The first thing a potential pen pal will do is see your picture. If she likes what she sees, she will read your intro. It is up to your intro to close the deal on getting you an initial response.

Now, when strategizing your intro, here's how you need to look at it

You are a product; you're trying to sell yourself. Your intro is your sales pitch. You need to convince the women overlooking the site why they should write you verses somebody else. Remember, there are a lot of prisoners competing in this market. It's up to you to be the most attractive – colorful, creative, persuasive, inviting, etc.

You also want to write your intro according to the type of pen pal you're looking for. If you're looking for a mature, professional woman, you will want to write a mature, professional into. If you're looking for a street-type girl, you should use a language that's more in her lane. Again, it is your ad. Just as companies create their ads to appeal to the market they are targeting, you need to create yours to appeal to the market (pen pal) you are targeting.

Show Qualities (sizzle)

Regardless of what type of girl you're aiming for, however, be sure to write an intro that's positive and upbeat, as well as one that showcases your qualities. If you have a sense of humor, show it. I you're creative, use creativity in your intro. You want to show your potential buyer (pen pal) that you are worth buying – that they will have a good experience with you. After all, that's what you're trying to sell – yourself; as an experience.

Extras (More sizzle)

Many of the pen pal services will allow you to add a piece of artwork and/or poem to your profile – usually for an additional fee of course. If you can draw, it's an added bonus for your pen pal, as most women love getting drawings from prisoners. If you're potential pen pal is trying to decide between you and another prisoner, the fact that you can draw and he can't might be the deciding factor.

When deciding on what kind of drawing to post, make sure you use one with an image that will appeal to the kind of pen pal you're targeting. Don't put a gangster-type drawing if that's not the kind of pen pal you're seeking. Instead, put something thematically relevant. For example, if you're looking for romance, put a romantic drawing.

Another thing that will better your chances is if you put a poem with your profile. Women love poetry, and if you can write or get ahold of the right poem, it, too, may just be the deciding factor of why a potential pen pal chooses you.

For an additional fee, there are services that will post you right on the front page of their website. From my experience, being posted on the front page where you are seen first is an extremely beneficial feature/option to take advantage of.

Leave no stone unturned

You obviously want to maximize your chances of success, so do as many of the options as you can afford. You need to stand out from hundreds (or thousands, depending on the site(s) you use) of other business/products/experiences (prisoners), so make sure you leave no stone unturned. And if you can afford to be on more than one website, do so, be on as many as you can afford.

Responding to a pen pal letter

If you do what I've explained thus far, it is very likely that you will start receiving mail from women who are interested in getting to know you. However, you aren't completely sold yet, as it is very likely those same women have each written to another prisoner or two, and is trying to decide which one of you will be the final purchase (choice).

At this point in the process, you will need to hit your pen pal with a response that will get you the final sale so-to-speak. You do this by further showing your pen pal why an experience with you is the best one for her.

To show her why you're the best one, you do just that – you show her. You don't tell her. You show her by giving her the best letter – the best written, the most intelligent, the funniest, the most creative etc. It will take some work, but if you want to be successful, you must go the extra mile.

There is a proper way to respond to an informal letter, no matter who it's from. And as we discussed in our writing chapter, it's to first start off with an upbeat greeting, and then to go over the letter you've received and respond to one paragraph at a time, until you have responded to everything in the letter. The only exception to this is if the letter you've received jumps back and forth from subject to subject; in that case, you should mark each subject/paragraph separately, and respond to one subject at a time.

Once you've responded to what you were written about, then it's time to write what you'd like to talk about, ask, etc. Using this process will make your letters much more thorough, detailed, organized, and pleasant to read; which, of course, will make your pen pal that much more excited to receive your letters.

Hopefully the person receiving your letters notices the organization and process of how you answered her letter and responds to yours using the same method.

Doing so will give you both the best pen-palling experience.

Note: Got a drifter? Yeah, it's fucking annoying, I know. It seems it's hard to make progress with a drifter because they always drift from subject to subject without even coming to a point with one or the other. Unfortunately, for you, not many of your pen pals are going to read a how-to guide like you're doing now. Instead, they will just write you whatever comes to mind, when it comes to mind, without much consideration to the difficulty it creates for you who is undoubtedly trying to make some form of progress...

So, since your pen pal is probably not going to read a how-to guide, you will have to teach her how to write you the way you want to be written. There are several ways to teach your pen pal how to improve their responses to your letters. However, I've found it best to do so in a roundabout way by describing how I respond to their letters. For example: I really enjoy your letters. I find them very interesting; attention grabbing. I'm happy that you're my pen pal; and I take a lot of pride in how I respond to your letters. I like to try to make sure that I leave no stone unturned, so I found it best to just go down your letters and respond to one paragraph at a time. I value the communication that we have; I created the little method to ensure my side of the communication process is thorough. I've never been much of a pen-pallor before, so if you see how I can improve my responding method, please feel free to let me know.

Doing this will let your pen pal realize that you are paying attention to things such as the quality of your response, which means it's likely you're paying attention to the quality of her response. This realization will make her question the quality of her own response, and if and how it can be improved. By telling her how you respond

– which, of course, you already know is good, as does she – it will teach her a way to improve her own.

The elements (satisfaction guaranteed)

You want to make sure that you always provide a good experience for your pen pal so they are always eager to receive mail from you. You must keep your customer (pen pal) satisfied at all times.

Here are a few key elements that you should try to include in each and every letter. If you do, the quality of your letters will be on point.

Be positive

Nobody wants to take time out of their busy life to write you (befriend you, help you, etc.), only to get a letter back that's negative and depressing. So, make sure that when you write your pen pal, you have a positive and uplifting attitude and energy. Your pen pal wants to feel happy when reading one of your letters, and you should want that too. The better your letters make her feel, the more anxious she'll be to receive another one. And that's what it's all about – keeping her anxious to receive your letters.

Be funny

If you don't know how to be funny in a letter, you'd better learn quickly. Women love to laugh, and even more than that, women love the men who make them laugh. You ever see a big fat guy with a super bad bitch and wonder how in the hell he pulled it off? That's how, he's a funny fat guy.

Look, you are in prison. As fucked up as prison is, funny-ass shit happens every day. Including a funny situation or experience in your letters to your pen pal. To you it might be everyday shit because you're used to the things that happen in prison, but to your pen pal, it's not only funny, but interesting, too.

Be Creative

If you want to hook your pen pal, be creative you need to provide your pen pal with an experience they won't get from anyone else. Furthermore, women love a creative man. You can impress a woman greatly with a little creativity....

True Story

I once got hooked up with a woman that I wanted rather badly. I knew she wasn't really the type to write someone in prison, so I really wanted to hit her with my best material in hopes I'd impress her enough to actually want/continue to write me.

Well, I'm a writer, and I'm super OCD when it comes to my writing, whether it be books, blogs, letters, etc., I like everything to be nice, neat, and organized. One thing I don't like is making mistakes in my letters, and what I hate even more is to have my letters look messy with all kinds of scribbled out words.

When I first began writing this woman, I wrote her very nice, long, and detailed letters that would literally take me an entire day of two. It was a ton of work and I barely had time to do anything else. Furthermore, every time I'd make a mistake, I'd start that page completely over. Yes; tons and tons of work.

After a while it just got to be ridiculous. All my other projects and responsibilities got put on the back burner, and it was all starting to pile up on me.

So, what I decided to do is come up with a way to use my mistakes to my benefit. And I did instead of writing 1½ pages and starting over because I made a small mistake, I started leaving my mistakes and making jokes out of them. For example, one time I was writing about getting out of prison, but when I wrote the word "out" I'd accidently spelled it "ot"; I got distracted and left out the "u." Stupid, right? Well, instead of starting over, I drew a real nice arrow from the side of the page (the margin), pointing in between "o" and the "t." On the other side of the arrow (in the margin) I wrote, "hey, u, get back in there!" accompanied by a little smiley face. Doing that allowed me to fix my mistake and let her know I was smart enough to spell the word "out"; I didn't have to start the page completely over to do it, I made her laugh, and I added character to my letter. She loved it, she mentioned it, she started doing it. It became part of my personal writing style.

Be intelligent

Women are attracted to intelligent men. So, since you are doing time in prison, you should use some of this time to read a few books, articles, etc., and expand your mind a little bit so that you can stimulate hers with the things you write about. And one of the biggest things you can do to show intelligence to a woman you're writing to is to be a great writer. Yes, like I've mentioned before, being a great writer is one of the best skills a prisoner can have... understand?

Now, please listen to me... What you don't want to do is try to sound more intelligent than you really are by using all kinds of big-ass words that probably neither you nor she really understands. For one, if she does know the word, you risk looking like a schmuck by using it in the wrong context (it's very easy to do). And for two, if she doesn't know/understand the word, you risk miscommunicating your point, and that's counter-productive. So, don't be a dumbass; show your true intelligence and be the authentic you.

Be   charming

You need to charm and flatter your pen pal – make her feel good about herself. There are a lot of women who are not properly complimented. Well, compliments feel good, right? We all like them. And if you're the one providing your pen pal with that good feeling, your letters will be like a drug to her and she will become addicted to them. The more you can get her to need your letters, the better of a position you will be in.

Look, let me explain something to you playboy. It is not hard for a woman to get a man. Even if she's not the most attractive, she still has a mouth and a pussy, and as long as she does, she has the ability to get somebody. So, with that said, not only are you competing with other people in prison whom she can be writing to, but you are – at least to some extent – competing with guys on the outside, too. The difference between you and a guy on the outside? He can give her dick whenever she wants it and you can't. Women like sex just as much as men, so the fact that he can give her dick creates some stiff competition for you (if you know what I mean).

Now, especially if she's not all that attractive, it's likely that the guy on the outside is only going to give her dick. Luckily for you, most women need more than just that. They need to be heard, romanced, loved, paid

41

attention to, complimented, respected, etc., and that, my friends, is where you come in.

Like any smart businessman, when you want to start a business, you want to find out what you can supply (to your target market) that's not being supplied by competing business – in this case, other men. And since other businesses (men) are not providing an ear, romance, love, attention, compliments, respect, etc., you need to specialize in those areas...

Business 101: Supply the demand; understand?

Be confident

Ask any woman and she'll tell you she finds confidence in men to be sexy. I don't mean that you should be arrogant and obnoxious, but be confident in who you are and what you're doing. After all, you're a big, bad prisoner; you're supposed to be strong and tough. That is probably one of the reasons that your pen pal is attracted to you – because she likes a strong, confident man. If she was looking to befriend a weak, wimpy guy, she probably wouldn't have looked for a pen pal on a prisoner pen pal website; she would've found one from an online knitting club.

Be interesting

You need to keep the attention of your pen pal, and the way to do that is to consistently remain interesting. Something in every letter you send her should capture her attention – intrigue her.

There are many ways to appeal to a woman's interest, and some of those ways are all around you and things that you do daily without even thinking twice about. You may hate your prison experience, but to people who don't have to live here, the inner workings of our reality/society can be quite intriguing. I've had a couple of pen pals find the way I put my soups together to be interesting. To me it's nothing; a daily thing. But to my pen pals, putting beans and crushed-up chips in my Ramen soup is something they've never thought of. And when they find something so basic (to me) to be so interesting, imagine how impressed they are when I describe to them how I make tamales, wine, a tattoo gun, etc.

The more you put into it, the more you'll get out of it

In regards to the music business, a guy once told me, "The more you put into it, the more you'll get out of it." I heard him, although I didn't fully understand what he was saying until years later when I learned more about the music business.

Anyway, that same concept applies to a lot of things in life; including other businesses, including the business of pen-palling. If you want to be successful at it, you're going to have to put in the work to be so.

The biggest misconception that many prisoners have is that, to keep a woman pen pal satisfied on a romantic level, they only have to write a two-page letter once every two weeks. Those are the same prisoners who're unsuccessful.

I learned a long time ago that the prisoners who are successful with women on the outside are the prisoners who write them letters almost daily, send cards and drawings, and who call as much as possible, too. Many prisoners who're successful put in 8-hour days, just like they would at a regular job. That's what women require, so that's what you have to do. Like I said its work. However, if you want full-time benefits, you have to work full-time; understand?

An even exchange

I know many prisoners who're what I consider professional pen pals, and they run their operation just like business. They are the product, they promote/market their products/business online (pen pal service(s)), and they provide a product/service (letters) in exchange for something they want and/or need. I hate to put it so bluntly, but it is what it is.

You'd be surprised what letters from a prisoner can do for a woman. Think about how good a woman feels when she gets letters of support, compliments, encouragement, or romance. Again, guys out there want sex; they're not too concerned with the woman's emotions. So, there are a lot of women who get sex from a jerk on the streets, but then get romance and emotional support from a guy in prison.

A lot of prisoners become almost like therapists to their pen pals. As a prisoner pen pal, we devote a lot of time "listening" to the woman pour her emotions out on paper. And not only do we "listen," but we respond with words of support and encouragement.

Some people put a negative light on prisoner pen pals as if they're just using woman on the outside. Well, sure, some prisoners do use women on the outside (just like some men on the outside use women on the outside), but there are many women on the outside who use prisoners. For example, many women turn to the comforting words of a prisoner when she is going through a rough time in her life. When she needs the attention and support only a prisoner is willing to give; only to leave the prisoner hanging once that time in her life is fixed/fulfilled some other way. There are also women who love the love and romance they can get from a prisoner, including the letters discussing their sexual fantasies in the greatest of detail, only to leave the prisoner hanging once that part of her life is being fulfilled by somebody else; as if the prisoner has no feelings...

So, when you really look at the reality of the situation, who's using who? In my opinion, it's an even exchange; it's business.

Looking for Love?

If you expect to find real, genuine love from a woman you've met from a prisoner pen pal site, you may be setting yourself up for disappointment. Don't get me wrong, I'm sure that real love can exist between a prisoner and a woman on the outside he's met via pen pal website; however, I'm also sure that it's not the norm.

When you and your pen pal first start "falling" for each other, it will probably feel like love. Your relationship will be new and exciting. However, you should be aware that a woman will usually stay on the team solid for about 18 months. After that you will probably notice things starting to fade. So, enjoy it while it lasts...

Anything's possible

When it all boils down to it, anything is possible. And if you are in prison, you should be trying to do anything that will improve your lifestyle.

I've seen many successful romantic relationships between prisoners and their pen pals. I've also seen some marriages between prisoners and women they met by pen-palling first. If you have a release date, and if you can get family visits, your chances of success increases drastically.

On the other hand, I've also seen many successful business relationships between prisoners and their pen pals. I've seen prisoners get thousands of dollars, lawyers, packages, weekly visits, you name it, and in exchange, those guys pretty much devote their lives to the women who're providing such things for them. They spend their days writing, drawing, calling whatever it takes.

CHAPTER 5

SURVIVING A CELLY (CELL-LIVING ETIQUETTE):

To live comfortably and peacefully in a 9x12 concrete cell with another man can be a challenge. It takes a bit of skill to pull off successfully, and it is a skill that is acquired mostly from experience. However, I have a bit of experience when it comes to living with a cellmate, so hopefully you can take what I've learned and use the information to give you a head start towards successfully living with a cellmate of your own.

A bit of perspective

To put it in perspective for you, living in a cell with another man is like a marriage; without the sex (unless, you're into weird shit). After all, you're going to be spending most of your days and nights with your cellmate, locked inside of a tiny, concrete storage room you both will be calling home. You guys will both be eating in that cell, sleeping in that cell, shitting in that cell, and probably having hours of dialog talking about what life was like for you on the outside before being sent to that cell.

Every cellmate you have is going to be different and you have to have some type of flexibility when learning how to adapt to each one. You have to have patience and understanding, because not only will your cellmates be different from each other, but many will also be different from you.

Sometimes you will be put into a cell with someone because you guys are the same race or have the same gang affiliation, but you may also be put into a cell with someone because his cell has an empty bed. It all depends on where you're at and how the prison you're in assigns housing. Sometimes you will be put into a cell with someone you know or have heard of through the grapevine, and sometimes you will be put into a cell with someone you don't know and have never heard of at all – a complete stranger. Sometimes you will have a lot in common with the person you are celled with, and sometimes he couldn't be more different.

Your best bet is to find someone whom you already know and are friends with, have things in common with and are compatible with, but sometimes that takes a bit of work and manoeuvring to accomplish, and until you do you're going to have to work with the situation you've been given.

Now, while each person is going to have his own set of pet peeves that you will have to learn and customize your program to (especially if he's bigger than you), there is a basic cell etiquette that is followed, and if you follow it you will increase your chances of a successful marriage regardless of who it's with.

Cell ownership

First and foremost, you should understand that the cell predominately belongs to who was there first. If you move or get moved into somebody else's cell, you cannot just go in there and change up his program. I'm not suggesting that he gets to control everything in the cell, but for the most part you should follow the pace he's set.

Prison is very big on respect; you're going to find yourself in a big problem fairly quick if you go into somebody's cell and show a lack of it. When you first go in, make sure you ask him what his daily program/schedule is like and if he has any pet peeves. That opens the door for your celly to explain to you how he likes to live, what he likes to do, etc. When you first go into his cell, it'll probably be a little awkward, and that will loosen things up a little bit and allow him to tell you what he really feels without him feeling like an asshole by doing so.

Show and check paperwork

The first thing every prisoner should do when moving in with a new cellmate is show him his paperwork – why he's in prison, that he's not a rat, etc. That will give your new cellmate a good impression about you, as he will know you're not trying to hide any funny business from him – a sex offense, a deal in where you snitched out your crime partner(s) to save you own ass, etc.

Not only should you present your new cellmate with *your* paperwork, but he should present you with *his*, in return. If he doesn't, then it is likely that he's trying to hide something and you should probably get out of the cell sooner than later.

Don't ask too many questions

Even if you are solid and not a rat, don't ask your cellmate too many questions – especially "personal" ones, and especially if you hardly know him. Doing so can make him suspicious of you. Mind your own business, and what he wants you to know he'll tell you.

Keep in mind that most prisoners like to brag about what they've done or what they're doing. After all, most people in prison are criminals, so they glorify crime and the criminal lifestyle. Sometimes, in fact, it's best to ask your cellmate to not tell you something. If he gets busted, you won't be a suspect. You couldn't have told what you don't know, right?

Note: Not only should you not ask too many questions, but you shouldn't talk too much, either. Especially when it comes to your case and/or other crimes. I don't give a fuck how cool you *think* your celly is, how many tattoos he has, or if his O.G. moustache is down to his nipples; *anybody* can be that rat.

What happens in the cell, stays in the cell

Whatever goes on in your cell – plotting, planning, scheming, scamming, arguments, minor scuffles, etc. – stays in the cell. Don't go around talking about what goes on in your cell; that's between you and your celly.

Don't expose your cellmate's business

Again, what happens in the cell, stays in the cell. Never go out to the yard and expose your celly's business. If your celly has a phone, or if he's knocked someone, don't go bragging about it. If your celly's hitting dope at visiting, don't go telling you friends. If someone asks you what CDs your celly has, tell the person you don't really fuck with your celly's shit like that and that they should go ask him. Or, just simply say, "I don't speak on my celly's business. You gotta ask him about his CDs."

Remember, prisoners are crafty. They may be asking you about your celly because when they asked him he didn't give them the answer they wanted, so they're asking you to see if he's lying. Prisoners are going to try to manipulate and play you and your celly against each other for their own benefit. Don't fall for it and risk having a falling out with your celly over it.

Never fuck with your celly's shit

One of the fastest ways to get stabbed in prison is by going through your celly's personal shit while he's gone. That's a scumbag move, and if he finds out he's liable to whack you. If your celly has a radio, TV, hot pot, etc., and you don't, he'll most likely make it clear that you're allowed to use those items any time you want. He may even give you access to his books, CDs, and/or canteen. But as far as getting into his personal stuff – paperwork, pictures, letters, etc. – don't ever do it.

Also, a little piece of advice... There are a lot of snakes and scumbags in prison, so for your own safety, in case your celly doesn't follow the same etiquette I just gave you, have your people get a PO Box and mail everything to you using it as their return address, instead of using their home address. And when you get letters from people who don't use a PO Box for their return address, tear the address off the envelope, rip it up into small pieces, and flush it. Never leave addresses laying around because there are those scumbags that will write them down and then write your people once you guys are no longer on the same prison yard.

Oh, and write the addresses in your address book in a way that only you understand them. It's much better to be safe than sorry.

True Story

I once had a celly named Ronnie. He was an older guy who lived on the bottom tier, the tier I wanted to be on, and one day his celly moved out, so I moved in. I didn't really know Ronnie too well before this, but he seemed decent. He was a porter, so he was hardly ever in the cell anyway. And when he was, we got along well; we'd chat and he'd tell me a lot of stories about 'back in the day,' etc.

Ronnie really liked to gamble, and I really like to make money. So, since Ronnie was pretty good at gambling and had a bunch of extra cosmetics and shit (prison money) sitting in paper bags under the bottom bunk, I'd let Ronnie gamble with my money. In exchange, when he won, we'd split the winnings. Sure, it was a no-lose situation for him, since he got to gamble with my money, but I didn't really care.

I always had a lot of shit coming from canteen and packages. Ronnie didn't really have shit other than what he'd hustle from the gambling table, most of which would go right back in the pot. So, since he was my celly and I thought we were cool, I'd give him soups, bags of chips, boxes of Nutty Bars, etc. This is on top of giving him money to gamble with.

Ronnie was a dope fiend. He loved heroin. I don't like living with guys who use like he did, but I had a little respect for him because he'd never actually cluck his shit for dope. He was kind of a "responsible" dope fiend; he'd only use when he'd hustle up money to buy it, or someone would kick him down something for free. Anyway, one time Ronnie slammed some heroin and overdosed. He fell flat on the floor, needle and everything. I immediately sat him up and started pouring cold water (from the toilet) over him; his head, nuts, etc. I also slapped him across his face a few times as hard as I could, which, I admit, I kinda liked because he had been getting on my nerves anyway. I thought the dude was going to die, but after 5-6 minutes he came to. Long story short; I gave him money to gamble with, food to eat, and I saved his life, ya dig?

During this time, I had a pen pal from Texas named Rose. She was a good-looking lady, a few years older than me and already settled down in life. Rose was very supportive and was going to help me with some online aspects of my business. She was a very valuable friend with only one requirement; that I never, ever give her address out to anyone. I assured her I never would, and I meant it.

After living with Ronnie for a couple months I

moved into another block to be with some of my folks. A few months after that I was sent to the hole for some bullshit. During this entire time, Rose was riding strong.

I'd been in the hole for about five months when in comes Ronnie. Since I was cool with him and I was already established, I sent him a bunch of food, cosmetics, magazines, etc.

It was about a month after Ronnie arrived that I received a letter from Rose telling me how I'd betrayed her, and that I'd never hear from her again because I did the one thing to her I swore I'd never do; I gave her address out, to some schmuck named Ronnie.

I wrote Rose back and tried to explain that I never gave her address to anyone. I explained that Ronnie was an old celly who had must've written her address down while we were cellies, or the cops gave him one of my letters after I moved out. I promised her I'm much too selfish to ever want to share her with anyone. However, to this day, I've never heard from her again.

Although aware that Ronnie had betrayed me in one of the worst possible ways of betraying someone in prison, I didn't let him know that I knew. Instead, when I'd be escorted past his cell on my way to the yard, I'd smile, tell him what's up, ask him if he needed anything, etc. I didn't want him to know I knew what he'd done because I knew I'd see him again someday.

A year later, back in general population, me and about five others were called out of our building to go pick up our quarterly packages. At the time we were called out, there was nobody on the yard; just us.

While waiting for the package officer to call my name, a line of about 8 new arrivals were escorted from the orientation building to the laundry room to get their state-issued clothing. Among the new arrivals? Ronnie. I cannot explain to you how happy I was to see him....

Being that I was about to get my package, it

obviously was not a good time to confront Ronnie. So, I pulled my hat down low, turned my back to the group he was in so he wouldn't notice me, and smiled. A few minutes later, he was escorted back to the orientation building. A few minutes after that I was issued my package and then went back to my own building.

When program opened up later that day, the first thing I did was go talk to a guy on the yard named Jay that knew both Ronnie and I and told him that Ronnie had just rolled up. I told Jay that Ronnie had not seen me, and if he asked about me at all, to say he hadn't seen me on that yard and didn't think I was there. I told Jay to even tell Ronnie that he – Jay – had a problem with me, and when he saw me he was going to fuck me up. I wanted Ronnie to really believe that Jay hadn't seen me, and also feel that he had an ally. This way, he would never see me coming.

Ronnie ended up being on a different tier than me so I never went to the yard at the same time he did. Days, weeks, and then months had went by and I still had yet to see him.

Then one day, while on the yard, Jay had come up to me and let me know that Ronnie had just went into the nurse's office and would be coming out soon. I told him to go wait for Ronnie to come out, and when he did, to convince him to walk the long way back, all the way around the track. In case Ronnie didn't go along with Jay, I went and sat down on the ground, in front of Ronnie's building, on the other side of a table where I could see him when he came out but he couldn't see me. If necessary, I would just intercept him before he made it to his building.

I sat there for about ten minutes, and then out came Ronnie. I saw Jay immediately walk up to him and start conversing. Instead of walking toward me, they started walking the other way -- the long way. The plan was going nicely.

Once they started walking away, I got up, pulled my hat low and followed. My plan was to wait for them to get as far away from the main tower as possible, so I can make my move and at least try to get away with it. Once they were about there, I sped up to a speed that would allow me to catch up with them as soon as they were exactly where I wanted to meet up with them at. My timing was perfect.

As soon as we all arrived to the spot where I'd make my move, Jay turned around to see what was going on; I was right behind him. When he saw me, he made a little space between himself and Ronnie so I could slide right in and do my thing.

Without Ronnie even realizing it, I'd stepped right in the middle of him and Jay; Ronnie was to my left. Ronnie was talking, and when he looked up and to his right, he no longer saw Jay, he saw me. At the exact time he saw me I said, "Hey, Ronnie; how you doin'?" and immediately crushed my fist into his mouth, causing him to drop like the sack of shit he is. While he was on the ground, I kicked him in the face and stomped on his head; and for good measure, I stomped on his glasses, too, crushing them into pieces. While Ronnie was splitting up teeth and blood, I said to him, "If you ever steal from me again, I'll fuckin' whack you."

I was about to jump back on top of him when I suddenly noticed that no alarm had went off. That meant that I had gotten away with what I'd done so far, and I decided I was content with that. I started walking away, but had I heard the alarm go off, my plan was to run back over there and smash him until they came. If I was caught; might as well get all the money, right?

For a while Ronnie had sat at the table near where everything had happened, trying to gain his senses. Then he went back to the nurse, and a few minutes after that he was escorted to the prison's main hospital to get himself put back together. I could've sworn he was going to tell on me, but he didn't. Turns out he got hit by a softball -- a softball game was going on and occasionally prisoners do get hit by a fly ball zipping through the air.

A few weeks later I got word that Ronnie had rolled it up off the yard. He told the guards his life was in danger. I'm not quite sure if he really felt that way, or was just embarrassed for getting it the way he did. Whatever his reason(s), I haven't seen him again, which obviously is something I'm OK with. I did what I had to do and that's that.

There are two morals to this story: 1) There are scumbags who will steal your addresses and write your people when they think they can get away with it. 2) Karma's a bitch; people who do this will eventually get hit by a softball zipping through the air.

Communicate (nobody can read your mind)

One of the most important things to have (in any marriage) is effective communication. Never assume anything; ask. And at the same time, don't hold things in. If something bothers you and you're not going to be able to let it go, express it. Just make sure you do so respectfully, and at the right time; maybe even in a roundabout way.

For example, while I write this section of the book I am in Tehachapi SHU, and for security purposes there are no mirrors in the cells. However, the outside of my sink is extremely shiny – so shiny I can see my reflection rather clearly.

Well, the other day I got a new cellmate; some guy I don't know, but who seems OK. Anyway, yesterday he took a birdbath in the sink, and after he was done he cleaned it using a green scrub pad. He was trying to be respectful by cleaning up after himself, which is cool, but the green scrub pad will scratch up the sink and I will no longer be able to use it as a mirror.

After he mentioned that he hit the sink with a scrub pad I said "OK, OK; that shit won't even scratch it up, huh?" He replied, "Oh, man, I don't know, I guess it could. Did it?" I told him, "I'm not even sure, bro; I think some pads scratch 'em and some don't. Here, let me check." I then went and examined the sink. While looking at it I said, "I can't really tell, but at least I can still see my ugly mug." His next reply was, "Yeah, we better not even chance it." I said, "Yeah, I think you're right."

Now, between you and me, of course he scratched the sink, and of course I knew a green scrub pad would do so. However, rather than seem confrontational which could've caused tension in the cell, I played the dumb role and lead *him* into suggesting that we no longer use the scrubber on the sink, which was my goal in the first place.

I don't have much in my cell right now. I am happy to have a shiny sink so that I can see my reflection when I wash my face, comb my hair, etc. Had I not said anything, frustration would've built up over him fucking up my sink/mirror. And not only would I possibly've built up resentment towards my celly that could've lead to other problems, my mirror would've eventually been gone. However, I ended up killing the whole situation quickly – before it lead to resentment and a fucked up sink/mirror, and without offending the person I have to live with.

Be considerate

Consideration goes a long way; it's a way of showing respect to your celly. Have some consideration for the guy you're living with, just as you expect him to be considerate of you. For example, if your celly is reading, writing, sleeping or watching a movie, don't start yelling to somebody way down the tier and hold a long conversation with them. That's rude. If your celly works all day or is gone for a couple of hours, handle your business *while* he's gone so you can be out of the way by the time he gets back. Nobody wants to go to work all day, and just when they expect to get back to the cell to wash up, make something to eat and relax, their celly is just starting their workout in the middle of the cell floor. Prison cells are small, there's not enough room for two people to be on the floor at the same time like that.

Another part of being considerate is making joint decisions – asking his thoughts and opinions before doing something that will affect the both of you. For example, before you start moving shit all around the cell and hanging stuff up wherever you want, ask your cellmate how he feels about your ideas. After all, he might not want to stare at a picture of your ugly fat bitch all day – the one you met in the county jail while she was fighting a dope case and your pretty bitch was running off with your best friend who ratted you out to escape 30 days in jail.

Also, if you make something to eat, ask your celly if he'd like a little bit – especially if he doesn't have anything to eat of his own. You wouldn't want someone eating one of the recipes in this book in front of you while your stomach was touching your spine without offering you a little something. Like your mother told you, share.

Oh, one more thing... Anytime you gotta fart, sit on the toilet and flush it. Nobody wants to smell your asshole, and flushing your farts will help take that ungodly smell away. And when you shit? Don't just leave a bunch of butt nuggets floating in the toilet, fermenting, while your celly is in the corner of the cell with a blanket over his face choking and gagging. Flush that shit. And in case you don't know, the "drop one, flush one" is called a "courtesy flush."

Have a positive attitude

I know you're in prison and things in life aren't necessarily the way you'd like them to be, but try to have as positive of an attitude as possible when you're around your celly. Nobody wants to be around a miserable person all the time; it's infectious. And besides, everybody else has their own problems they're dealing with – probably ones very similar to yours. Your celly doesn't want to hear about how your girl ran off with your best friend after your best friend ratted you out. Nobody wants to hear about all the details of your case – how you didn't do it, how the DA lied, and how the system screwed you over. Hearing about that all the time is depressing and heavy. Why? Because *our* girl ran off with *our* best friend after he ratted us out; *we* have a case that *we're* worried about; *we* didn't do the crime *either:* the DA lied on *us*, too; and we were all fucked by the system.

Despite how you truly feel inside, at least project a positive attitude/energy. You're going to bump heads with your celly if you're bitter and grouchy all the time.

Rotate cleaning duties

Usually cellmates rotate cleaning duties – you wash the floor and walls one day, your celly does it the next; unless otherwise agreed upon, of course. For example, if your celly was there first and it's his cell, he may have a specific way he *likes* to do it, so he'll only ask you to clean up after yourself as *he* will do the daily wipe-down. Or, maybe your celly has a job but you don't – he works all day while you sit in the cell. In that case, maybe *you* should do the daily cell cleaning and relieve *him* of it.

Regardless of who does the daily cleaning duties – you, him, or the both of you – make sure you always keep your stuff clean. If you make something to eat, clean up after yourself. If you use the sink, wipe it down when you're done. When you get up in the morning, fold up your blanket(s) and roll up your mattress. Make sure your locker is nice and neat and that you're not living like a filthy fucking pig. Nobody wants clean up after you or live in your sloth.

Note: Believe it or not, many prisoners have a rule that they/you sit when they/you piss. That way all the piss goes into the toilet and nothing splashes out of it. Another rule that many prisoners have is that they/you clean the inside of the toilet after each shit they/you take. That way, you're in charge of washing your *own* shit and nobody else's, and the toilet is always clean.

Alone time

Everybody needs to be alone from time to time. No man wants to be around another man 24/7. No man even wants to be around his bitch 24/7, so you *know* he doesn't want to be around *you* that much. So if you and your celly have been around each other too much and your door gets cracked open for you to go somewhere, go. Let your celly jack off, take a shit, and have some time to meditate. It's good for the both of you. If you guys are around each other too much, you guys *will* start bumping heads; trust me. Even if you and your celly are cool, the littlest things will start getting on your nerves. You guys *need* time apart.

CHAPTER 6

SOCIAL GAME: THE STRATEGIES

Having a great social game is extremely valuable in prison. The more people you can get to like you, the better off you will be.

Keep you safe

The more your fellow prisoners like you, the less you have to worry about them plotting to harm you. Sure, you always have to be careful and watch your back (and front), because there will always be somebody who doesn't like you – especially if you have something going for yourself – but you will have *less* people out to get you if you are well-liked and popular.

Furthermore, when people like you, they want to protect you. So if they hear of somebody else plotting to harm you in any way, they will let you know; often times, even at their own risk. Having a heads up that somebody wishes you harm is obviously in your best interest; it allows you to prepare your defense (or, your offense, which can be another form of defense).

Keep you in the know

Most prisoners are plotting on different come-ups or have some type of resource that can be of use to you. Building great relationships with such people, to where they like and trust you, will make them more likely to offer their connection(s) and resource(s) to you. In a place like prison, where we are forced to make the most out of the very little we have, you want as many people as possible to trust you and offer you their resources.

Be personable and polite

You may think that, if you're quiet and mind your own business, you will have less problems and be able to stay out of trouble. As much as that seems logical, it's not true. Maybe you can get away with it if you are 45+, but if you are a younger guy and you are quiet, people will see you as standoffish, sneaky, one who thinks they're "better" than everyone else, or possibly even weird, or weak.

Your social game has to be on point if you want to make your time easier. You have to associate with people, talk to them, etc.

Even if you don't like someone, act like you do. Never let anybody know how you truly feel, because if you do, you will be making a big mistake. You want *everyone* – even those who would typically be your "enemy" – to feel inside like you guys are actually friends.

It may seem two-faced to act as if you like someone if you don't – and it is, really – but that's just what you have to do in prison; even if you prefer to be a genuine, sincere, and honest person. After all, we're talking about the devil's playground, and the devil's playground is not full of genuine, sincere, and honest people, so it is not a place for your genuine, sincere, and honest qualities. Prison is a dog-eat-dog environment. The longer it takes for you to accept this fact, the harder your time will be. Because even if you are not willing to do it to the next prisoner, you can believe he is willing to do it to you.

People want to be lied to

The majority of prisoners have an inflated ego, and they think they are much better and more important than they really are. Prisons are full of know-it-alls, masterminds, and people who have it "all figured out." To tell them any different – even if you're being honest – will be insulting to them.

When somebody shows you a drawing they did and asks you if you like it, say yes – even if it looks like shit. Tell them it's really nice, and that you like the way they do their shading – even if you don't. Doing so will make them feel good about themselves, and since you were the one who complimented them, they will like you for it.

If somebody wants you to hear their new rap song, or they want to read a poem to you that they wrote, give them the time it takes to listen to what it is they want to share with you. And when they're done, tell them that they did a great job. Don't make them feel shitted on by not listening to what they have to say or by telling them it needs work. Tell them that they should contact Jay-Z because they can probably make a ton of money selling their lyrics. Or tell them that they should write a book consisting of their very well-written, creative, and crafty poems, because they will make a lot of money with their skill – even if you know poetry books don't typically sell a whole lot. And if *they're* aware of that fact, make them believe that they are an exception to the norm. That's what they want to hear, and they will like you for it.

Furthermore, in their mind, they already think they're the best; they just want *you* to think they are, too. So if you tell them anything different, they won't believe you; they will think you're jealous and hating, and they won't like you.

If you are somebody who's honest and thinks that, as a real friend, you need to tell your "friend" the truth, you are wrong. Maybe that's the right thing to do in the free world, but in prison, if you do that, you will be hated. Believe me, people *want* to be lied to.

Learn to arrange

Most prisoners think they're master manipulators. They love reading books like "The 48 Laws of Power," "The Art of Seduction," and things of that nature. The majority of prisoners, however, brag about how they've read those books inside and out. I never really understood this. I think most prisoners are more concerned with seeming intelligent and letting everyone know they, too, have read those books, rather than keeping the information to themselves and acting as if they're unfamiliar with the kind of information those books teach, which, I'd assume is something those type of books would recommend....

Let the prisoners around you think they're mastermind manipulators, and then use their arrogance against them. Play dumb; never let anyone know your true level of intelligence. Instead, let them think they're smarter than you (which I *promise* you they already think anyway), because not only will it give you an advantage in your game (they will be less defensive), they will like you more.

Be neighborly

Be good to all of your neighbors. And I don't just mean the guys in the cells to your immediate right and left, I'm talking about, maybe, *four* cells to the right, and *four* cells to the left.

The prisoners in your section are not the ones you want to be feuding with. If you think it's bad feuding with your neighbours on the streets, well, it's much worse when feuding with your neighbors in prison who're most likely bullies, brutes, head-bussas, gangsters, killers, etc.

Being neighborly doesn't take much effort, just be friendly with those who surround you. Greet them when you see them in the morning; all you have to do is smile and say "Good morning." Do this even if your neighbors are grouchy. Even if you don't like them, appear as if you do. Even if you're not in a good mood that particular morning, appear as if you are.

If you are a more fortunate person who lives more comfortably than the majority of those around you (go to canteen and get packages regularly, etc.), don't brag, show off, or floss what you have. That will make your fellow prisoners hate you. Regardless of the front that most prisoners put up, most of them will hate you if you have more than they do; especially if you brag about it, or too openly let it be known. For whatever reason, a lot of guys in prison feel as if they are owed something, and on top of that, they are often frustrated. If you don't give them what they feel they have coming, they will turn their frustration towards you; they will begin to hate you, and being hated could possibly put you in danger.

If you are somebody who has a lot, it is wise to share with your neighbors. If you share, it is less likely that they will hate you because of jealousy.

When it comes to newspapers, magazines and books, you should always share them with your neighbors. Anything that's not going to hurt you financially or jeopardize you in any way, you should share.

As far as food and other items, give what you can but don't do too much. Just ask your neighbors if they are all right and if they need anything. If they do – and you should already *know* who does and who doesn't, because you should be *paying attention* to who gets canteen, who has money, who has family support, etc. – give them a couple of soups (Ramen noodles) and a few shots of coffee. Maybe even open up a bag a chips and let everybody pass it around.

There's no set amount on what you should give; it all depends on what you can afford. If you have a lot of money and can afford to pass out whole bags of chips, or whatever, then, do what you do.

However, and as crazy as it may seem, in prison you have to be very careful when being generous. It's good to share a little bit with your neighbors, *but*, at the same time, you don't want to give off the impression that you're a pushover, or that you're trying to *buy* friends. If prisoners' sense that that's the case, they will try to take advantage of you and use you for what you have. Then your attempt to be generous will backfire. You will either get used for your stuff and be seen as weak, or you will have to deny giving someone something they feel they have coming, and in turn, they will hate you – what you're trying to avoid in the first place.

Do not look into other prisoner's cells

A lot of people have a very bad habit of looking into other prisoner's cells. Do not be one of those people. When you go to another prisoner's cell, go to the side of the cell door, knock on the door (lightly, respectfully – not like the fucking police), and call their name. When they answer, say excuse me, state your business, and keep it moving.

There are several reasons why you don't want to just start popping your ugly face into another prisoner's window. For one, it's just disrespectful. For two, you might end up seeing something you don't want to see – like a man pulling on his dick (unless you're weird and you *do* want to see some shit like that). And for three, you might see something the prisoner inside the cell doesn't want you to see, and that can lead to a problem.

Prisoners do all kinds of things in their cells. You don't want to pop your mug in another prisoner's window and catch him doing something you are not meant to see. That will upset the person doing it and they will dislike you. Furthermore, if shortly after you leave they get busted, guess who the suspected rat is going to be? That's not a good thing for you.

So, keep your face out of other prisoner's windows. It's offensive and disrespectful. Leave all that sneak attack shit to the police.

Be respectful to guards and staff

Even if you are one of those people who hate the police, be respectful to the guards and free-staff. It will not benefit you one bit to show your lack of respect towards prison staff of any kind; and since it will not benefit you, you have no purpose for doing it. Right?

Relationship building in prison goes further than with just your fellow prisoners. After all, most prisoners are in the same position you are and have limited power, access, money, resources, etc. The ones who do have more power, access, money, and resources, however, are the people who will go home at the end of their day: them. Therefore, having a cordial relationship with them can be *extremely* valuable.

Keep them out of your cell

One of the most obvious reasons to be respectful to the guard on your yard, and especially in your building is to keep them out of your cell. The most common form of reprisal from a disrespected guard is to search your cell and take all the extra things you've hustled up and really aren't supposed to have, or, to just disrespect you back by trashing your belongings.

Most of the time, and guards are very aware of this, you are going to have stuff in your cell that you are not supposed to have: extra property; canteen that you don't have receipts for; appliances that you bought off of another prisoner, and therefore, it is not on your property card; or, other forms of contraband. It's hard to come up on stuff, so when you do, you don't want to lose it for disrespecting a guard.

Warnings

If you're "under surveillance" in any way – if your mail is "flagged," if your visitors are being watched closely, if your prison's security squad is trying to build a case against you, etc. – you would want to know, right? Well, that is another reason why it's wise to be "friendly" with them, as *they* are the ones who will be able to give you that kind of information.

Now, being "friendly" with them doesn't *guarantee* that they will give you a heads up when something is going on, but it does increase your chances.

The blind eye

Being that there are so many petty rules in prison, it is likely that you are doing something you're not supposed to be doing. Some things that are basic, everyday activities for folks in the free world are considered crimes in prison. So breaking rules in prison is extremely easy to do.

You don't want any angry, bitter, bored guard hawking you and waiting for you to do something so he/she can write you up or punish you in some way. Little, minor confrontations can lead to big problems – including assault accusations, etc.

Having a good rapport with them will make them less likely to stalk you while waiting for a slip-up. In fact, it is likely that, when they do see you slip up in some way, as long as it's not something that will front *them* off, they will act as if they didn't see it and let you go about your business.

CHAPTER 7
SURVIVING PRISON FOOD

Surviving prison is one thing. But surviving prison *food*? Well, that's something entirely different. I mean, we all know that prison is full of brutes and bullies, but there's a solution for that. We all know that prison can be depressing, but there's a solution for that, too; go to the mental health chapter, learn some techniques to keep the mind healthy, and apply them. And if you need money? Go to the section of this book where I teach you different hustles, learn/do one, and get paid. I can show you how to do *all* that, and a couple of other things, too, but what I can't show you is how to *enjoy* prison food. I'm just not sure it's possible....

I've been to my fair share of prisons over the years, and while the quality of the food usually varies from place to place, for the most part it's never good; the quality variations being between bad and worse. And although one might think you'd get used to it after a while, it actually works quite the opposite.

See... the prisons meals are made up according to a "nutrition/caloric" "guideline." In other words, "by law," the prisons have to provide us with a certain amount of "nutrition" and "calories." No part of that has anything to do with *taste* quality or variation, so most prisons have created a few meals that meet the "nutrition/caloric" "guideline," at the least amount of expense to them, then they rotate the meals around and around.

However, the creativity of those in charge of designing the meals is quite impressive, as our meals usually consist of one or more of the following: beans, potatoes, beans, bread, beans, eggs, bread, potatoes, eggs, baloney, beans, baloney, potatoes, and, if you're lucky, a side order of beans, potatoes, and/or bread. Now, do you really think anyone is going to get used to that?

I must admit that the prisons do serve other meals. However, like I said, they are usually served with one or more of the above-mentioned items, and they (the other meals), too, are less than desirable. I mean, I've been eating greasy pancakes every Monday for so long, even the *smell* of the grease turns my stomach....

I'm sure by now you understand the pain and suffering capable of being caused by years and years of prison food. So, with that point being made clear, the question becomes: How does one survive such an abusive and torturous menu? Well, here is the answer...

For 1) Prison food isn't going to actually murder you until sometime after the 10th year, so you have *some* kind of a "grace" period; sure, you may not enjoy your meals, but you will survive them (hopefully). And for 2) Most prisons allow the purchase of canteen items. Therefore, you better A) Figure out a way to get money to purchase canteen, as it does get expensive; and B) Learn how to cook a variety of good meals using the food sold on canteen. (And yes, I said a variety; because even those meals become deadly after eating them over and over for 10, 15, or however many years.)

Now, nobody knows what you like to eat better than you, and over time I am sure you will get creative and become your own master chef. However, until that time comes, here are some of the more popular prison recipes created by yours truly – your fellow prisoners. Read them, learn them, try them... It might just save your life.

Bean and Cheese Burritos

Materials required:

Hot pot, bowl, spoon, cooking bags

Ingredients:

6 chili-flavored Ramen noodle soups
2, 8-ounce bags of instant refried beans
1, 12-ounce bag of hot and spicy corn chips
6 ounces of cheese spread
2 packs of flour tortillas (16-20)
1, 5-ounce bottle of Tapatio hot sauce

Preparations:

Fill your hot pot with water and plug it in. While you're waiting for the water to boil, crush all 6 of your Ramen noodle soups while still in their individual packs, open them, set the seasoning packs aside, and pour all the crushed noodles into a bowl. Then, open both bags of beans and pour them into a separate bowl. Put 6 ounces of cheese spread into a cooking bag and tie the bag at the top. Set both bowls of beans and the bag of cheese aside.

Cooking:

Once your water is boiling, pour the necessary amount into the bowl of crushed noodles, as well as your bowl of beans, and put a lid on each bowl. Fill the hot pot back up with water, and while you're waiting for the noodles and beans to cook, put the bag of cheese into the hot pot so that it will melt.

Once the noodles have finished cooking, drain any/all remaining water, and pour all of the noodles into a cooking bag. Add the desired amount of seasoning salt and mix it up with the noodles real good by tossing it all around in the bag.

After the seasoning is evenly mixed throughout the noodles, check to see if the beans are finished cooking. If/when they are, scoop them out of the bowl and into the cooking bag with the noodles. Mix the noodles and beans thoroughly and evenly.

By this time the cheese will be melted, so take it out of the hot pot, rip a small opening in the corner of the bag so you can squeeze melted cheese out of it, and set it aside. Then, open the pack of tortillas and lay them out flat, 4 at a time, on your <u>clean,</u> metal bunk. Put the desired amount of noodle/bean mix through the center of each tortilla, squirt the desired amount of cheese over the noodle/bean mix, and then sprinkle a handful of hot and spicy corn chips over that, followed by a bit of Tapatio hot sauce. Roll the burrito up, put it in a cooking or tortilla bag, and repeat the process until all of the burritos are made.

Note: Some prisoners like to heat up their tortillas by placing them on top of the hot pot and steaming them. This is a good idea as it will not only heat the tortillas, but allow you to roll the burritos without the tortillas cracking. If you don't want to heat/steam the tortillas, you might just want to fold them in half like a soft taco.

The reasons why you are putting all of the burritos into a cooking bag is because A) You will likely have more burritos than you and your celly will eat in one sitting; B) You can then set the cooking bag full of burritos on top of the hot pot to heat them up before eating them.

Chicken Fajitas

<u>Materials required:</u>

Hot pot, bowl, spoon, cooking bags

<u>Ingredients:</u>

4 chili-flavored Ramen noodle soups
3, 4.5-ounce pouches of chicken breast cuts
10-12 flour tortillas
1, 12-ounce bag of hot and spicy corn chips
2 ounces of sliced jalapeño peppers

Preparations:

Fill the hot pot with water and plug it in. While you're waiting for the water to boil, crush all 4 of the Ramen noodle soups while still in their individual packs, open them, set the seasoning packs aside, and pour all the crushed noodles into a bowl.

Open the 3 pouches of chicken breast cuts and pour them all into a cooking bag. Dump out all the chili peppers and jalapenos into a bowl, cut them down into a size of your desire, then dump them all into the cooking bag with the chicken breast cuts. Tie the cooking bag at the top and shake all the chicken, chili peppers, and jalapeños around until it's all mixed together thoroughly.

Cooking:

Once the water is boiling, pour the necessary amount into the bowl of crushed noodles and cap the bowl with a lid. Then, while you're waiting for the noodles to cook, fill the hot pot back up with water, and set the bag of chicken, chili peppers, and jalapeños inside the hot pot so that it will heat up.

Once the noodles have finished cooking, drain any/all remaining water, and pour all of the noodles into a cooking bag. Add the desired amount of seasoning salt, and mix it up with the noodles real good by tossing it all around in the bag.

Next, take the bag of chicken cuts, chili peppers, and jalapeños out of the hot pot, tear open the bag, and dump everything into the cooking bag with the noodles. Shake the noodles, chicken cuts, chili peppers, and jalapeños around inside the bag so that everything is mixed thoroughly.

Lay the flour tortillas out on top of your *clean*, metal bunk, and cover half of each tortilla with fajita mix. Put a handful of hot and spicy corn chips on top of each pile of fajita mix, fold the flour tortillas in half (like a soft taco), and stack each fajita in a cooking or tortilla bag. When you are ready to eat, simply set the bag of fajitas on top of the hot pot to heat them up, and enjoy.

Meat Teriyaki Bowl

Materials required:

Hot pot, bowls, spoons, cooking bags

Ingredients:

4 hot-n-spicy vegetable-flavored Ramen noodle soups
1, 7-ounce pouch of shredded beef
8 ounces of Chinese sausage
16 ounces of mixed vegetables
6 ounces of chili corn chips
1, 6-ounce bottle of teriyaki sauce

Preparations:

Fill the hot pot with water and plug it in. While you're waiting for the water to boil, break all 4 Ramen noodle soups in half and put 4 halves into each bowl. Set the seasoning packs aside.

Open the pouch of shredded beef and put it all into a cooking bag. Break down the Chinese sausage into small chunks and put it all into the cooking bag with the shredded beef. With your hands, spread all the meat around the bottom of the bag, and then pour the bottle of teriyaki sauce over the meat. Tie the top of the bag and set it aside, allowing the meat to sit and marinate. Put the mixed vegetables in a separate cooking bag, tie the top, and set it to the side as well.

Cooking:

Once the water is boiling, pour the necessary amount into each bowl of noodles and cap the bowls with their lids. While the noodles are cooking, put the bag of meat/teriyaki-sauce and the bag of mixed vegetables in the hot pot so that they will heat up; put more water in the hot pot if necessary.

Once the noodles are fully cooked, drain any/all remaining water. Then, add the desired amount of seasoning to each bowl of noodles and stir until the seasoning is completely mixed throughout.

By this time the meat and vegetables will be done cooking. Take out the meat and tear a small hole in the corner of the bag, allowing all the teriyaki sauce to drain into the sink or toilet. Take a spoon, make an opening in the middle of each bowl of noodles, and pour one half of the meat into the center of one bowl, and one half of meat into the other. Take the bag of mixed vegetables out of the hot pot, tear it open, and spread half of the vegetables over the top of one bowl, and half over the top of the other. Lastly, get yourself a couple of pencils, and enjoy.

FYI: Just kidding about the pencils.

Beef and Bean Burritos

<u>Materials Required:</u>

Hot pot, bowls, spoon, cooking bags

<u>Ingredients:</u>

6 Chili-flavored Ramen noodle soups
2, 8-ounce bags of instant refried beans
1, 8-ounce bag of instant rice
1, 10-ounce summer sausage
1, 11.25-ounce pouch of chili beans
6 ounces of jalapeño cheese spread
4 ounces of mayonnaise

<u>Preparations:</u>

Fill the hot pot with water and plug it in. While you're waiting for the water to boil, crush all 6 of the Ramen noodle soups while still in their individual packs, open them, set the seasoning packs aside, and pour all of the crushed noodles into a bowl, followed by the rice. Pour all of the instant refried beans into a separate bowl and set the bowl of noodles/rice and the bowl of beans to the side.

Now break the summer sausage up into small chunks and place them inside of a cooking bag. Open the pouches of roast beef, pour them into the cooking bag with the summer sausage chunks, mix all the meat together, and tie the top of the bag. Put 6 ounces of cheese spread into a separate cooking bag, followed by the 4 ounces of mayonnaise, and tie the top of that bag, too. Set both the meat and cheese/mayo bags aside.

<u>Cooking:</u>

Once the water is boiling, pour the necessary amount into the bowl of noodles/rice, as well as the bowl of beans. Put a lid on each bowl.

Fill the hot pot back up with water and let it boil. Set the pouch of chili beans in the bottom of a bowl, flat, and set the bag of meat on top of it. Once the water is boiling, pour the necessary amount into the bowl to allow the pouch of chili beans and bag of meat to heat up, and then set the bag of cheese/mayo inside the hot pot so that it will melt and mix together.

Once the noodles/rice have finished cooking, drain any/all remaining water, and pour all of the noodles/rice into a cooking bag. Add the desired amount of seasoning salt, and mix it up with the noodles/rice real good by tossing it all around in the bag.

After the seasoning is evenly mixed throughout the noodles/rice, check to see if the beans are finished cooking. If/when they are, scoop them out of the bowl and into the cooking bag with the noodles/rice. Mix the noodles/rice and beans thoroughly and evenly.

By now the bag of meat and chili bean pouch should be heated up. Open the chili bean pouch, squeeze all the chili beans into the cooking bag with the noodles/rice/refried-beans and mix it all together. Once it's all mixed thoroughly and evenly, do the same with the bag of meat.

Now you have a cooking bag full of burrito filling. Take the bag of cheese/mayo, mix both substances together inside the bag, rip the bag open, squeeze it all into the burrito filling, and mix everything together thoroughly.

Lay out the tortillas on your *clean,* metal bunk, put burrito filling down the center of each tortilla, roll or fold, and place each one inside of a cooking or tortilla bag. Once you have finished, you can heat them up by setting the bag of burritos on top of the hot pot, and then eat them at your leisure.

Beef Soft Tacos

Materials required:

Hot pot, bowl, spoon, cooking bags

Ingredients:

6 chili-flavored Ramen noodle soups
1, 7-ounce pouch of shredded beef
1, 6-ounce pouch of beef crumbles
1, 10-ounce beef summer sausage
1, 11.25-ounce pouch of chili beans
6 ounces of cheese spread
4 ounces of mayonnaise
10-12 flour tortillas

Preparations:

Fill the hot pot with water and plug it in. While you're waiting for the water to boil, crush all six of the Ramen noodle soups while still in their individual packs, open them, set the seasoning packs aside, and pour all the crushed noodles into a bowl.

Open the pouches of shredded beef and beef crumbles and pour everything into a cooking bag. Break the summer sausage down into small chunks, and put it all into the cooking bag with the other meat. Tie a knot at the top of the bag, shake all the meat up thoroughly, and set it aside. Once that is complete, scoop out 6 ounces of cheese spread and put it into a cooking bag. Add 4 ounces of mayonnaise to the cheese spread, and tie the bag off at the top.

Cooking:

Once the water is boiling, pour the necessary amount into the bowl of crushed noodles and cap the bowl with a lid. Lay the pouch of chili beans in the bottom of a bowl, flat, set the bag of meat on top of it, and pour the remaining water into the bowl so that the chili beans and meat heat up. Fill the hot pot back up with water, plug it in, and set the bag of cheese/mayo inside so that it heats and melts together.

Once the noodles have finished cooking, drain any/all remaining water, and pour all of the noodles into a cooking bag. Add the desired amount of seasoning salt, and mix it up with the noodles real good by tossing it all around in the bag.

Take the bag of mixed meat, tear it open, and dump it all into the cooking bag with the noodles. Open the pouch of chili beans and put them into the cooking bag with the noodles and meats, and then mix all the ingredients together evenly and thoroughly.

Lay the flour tortillas out on top of your clean, metal bunk, and cover half of each tortilla with soft taco mix. Take the bag of cheese/mayo out of the hot pot, and kneed the bag until the cheese and mayonnaise is mixed together thoroughly. Tear a small hole in the corner of the bag so you can squeeze cheese/mayo sauce out onto your soft tacos, and squeeze the desired amount onto each. Fold the tortillas in half and stack each soft taco inside of a cooking or tortilla bag.

When you are ready to eat, simply set the bag full of soft tacos on top of the hot pot to heat them up, and enjoy.

Spaghetti and Meat balls

Materials Required:

Hot pot, bowl, spoon, cooking bags

Ingredients:

4 beef-flavored Ramen noodle soups
1, 12-ounce pouch of meatballs and tomato sauce
1, 8-ounce beef summer sausage
6 ounces of nacho cheese chips
6 ounces of cheese spread
4 ounces of mayonnaise

Preparations:

Fill the hot pot with water and plug it in. While you're waiting for the water to boil, break all six of the Ramen noodle soups in half while still in their individual packs, open them, set the seasoning packs aside, and put all 8 halves of Ramen noodle soup blocks into a bowl.

Break the summer sausage down into small chunks and put it all into a cooking bag. Open the pouch of meatballs and tomato sauce and pour the entire pouch into the cooking bag with the summer sausage chunks. Tie a knot at the top of the cooking bag and mix the summer sausage chunks evenly throughout the meatballs and tomato sauce. Put 6 ounces of cheese spread into a cooking bag, add 4 ounces of mayonnaise, and tie a knot at the top of the bag.

Cooking:

Once the water is boiling, pour the necessary amount into the bowl of noodles and cap the bowl with a lid. Set the bag of cheese/mayo inside of a bowl, and pour the remaining water into the bowl so that the cheese/mayo will melt and mix together. Fill the hot pot back up with water, plug it in, and set the bag of meatballs, tomato sauce, and summer sausage inside so that it will heat up.

Once the noodles are done cooking, drain any/all remaining water, and then dump the noodles into a cooking bag. Sprinkle only two of the beef seasoning packets over the noodles, and mix it up real good by tossing it all around in the bag.

Check to see if the bag of materials, tomato sauce, and summer sausage is hot. If so, rip a little hole in the bottom of the bag and allow all the meat and sauce to spill into the bag of noodles. Then, pick up the bag of ingredients; hold it up with one hand by the top of the bag, and with your other hand, shake all the noodles, meat, and sauce around until it's mixed thoroughly.

Take the bag of cheese/mayo sauce, tear a small hole in the bottom, and squeeze all of the cheese/mayo sauce into the cooking bag with the noodles, meat, and tomato sauce, and repeat the process of holding the top of the bag up with one hand and shaking the bottom around with the other until all of the ingredients – noodles, meatballs, tomato sauce, summer sausage chunks, and the cheese/mayo – are mixed together thoroughly.

You now have a cooking bag full of spaghetti and meatballs. Put half into one bowl, and the other half into another bowl. Throw 3 ounces of nacho cheese chips on top of each bowl, and enjoy.

Hot and Spicy Fish Dish

Materials Required:

Hot pot, bowl, spoon

Ingredients:

2 chili-flavored Ramen noodle soups

1, 8 ounce bag of instant rice
1, 4.5-ounce pouches of tuna
2, 4-ounce pouches of fish steaks (any flavor)
1 bottle of hot chili Sriracha sauce

Preparations:

Fill the hot pot with water and plug it in. While you're waiting for the water to boil, put one soup and one half bag of rice into each bowl. Set the seasoning packs aside.

Cooking:

Once the water is boiling, pour the necessary amount into each bowl, and then cap each bowl with a lid. Fill the hot pot back up with water, plug it in, and then put the fish steak pouches in the hot pot to heat them up.

Note: Depending on the size of the hot pot, you may have to heat the fish steak pouches separately.

Once the bowls of noodles/rice are fully cooked, drain any/all remaining water, and sprinkle the desired amount of seasoning into each bowl. Then, drain the water out of the tuna pouches and pour one pouch into each bowl. Stir the noodles, rice, seasoning and tuna until each bowl is mixed thoroughly.

Once the noodles/rice is cooked and mixed thoroughly with the tuna, take the fish steaks out of the hot pot and put one into each bowl. Squirt the desired amount of Sriracha sauce over the top of each bowl, and enjoy.

Beef Tamales

Materials Required:

Hot pot, bowl, spoon, cup, cooking bag

Ingredients:

16 ounces of nacho or corn chips
1, chili-flavored Ramen noodle soup
1, 8-ounce bag of instant rice
1, 8-ounce spicy summer sausage
1, 7-ounce pouch of shredded roast beef
1.5 ounces (or desired amount) of diced chili peppers
1.5 ounces (or desired amount) of diced jalapeños

Preparations:

Fill the hot pot with water and plug it in. While you're waiting for the water to boil, crush the Ramen noodle soup while it's still in its pack, open it, set the seasoning pack aside, pour it into a bowl, then open the bag of rice and pour it into the bowl, too. Next, pour the bag of instant refried beans into a separate bowl and set both bowls aside.

Open the pouch of shredded beef and dump it all out into a cooking bag. Break the summer sausage down into small chunks and mix it in with the shredded beef. Tie the top of the bag and set it to the side.

Grab the bag of chips, let the air out of the bag, and while leaving the chips inside the bag, crush them all down into dust.

Cooking:

Once the water is boiling, pour the necessary amount into the bowl of noodles/rice as well as the bowl of beans, and put a lid on each bowl.

Next, you need to pour a little bit of water into the chip bag with the crushed chips. You need to do so gradually so that you don't add too much, as you only want an amount of water that will allow you to knead the crushed chips into a dough-like substance. So, pour a little bit of water, then knead the crushed chips into "dough," and if you need a little more water, add it at that time.

Once you've poured the necessary amount of water into the crushed chips, fill the hot pot back up, and put the bag of meat into the hot pot so that it will heat up while you finish kneading the crushed chips into "dough."

After you've kneaded most of the crushed chips together through the chip bag, tear down one side of the bag, and then along the bottom, so that it becomes one large piece of flat plastic. Doing this will allow you to knead the crushed chips thoroughly and into a big, flat piece.

Note: Many prisoners like to use the edges of the bag, or an entirely different bag/piece-of-plastic to flatten and shape the dough.

Once you have formed the dough into one big piece (about a quarter-of-an-inch thick), you should cut it into pieces *twice* the size of what you want each tamale to be. (Keep in mind that it's easier to make larger-sized tamales – about 3 inches by 6 inches.)

Check to see if the beans are done cooking. If/when they are, spread beans over half of the dough pieces. Check the noodles/rice to see if it's finished cooking. If/when it is, drain any/all remaining water, add the desired amount of seasoning salt, and stir thoroughly. Then, spread the noodles/rice over the same dough pieces that you have spread beans over.

Once that step is complete, take the bag of meat out of the hot pot and mix it all around inside the bag. Then, open the bag, and pile an even amount of meat on the dough pieces you've put beans, noodles, and rice on. Take the peppers and jalapenos, and sprinkle the desired amount of top of the meat.

Lastly, cover the filling-full pieces of dough with pieces of dough you did not put anything on, and seal the sides by pressing them together. In the end, you should have something that resembles a hot pocket and tastes deliciously.

Meat and Cheese Nachos

Materials Required:

Hot pot, bowl, spoon, cooking bag

Ingredients:

1, 16 ounces of nacho chips
1, 4-ounce bag of instant refried beans
1, 11.25-ounce pouch of chili beans
1, 7-ounce pouch of shredded beef
1, 5-ounce spicy summer sausage
1, 8-ounce container of cheese spread
4 ounces of mayonnaise
2 ounces of sliced jalapeños

Preparations:

Fill the hot pot with water and plug it in. While you're waiting for the water to boil, put all of the cheese and mayonnaise into a cooking bag. Tie a knot at the top of the bag and set it aside. Open the refried beans, pour them into a bowl, and set it to the side, too.

Next, open the bag of chips (the standard way), and then tear carefully down one side and along the bottom so that what you end up with is one, flat, large piece of plastic that will serve as a plate.

Open the pouch of shredded beef and dump it all into a cooking bag, and with your hands, make sure the beef is shredded apart nicely. Then, open the summer sausage, break the entire sausage down into little pieces with your hands, and put the pieces into the cooking bag with the shredded beef. Take out the sliced jalapeños, cut each one in half, and throw those in the bag, too. Mix the shredded beef, summer sausage, and jalapenos up really well, then tie a knot at the top of the bag and set it aside.

Cooking:

Once the water is boiling, pour the necessary amount into the bowl of refried beans and cap the bowl with a lid. Then, fill the hot pot back up with water, plug it in, and put the pouch of chili beans inside.

As soon as the refried beans have completely cooked, take out the pouch of chili beans, open it up, dump it all into the bowl with the refried beans, and mix both kinds of beans together. Once the beans are mixed together thoroughly, put a lid on the bowl to keep them warm.

The next step is to put the bag of meat/ jalapeños and the bag of cheese/mayo into the hot pot so that the meat/ jalapeños will heat up and the cheese/mayo sauce will melt into one, nice cream.

It should only take a few minutes for the meat/ jalapeños to heat up and the cheese/mayo to melt, so as soon as you see it's ready, open the bowl of beans and pour them evenly over the chips. Then, take out the meat/ jalapeños, tear open the bag, and spread it out evenly on top of the beans.

For the final step, take out the bag of cheese/mayo, and make sure it's mixed together nicely by kneading the bag. It will be very hot, so you may want to put a towel over your hand while doing this. Then, once it's mixed thoroughly into a cheese/mayo cream, tear the bottom corner of the bag open, squeeze the creamy sauce all over the top of the chip/bean/meat/ jalapeños pile, and enjoy.

CHAPTER 8

THE JUVENILE'S GUIDE TO SURVIVAL IN PRISON: 10 EASY STEPS TO ENSURE YOU RETURN TO SOCIETY IN ONE PIECE

By James Adrian (Jackson, Michigan)

I would like to thank you for picking up this book. I will attempt to give you all the lessons I have learned in my 20 years in prison. I know that the art of convicts sticking together or trying to help each other has pretty much went out the window. I am one who still believes in helping my fellow brother. I was a juvenile when I left society, so the many lessons I've learned came while I was in prison. When you step through those doors you are on your own. You are what we call "a fish." You are tossed in the water with sharks, alligators and many other creatures that will devour you. With my help you will have a chance to not only avoid the many pitfalls that await you, but find the most efficient way to be successful once you return to society.

Lesson 1
The first thing you are to do is erase that stupid look off your face. We already know you are scared, so it's best not to look it. You have to appear to have a little rough edge to you. When you get to your cell, don't ask a bunch of questions. There's going to be a guy in your cell who is your bunky. He don't want you in the cell because you don't know how to "jail". Which means you don't know the many rules to living in such tight quarters with another man. You don't have any appliances, and 9 times out of 10 he was about to move someone who he knows into the cell but the move was not done before you came into the cell.

Once you have made your bed it's time to step out of the cell and see what's going on. I would recommend that you go into the dayroom where everyone playing cards and look on the wall for the rules. You have to know the rules of the prison before anything. You never want to start off by having the COs telling you what you can't do. They know you are new here also, so you can become their project real quick. They want to welcome you to prison by writing tickets on you. A ticket is what you get when you violate the rules of the prison. When you receive a ticket, you can be sanctioned. You can be placed in your cell for a certain amount of days. You will only be allowed to go eat your meals in the chow hail or use the shower or bathroom if there is not one in your cell. The tickets can also affect your release from prison. The parole board monitors your behavior by the amount of tickets you receive while you're in prison, so avoid them at all cost.

Lesson 2
The best weapon you have is your eyes and ears. The easiest way to avoid conflict is to stay out of people's business. You don't see anything, you don't hear anything. The things you need to know, you figure out on your own. When it's time to go eat, follow the line of other inmates and stay out of people's way. You have to respect people's space, and have good manners. It's OK to say excuse me, or thanks. When you get to the chow hall make sure you don't sit in anybody's seat. There are going to be sections that belong to different organizations, so find a spot by yourself.

You're getting into the thick of things now and you are starting to mingle in the dayroom and enjoy the yard. This is when someone will approach you. They want to know where you're from. If you look young, how old you are. The thing you have to figure out is what is their angle, better yet, what do they want? Are they just trying to be friendly? Are they trying to see what they can get out of you? Are they trying to get you to join an organization? Are they trying to get you to do something for them? This is what you have to figure out, and fast. You never want to share too much of your personal information, but you should be willing to engage in some friendly conversation. If nothing else, remember this; everyone needs a friend in prison. I said EVERYONE. It doesn't matter how big and tough you think you are; you have to be able to trust someone.

Lesson 3

There is a big picture here, and as the old saying goes, birds of a feather flock together. You have to choose your company correctly. There's going to be many different groups all around you, most you will never know. You have the Christians, Muslims, the Gangs, the Cities, and those who just build friendships over the years. You have to find out where you fit in in all of this. That is on the more positive side. You also have the guys who deal in homosexuality the guys who are labeled snitches, and guys who are stealing. You have the guys who are drug addicts and alcoholics. You have the hustlers and the guy who just wants to run scams. You can be anything you want in prison and everyone has a story. It is about how you want to be viewed and this is done by how you carry yourself and who you spend your time with. You never want to find yourself spending a lot of time at the CO's desks; in here, perception is reality. You may not be giving them information about things going on in prison, but that is how you will be viewed if this begins to be a pattern. I am one to believe it's best to do your time the easiest way possible, without conflict.

You have to know how to communicate and talk to your peers. The most asked questions you will receive is how much time are you doing? What are you in here for? This is very important. In here, murder is looked at as being respectable and rape is frowned upon. I would say any crime against women or children immediately makes you a target for anything, and I mean anything. The problem with crime is that it's always done to someone else's family member. You must keep that in mind when you speak about why you are in prison. That was someone's mother, brother, aunt, cousin, friend, daughter or significant other. I would recommend that you keep the details to a minimum.

Lesson 4
There are certain rules that have to be followed, and the only way you will know them is by someone telling them to you. When it comes to your living conditions, you have to be considerate to the person you are sharing a cell with. The cell is already too small for two grown men to live in to begin with. You have a bunk bed and two desks and two chairs, you may even have a toilet. You have to keep your area clean and neat. You have to make your bed when you get out of it. Make sure you keep your sheets and clothes clean so there's no odor in the cell. This may mean you have to get you a laundry man to wash your clothes. You will have to work out a payment plan with him to get your stuff washed on a daily basis. You may also want to do the same with your barber. These are the two people you never want to have a misunderstanding with. The most important thing to never forget is you have to share a cell. You should always set your schedule around your cellmate's. This will allow you both to have the cell to yourself sometimes. When your cellmate gets off work, comes from school, visits or any other call-out, give him the cell for a while. When he gets out of the shower, leave the

cell. This gives him some time to lotion up or do what he needs to do.

You never wake a person up under any circumstances. The only time that we are able to escape our harsh reality of prison is in our dreams. It has to be an emergency. You don't cut your hair in the cell, you don't have no one else in the cell, and you respect your cellmate's property like you do your own. You don't touch anything of your cellmate's without his permission. You never leave the cell door open, or give anyone your key. It is always best to have all your own appliances. You have to get you a TV first. It is the most important pacifier while you are doing time. You can go to the store and buy the food and hygiene you need. You never want to borrow anything from anybody. That is one of the easiest ways to run into trouble. Make sure you buy you a few locks to keep all your property safe. This will limit the opportunity to have your things stolen. You never give out things that you can't afford to lose. Whenever you let someone borrow something, there is a possibility you may never see it again. You should always try to keep in mind that you can't bring attention to the cell. This means that you should not give the COs a reason to "shake it down" (search). When your cell is shook down, your personal belongings are searched thoroughly and often left in a worse position that you would like. This is a tactic that is used by COs to frustrate you and your cellmate, and this could cause you and your cellmate to have conflicts with each other. This could lead to you catching tickets and having to spend time in the cell. This is an inconvenience to your cellmate because he can never get any time alone in the cell. This is why it is best to find someone you know or feel you have more in common with to live with.

Lesson 5

You will ultimately start to find your way around and start to play sports, lift weights or play cards. You will learn fast that sports are very competitive. It is the quickest way to get into a fight. You can show a guy up by playing better than him or you can foul him too hard on the basketball court. You should always keep your cool when playing sports. You will have to show that you can play because it's hard to get on the court. You can go to the dayrooms and find all type of stuff to do. You can play poker, spades, or blackjack. There is always going to be someone who wants to gamble with you, because you are the new guy who more than likely has money coming from the streets and you are not that good at gambling anyway. I want you to just remember this; what you think you know about gambling, you don't know. If you are going to gamble, never gamble with what you don't have. You never want to owe anyone. If it's not in your cell, don't bet it. This goes for any substance that you may find also. I would recommend that you don't gamble on any substances because you never know the effect it may have on you, and plus we are supposed to be trying to better ourselves.

Lesson 6
The hardest thing in prison to keep up is your health. We are subject to the worst of everything. The worst food, water, dental and health care. The items on the store list are filled with preservatives. We eat a lot of Ramen noodle soups which is high in sodium. We have chips, cookies and candy. We have to find the best way possible to survive with these items. There is no way possible that you can go to the chow hall and leave satisfied. The rations that you get are equivalent to a McDonald's Happy Meal. You get sick in prison if you are kind of on your own. You have to fill out a kite, which is a special document used to make an appointment with. Then you

will be called out 3 to 5 days later. The care is minimal. They used to blame every problem on smoking. They want to give you the least amount of care, to save money. The answer for all your dental issues is getting your tooth pulled. The best option is to wait until you are free to get anything done. They also charge you $5.00 for every time you get checked out. They will give you a flu shot and they check you for tuberculosis every year. The sad thing about prison is that there has been a rise in mentally challenged inmates lately. The effect of closing the mental hospitals and prisons that properly deal with these inmates has a lot of inmates not getting the care they need. You have to be more mindful of some of the guys around you that are not functioning properly and are subject to some strange behavior that could affect you sometimes. It's just hard for all of us to work together to better our condition when we are given less and expected to do more, all for the sake of attaining our freedom.

Lesson 7

The most important thing to a man while he is in prison is family. This is when we do all we can to stay connected. This is by far the most motivating force in prison. While you are in prison you are allowed to have contact visits with family member and friends. You have to go through the process of getting visiting applications and sending them out and having them returned. You have to place that person on your visitor's list and then you are ready to go. You are allowed 5 to 7 visits a month, and only two for the weekends. It changes for different levels. You get to hug and kiss at the beginning and the end of the visit. The part that is not fun at all is being strip searched after the visit. You have to wear your state issue shoes, but you can wear your personal clothes which you can order through approved catalogs. These catalogs can be attained through your unit block representative. You get to sit on the visit and hold hands. You are allowed to purchase vending machine food and take pictures with the money your family puts on a debit card before entering the prison. This is all very fulfilling and the closest thing to being free under the circumstance. The only other options you have of communication is through 15 minute phone calls at a time and letter through snail mail and Jpay. The Jpay machine allows you to send letters to family and friends who have set up accounts to reach out to you first. These messages are sent within 48 hours most of the time and speeds up the process of communication. The phone calls are good also, but they are so expensive, you have to pay almost $3.00 for each 15 minute call. You can put money on your phone through disbursement in $5.00 increments. There is also a number for your family to call to put money on their phones also. If you put the money on your phone through the prison, you can call any number you like. If your friends or family put money on their phones, you can only call the number they place the money on.

You have to explain the condition of your imprisonment to your support team in society because their understanding of prison is based on TV and it's a bunch of little details that they will never understand. The best way to do this is to let them know you need pictures and money on a regular basis. You have to keep contact with your siblings and children and steer them in the right direction by letting your life be an example. This will be the best advice you could ever give anyone.

Lesson 8
The down-side to prison is the fact that there is a place to put inmates who don't follow the rules or find themselves unable to get along with staff or other prisoners. This place is called "The Hole" by inmates and

Administrative Segregation or Ad-Seg. When you are placed in the hole you are disconnected from the prison population. You're put in your cell with nothing but your bed and a toilet. You get your meals brought to your cell and you may shower three times a week. That depends on which prison you are at. You are only allowed to write letters to communicate. There is no phone, appliances or contact visits. You have to go on your visits in handcuffs and belly chains wearing a jumpsuit that is provided by the prison. There are different penalties for violations ranging from contraband to assault with deadly weapons. The reason that this is so very important for you to pay attention to is because many have lost their lives here. One thing I have realized is that no one gets stabbed for minding their own business. You have guys who have been in the hole for years. It's very easy to lose your sanity sitting in those cells by yourself for long amounts of time, so it's best to avoid this part of prison at all cost.

Lesson 9
I have told you the goal is to get out of prison. A wise man once told me that if you are not doing everything to get out of prison, you are doing just enough to stay in. There are three ways out of prison: dead, the courts, or earn your way out. That is what I am going to talk about right here. There are going to be opportunities for you to take classes to help with your behavior and thinking process, you just have to be willing to take the time to settle down and get involved. This is the time for you to sit down and see what is required from the parole board that will raise your probability of freedom. They have classes like Thinking For Change, Violence Prevention Program, Cage Your Rage, Chance For Life. There's organizations that can help you with building character skills like NAACP, National Lifers of America, and The Prison Creative Arts Program. You can check out books

form the library and study from colleges if you choose to. The power is all in your hands to take back the power of your destiny. You don't have to let one mistake define who you are and how you're perceived. The power lies in you to change and it has to come from the inside. You can find your spiritual calling through studies. You can take vocational classes. Most people complain about their condition as opposed to taking advantage of what is here. If I would have done this, you never would have had a chance to read this and possibly change your life or avoid the pitfalls set to bring you down.

Lesson 10
This part is to remind you that you can't raise hell all your life. You have to think about who you are, and what you can do to give back to the same community you once terrorized. If you can get involved in any programs that donate or fund raiser for the needy, you should get involved. You can reach out to churches in your community and write letters.

CHAPTER 9

BEHIND THESE WALLS – A WOMAN'S PERSPECTIVE

By Victoria Lynn Simms (Salem, Oregon)

Hear my pain! As I am a Survivor. I have managed to stay in control on my mind. The negative effect they tried to place on my life I instead turned it into something quite positive. When they tried to make me go insane, it only made me wiser. When they tried to break my spirit and steal my sense of being, it only made me stronger. It's true I may have given them a little too much fuel and energy, but the whole time I was scratching, kicking and fighting the destruction of conformity to and of my mind. And with the fight I fought there was no such thing as comfort from anyone because even though, true enough, there may have been a few prisoners and guards alike with a real and genuine concern for my struggle and plights, their contempt of fear to help or express their agreement with my "causes" in any way only made me feel that much more alone, though bolder.

It's time to break the silence! Not that I have been silent since in. I would just now like to spend my time and energy bringing society up on their awareness. I would like to "write", and "talk", and write some more to anyone who will listen, hear, and read. I am a proud prisoner activist/litigator and have no shame in mine! And being as how I will shortly be released, I will be even more active once free to do so.

I had to turn to stone in order to survive prison and it's all too many daily humiliations and indignities, but that was my safety net and shield. It was to protect myself from the circumstances which were too far beyond what I could control. Though often times I felt pain and fear, I just put on a tough face and took it, whatever it was. I have in fact swallowed sooo many tears, as well as learned to be good at hiding my many, many emotion of hurt while busy being a stone. I have learned so many things since being in prison, but most of all how ignorant I had been to real prison life. It wasn't like anything I was taught and led to believe on TV. I thought I was "sharp", "cool", "smart", and knew it all, much like the rest of society think they do. They just have no idea what prison is really like and all about.

There is many things that go on behind these walls – different things, for sure – and not all are correct, nor on any kind of rehabilitative level at all. We are understandably brought to prison due to wrongs or illegal activities which we engage in; however, once in prison, "rights" and "wrongs" no longer exist nor count. Prison has been a living nightmare for real. I have been hit for years and wounded by the daggers of words put on me by the authorities, most of whom are dysfunctional and hateful, and go into these professions due to a driven by their own personal inadequacies. Both male and female guards have usually at one point or another in their lifetimes been abused in their pasts, and it's the cycle of repeat and recurrent effect that we prisoners reap! Racism is also freely and legally used in prisons. Black people, both women and men have always been treated unequal, at all times and places in the history or time. In prison I learned to be inhumane to some degree by not giving and sharing as God so much intended and commanded us to do. It is one of the most immediate rules of the prison not to give, care, nor be concerned about another unfortunate human being. If they should need or ask for a bar of soap to wash their ass, toothpaste to brush their teeth, shampoo to wash their hair, deodorant to keep from stinking, etc., you are to tell them "no". It is a shame and all a part of the humiliation and tearing down of one's self which is a programming and brainwashing in and of itself, these crucial types of necessities they would rather see you do without than to display a good heart or good will act of kindness. Corrections does not consist of what is good, or what is right for the harmony of the orderly operation of the facility, but it is instead more about the on-going tribulation of daily difficulties in making it through the day, from morning till night, from point "A" to "Z" without receiving some sort of punishment. Many prisoners won't even venture out of their cells at all unless they absolutely have to in attempts to avoid the daily petty, frivolous, knit-picking of and by the guards. You are constantly harassed for not only the most minor of things, but some totally invented and fabricated. It is even more common for the officers to prey on the weak, the minorities, the mentally-challenged, and even the elderly. If you can imagine what it would be like to rise awake every morning, get dressed all up in your little drab grey uniform, and look yourself in the eye of your mirror and say and ask yourself, "Let's see now; who can I go to work to humiliate, badger, and disrespect today?" Well, if you can imagine "that" then you must know that they are people who do not respect themselves, and you and I both know that has got to be a terrible way to feel.

There is no doubt about it, a prisoner must establish a pastime of different things in order to do their time. Something to take their mind away and to avoid the consistent daily nit-picks, harassments and other poppycock. Sleep is your only real peace of mind, but you can even be written up for little things while you're sleeping. Other mind escapes are radio, artwork, reading, physical fitness, crafts, etc.; however, I myself found my peace of mind through writing. It became my tool and way of keeping my dignity and bearing on who I really am. It became my own cognitive awareness on what power and control I had left on myself. And no matter how much power they had over me, I never bowed down nor surrendered to the point of allowing myself under their firm hold, and for that I am proud.

It was my writing which connected me to a different world and a therapy to help me rise above my pain. I learned to nurture myself in the art of gaining and maintaining a psychological advantage over their negative influences they yoke upon me. I may have been captured as their property; however, I graduated from being their prey to an egalitarian real quick like. I hold the principle of expecting whatever rights are due me under the Constitution be given to me. The world of the Department of Corrections is not what it is professed to be at all. And the truth be told, there is nothing correct about it, and it should have in fact been called the Department of Wrongs. It is majorly corrupt and run by professional sidewinders.

Upon entry to prison, I went from straight denial to becoming a straight rebel. I was about correcting the "correctional" guards within compliance of their own many rules, and then I went on to challenging the rules of the prison which I felt was total whack! I moved from those stages to studying all the law books I could get my hands on, and once knowledgeable enough I began to file suits and claims for the wrongs and illegal activities imposed upon me. I was making major moves, receiving publicity from the problems behind these walls, etc. However, it mostly proved to me how much more underhanded and dirtier that the prison officials could be. They reached out and touched me with harassment and retaliations that you couldn't even imagine. Segregation, excessive force, fabricated misconduct, disciplinary reports and much, much more. Your mail gets monitored and tampered with. The same with your visiting. They can basically cut you off illegally from the outside world.

My time remaining in prison is short now, and I hope to never return to a locked cell behind these walls again. My aim now is to inform society of what a nightmare prison really is. Living under the care of a bunch of busters and sidewinders is hard to do, but what's even harder is being away from your family and children. In my fifth year down, with one remaining, my baby boy committed suicide. Being without his mother for all those years proved to be too great for him. And my only surviving son just received a prison sentence; something common for the children of incarcerated mothers. I know and realize that many of my scars and the damage that I have acquired while being in prison will have a lasting effect on me, produced by the significant grief of tragic events. There may never go away at all. However, I know that some restoration and healing will take place and occur through what attention and awareness I intend to provide of the truth to what goes on behind bars. From a woman's standpoint and perspective. And through my real and personal experiences, I expect to deliver the scoop and the skinny of things real swell! They are not playing fair in here and I am sincerely in hopes that what survival skills helped me will help and work for others.

At this particular point I am working as an independent, representing reform by and of my own powers to detour and aid in preventing and discouraging more humans from falling prey to the prison system as I did. It is a perpetual-prison-machine and we are in fact an industry, a commodity and product! We are actually worth more per head in capital than cattle now-a-days. We have become the bigger and better goods and stock. We are rented out, sold and traded, every day. We are the investment for value and profit and are calculated according to dollar signs as to how much they expect and project to bring in from us down the line. Sad, but true. And due to the "best to warehouse humans" mentality many new scandalous and ridiculous laws have gone into effect, such as the three strikes, the habitual criminal act, the mandatory minimums, etc., all of which to capture, attract and reproduce more prisoners. The courts seem to be particularly targeting America's youth, and have been giving them phenomenal amounts of time, if not life sentences, without even batting an eye when handing it down to them. There is something terribly wrong with this picture, in which our society has become a party to, and this is why it is inevitable that they must be schooled to what's really going on. We have a problem here and it needs to be acknowledged in a major way before anything could possibly even begin to change or be done about it.

I, being a prisoner, have had to stuff many things – feelings, views, opinions, etc. – inside, but no more! I have stacked it all up and am more than eager to let it out. My stay in prison has inspired me and I am enthusiastic in my plight and eventually intend to write a book. It will be a much more detailed account of my prison experiences or what prison is really like – its inhumane and barbaric conditions, medical neglect, transfers to rental bed facilities and privatization joints, mental neglect, excessive force; on being a mother behind bars, the prison's legal services, and the corruption as a whole. The whole ball of wax. I have weathered the storm; however, there are many unfortunate souls who could not manage to turn the destruction and damage done to them into a positive aspect and direction. Those are the types who will come out to society mad at the world, or those responsible for their injustices. Society has just been so easily influenced by false propaganda, and will not only vote, but will rally for shit that ain't even just not right. The biggest and foremost problem is that they are blinded by what they desire to believe, which is if you lock everybody up, the world will be a better and more safe and peaceful place to live, but instead they are being fooled, hoodwinked and lied to about that of which they are supporting. And you know something, one of these days they are going to vote their own selves a bad hand because they would just be too brainwashed to realize it. Wouldn't that be ironic, to say the least?

I could not do much from prison because it's a place where you really have nowhere to turn because the corruption is nearly always core deep. From any kind of grievance system, all the way up to the top. They are underhanded and scratching each other's backs. It's a hell of a thing, and more often than not, if you do make it up to the courts, they too will usually go along with the DOC judgement or determination. And as you work your way up with your claim to the court justice levels, the harassment is great. So great that most of your fellow prisoners think that you must be crazy for even attempting to challenge the prison system about their wrongdoings in any way. It scares the other prisoners and they no longer want to be around you. They will back off from you and no longer want to affiliate with you. You would have to be in the situation for you to see how truly ridiculous and strange it seems. They would rather defend the guards if and when it comes to choosing up which side to take. I was involved in the class action suit and it was against a privatization corporation; however, all it took was a slice of pizza and some chicken to move my fellow prisoners to write statements to support the corporation. I couldn't believe it! There is no more honor among these new brand of thieves, nor is there any unity. They in fact have made a believer out of me that your fellow prisoner actually rates #2 on your scale of enemies. They will set you up in a heartbeat and give up the goods on you for nothing at all -- free of charge! They wouldn't have to get a nickel, any promises of an early release date, nor one red cent.

They just want to be good Samaritans, wannabe cops, and their noses are so far up the guards' asses that they don't know which way is out. It would just be so proper if prisoners could stick together at least long enough to get some things done. But it first takes you real work to study and figure out the "haters" from the "genuine", and even then, as mentioned earlier, when you do distinguish the genuinely concerned from the sidewinding busters of hatred, they are much too frightened to matter.

These shackles on my feet has been by far the biggest load I have ever had to carry in my lifetime. However, it has given me a very strong backbone. And with all the weight and baggage that one must carry upon exiting prison, they could not possibly be expected to snap, crackle, nor pop back into society without some sort of transitional counseling and a reality check. And as if they weren't punished and treated bad enough during their sentence in prison, once out they go through a whole new series of discriminating treatment. You can't land a job, the housing authority has new rules against prisoners getting any housing assistance upon release, and though you have done your time and paid your price and filled your debt to society, an ex-con is just treated badly in general, as if they are supposed to be punished the rest of their lives. I personally have redirected my attitude before being released and am using all of any negative bottled-up energy and fuel for constructive results and a positive outcome. I have faith in myself and the difference I intend to make when I bounce, and feel that if I did leave prison in the confused state and mixed-up mode which they expect us to; well, then, they really would have "won" the game after all, now isn't that right?

CHAPTER 10

HOW TO SURVIVE IN FEDERAL PRISON

By Unknown

If you have been sentenced to federal prison, you will become the property of the Bureau of Prisons (BOP). If you have been given a federal sentence, then it's likely that you'll be spending several years behind bars, but if you know what to expect right away, your life in prison will be much easier. If you want to know how to prepare for federal prison and how to survive in your new environment, just follow these steps.

Bite your tongue. If the judge doesn't allow you to self-surrender to the prison where you have been designated, you will be handed over to the U.S. Marshal services. Do not speak to a Marshal, or let him overhear a conversation, about your case or anything else for that matter. Nothing you can say will make the situation any better and it might even make things worse: just because you have already been convicted doesn't mean that you can't be charged with something else.

Don't ever forget that anything you say can be taken down in evidence and used against you. So, keep your mouth shut as much as possible.

Take advantage of medical care outside of prison if you have time. The choice and quality of care is significantly better outside of prison. Certain treatments that you take for granted might not be available in prison, or won't be as good. After all, if you're in prison and you don't like the prison dentist, where else are you going to go to have your teeth fixed? So, if there's time to do it, consider having a dental check-up before you self-surrender, and get anything important fixed.

- Also, if you wear glasses you may want to have an eye test and get new lenses, assuming you need them. As with dental care, you've got a better choice of lenses and frames outside prison.
- If you're lucky enough to have some time before prison, get a check-up or address any medical issues you've been having. Though you'll get medical care in prison, it's better to get medical attention before you're locked up.

Line up some reading material. Most federal prisons allow magazines and books to be sent to inmates – on condition that these are sent directly from the publisher or a retailer like Amazon. If you're self-surrendering and you know which prison you're going to be in, consider taking out a subscription for magazines/journals, and order a couple of books from Amazon to read. Do this a couple of days before you self-surrender.

- Alternatively, give your friends and family a shopping list of books/magazines and let them take care of ordering things. There's no web access in prisons, so make your selections before you enter prison.
- Though choosing reading material may be the last thing on your mind before you start your time in federal prison, being prepared for reading material (as soon as you're allowed to have it) can help you feel less lonely and more comforted when you begin your sentence.

Keep your guard up if you are sent to a hold-over facility or a prison camp. If you are placed in transit to prison, you may be sent to a hold-over facility. The facility you are sent to may be determined by whether you are designated for a low, medium, or high-level prison. Some of the living conditions in these facilities are not ideal, such as being placed in a two-man cell with up to three other inmates for 23 hours a day, being allowed out to rec in an enclosed area for one hour, and only being allowed to shower for five minutes twice a week.

- Each facility has its own rules -- just be prepared for the extreme conditions you may face.
- Be especially cautious during this time. You will be with other people who are in a state of uncertainty and are more likely to be volatile than they will be once they get settled in to the prison routine.

Learn the rules. Try to find out as much as possible about how the system works in the prison you will be living in. If there is an official rule-book for the prison, read it. You can be punished for breaking a rule that you didn't know existed. Breaking the rules will not only piss off personnel but inmates as well. It makes life harder for everyone. Ignorance of the rules is no defense. Information is power.

Bring the maximum amount of money that you are allowed to take to prison. You may be allowed a certain amount of money (up to $500). This money will be used to buy supplies you may need while incarcerated. This is called putting "money on your books." You will need money for supplies such as stamps, envelopes, snacks and also hygiene supplies.

- Cash is not necessary and will be confiscated. It's best to go in with a US Postal Service money order as they are widely accepted in all prisons (federal and state).
- Additionally, don't let anyone know that you have money. Pretend that you're poor and penniless. That way there's no danger of other prisoners trying to extort money from you.

Surviving In Prison

Don't trust anyone. That goes for guards, other prison officials, and the person in the cell next door. If someone is being nice to you, ask yourself "What's in it for him or her?" They almost always have some hidden motive that you don't know about. In prison, nothing is free. For example, if someone gives or loans you something, you will probably have to pay it back with a hefty rate of interest added. If you can't pay, they may demand a favor that could get you into big trouble, like hiding contraband in your cell.

Hide your emotions. If you want to look tough, do not show fear, anger, happiness, or pain. Emotions are your worst enemy because they reveal your weaknesses. Both inmates and guards prey on weakness. Don't give them the opportunity to do so. If someone can figure out what makes you angry, they can use that knowledge to manipulate you. In the same way, if someone knows what makes you happy, they can try to ruin it for you. And because they are around you 24/7, they have unlimited opportunities to test their manipulative skills on you.

Make use of your cellmates. Do not be overly friendly with your cell mates but do ask some questions. Many have been in prison before and will be able to give you information about the prison you are being sent to as well as the system itself. You will have to judge for yourself whether to believe any of the information. Use common sense and try to figure out if that person has a reason to lie or mislead you. Some convicts will try to intimidate new inmates or mislead them for fun. Be careful.

Choose your words carefully. Potentially, anything you say to guards or prisoners, no matter how innocent you think it is, can be used to hurt you, manipulate you, or be taken out of context. Avoid discussing dangerous conversational topics. Otherwise, it can easily get you into trouble. Obvious subjects to steer clear of are religion, politics, racial issues, or your own personal feelings about someone or their family and friends. #*Some of the prisoners you'll encounter may have a short temper, or are mentally ill, of low intelligence, or just plain bad. Prisoners like that don't have a warning written on their forehead – they look like regular guys.

- You can easily be misunderstood or deliberately misquoted by someone who's trying to stir up trouble. What starts out as a petty argument over a trivial issue can turn into someone bearing a strong personal grudge against you.
- Don't be paranoid. Just be aware that things may not be what they seem, such as the prisoner who tells you that gay or black people are just like everyone else, then asks what you think may in reality hate homosexuals or black people – he's just testing your attitude or yanking your chain.

Always be polite and respectful to guards and other prison employees. If you give them a reason to hate you, they can make your life even harder than it already is. So, don't give them a stick to beat you with. It's true that some prison employees are better than others. Even so, never forget whose side they're on – it certainly isn't yours. You need to get it in your head that the staff are always right and you need to do what they say. Even if you know it is wrong at the time, it is best to just follow the order, and if you have a problem with it, you can address it at some later point.

- For example, if you work as a server in the kitchen and a staff foreman tells you to go clean tables in the dining room though you know it's not a part of your duties. The best thing to do is to just go clean the tables, because you are an inmate and you are not going to win an argument with a staff member.
- Don't do anything that makes staff feel challenged or intimidated; they have various ways of making you pay for that mistake.

Don't stare at the other prisoners. Although you're simply curious about them, the other person can completely misinterpret what's happening. In prison, if someone stares at you it usually means they feel intense hostility or disapproval towards you. Alternatively, staring is a way of showing sexual interest. It's OK to look at people, but don't stare at them. There's a difference between looking and staring.

- When you're walking to your cell, do not stare into the other prisoners' cells. This is considered an invasion of privacy and can get you in big trouble.

Don't be a snitch. People who tell tales to the guards or other prisoners are despised by everyone and can be physically attacked. The best thing you can do in prison is to see everything, hear everything, and say nothing. If the guards ask you for information about some incident involving other prisoners, claim that you were looking the other way and didn't notice or hear anything. While this may irritate the staff on some level that you aren't willing to snitch, they will likely understand.

- Avoid being seen talking to guards in a friendly way because other
prisoners could assume (wrongly) that you're a snitch.
- Don't talk to prison staff any more than absolutely necessary, because while it may be just innocent conversation about the weather, other inmates won't perceive it that way.

Don't ask the staff to solve your problems. Truth is, you can never go to staff for assistance with issues you may have, or else you will have problems with inmates if you do. If you go to staff with a problem, the only thing they can do for you is put you in the SHU as a protective custody inmate, and that will cause you trouble throughout your entire incarceration.

- If you complain to staff, you're stuck out in no-man's-land between the staff and inmates. Neither group will help you. Try to get used to the fact that you have very few human rights in prison, and that you're largely powerless to change your circumstances.

Ask to be placed in the Secure Housing Unit (SHU) only in extreme circumstances. When fights occur in prison, the participants may be punished by being put in a segregation unit or be moved to a higher level of confinement, but it is extremely unusual for them to be charged with a crime, as long as all the participants were prisoners. Your legal protections in prison are severely curtailed by the system. The guards and administrators do not want anyone to make waves.

- Prison employees will punish you for making waves much more quickly than they will come to your aid. Sometimes the punishment will be official, in other cases it will be more subtle e.g. "forgetting" or "misplacing" something that you need.
- You always have the option to ask to be put in the hole for your own protection. The hole is unpleasant, but it is relatively safe. Don't ask for this kind of protection unless you fear for your life because if you go to the SHU you'll spend 99.9% of your time locked inside a cell.

Don't join a prison gang. Just like in the real world, in prison there are gangs. But in prison, gangs are far more prevalent. These gangs work very differently on the inside than on the outside. Be mindful of gang members, but avoid joining a gang; gang members are soldiers, and gang leaders demand absolute loyalty. If you join a gang, you may be ordered to do something that will keep you in prison a lot longer; a gang member has no choice, because aside from getting out of prison, there's only one way to quit a prison gang while in prison: to die.

- All prison gangs are separated first and foremost by the races they are typically associated with. Bloods/Crips/Black Guerrilla Family (African-American); the Mexican Mafia (Mexicans); MS-13 (Salvadoran/Honduran/Guatemalan/Nicaraguan); White Supremist/Nazi (Caucasian), etc. There are many different divisions.

Show allegiance to your race. It is crucial to your survival in the prison system to immediately show your allegiance to your race -- though this doesn't mean you have to join a gang to do it. If you are some white suburbanite 19-year-old kid that pledged yourself as a crip, and you used to buy the dope you got busted selling from your crip homeboys in the projects, that doesn't mean you can link up with them in prison. If you're white and you walk in slapping high fives with the brothers before you shake hands with the white dudes, you're going to send a rift through the whole community.

- This doesn't mean you have to get a swastika on your forehead or "Blood for Life" tattooed on your chest. It simply means whichever race you are associated with, you seek them out first and introduce yourself.
- You get to know inmates of your race first. Especially the "important" figures within your race. You can be "friendly" with people of other races after that.
- In prison, blacks, Mexicans, Chicanos, Asians, and whites all look after their own. This isn't the time to be colorblind.

Seek out people from your hometown. In most federal facilities, there are inmates from all over the country. You can do an inmate search prior to turning yourself in. You'll be able to look through the prison inmate listing to see if you know anyone or where their home state is. When you get to your designated facility, you need to find other inmates who are from your city or state; these are your "home boys" and they will usually help you with things you have an immediate need for, such as basic hygiene items and shoes.

But beware of your home boys if there is anything wrong with you or your case, like if you are an informant, sex offender, or anything else frowned upon by inmates, in which case your home boys will probably be the ones that will confront you on it. This could include assault, stabbing or whatever else they think you deserve.

Respect the personal space of the other prisoners and don't let them invade yours. You will be tested and if you allow others to get too close to you for comfort, they will just get closer and closer until your subservience is obvious. Have respect and never reach over someone else's plate at the mess hall for the pepper, salt, etc. Don't allow others to reach over your plate either, or you'll look like a pushover.

- Personal possessions like photographs, letters and other stuff are very important when someone is in prison. So, never borrow or use something that belongs to another prisoner unless he's told you it's OK to do it. Touching someone's personal possessions without their permission is a no-no.

Get used to the new rules. Above all, remember that the normal rules of the outside world simply don't apply any longer. When you're in prison, you're living on a different planet where all that matters to you is surviving the experience with as little damage as possible.

TIPS

- Letters and phone calls going in or out of a prison are routinely monitored. That's because the prison authorities are always looking for "dirt". If they spot something interesting, a copy or recording will be made for future investigation. Warn your friends and family that there's no such thing as privacy when you're inside prison.

- Bear in mind that anything you say, especially on the phone, is likely to be overheard by both prisoners and guards. There are snitches among your fellow inmates that are looking to trade

- Information for favors with the staff (this is encouraged by people like case managers). Be especially careful about criticizing another inmate as you can pretty much guarantee that it will get back to him.

- Keep a low profile and try to blend into the background when you are in prison. Stay under the radar of guards and other prison employees. Basically, don't draw attention to yourself if you can avoid it. Remember that the nail that stands out gets hammered in. Watch and learn.

- When you enter prison, try to concentrate on what's going on inside prison, because time will seem to pass faster that way. It's difficult not to think about the things you're missing out on in the outside world, but torturing yourself with it will just make you miserable. It certainly won't get you out of prison any faster. Instead, concentrate on the things you can control in prison, not the things that are out of your reach outside the prison fence.

- Inmates who are homosexual are usually looked down upon and are ostracized by other inmates. If you are gay, you best keep it to yourself while in prison, because it will only cause you problems. Inmates who are unusually young or cute-looking may be approached sexually by others who are testing the waters. If you are approached, it is best to decline; you do not want to become the property of some other inmates.

- Start eating like a horse, workout and study/practice street fighting techniques. At some point soon you are going to be tested and you'll need to show that you can look after yourself.
- Don't forget to get vaccinated for everything possible before sentencing, your county health service will do it at a reduced cost and it could save your life.
- When you have to go to the showers with 12 to 20 other inmates, wear boxers.

WARNINGS

- Hopefully you will never be physically attacked during your time in prison. However, if you are, here are some points to bear in mind. You can be attacked anywhere in the prison, though usually it will happen in a place where there is no direct surveillance by guards, e.g., a corridor. Obviously, you could be attacked in a cell, though a classic place for an attack is the toilet or shower, when you are distracted. An attacker can seize a time-window of just 30 seconds to attack you, then walk away nonchalantly. So, watch their hands because that's where the attack comes from. If someone has their hands in their pockets or behind their back, they could be concealing an improvised weapon such as a home-made knife. Don't let yourself get backed into a corner where you have no escape route away from your attacker.
- This may sound weird and uncomfortable, but could be life-saving: If you are concerned about getting attacked, sit when you go to the bathroom, and take your pants off completely. Since many attacks

happen when you are using the toilet, it's easier to defend yourself without your pants around your ankles, so you would not trip.

- Be careful to never call anyone a "punk" or "bitch", as they have a much different meaning in prison. If you should ever call someone either of those, be prepared for a nasty fight. If the attack doesn't come immediately, it doesn't mean it's not coming. If someone should ever call you a "punk" or a "bitch", it may seem logical to be the better man and walk away; however, while in prison, you have to show that you won't allow yourself to be punked, and it is almost certainly expected of you to put up a fight when called either one of these two names. Prison is a violent place; watching what you say can save your life.

CHAPTER 11
PRISON JOBS

Most jobs in prison don't pay very much – 17¢- 23¢ an hour, typically. And if you owe restitution, the state's taking a portion of your pennies right off the top (in California it's 55%!). With that kind of chump change, you're not even going to be able to buy the basic necessities off of canteen let alone live comfortable.

However, most prison jobs come with their own set of "perks." Some bosses allow the job perks because they know how difficult the work is for the little pay prisoners receive, so they look at it as part of the prisoner's salary and an incentive to work hard. Sometimes, though, perks are not provided, so you have to create your own perks, which, usually consists of having to be creative.

Kitchen

Many prisoners like working in the kitchen because the boss will usually let you eat extra food. Getting extra food is a good perk because the standard-sized portions are so small that you're often left hungry. Being hungry all the time will leave you feeling miserable, and if you don't have another hustle or someone sending you money for canteen, working in the kitchen will usually solve your problem.

Another perk you can get from working in the kitchen is that some bosses will actually let you take the day's leftover food with you when your shift is over and you can sell it to other prisoners. And even better than that, there are bosses who will let you use the extras to make big, Subway sandwiches, burritos, and similar things that prisoners normally wouldn't get, and you can sell those to your fellow prisoners as well. You can make a lot of money this way.

Note: Food items like tomatoes, onions, peppers, and cheese are always in high demand!

If your boss is an asshole (as plenty of them are) and he'd rather throw the leftovers away instead of letting you eat or sell them on the side, then you will have to find a creative way the demanded items. I can't tell you exactly how to do this because all circumstances are different, but I am sure there's a way it can be done. There is *always* a way; you just have to find it.

Other highly demanded items that come out of the kitchen are sugar, syrup, and jelly. Many prisoners are interested in these items because they are used to make wine. Most likely, though, even the cool bosses aren't going to let you take these items, because they know they're used for making wine, and if somebody tells that the bosses are letting it happen, they'll get into trouble that they won't get in for letting you take the leftover food. With that said, sugar, syrup, and jelly are good items to get from the kitchen, but you're most likely going to have to get them via creative means.

Education

If you get a job in education, there's a good chance you'll have access to items that you can sell to other prisoners. From my experience, getting the teachers and school staff to actually allow you to take items and supplies is not as easy as it is with the kitchen staff – probably because the school supplies are accounted for and actually needed for the prisoner students, whereas leftover food is just going to go in the garbage anyway.

Education staff might let you take an extra pad of paper, maybe a couple of ink pens and things like that, but more than likely you're going to have to get creative in order to make any real profits. In education you can usually get items like glue, glue sticks, writing paper, typing paper, paper clips, ink pens, pencils, dictionaries and other items of that nature – all of which are valuable to prisoners.

Program office

Working in the program office can provide you with its share of perks; however, you will be working with, for, and around guards – including sergeants, lieutenants, and captains. A lot of prisoners don't like working in the program office because it's easy to be pegged as a rat – even if you're not. Since you will work so closely with the officers, other prisoners will often suspect you of possibly working with them a little closer than you should be, and that's not something you ever want to be suspected of.

I will say that, one good thing about working in the program office is, even if you don't snitch, you can usually get some kind of juice-card with the officers – including the sergeants, lieutenants, and captains – because they get to know you a little bit and start to see you as more than just a number. Sometimes this is helpful, because if you get into some kind of trouble in the future, there's a decent chance they will give you a little leniency.

Furthermore, when you're always around all the officers, you can listen to their conversations and learn inside information. You might overhear guards talking about a prisoner and you can warn him. You can act as somewhat of a spy and try to get information for your partners on the yard who're doing their thing.

As far as the items you can usually obtain to sell, they will be similar to what you can get from education: glue, glue sticks, paper, pens, pencils, markers, typewriter ribbons, masking tape, scotch tape, etc.

Law library

If you get a job in the law library, it's likely going to be because you applied for the position and are knowledgeable about law. If you're knowledgeable about law, you're probably already going to be making money doing legal work for other prisoners on the yard. However, there are still perks you can usually get from working in the law library.

Working in the law library will not only give you lots of access to the law books you need in order to do your legal work hustle, but you will also usually have the ability to make photocopies. Prisoners always have a need to get things photocopied: Porn, tattoo patterns, gambling tickets and master sheets, manuscripts, etc. Furthermore, from working in the law library, you should also have access to items like manila envelopes, filing folders, typing paper, and things of that nature that you can sell to other prisoners.

Maintenance

Like the others, maintenance jobs have their perks. From working on a maintenance crew, you can usually come up on supplies prisoners use to fix their cells up with.

For example, if you work on the paint crew you can usually get a hold of extra paint. Your boss might let you take a little here and there, or, maybe he'll just turn around long enough so that you can borrow some. If not, however, you can always figure out a way to "get" paint. Paint is valuable to prisoners because a lot of prisoners like to paint their cell. Having a nicely painted cell in prison is equivalent to having nice furniture in your house on the outside.

Another thing of value maintenance workers can usually get a hold of is wax. Well, we call it wax, but it's really floor sealer for concrete floors. However, it makes the concrete extremely shiny; the more coats you put on, the shinier it will get.

Like paint, prisoners use wax to fix up their cell with. Not only do a lot of prisoners like to wax their concrete floor, but their concrete walls as well. If you add coat after coat after coat, you can make your walls have a thick layer of wax so shiny that it will resemble the clear coat gloss of an automobile's expensive paint job. And if you get a hold of paint to paint your cell with (usually just your lockers, bunks, desk, and door – not your walls), you can put a bunch of layers of wax over the paint so that it gives it a nice shine as well as protection from getting scratched. (Putting wax over your paint to protect it from scratching is a good idea because wax is typically much easier to get a hold of than paint.)

Working in maintenance will also usually give you access to sandpaper. This can be sold to prisoners who like to go the extra mile when fixing up their cells. The toilets and sinks in a prison cell are usually made out of a dull stainless steel. However, if you sand it with very fine sandpaper, you can make it as shiny as set of chrome car rims. It takes a bit of time to get it super shiny, but a lot of prisoners won't have their sink and toilet any other way. Hey, we have to turn what little we have into the most we can make it, right?

Building porter

Building porters usually have access to supplies like disinfectant; Ajax; hand soap; green scrub pads; sponges; buckets; toilet paper; and, if you're in a prison that has them, shaving razors. However, with the exception of buckets, which typically go for about $3.00 – $5.00 each, you probably aren't going to want to charge your fellow prisoners for these items. Prisoners feel like they have these items coming, and they will likely be offended if they are charged for them. The reason why you might be able to get away with selling buckets is because buckets are usually limited – only a certain amount is issued out to each building. And although prisoners typically aren't allowed to have buckets in their cell, they're a hot item because we like to use them to wash our clothes in. Therefore, sometimes prisoners won't mind paying for a bucket. I guess, like anything else, it all depends on where you're at.

Laundry

Working in the laundry is a great job to have because prisoners are always in need of a laundry hook-up. Prisoners especially like to have brand-new clothes for visiting, and for the most part nobody will mind paying for them.

Some laundry job bosses will let their workers take new state clothes to sell on the yard. However, if they don't, then like anything else, you can always find a way to get laundry via creative means.

I'm sure laundry goes for different prices depending on where you're at, but just to give you some kind of idea, I typically pay about 50¢ for a T-shirt, pair of socks, or boxers; $2.00 for a blue button-up shirt; $3.00 –$4.00 for a pair of pants or jacket; and $3.00 – $4.00 for a pair of shoes. This, of course, is for brand-new items.

As you can see, although the state doesn't usually pay prisoners even a decent amount of money for the jobs they're assigned to, there are often other ways you can make up for it; sometimes you will have access to items you can sell on the side, or sometimes you will be given other perks that take place of payment. And sure, sometime you may have to resort to being creative in order to get what you should get for the hard labor you do, but, hey, this book is about surviving prison... by *any* means.

If you do have to resort to creativity, be careful that you don't get caught. If you do get caught, you will most likely be written up and given some type of consequence to deal with. And sometimes even the decent guards and free-staff will write you up if they are fronted off to their superiors by you getting caught. Decent or not, when it comes down to it, they are obviously going to protect themselves over you; but, hey, that's understandable, right?

CHAPTER 12
STORE

If you do it right and have discipline, running a store can be profitable. However, it can also be a headache – a lot of drama and activity....

It takes money to make money

In order to build a store, you're going to need to have a little start-up money. There's no set amount to how much you need in order to start your business up with, it all comes down to how much you can afford to invest.

The concept

The concept of running a store is fairly simple: you buy items off of the canteen, and when prisoners run out of their own items, and can't wait until they go to the store (canteen) during their own designated time to get what it is they need, they can get the item(s) from you at a price increase. What is the usual charge for prisoner-ran store items? Usually it's one item in exchange for two of the same item back; it's called a two-for-one. However, if there's other stores in your building, you may need to offer a more competitive price – two items in exchange for three back. That's a little better deal for the barrower.

Problems

One problem that often arises when running a store, is that a lot of prisoners like to barrow items, but don't necessarily like paying them back – especially your "friends" who will always want you to "hook them up." A lot of prisoners are full of drag, and if you're not careful, you can end up with at least a headache – possibly even a situation to deal with.

In order to avoid getting yourself into some bullshit (having to fight or stab someone over a bag of chips is bullshit to me), you will either have to deal only with people who are good for it (if there is such a thing), or always get some type of collateral. If you front items you're taking a chance. However, if you get collateral from a bunch of people who only owe you $5.00, you're going to have all kinds of miscellaneous stuff in your cell that belong to other prisoners... It's up to you to decide which method is the lesser evil.

My advice to you is, if this is something you're interested in doing, build a reputation for *how* you run your business. Never make deals or shift, and prisoners will eventually understand exactly what is required in order to shop at your store.

Another problem that can occur when running a store is the temptation to start eating the food items when you're hungry. You have to be disciplined; you have to keep your product separate from your personal stash. It's kind of a don't-get-high-on-your-own-supply type of concept. If you eat all your chips and drink all your coffee, you aren't going to have anything left to loan. It's real easy to eat yourself storeless.

If you decide to run a store, you should be careful that you don't front yourself off to the guards in your building. Some officers don't allow prisoners to run stores; they know the kind of problems they can lead to. In addition to that, you don't want to be suspected of selling drugs (whether you are or not) because you have so much extra stuff inside of your cell.

However, some officers don't mind if they know a prisoner in their building is running a store, which is a good thing, obviously. They'll know where all your extra money is coming from and won't sweat you for it.

If you're willing to deal with the problems that often come along with running a store, then maybe it's a good idea for you to do it. You can easily turn your product from one to two (double your money).

The most demanded items are usually coffee (most prisoner's fiend for coffee), Ramen soups, hard candy, and sweets. Try to stack up on those and other non-perishable items.

Also, make sure you always keep an accurate, detailed log of who owes what so that you increase your chances of avoiding misunderstandings.

CHAPTER 13

PRISON ART

Prison is known for the artwork produced by its prisoners. Art has always been a big, famous part of the prison culture. There are a lot of artists in prison, including some very, very talented ones – maybe even some of the best in the world.

Drawing

Some guys are natural artists, true, but that's a very rare case. Most prison artists start off with nothing more than a desire to learn how to draw; OK, and maybe a little bit of time to kill, too. The point is, if you don't know how to draw already but you desire to learn, there's no time like when you're doing time.

In prison, artists are in high demand. Prisoners are always looking to buy things like home-made greeting cards and portraits to send to their wives, kids, mothers, pen-pals, etc. So, if you know how to draw, you will *always* have a hustle in prison.

There's no set amount you can charge for your drawings. The better you are, the more you can charge. However, you should keep in mind that most prisoners don't have a ton of money, so it's good to try to keep your prices realistic – what people can afford. With that said, if you are very, very, *very* good at drawing, you can set your price(s) and then make prisoners get creative in coming up with the money in order to afford you. They might have to make more sacrifices to buy your art than what they'd have to make to buy the next artist's, but that's their problem – if they want your work.

Practice makes perfect

I have seen some amazing art in prison. Sure, I've seen a lot of great art, but I've also seen some art so amazing that it makes even the *great* art not so impressive. It is rare to find artists as great as what I'm talking about, but if you can become one yourself you will make a lot of fucking money.

Like most things in life, in order to be a great prison artist you have to practice, practice, practice. You have to be serious about your craft, you have to *want* to be the best, and you have to be willing to put the necessary time into it.

The easiest tool to draw with for most people is a pencil. Using a pencil is the best way to learn because it allows you to erase your mistakes. Always start by sketching the outline of your image as lightly as possible so that the markings you do not want can be easily erased, and so that you don't damage the texture of the paper.

Making a pattern

A lot of prison artists use what we call "patterns." A pattern is the outline of an image that you either trace or ditto onto the paper you are drawing your image on. A lot of prison artists use patterns to get the outline of an image down and then they just add the shading to it.

You can make your own pattern(s) fairly easy. All you need to do is get tracing paper and trace an image you want to draw: a girl, a rose, a dog, a car, etc. – usually something out of a magazine. Once you have a hard outline, you can trace or ditto it over and over.

If you can't get tracing paper, sometimes you can use the thin, transparent paper that your toilet paper is wrapped in. And if you can't get that, you can stick a regular piece of writing or typing paper over the image, then put it up to a light (TV, window, etc.) and trace it that way. The light behind the two pieces of paper – the one your image is on and the one you're tracing it onto – allows you to actually see what you're tracing.

Most prisons don't allow ditto paper because they know we use it to put tattoo patterns on skin. However, it's not difficult to make home-made ditto paper. All you have to do is take a regular pencil and color in the back of the paper your pattern is on, and dark. When you do this, and then put your pattern on top of the paper you want to ultimately draw your picture on and trace your image, the pencil will transfer from the back of the pattern to the page you want your pattern on, and you will have a light outline of the image you wish to draw.

If you want to learn how to draw, my advice to you is to start with a pencil, a piece of art paper, and a pattern – either somebody else's or your own – and then learn how to add the shading to images. Once you have learned how to draw well with a pencil, you can then start learning how to use colored pencils, ink pens, and whatever else you can get a hold of.

Greeting Cards

As I mentioned earlier, greeting cards are always in demand. Most prison artists like to use card stock or thick drawing paper to make their greeting cards out of.

When making greeting cards, prison artists usually fold their card stock or drawing paper one of two ways: in half, like the typical greeting card, or in thirds – like how you'd fold a business letter (this way it can be sent out in a regular business envelope). Of course, there is no set rule with this. You can do whatever you want, however you want; whatever looks good, and, ultimately, whatever your fellow prisoners will *buy*.

What you can charge will depend on how good you are; however, greeting cards usually go from $2.00-$6.00.

Portraits

Portraits are also in high demand. Prisoners love to send portraits to people because people love to receive them. To learn how to draw portraits precisely will take some practice, but once you have it down you can really make some big bucks. A portrait of someone's face the size of a softball can easily get you $15.00-$20.00; sometimes more. Learning how to draw portraits is a great investment of your time because it will certainly pay off.

Patterns

As we all know, tattoos are extremely popular in prison. But, believe it or not, not all tattoo artists actually draw. It's true! Most can draw at least a little bit, but a lot of them won't, as they'd rather spent their time tattooing – where they make more money.

If you have creative ideas and designs, you can make decent money drawing tattoo patterns for people to take to their tattoo artist. A lot of prisoners who're getting tattoos like to do this to save time – they have one artist creating all their patterns, so the tattoo artist can use his time for tattooing.

I know a guy named Playboy who can draw extremely well. He can draw in pencil and pen, he can paint and tattoo. But the best thing about Playboy is his creativity – his imagination. He's very good at making images transform or "melt" into other images. For example, he'll draw a skull with smoke coming off of it turning into some prison bars, and then the bars will flow into the hair of a sexy woman. In the woman's hair will be a rose, and the rose petals will turn into $100 bills. Playboy made himself the go-to guy for tattoo patterns. His designs were in demand by the entire yard.

A lot of people want creative, intricate designs for their tattoo patterns. So, if you have a great imagination and a lot of creativity, you can specialize in this and sew your entire yard up.

Handkerchiefs/Paños

When you learn how to draw using an ink pen and colored pencils, you can start collaging handkerchiefs – also known as "paños." Believe it or not, handkerchiefs are fairly easy to draw on because they take the ink and colored pencils really well.

You can usually purchase plain, white, 16x16 handkerchiefs from the package companies for about $1.00. If not, you can get a brand-new sheet, cut a piece off of it and have the tailor sew the edges. However, be careful when using a home-made handkerchief because some guards will confiscate them. You don't want to spend all that time on it just to have some asshole guards come and take it.

Collaged handkerchiefs usually go for $25.00 – $100.00. However, like anything else, you can charge what you want – whatever people will pay for your work.

I can go on and on about drawing and other forms of prison art, and learning how to do it properly, but I would have to write several books in order to explain everything thoroughly. The best advice I can give you, however, is to get together with some of the more experienced artists around you and ask them each to teach you their little "tricks." Once they do, practice, practice, practice, and learn to be the absolute best you can be. You *must* dedicate yourself. And if you have someone who will send you books, ask them to send you *Drawing for Dummies*; it's full of great information.

There are many reasons why drawing is a good hustle. Not only is prison art in high demand, but you can almost always come up on a pencil or pen and a piece of paper to create your hustle, *and* it's legit. You can't get in trouble for being a great artist; you're not going to go to the hole because you draw too well. In fact, if you're a good artist, a lot of times even guards will want art from you. Usually they will either put money on your books, or you will get special privileges (be given a juice card) for doing a piece of work for them. The opportunities for a great artist are endless.

CHAPTER 14

SURVIVING THE HOLE: THE STRATEGIES

Let me begin by explaining the following...

The hole is technically an informal name given to units where prisoners are locked down and usually in some form of isolation. Other informal names you may hear are solitary confinement, lock-up units, or lockdown units. The formal name may differ depending on what state you're in but the most common name is "Administrative Segregation" (Ad-Seg). Prisoners are sent to the hole (Ad-Seg) for disciplinary, security, or safety purposes.

SHU stands for "Security Housing Unit." And while the hole is often a temporary placement, if one is found guilty of a SHUable rule violation or deemed a security threat to the general population – maybe because he has been validated as an associate or member of a prison gang and is said to have a high influence among other prisoners – one will be sent to the SHU. Other names you might hear of SHU-type facilities are "management unit" or "control unit." However, program and concept-wise, all lock-up units are similar in nature.

A bit of perspective

When you're in prison, going to the hole is kind of like going to the county jail; whereas going to the SHU would be like going to prison. What I mean by that is, when you are free, on the streets, and you are accused or suspected of a crime, you are sent to the county jail while you fight your case. If you are convicted and the crime carries prison time, you will then be sent to prison. Well, when you're in prison, on a general population yard, that is prison's equivalence to being free. However, if you are accused or suspected of a "crime" (rule violation) while in prison, the guards will arrest you and lock you up in the hole – where you will lose most of your privileges/freedom – while you wait to have your crime (rule violation) heard by a judge (Senior Hearing Officer). If you are convicted (found guilty) and the crime (rule violation) is SHUable, you will go to the SHU.

However, for the purpose of this chapter, I am going to use the common, generic name "the hole" to refer to any unit with a lockdown/isolation concept.

The concept

Prison's concept, in general, is to punish its prisoners by depriving them of freedom. The hole, however, takes punishment to another level, as its concept is sensory deprivation – to deprive prisoners of their five basic senses: sight, sound, smell, touch and taste. The idea of prison's administration is that, if they cannot break of control you by prison alone, where all of your rights as a free human being are stripped from you, they will break and control you by putting you in the hole, often for long periods of time, and strip you of all basic human senses. However, whether they are successful or not is often up to you....

How/why does this pertain to you?

Well, if you are doing a stretch in prison, odds are you will at some time end up in the hole for one reason or another. After all, it's not very difficult to find yourself in the hole, as some prisons will send you there for something as simple as a fistfight, which, in some prisons are a daily occurrence.

The experience

While in the hole, with the exception of three showers and a few hours of yard a week (in most places), you will spend all your time locked down in your cell. You will have little or no contact with other prisoners – with the exception of your celly, if you have one, as some holes are single cell – and you will also have very little or no contact with the outside world, as prisoners in the hole are typically not allowed to use the phone, and only allowed two 1-hour, no-contact visits per week.

You will also have very little property – even less than the already little amount you are allowed in general population. Regardless of your reason for being in the hole, whether you killed somebody on the yard, you're under investigation for selling drugs, or you're there because you feel your life is in danger and you've requested protection, all prisoners are treated the same.

Personally, I don't necessarily mind being in the hole. I would rather be in general population because I have more access to things and can maintain my relationships better with people on the outside, as I have access to contact visits and phone calls; however, I have done a lot of time in the hole (SHU, Ad-Seg, etc.), so I have learned how to take advantage of the situation. Being in the hole allows me to escape the daily distractions that occur in the general population and focus on my work, which is what I like to do anyway. In fact, while I write/work-on this very chapter of "Surviving Prison," I am actually in CCI SHU, in Tehachapi, CA.

However, not everybody is able to survive the hole as well as others. The lack of human interaction (except for one's celly, if he has one, which can actually become a problem because of *too* much time together); the lack of contact with family and friends on the outside (which often leads to a loss of relationships); the feeling of being trapped in a cell for most of every day; the sometimes dead quietness, yet sometimes loud chaoticness; the constant hunger; the strip searches that take place every time one comes out the cell; etc., is often just too much for even a strong man to handle. Such a situation often leads to frustration, depression, and hopelessness.

If you find yourself in this situation there *are* things you can do to help yourself cope a little easier. In concept, this entire book will help you survive your time in the hole, but you should "up" the concepts to a more intense level, as doing time in the hole is much more intense (especially mentally) than doing time in the general population. In order to maintain your composure, you must learn to exercise extreme discipline and you must learn to survive on even less than you do in general population, oftentimes in even animal-like conditions.

Here are some things that I incorporate into my strategy when doing time in the hole, and I suggest you try to incorporate them into your strategy as well. You will notice that many of my suggestions appear elsewhere in this book, but for the specific purpose of surviving the hole I have listed them here for you...

Use your time wisely

It is very important that you take advantage of your time in the hole, and, like in any situation, turn what is perceived as a negative into a positive. Don't just go to the hole and sleep. Instead, set goals for yourself, come up with a plan, and execute it. While in the hole is a perfect time to focus on your legal case, the book you've wanted to write, or study the subject(s) you've wanted to learn about. You are going to have a lot of time on your hands. However, time is valuable; use yours wisely and you will prosper.

Stay busy

You are only using your time wisely if you are constantly busy. You should have no time to just sit around aimlessly. You will notice that a lot of prisoners who break under the pressure of being in the hole are the same ones who just lay around and/or talk out of their doors and/or in their vents all day. They are ambitionless and do nothing but sulk in their reality, allowing it to eat away at their sanity. Staying busy will help you mentally escape your environment, which is key to surviving one as hellish as the hole.

Reflect; organize your thoughts

Use this down-time to get your thoughts in order. Reflect on the situation(s) that lead up to you being placed in the hole, what you may have done wrong, and how you can improve your strategy upon being released (if you're lucky enough to be released).

Furthermore, you should also use this time to reflect on your life as a *whole,* and how you can improve *yourself* from this point forward. Look deep into who you are as a man, decide exactly who and what it is you want to be, and *how* you can become the best *you.*

Correspond/Communicate

If you were never into letter writing before, I suggest you learn to get in to it now, because it is extremely important to have regular correspondence with your family and friends on the outside. You being in prison is hard on your relationships, but you being in the hole is much, much harder. You must do all you can to maintain your relationships on the outside.

Furthermore, maintaining contact, communication, and support from your family and friends is extremely important in regards to your survival. Such correspondence will provide you with hope, and hope will help you push forward. I suggest that you also use this time to reach out and try to connect with other forms of outside support such as pen pals, network organizations, etc., so that you are in as much contact as possible with people in the *free* world.

Note: If you plan on doing something that you *know* is going to land you in the hole, I suggest you mini-write all your addresses and kiester them – wrap them in plastic and stick them up your asshole. You want to make sure that you can always maintain contact/communication with your people/resources.

Express yourself

Being in isolation can limit the ways you are able to express yourself – both emotionally and creatively – but it still can and *should* be done. Keeping a written journal about your experience, writing down your personal ideas/philosophies, writing poetry and/or song lyrics is a good way to express yourself emotionally. Writing things such as magazine articles, plays, short stories and/or books is a great way to express yourself creatively; as is drawing.

Create a way to express yourself both emotionally and creatively. Doing so will help you release built-up emotion as well as give you something to focus on. Use your imagination and creativity to escape the boundaries of your cell's four walls.

Read

Read as much as you can while in the hole. Reading will not only provide you with great knowledge, but also take you to another place mentally.

142

I suggest that you read books that are educational and relevant to your studies, but I also suggest that you read newspapers and magazines that will keep you up-to-date with news and interests that you have in the *free* world. You must never accept nor get used to prison. Keeping a piece of your thoughts focused on the *free* world will help you do so, as it will remind you that something much greater than your immediate environment exists.

Exercise

Being cramped in a cell all day is unhealthy, so it is very important that you exercise regularly. Develop an exercise program and follow it. Try to stretch and use your muscles, as close to as much as you would if you were *not* in the hole.

Furthermore, exercising provides a way for you to release unwanted energy and stress. Not only is exercising good for your body physically, but mentally, too. While exercising is a great time to block out your environment, get your thoughts in order, and even meditate.

Lastly, even though you will have very little or no contact with other prisoners, you must keep yourself combat-ready at all times. You never know when your door will "accidently" open along with the door of a prisoner with whom you are at war with. Believe me, it happens; *always* be prepared for it.

Meditate

It is very, very important that you take time out of each day – at least 15-30 minutes – to meditate. Meditating will allow you to release a lot of physical and mental stress. Study various meditation techniques and use the ones you feel work the best for you.

CHAPTER 15

SUPERMAX SURVIVAL SECRETS: A MIND AND BODY IN MOTION STAYS IN MOTION; A MIND AND BODY AT REST STAYS AT REST

By Bro. Khalfani Malik Khaldun (Indiana)

Part 1: Being Used to Legitimize These Units

Society must start to look closely into the intentions being used to operate and legitimize solitary confinement units. All across America today, U.S. prisons are isolating prisoners who are labeled "high security risk" or prison organizers, activists, and lawsuit litigators. Prison administrators are screaming the need for more security and money provided by State legislators which opens the flood gates for more control units.

Prisoners who have displayed the integrity and guts to challenge the oppressive conditions of the many controlled environments they are forced to live in [are the targets]. Once known as an agitator, prisoners are placed in these categories and named as problems or potential problems. Once placed on the list as a high-risk prisoner you can be placed under administrative watch by the State's Prison Commissioners Office. This status will allow a classification committee to bounce you around from control units all across the state you are imprisoned in. The thing that is important to understand about this placement in solitary confinement is they are properly selecting prisoners whose names are recognized all around the Prison Department of Corrections of the state the prisoners are housed in. These moves are being made now, even when the targeted prisoners have not committed a prison violation or rule. They are being isolated because they are feared for being too influential

144

inside the general populations of state or federal facilities.

Some of these administrators claim that they suspect certain prisoners will do it again or in the future commit acts of violence. So their rational is that they will not let prisoners ever do it again. For example, you're Attica Rebellion, Resistance Days of San Quentin, Lucasville Ohio uprising, and so many others. The State Prison administrators all across this racist country don't ever want to see another Attica. This I am sure of. There is another relevant point to be made in this section on how they use big named activist prisoners to legitimize the existence of these control units.

There are a lot of prisoners gifted in challenging the violations which exist in many SHU units, Supermaxes, etc. Such challenges, however good, ultimately result in helping these people create new ways to enhance their torture, abuse, and isolation. Why do I say this? Many prison litigators will admit that our work forces prison violations to surface and the courts sometimes issues orders of correction. But in other cases, the courts leave the discretionary racist "rule" in the hands of prison administrative commissioners to do things they please. This opens a window of opportunity which allows time to bring violations up to par and undermines the legitimate grounds we raised in legal battles. So there is always a need to be mindful of this as a reality for the challenges we expose. Taking a stand in prison results in most cases in prisoners being placed further and further into the trenches of the belly of the American prison plantations. Prison administrative committees know that historically, isolation has been used to drive prisoners insane and break their will to resist. To conclude this section, I will outline some "points to ponder." Remember this to survive this madness.

Points to Ponder:

- Learn exactly why you are being held in, or being classified for, the placement in Administrative Segregation, Control Units, or Security Housing Units.
- Maintain your personal file on all your complaints, grievances, reviews, and keep copies of every letter you send to facility heads.
- Don't ever be afraid to question the legitimacy of your placements from the Superintendent Office, or to the commissioner's office, on up to the Governor of your respective state.
- Write your local Senators, State Representatives, who represent the closest district near the prison you're in. Expose to them the violations that are taking place.
- Write letters to editors on the local newspapers describing to them what the living conditions are like. Also contact the news media and suggest that they come in to inspect the units.
- These points are not complex. In fact, they're rather simplistic and should be incorporated into prisoners' daily programs while isolated in solitary confinement units across this country. Prisoners much do the required research and study to arm themselves with the wealth of information in circulation on control units. The prison administrators in control of these units are putting men away like "unusable goods" to deteriorate, rot away, and then ultimately die. If you're wanting to live, then build the nerve to fight for your survival.

Part 2: Study and Learn What Rules and Policies Which Govers the Operation of Control Units

Prisons all across this country that now operate solitary confinement units are all governed by state statues, prison operational procedures, mandatory rules, all of which are in state law. Many prisoners who are being transferred to these units are basically unaware of these realities. This has been one of the biggest faults of ours, because when you don't know a civil right or law has been violated, there is no way to make anyone be held responsible for these violations.

Prisoners must obtain copies of these state codes and statues governing all laws for the treatment of prisoners. This is imperative. After a careful review of such, then and only then may you understand what they can and cannot do. Prison administrators often know that rookie guards are inclined to violate prisoners' rights. But most have a "code" amongst themselves that if you fail to document your complaint or allegation of abuse, it's like it never happened. So, to not keep your records or file your complaints, it's like defeating your own self before even starting. Do your homework.

These control units operate on these policies which in most cases vary from facility to facility or unit to unit. Their characteristics are extreme isolation, reduced environmental stimulus, scant recreational, vocational, or educational opportunities, and extraordinary levels of surveillance and control of movement. All policies are not always followed, and when this happens you anticipate abuse and dehumanization of prisoners almost every day. So, you must study these policies because it allows those of us under attack to place a shield around ourselves. Also, it helps us to keep those prone to abuse in check.

Being confined to the cell for 23 to 24 hours a day gives one a lot of time to study and internalize all the rules, policies, procedures, state laws or codes and use them to confront those responsible for our placement in these units. The state code violations must be exposed because these codes mandate the laws all citizens inside the state must follow. State employees, which includes all prison guards, operate under the color of state law. So to obtain copies of the state codes for your state where it applies to the treatment of prisoners would be helpful to any prisoner. Having spent countless years in prison already, I am clear on how this work can exhaust anyone after a period of time.

However, most times it is our self-determination and consistency that helps us get the attention of our captors. When we start a pattern of giving up easily, or simply never challenge the wrongs waged against us, prison administrators will never view anything we challenge as a recognizable threat to their violations of state and federal law. They are doing what they please to us now simply due to our overall lack of legal law knowledge. We must become more diligent in learning how to interpret the law. Learning these things will be like loading your gun. Without your bullets your weapon is useless. Arm yourself so you will bring forth an effective challenge.

Points to Ponder:

- Prisoners must create an active file of all the prison regulations, rules, policies, state statues, and codes that govern your custody.
- Look for mandatory language like "they shall" or "they must" because this is what gives us our leverage to challenge violations of their own mandates.
- Most prison libraries and law libraries have prisoners supplying the control supermax or security housing units all over this country. We must establish respectful relations with these prisoners to help us secure the legal cases, etc. we will need. Communication in this sense means everything.
- We must send copies of these rules, policies, etc. to our loved ones and other extended family members.

148

Educating them about these things can only help us win the war for our lives in the long run.

- Control units are claiming lives and stealing the souls of men. We must continue the work others have started to control or stop the construction of these units and providing the outside with the truth behind the lies being told by prison administrators as to why they need such environments of control and psychological manipulation.

Part 3: Building a Basic Solidarity With Prisoners in Your Environment

Prisons have always been places where hostilities can be created by those who run them, solely for the purpose of keeping a perpetual wedge between white and black prisoners. Why? This question is easily answered by acknowledging their agenda. To perpetuate racial violence inside prison, prison administrators prevent us from seeing who the real source behind the problems are, which them is. This is classic divide/conquer tactics and in most cases it works.

These tactics not only prevent us from seeing the real picture, it also prevents us from development/sound relationships of solidarity. When we don't work together, we become vulnerable to being attacked without them fearing retaliation. When we are trying to come together for the better of our conditions, none of this can be done without mutual respect being established. This is not always an easy job, due to prisoners having different ideologies religions, political beliefs, etc., and sometimes these differences get in the way. This has been a stumbling block when we try to build collective unity on control units in very reactionary environments.

But due to the growing levels of consciousness and development in all U.S. prisons, collective unity and understanding amongst targeted prisoners is growing day by day. We must move with this momentum when it exists and build unshakable foundations of solidarity. All prison organizers must know and come to terms with not being able to galvanize 100 percent support from prisoners; even when it is those who don't participate in the struggle-related efforts who benefit most sometimes.

Prisoners who work to expose violations are those who sometimes suffer the most. This is why we must have respectable communications with at least a majority of the prisoners in our environment, no matter where we are -- Ad Seg unit, SHU, Supermax, or even General Population. Those prison administrators who despise being sued, exposed, written about will display reactionary tendencies. They will approve staff to beat you up, set you up, or even kill you.

This is a fact, and you don't ever want to isolate yourself from your fellow prisoners. Because when you need to have someone call or contact your family to inform them of your abuse, no one will care to assist you.

So, it is very crucial to be established as a principled person who would help them if they needed you. This way, even if you're envied or prisoners hate you out of misguided jealousies, they still will feel compelled to honor/aid you. This is KEY and must be established by all. We must be more observant of our current situation, and become masters in whatever we know our gifts to be. We all have a purpose. Some of us, through trial and error, have grown to know what are purpose is; while many of us remain trapped in a whirl-wind of misguided emotions and utter blind confusion. This is not to say the latter person(s) will not discover what your life's is. Everyone has a purpose, and through the host of your countless experiences, this purpose is discovered. Without ever discovering our purpose in life, our souls will drift as a ship as sea tossing and turning.

Points to Ponder:

- Don't play into the games of the administrators when they promote the divide and conquer tactics.
- When trying to create unity among prisoners, always show them what they have in common with each other as prisoners similarly situated in the same oppressive conditions.
- All prisoners have a voice and should be heard when discussing the challenges, they must prepare for in confronting the host of violations inside these units. That is real democratic centralism.
- Encourage collective work and responsibility among prisoners you may have influence with. Everyone has a role to play in prison activism.
- Create a basic political library and do your best to make sure such materials that are legal-related or educational are available to all who desire to learn more. We are supposed to be creators, so this is our job.
- Develop a policy among yourselves that if one prisoner comes under attack, then it symbolical means all of you are under attack. This way you will build a solidarity that extends beyond the racial expectations of prison life.

Part 4: To Organize an Educational Program

Solitary confinement in our current state of incarceration still breeds insanity and body deterioration. One of the key components for countering mental instability is a solid study program.

It's been said that an idle mind is the devil's workshop. So when we fail to create various forms of release we can leave ourselves vulnerable for a host of psychological disorders. These units are creating psycho-active psychosis and the results end in men slowly falling apart.

151

In most of these units prisoners are allowed to order radios or televisions. These avenues of release helps to serve as social distractions and avenues of escape. But too much of both can serve to keep one too content with TV shows and one loses focus on legal work and your freedom. Prison administrators use many social distractions as pacifiers to maintain control of the prison populations/units as a whole.

Too much humility can become cowardice, so we must stay strong in mind, body and spirit. Prisoners must acquire a host of reading materials on subjects that helps to empower them with wisdom, knowledge and understanding. We all have a purpose to our overall existence. If you're not willing to surrender your soul or become a victim of 23- or 24-hour isolation status, build yourself an educational awareness program to stimulate individual or collective growth and development. Group dialogue is really helpful if closed up units like SBUs, supermaxes and ad-segs.

The sensory deprivation that overwhelms and impacts the minds of prisoners in these places makes the effects of isolation that much more critical. A constant reading, writing, and communicating with family and friends are the weapons we use to combat the intentions of this form of isolation. We must maintain a healthy balance of mental stimulating information. Reading helps us develop new ideas as well as keep the mind active. A body and mind in motion stays in motion. A mind and body at rest stays at rest.

Solitary confinement has the potential to rob a person day by day of some of their ability to rationalize and think critically. So I can't stress the importance of developing a sound system of basic and advanced education programs. I have spent many years in 23-hour isolation units to know exactly what works and what will ultimately fail in the end. I suggest prisoners inside these units make their isolation work for them. Make it a companion. Instead of falling apart, pull yourselves together and do all the necessary things you can to preserve your life. My early years of isolation allowed me time to discover that I had a creative writing spirit. Those were times when some of my best essays were created. It was then that I learned how to use isolation as a tool toward my own growth and development. We must steadily and consistently feed our brain the necessary stimuli with quality materials. A healthy study habit helps tremendously in combating the ills of insanity. So many prisoners have succumbed to the conditions of these types of reactionary environments many prisoners are being made subject to spending decades and entire prison terms on these units. You will be their next victim if you don't prepare yourself right now.

Points to Ponder:

- Prisoners who like to read and do their own research and share their political or non-political materials should organize a people's library for the unit.
- Prisoners could make use of idle time by developing "spelling bee" contests on your unit as a way to upgrade and better one's spelling.
- Prisoners can build a strong vocabulary by studying the dictionary. This helps to also better our ability to communicate with everyone we write or come into contact with. The use of properly used language can be very persuasive.
- Prisoners who believe that there is a higher being or higher power should do what is necessary to get in tune with their spiritual side. This helps to balance out the stress one endures on these units.
- Prisoners should find one or two people we have things in common with in the free world and maintain a connection to the streets. This is very crucial to your continued stable mental health.

Part 5: Building a Strong Support Base Around Yourself

Prisoners who are being housed in solitary confinement must come to terms with their need to build a strong outside base. Many of us still have close relationships with our families. While on the other hand, some of us don't have anyone out in society who cares enough to help us. This is why it's extremely important for us to build extended family ties with people who care for the survival of prisoners across the country.

Personally, prison administrators' mission in most cases are to destroy the ties and relationships we have developed with freedom loving people who's on our team. These ties are crucial in times of support and assistance. We all need people who are not overly judgmental and who will embrace us as we are and stand by us in our fight for freedom. So we must bring all of our supporters together with our loved ones and build a movement. When you don't have anyone to make a call to the warden, governor, or commissioner's office, who will expose what is occurring on your unit, or to you, by prison guards, these people are more likely to violate your rights.

When harassment goes unchallenged, prison administrators tend to get out of control. So we as prisoners must educate and inform people on the things they can do from the free world to keep prison administrators at bay. Over the years this has been an effective process because when the people on the outside have all the informational tools to assist us they will almost always respond correctly. Sometimes this can be a not-so-easy process, because all people don't work well together. Personality conflicts, ego flare ups, insecurities, and a variety of other factors prevent such collective efforts.

Prisoners' families and those who care and support them share a common connection that must be revealed to them when we begin the process of encouraging them to work together for our freedom. Our friends and families want the same thing; to see us return home through the gates we entered. This is a common relationship they share on the outside.

Building or organizing yourself a freedom defense committee of people loyal to you is a must. This committee on your behalf would be to keep the courts, attorney on your case, prosecutor, etc., on notice that you have people who have your back. They would help you solicit funds to build a strong financial base to pay your attorney, or securing one if you don't have reliable legal representation. They would help to publicize and inform society about your current prison reality and legal battles as you push for freedom from Amerika's prisons.

A strong base of support is very important for many reasons. No one in prison should be in prison without some kind of support. But prisoners who are the constant targets of prison administrators deserve it more so than others, for it is these men or women who are trying to change their oppressive environments. They are not targeted due to reactionary behavior in prison. They are constant victims of manufactured set-ups, harassment, slander, and even attempts made on their lives because they are revolutionary and politically conscious. Also these men and women work to expose violations of policy and law.

Points to Ponder:

- Build yourself a support freedom committee to help you maintain, survive, promote your freedom, and expose the conditions of the prison or control unit you're in.

- Try to establish a consistent relationship with friends who will visit you regularly. It helps to keep one focused and uncontrolled by the conditions of your environment.
- Always send a card or warm respectful letter of appreciation to those outside who support and show their love and concern for your wellbeing. Never abuse the relationships or you may live to regret it when you're alone and depressed.
- If you are in need of money for legal representation, build a creative fundraiser. They can sell some buttons, T-shirts, hats, that reflect consciousness that say support that innocent inside.
- Prisoners can write booklets of poetry, history, prison life, their lives, and once formatted correctly, they can be sold on E-Bay or some other venue to raise money. If you want the winning formula to writing urban books, be sure to purchase *How To Write Urban Books for Money and Fame* by Mike Enemigo and King Guru today by sending $19.99 + $5 s/h to: The Cell Block; POB 1025; Rancho Cordova, CA 95741.

Part 6: Becoming Proactive About Being Housed in Solitary Confinement

Some years ago a fellow prisoner gave me some wise advice about combating prison abuse from those who run these prisons. He said you must become "proactive" in the ways you challenge and oppose oppressive conditions. For a long time, many of us who have 10 years or more in saw the coming of hard times and prison changes. We also saw the potential for the construction of the proliferation of control units we see popping up all across the country. We failed to prepare ourselves, and now we are the ones being buried inside solitary tombs.

Preparing ourselves would have meant that we were taking a proactive stance.

Today, many of us are not being proactive when it comes to really preparing and exposing these units and those who run them for fear of retaliation or some false charges being brought against them. But this must change if we are ever going to present an effective challenge to the way they are classifying us on these units. Their actions are arbitrary and meant to cause undue mental harm on many prisoners. Historically it has been stated that too much isolation does and will cause insanity. Such isolation also causes and preexisting mental health conditions to enhance themselves.

Without any meaningful mental stimulation or physical release of pent-up frustrations, the entire existence of the human begins a deterioration process. This writer has been housed in controlled environments for the past 16 years. I can personally say that prison administrators have used my isolation to punish and break my will to resist. I remain strong and am resisting, but I would be openly lying if I said I am not being affected by long term isolation.

Prisoners must be more proactive and challenge being housed in control units on indefinite terms. This is unnatural and abnormal, but it openly shows the barbaric nature of prison control unit administrators. They are violating our human and civil rights every day. We are the victims of premeditated arrogance and bald racist tendencies at the hands of these prison officials. Don't you all agree that we must learn how to protect ourselves sometimes without the use of violence?

Media outlets and newspaper publishers are always interested in hearing or reading stories about prison conditions. Prisoners must do what it takes to get their words in the hands of people who are in real positions to help. We are dying in these units. Some due to deteriorating health troubles, while others are being beat to death or shot up with psychological "mind controllers" that destroy one's ability to focus and be rational. We will benefit in the long run for exposing prison abuse, poor conditions, bad food, and all violations as a whole. This establishes a clear record documented by those of us who don't fear retaliations. Prison administrators have made it a practice to intimidate prisoners who file successful complaints against them by launching false conduct reports or infractions, placing restrictions on our movements, destroying our mail to the outside, random cell searches, petty confiscations of reading and legal materials, or even making attempts on our lives by manipulating prisoner collaborators. We can live like men on our feet challenging these injustices, or die off slowly like cowards on our knees. We must never feel like we don't have a right to protest and speak out about prison violations.

Points to Ponder:

Pay close attention to all gradual changes in your units. Doing this will prepare you to organize new changes to the challenges you make to oppose those meant to be repressive.

Write stories and letters to social groups, media personalities, news editors, etc., describing your being housed in solitary confinement. Share with these men or women what the living conditions are like and how they can be helping in doing investigations into your claims. Notify your state's health department if you have issues of poor sanitation.

- Encourage prisoners in your unit to compel their loved ones to organize press releases and address the overall conditions to the various news channels active in your area. Getting the word out is important.
- Write letters soliciting support for your claims and complaints to groups such as Amnesty International

and Human Rights Watch. Keep a file of everything you file for your record.

- These people are trying to kill us men. These points are not complex, they are easily understood. We must remain active by staying extremely proactive. I hope you will stand in solidarity with me and take control of your own survival or you'll die in isolation.

Part 7: Making Use of Your Access or Limited Use of the Unit's Law Library

I am almost certain that all across this prison industrial complex and country as a whole inside the SHUs exist a small unit law library. There are state prison policies, state law, and federal law and regulations control units must comply with.

Except for the right to life, the most fundamental right of prisoners, and one that is often at risk is the right not to be subject to torture and cruel, inhumane or degrading treatment or punishment. This right is protected by both the ICCPR and the convention against torture and other cruel, inhumane or degrading treatment or punishment, another treaty to which the U.S. is a party. It is also clear that solitary confinement, particularly for long periods, and particularly when combined with extreme deprivation of sources of stimulation, may cause mental suffering severe enough to violate international standards.

Article 1 of the Convention Against Torture defines torture as: "any act by which severe pain or suffering, whether physical or mental, is intentionally inflicted, on a person for such purposes as obtaining from him or a third person has committed information of a confession, punishing him for an act he or a third person, or for any reason based on discrimination of any kind, when such pain or suffering is inflicted by or at the instigation of or with the acquiescence of a public official or other person acting in an official capacity."

The Prison Industrial Complex by choosing to subject hundreds of us to prolonged periods in extremely harsh and potentially harmful conditions that cannot be justified as reasonable necessary to ensure security or to serve the legitimate goals of punishment, the prison industrial complex has violated prohibition on cruel, inhumane or degrading treatment contained in the international covenant on political and civil rights and the United Nation's standard minimum rules for the treatment of prisoners.

It is more accurate to describe life in these units as one of extremely limited environmental stimulation, one in which perceptually informative inputs are limited. Our worlds in here are cramped, claustrophobic, and austere. We are spending years of solitary lives, surrounded by the noise of others, but without the opportunity to develop normal social relationships. In a federal administrative segregation case called Bono v. Saxbe 450 F. Supp. 934 E.D. 111. 1978 the Court said: "Since by virtue of the prison's own rules, prisoners have protected liberty interest in remaining in the general population rather than being placed in the control unit U.S.C.A. Const. Amend. 5"

Before we can be placed in control units they must begin by giving written notice of the acts which led prison officials to contemplate taking the measure of confinement in the control unit, must be given a personal hearing with the right to present documentary evidence and with an impartial decision maker, must be given written notice for the action, and must have an opportunity for review at the time of the determination and for later periodic review.

Most control units don't provide a criteria, and terms you're forced to live in such confinement may be said to be permanent. Prison administrators claim that placement in administrative segregation in control units are not to be punitive when in fact it's clearly a form of punishment. For the most part our placements in such units are arbitrary. In Wright v. Enomoto 462 F. Supp. 397 (N.D. Cal. 1976): Though prisoner's rights may be diminished by the needs and exigencies of the institutional environment, a prisoner is not wholly stripped of constitutional protections when he is imprisoned for a crime. There is no iron curtain drawn between the constitution and the prisons in the country...prisoners may not be deprived of life, liberty, or property without due process of law.

Points to Ponder:

- Secure yourselves copies of all relevant cases dealing with administrative segregation where prison authorities were ruled against by the courts in the prisoner's favor.
- Learn all state prison policies that have rule over the environments in which you live. This is how we keep the officers in place when they violate facility rules.
- Never miss your opportunity to visit or send for legal state codes from your law libraries on those that govern your state or federal prison.
- Learn what your rights are as a prisoner so that you can expose to the media and courts how they are being violated.
- These are some simple key points to incorporate into your everyday lives while many of you are housed in control units. Today in Amerika we are being called hot-heads, terrorists, and the Amerikan Patriot Act is opening the door for all of our rights to be eroded. Learning how to apply state and federal law in defense of your rights could only be helpful down the road.

- The inhumane treatment and overall prison conditions can lead to a lot of bitterness and the loss of self-esteem. After doing any significant amount of time in these units, prisoners' character defects seem to grow until they literally dominate the persons' entire personality. Such closed confinement makes it extremely difficult to function in a civil environment. Prison authorities all across this country will have to come to terms with the pathological problems that are arising out of long term incarceration. Trying to reconnect with loved ones once released from these units back out into society is extremely hard.

Part 8: Proactive Participation in All Available Educational, Religious, or Correspondence Programs

There is nothing more solid than he or she who's confined in prison or housed in control units than to take an active stand and participate in all meaningful, positive, and wholesome activities. Many prisoners segregated on control units are being denied access to actually attend class for college. But they are granting us access to take our G.E.D. and pay to enroll in courses through mail correspondence. Also we can obtain a host of certificates of achievement by taking courses from the federal emergency management institute free of charge.

Also, there are a wide variety of religious schools of thought that offer prisoners a chance to earn a lot of great certificates. They too are free of charge when a prisoner is convicted and sent to prison. When going back into the court room, it's proven beneficial for many to produce certificates before the judge ruling on your appeal or modifications of sentence motions. Each prison also offers substance abuse and anger management courses where you can obtain a certificate of achievement once the course is completed. Many of the federal grants once readily available are now bankrupt and prisoners are hindered in their pursuits of higher education. Prisoners who are housed in control units, for the most part can't attend actual college classes, and must pay for a college through mail correspondence.

When a prisoner becomes proactive and not reactive, it's like taking back their lives. So it's very important to play an active role in your own survival and emotional, social, and political development. Society on a daily basis is being influenced by the Amerikan media's social commentary. Much of this propaganda is overwhelmingly anti-prisoner. So when prisoners are all being castigated 24/7, citizens are not quick to want to assist us. But being able to show your achievements while on the inside, prisoners can destroy the many myths or stereotypes being propagated. This is extremely important. Take charge of your life by taking your life back.

Prisoners have a right to write in to their local governors, state representatives, legislators, and others to complain about non-existent educational programs. State law and state codes require all state/federal facilities to operate a program service and educational outlet for its prisoners. If prisoners fail to hold those officials responsible, educational advancement will be non-existent in these units.

Points to Ponder:

- Write letters to correspondence schools and request an application to participate in obtaining certificates by completing their variety of courses.
- Write letters to colleges in your area and attempt to establish relationships with college professors and professionals who may empathize with your situation

and want to take a personal interest in helping you further your education.

- When you start collecting your certificates, you may want to make copies of them and send a copy home and have one placed in your facility packet.
- Engage yourself in any self-help and self-improvement opportunities that are available to you and encourage fellow prisoners to participate as well.

Taking action is "proactivity." We must always do for ourselves first, and then maybe someone would be encouraged to help us as well.

Anyone who desires to obtain a G.E.D. should do so. We are actually the ones capable of rehabilitating ourselves. We must first be transformed internally before actual changes can be made.

This is simple, and if you are genuine, it can be helpful to anyone who takes charge of the direction of their lives. Stop wasting time and energy engaging in activity that isn't conductive to your development as a whole. Inside Amerikan prisons, there exists a high level of hopelessness that will overwhelm most prisoners. This hopelessness cripples many to the point of discouraging men from fighting for their freedom. No one will help prisoners until they know we have a desire to fight for our own selves.

So, as we struggle to endure the madness that comes with being in prison and isolated in these control units, strength and perseverance must become our weapons of choice. The prison industrial complex is hoping to steal souls and lives of prisoners who are isolated in their custody. If you're not ready to die, stand up and become more proactive.

Part 9: On Turning Your Cell Into Your Own Laboratory

Sensory deprivation is alive and well and is used by prison authorities who run and operate control units all across this country. Most prisoners who are sanctioned to indefinite terms will more than likely be forced to live in conditions isolated to a cell 23 hours a day. Sometimes even 24 hours.

Closed inside these units, prisoners are being compelled to turn their cells into their very own laboratory. We have to study, write, exercise, and create right in these cells. In most cases you will have a cell to yourself. Some other units run the double man cells which ultimately can become very cramped for real active prisoners. These cells are the size of some big closets. Most of our time is spent in these cells so we have no other choice than to come up with creative ways to use the isolation to our advantage. Personally, it is crucial to use your moments of isolation to develop self-control. When we control our inner-self, we have won our first battle for freedom. Because without internal freedom, you'll never know real freedom at all. Working on our inner-selves enables us with the ability to conquer the sensory deprivation of being in a cell 23-24 hours a day.

Another very important issue we must develop is a good study and spiritual program. Doing so helps us to release the negative feelings we have inside. This small cell must become your laboratory where you create your unshakable foundation. Where you develop your maturity as a person, and where all the necessities you need are right there in arm's reach. We should never leave our rehabilitation in the hands of prison authorities. We are our own liberators -- we educate and teach ourselves. The credit goes to those of us who possess the self-determination to guide our survival in these oppressive control units all across the U.S. These units are built to contain and repress prisoners' resistance in the general populations across this country in Amerikan prisons. They are torturing and dehumanizing prisoners every day inside secured housing units all across this country. The ugliness of what the Amerikan people witnessed in the prison Abu Ghraib over in Iraq is nothing new to us here in Amerika. Torture and dehumanization are "tools of the trade" in U.S. prisons and supermax control units to destroy dangerous people. Prisoners are being suffocated, strangled, hanged, and hit with electric stun guns. They are dying and no one in society seems to feel this is a serious problem, but only a few staunch activists. We owe it to ourselves as revolutionary and aspiring revolutionary prison activist to work diligently to expose all prison abuse. Prisoners must learn all they can about existing violations inside the units they are isolated in, then expose it to the local public in the city and states you're located in. Turn your cell into your personal laboratory.

Points to Ponder:

- Build your own personal library of good quality up-to-date books and materials that can help you stabilize your foundation. This includes spiritual books also.
- Develop yourself a real meaningful line of communication with a love interest and others who share a real concern for your freedom and your survival.
- Get yourself a stimulating physical exercise program; one that works the cardiovascular, abdominal, legs, arms, etc. A well-rounded workout does wonders for the mind, body and soul, and it reduces high blood pressure.
  Surround yourself with positive thinking people at all times and your state of mind will always be positive.

Part 10: Educating Family on Building a Support Group

Building a support group isn't a new idea, to say the least. But many of us seems to feel we deserve one, yet we are not willing to put in the necessary work to bring this into a reality. WE must first possess a vision of what this support group's overall objectives will be, what types of people it will consist of and if these people involved are qualified to represent you entirely outside of your presence. When we hope to create a support group that's specifically focused on our freedom from prison, it's imperative that we educate and provide family with paperwork on concrete ways they can conductively help us. A person support group is extremely important because they will serve as your voice in the streets. They will be able to make your phone calls to judges, lawyers, prosecutors, and anyone else that must be contacted. So, you should work hard to develop an understanding with people as to what their commitments are to you. When you're being held hostage in these control units, your support group will be helpful in advocating for you. Many of us who come under attack by prison authorities need the help of support groups to raise factual complaints of abuse, torture, and violations of state or federal law or prison policies which are governed by state codes or statues.

A support group will be able to galvanize media support and publicize your struggles on all levels. The media will be more willing to listen to free people, and opposed to prisoners, so you must direct your people on what must be done. A support group can also help you solicit funds so that you may retain credible legal representation. Other funds may be used for your personal survival while fighting for your freedom from prison. These control units are dismal desolate places, where men and women prisoners alike are languishing in these places. Prisoners who have support groups already should encourage others in the ways of organizing a support group. Everyone in prison needs and desires a safety net; having a group of people out in society that will help is very important. Our survival is dependent upon help from outside sources.

Points to Ponder:

- Build your support group and involve family members that you trust.
- A post office box number should be acquired to use as the address for correspondence. Personal addresses should never be given to strangers.
- Your support group must obtain a computer/printer/scanner to advertise your case or whatever.
- Your support group should establish you a personal website that can display relative and factual information you want shared with the public.
- All art of poetry and other things you're into should also be displayed on your website.
- Your group should organize fundraisers and take out a personal account to put any donations that come in to support you.

Requested Understanding...

I am currently fighting a prison related murder charge of a prison guard. I've served my original sentence already, but now due to this new charge the state of Indiana successfully manufactured I've been given another 60 years. All of my initial appeals have been denied. I am now on the second level of appeals.

Donations are welcomed and should be made out to the freedom campaign of Khalfani Malik Khaldun in the name of Mark Thiel; 30 N. 19th Street; Lafayette, Indiana 47904. Your help, assistance and compassion will be much appreciated. Without your help there is no way I can gain an advantage on my fight for freedom.

CHAPTER 16
MENTAL HEALTH: THE SECRETS

Not only is it important that you stay physically healthy in order to survive prison, but it is as equally important that you stay mentally healthy. The prison experience/environment can easily take its toll on the minds of its men, so if you wish to survive, you must learn to overcome the challenges you are sure to face. No matter how strong your body is, prison will eat you alive if your mind is weak.

Despite what people on the outside may or may not think, it is important for *you* to understand that prisons are *designed* to mentally break its prisoners (you!) down. Once a man is broken down mentally, he starts to break spiritually. And one he's spiritually broken, he's as good as dead....

Furthermore, a mentally broken man is easier to control, as being mentally broken is to be tired. When he is tired, it's harder for him to fight. When it's harder for him to fight, it's easier for "them" to win. It is obviously to "their" benefit that *you* are weak; therefore, "they" have intentionally designed "their" system to exhaust you, and it is up to *you* to fight against falling a victim to that. In addition to the above, your psychological battle is not only with the depressing predicament that you find yourself in or the mental roller coaster designed by prison to suck out your energy and steal your spirit, but with your fellow prisoners, as well. Prison is a bloody shark tank full of great whites, and your fellow prisoners wish to suppress you just as much as anyone else. As explained in the mental warfare section of this book, you must learn to spot mental attacks from your fellow prisoners as well as defend yourself from them; and, just as importantly, you must also learn to spot and defend yourself from the mental attacks/wars waged against you by prison itself.

Here are my tips to staying mentally healthy and strong while you are in prison.

Keep your cell light on

For some reason, many prisoners like to keep their cell light off so that their cell remains dark all day. Why someone would want to live in the dark is beyond me, but it is an extremely common thing to do in prison.

Don't fall into this kind of program. Instead, keep your light on and *live*. Look at it like this: Light is life, and dark is death. When my celly wants to keep the light off all day I can *physically* feel a difference in my body. Too much darkness will bring upon depression. We are like plants: put us in sunlight, we will grow and live; put us in the dark, we will wither and die.

Don't sleep too much

Another thing a lot of prisoners like to do is sleep all day. However, it's a mistake; don't do it. Sleeping too much will not only make you always feel sluggish and sleepy, but it, too, will bring upon depression.

Exercise

Make sure you physically exercise at least a little bit each day. You have to keep yourself active. If you let a car sit too long without starting it, driving it around, etc., it's not going to run right. Well, the same thing goes for your body. A healthy body will help you keep a healthy mind, exercising will help you release tension and stress.

Don't dwell

I know life isn't necessarily going your way right now. However, don't sit around and dwell on your situation all day. It won't change anything, it will only *add* to your misery.

Instead of dwelling, turn whatever injustice has been done to you into a reason to fight. Rather than dwell or get depressed, get angry and channel that energy into something positive and/or beneficial; let your situation fuel your fire. Rather than dwelling on your situation, change it.

Stay positive

Despite your situation, you *must* remain positive. Too much negativity will kill you. Positivity (+) will *add* to your life; negativity (-) will take it away....

In addition to that, avoid negative people. They are like "energy vampires"; they will suck all the positive energy right out of you with their constant pessimism.

Have a sense of humor

It's important and healthy to have a good sense of humor. No matter what your situation is, always try to look for the humor in things. Laughter heals.

Have a Focus

Set goals for yourself and *focus* on them. Whether it's writing a book, studying something you're passionate about, or getting into something else that's time-consuming, escape prison by finding something positive and beneficial to do and *focus* on it. When you are focused on something, you will be too busy to dwell, stress, feel sorry for yourself, etc.

Read inspirational stories

Another thing I think is a good idea is to read inspirational stories. Whether you're religious or not, I find that "Guideposts" (magazines) have a lot of stories that give me a good feeling each time I read them. The "Chicken Soup for the Soul" is a good series too. And they even have a "Chicken Soup for the Prisoner's Soul."

Taking in good, positive, inspirational information is healthy. Whether it's reading books with these kinds of stories, or even watching TV shows like "Secret Millionaire" or "Home Makeover," intake as much positive and healthy information as you can.

Keep the faith; remain hopeful

Despite what your reality is today, you *must* remain hopeful. You'd be amazed how far faith and hope will take you. You must *never* give up. As long as you remain hopeful and continue to fight, you *will* have a chance of succeeding. If you lose hope and stop fighting, you will for sure *not* have a chance of succeeding. It's kind of like the concept, "you can't win if you don't play."

Religion

I cannot say that I am a real religious man. However, as I get older, I have a much clearer understanding of the essence and concept of religion. It now makes sense to me *why* people find so much strength in religion, and it all comes down to keeping faith and remaining hopeful.

If you have a religion, practice it. Religion is a *positive* intake. Therefore, it will help you stay on a positive path and remain faithful.

Mental relaxation

Finding time to relax your mind is crucial. You should dedicate at least 15 minutes a day to practicing some kind of relaxation technique – meditation, etc. In prison's chaotic environment, it is very important that you maintain peace of mind.

Note: I find calmative breathing to be a great, simply way to reduce anxiety, and it can be done anywhere, anytime. All you have to do is inhale through your nose, hold it for a count of four, and exhale *slowly* through pursed lips until you have expelled all of the air in your lungs. Try it; you will immediately feel more relaxed.

CHAPTER 17

THE PSYCHOLOGICAL IMPACT OF INCARSERATION: IMPLICATIONS FOR POST-PRISON ADJUSTMENT

By Craig Haney

Introduction

This paper examines the unique set of psychological changes that many prisoners are forced to undergo in order to survive the prison experience. It argues that, as a result of several trends in American corrections, the personal challenges posed and psychological harms inflicted in the course of incarceration have grown over the last several decades in the United States. The trends include increasingly harsh policies and conditions of confinement as well as the much-discussed de-emphasis on rehabilitation as a goal of incarceration. As a result, the ordinary adaptive process of institutionalization or prisonization" has become extraordinarily prolonged and intense. Among other things, these recent changes in prison life mean that prisoners in general (and some prisoners in particular) face more difficult and problematic transitions as they return to the free world. A range of structural and programmatic changes are required to address these issues. Among other things, social and psychological programs and resources must be made available in the immediate, short, and long-term. That is, modified prison conditions and practices as well as new programs are needed as preparation for release, during transitional periods of parole or initial reintegration, and as long-term services to insure continued successful adjustment.

This paper addresses the psychological impact of incarceration and its implications for post-prison free world adjustment. Nearly a half-century ago Gresham Sykes wrote that "life in the maximum-security prison is depriving or frustrating in the extreme," and little has changed to alter that view. Indeed, as I will suggest below, the observation applies with perhaps more force now than when Sykes first made it. Moreover, prolonged adaptation to the deprivations and frustrations of life inside prison – what are commonly referred to as the "pains of imprisonment" – carries a certain psychological cost. In this brief paper I will explore some of those costs, examine their implications for post-prison adjustment in the world beyond prison, and suggest some programmatic and policy-oriented approaches to minimizing their potential to undermine or disrupt the transition from prison to home.

One important caveat is important to make at the very outset of this paper. Although I approach this topic as a psychologist, and much of my discussion is organized around the themes of psychological changes and adaptations, I do not mean to suggest or imply that I believe criminal behavior can or should be equated with mental illness, that persons who suffer the acute pains of imprisonment necessarily manifest psychological disorders or other forms of personal pathology, that psychotherapy should be the exclusive or even primary tool of prison rehabilitation, or that therapeutic interventions are the most important or effective ways to optimize the transition from prison to home. I am well aware of the excesses that have been committed in the name of correctional psychology in the past, and it is not my intention to contribute in any way to having them repeated.

The paper will be organized around several basic propositions – that prisons have become more difficult places in which to adjust and survive over the last several decades; that especially in light of these changes, adaptation to modem prison life exacts certain psychological costs of most incarcerated persons; that some groups of people are somewhat more vulnerable to the pains of imprisonment than others; that the psychological costs and pains of imprisonment can serve to impede post-prison adjustment; and that there are a series of things that can be done both in and out of prison to minimize these impediments. Each of these propositions is presented in turn below.

I. The State of the Prisons

Prisoners in the United States and elsewhere have always confronted a unique set of contingencies and pressures to which they were required to react and adapt in order to survive the prison experience. However, over the last several decades – beginning in the early 1970s and continuing to the present time – a combination of forces have transformed the nation's criminal justice system and modified the nature of imprisonment. The challenges prisoners now face in order to both survive the prison experience and, eventually, reintegrate into the free world upon release have changed and intensified as a result.

Among other things, these changes in the nature of imprisonment have included a series of interrelated, negative trends in American corrections. Perhaps the most dramatic changes have come about as a result of the unprecedented increases in rate of incarceration, the size of the U.S. prison population, and the widespread overcrowding that has occurred as a result. Over the past 25 years, penologists repeatedly have described U.S. prisons as "in crisis" and have characterized each new level of overcrowding as "unprecedented." By the start of the 1990s, the United States incarcerated more persons per capita than any other nation in the modem world, and it has retained that dubious distinction for nearly every year since. The international disparities are most striking when the U.S. incarceration rate is contrasted to those of other nations to whom the United States is often compared, such as Japan, Netherlands, Australia, and the United Kingdom. In the 1990s, as Marc Mauer and the Sentencing Project have effectively documented – the U.S. rates have consistently been between four and eight times those for these other nations.

The combination of overcrowding and the rapid expansion of prison systems across the country adversely affected living conditions in many prisons, jeopardized prisoner safety, compromised prison management, and greatly limited prisoner access to meaningful programming. The two largest prison systems in the nation – California and Texas – provide instructive examples. Over the last 30 years, California's prisoner population increased eightfold (from roughly 20,000 in the early 1970s to its current population of approximately 160,000 prisoners). Yet there has been no remotely comparable increase in funds for prisoner services or inmate programming. In Texas, over just the years between 1992 and 1997, the prisoner population more than doubled as Texas achieved one of the highest incarceration rates in the nation. Nearly 70,000 additional prisoners added to the state's prison rolls in that brief five-year period alone. Not surprisingly, California and Texas were among the states to face major lawsuits in the 1990s over substandard, unconstitutional conditions of confinement. Federal courts in both states found that the prison systems had failed to provide adequate treatment services for those prisoners who suffered the most extreme psychological effects of confinement in deteriorated and overcrowded conditions.

Paralleling these dramatic increases in incarceration rates and the numbers of persons imprisoned in the United States was an equally dramatic change in the rationale for prison itself. The nation moved abruptly in the mid-1970s from a society that justified putting people in prison on the basis of the belief that incarceration would somehow facilitate productive re-entry into the free world to one that used imprisonment merely to inflict pain on wrongdoers ("just deserts"), disable criminal offenders ("incapacitation"), or to keep them far away from the rest of society ("containment"). The abandonment of the once-avowed goal of rehabilitation certainly decreased the perceived need and availability of meaningful programming for prisoners as well as social and mental health services available to them both inside and outside the prison. Indeed, it generally reduced concern on the part of prison administrations for the overall well-being of prisoners.

The abandonment of rehabilitation also resulted in an erosion of modestly protective norms against cruelty toward prisoners. Many corrections officials soon became far less inclined to address prison disturbances, tensions between prisoner groups and factions, and disciplinary infractions in general through ameliorative techniques aimed at the root causes of conflict and designed to de-escalate it. The rapid influx of new prisoners, serious shortages in staffing and other resources, and the embrace of an openly punitive approach to corrections led to the "deskilling" of many correctional staff members who often resorted to extreme forms of prison discipline (such as punitive isolation or "super max" confinement) that had especially destructive effects on prisoners and repressed conflict rather than resolving it. Increased tensions and higher levels of fear and danger resulted.

The emphasis on the punitive and stigmatizing aspects of incarceration, which has resulted in the further literal and psychological isolation of prison from the surrounding community, compromised prison visitation programs and the already scarce resources that had been used to maintain ties between prisoners and their families and the outside world. Support services to facilitate the transition from prison to the free world environments to which prisoners were returned were undermined at precisely the moment they needed to be enhanced. Increased sentence length and a greatly expanded scope of incarceration resulted in prisoners experiencing the psychological strains of imprisonment for longer periods of time, many persons being caught in the web of incarceration who ordinarily would not have been (e.g., drug offenders), and the social costs of incarceration becoming increasingly concentrated in minority communities (because of differential enforcement and sentencing policies).

Thus, in the first decade of the 21st century, more people have been subjected to the pains of imprisonment, for longer periods of time, under conditions that threaten greater psychological distress and potential long-term dysfunction, and they will be returned to communities that have already been disadvantaged by a lack of social services and resources.

II. The Psychological Effects of Incarceration: On the Nature of Institutionalization

The adaptation to imprisonment is almost always difficult and, at times, creates habits of thinking and acting that can be dysfunctional in periods of post-prison adjustment. Yet, the psychological effects of incarceration vary from individual to individual and are often reversible. To be sure, then, not everyone who is incarcerated is disabled or psychologically harmed by it. But few people are completely unchanged or unscathed by the experience. At the very least, prison is painful, and incarcerated persons often suffer long-term consequences from having been subjected to pain, deprivation, and extremely atypical patterns and norms of living and interacting with others.

The empirical consensus on the most negative effects of incarceration is that most people who have done time in the best-run prisons return to the free world with little or no permanent, clinically-diagnosable psychological disorders as a result. Prisons do not, in general, make people "crazy." However, even researchers who are openly skeptical about whether the pains of imprisonment generally translate into psychological harm concede that, for at least some people, prison can produce negative, long-lasting change. And most people agree that the more extreme, harsh, dangerous, or otherwise psychologically-taxing the nature of the confinement, the greater the number of people who will suffer and the deeper the damage that they will incur.

Rather than concentrate on the most extreme or clinically-diagnosable effects of imprisonment, however, I prefer to focus on the broader and more subtle psychological changes that occur in the routine course of adapting to prison life. The term "institutionalization" is used to describe the process by which inmates are shaped and transformed by the institutional environments in which they live. Sometimes called "prisonization" when it occurs in correctional settings, it is the shorthand expression for the negative psychological effects of imprisonment.

The process has been studied extensively by sociologists, psychologists, psychiatrists, and others, and involves a unique set of psychological adaptations that often occur – in varying degrees – in response to the extraordinary demands of prison life. In general terms, the process of prisonization involves the incorporation of the norms of prison life into one's habits of thinking, feeling, and acting.

It is important to emphasize that these are the natural and normal adaptations made by prisoners in response to the unnatural and abnormal conditions of prisoner life. The dysfunctionality of these adaptations is not "pathological" in nature (even though, in practical terms, they may be destructive in effect). They are "normal" reactions to a set of pathological conditions that become problematic when they are taken to extreme lengths, or become chronic and deeply internalized (so that, even though the conditions of one's life have changed, many of the once-functional but now counterproductive patterns remain).

Like all processes of gradual change, of course, this one typically occurs in stages and, all other things being equal, the longer someone is incarcerated the more significant the nature of the institutional transformation. When most people first enter prison, of course, they find that being forced to adapt to an often harsh and rigid institutional routine, deprived of privacy and liberty, and subjected to a diminished, stigmatized status and extremely sparse material conditions is stressful, unpleasant, and difficult.

However, in the course of becoming institutionalized, a transformation begins. Persons gradually become more accustomed to the restrictions that institutional life imposes. The various psychological mechanisms that must be employed to adjust (and, in some harsh and dangerous correctional environments, to survive) become increasingly "natural," second nature, and, to a degree, internalized. To be sure, the process of institutionalization can be subtle and difficult to discern as it occurs. Thus, prisoners do not "choose" do succumb to it or not, and few people who have become institutionalized are aware that it has happened to them. Fewer still consciously decide that they are going to willingly allow the transformation to occur.

The process of institutionalization is facilitated in cases in which persons enter institutional settings at an early age, before they have formed the ability and expectation to control their own life choices. Because there is less tension between the demands of the institution and the autonomy of a mature adult, institutionalization proceeds more quickly and less problematically with at least some younger inmates. Moreover, younger inmates have little in the way of already developed independent judgment, so they have little if anything to revert to or rely upon if and when the institutional structure is removed. And the longer someone remains in an institution, the greater the likelihood that the process will transform them.

Among other things, the process of institutionalization (or "prisonization") includes some or all of the following psychological adaptations:

A. Dependence on institutional structure and contingencies.

Among other things, penal institutions require inmates to relinquish the freedom and autonomy to make their own choices and decisions and this process requires what is a painful adjustment for most people. Indeed, some people never adjust to it. Over time, however, prisoners may adjust to the muting of self-initiative and independence that prison requires and become increasingly dependent on institutional contingencies that they once resisted. Eventually it may seem more or less natural to be denied significant control over day-to-day decisions and, in the final stages of the process, some inmates may come to depend heavily on institutional decision makers to make choices for them and to rely on the structure and schedule of the institution to organize their daily routine. Although it rarely occurs to such a degree, some people do lose the capacity to initiate behavior on their own and the judgment to make decisions for themselves. Indeed, in extreme cases, profoundly institutionalized persons may become extremely uncomfortable when and if their previous freedom and autonomy is returned.

A slightly different aspect of the process involves the creation of dependency upon the institution to control one's behavior. Correctional institutions force inmates to adapt to an elaborate network of typically very clear boundaries and limits, the consequences for whose violation can be swift and severe. Prisons impose careful and continuous surveillance, and are quick to punish (and sometimes to punish severely) infractions of the limiting rules. The process of institutionalization in correctional settings may surround inmates so thoroughly with external limits, immerse them so deeply in a network of rules and regulations, and accustom them so completely to such highly visible systems of constraint that internal controls atrophy or, in the case of especially young inmates, fail to develop altogether. Thus, institutionalization or prisonization renders some people so dependent on external constraints that they gradually lose the capacity to rely on internal organization and self-imposed personal limits to guide their actions and restrain their conduct. If and when this external structure is taken away, severely institutionalized persons may find that they no longer know how to do things on their own, or how to refrain from doing those things that are ultimately harmful or self- destructive.

B. Hypervigilance, interpersonal distrust, and suspicion.

In addition, because many prisons are clearly dangerous places from which there is no exit or escape, prisoners learn quickly to become hypervigilant and ever-alert for signs of threat or personal risk. Because the stakes are high, and because there are people in their immediate environment poised to take advantage of weakness or exploit carelessness or inattention, interpersonal distrust and suspicion often result. Some prisoners learn to project a tough convict veneer that keeps all others at a distance. Indeed, as one prison researcher put it, many prisoners "believe that unless an inmate can convincingly project an image that conveys the potential for violence, he is likely to be dominated and exploited throughout the duration of his sentence."

McCorkle's study of a maximum-security Tennessee prison was one of the few that attempted to quantify the kinds of behavioral strategies prisoners report employing to survive dangerous prison environments. He found that "[f]ear appeared to be shaping the life-styles of many of the men," that it had led over 40% of prisoners to avoid certain high risk areas of the prison, and about an equal number of inmates reported spending additional time in their cells as a precaution against victimization. At the same time, almost three-quarters reported that they had been forced to "get tough" with another prisoner to avoid victimization, and more than a quarter kept a "shank" or other weapon nearby with which to defend themselves. McCorkle found that age was the best predictor of the type of adaptation a prisoner took, with younger prisoners being more likely to employ aggressive avoidance strategies than older ones.

C. Emotional over-control, alienation, and psychological distancing.

Shaping such an outward image requires emotional responses to be carefully measured. Thus, prisoners struggle to control and suppress their own internal emotional reactions to events around them. Emotional over-control and a generalized lack of spontaneity may occur as a result. Admissions of vulnerability to persons inside the immediate prison environment are potentially dangerous because they invite exploitation. As one experienced prison administrator once wrote: "Prison is a barely controlled jungle where the aggressive and the strong will exploit the weak, and the weak are dreadfully aware of it." Some prisoners are forced to become remarkably skilled "self-monitors" who calculate the anticipated effects that every aspect of their behavior might have on the rest of the prison population, and strive to make such calculations second nature.

Prisoners who labor at both an emotional and behavioral level to develop a "prison mask" that is unrevealing and impenetrable risk alienation from themselves and others, may develop emotional flatness that becomes chronic and debilitating in social interaction and relationships, and find that they have created a permanent and unbridgeable distance between themselves and other people. Many for whom the mask becomes especially thick and effective in prison find that the disincentive against engaging in open communication with others that prevails there has led them to withdrawal from authentic social interactions altogether. The alienation and social distancing from others is a defense not only against exploitation but also against the realization that the lack of interpersonal control in the immediate prison environment makes emotional investments in relationships risky and unpredictable.

D. Social withdrawal and isolation.

Some prisoners learn to find safety in social invisibility by becoming as inconspicuous and unobtrusively disconnected from others as possible. The self-imposed social withdrawal and isolation may mean that they retreat deeply into themselves, trust virtually no one, and adjust to prison stress by leading isolated lives of quiet desperation. In extreme cases, especially when combined with prisoner apathy and loss of the capacity to initiate behavior on one's own, the pattern closely resembles that of clinical depression. Long-term prisoners are particularly vulnerable to this form of psychological adaptation. Indeed, Taylor wrote that the long-term prisoner "shows a flatness of response which resembles slow, automatic behavior of a very limited kind, and he is humorless and lethargic. In fact, Jose-Kampfner has analogized the plight of long-term women prisoners to that of persons who are terminally-ill, whose experience of this "existential death is unfeeling, being cut off from the outside... (and who) adopt this attitude because it helps them cope.

E. Incorporation of exploitative norms of prison culture.

In addition to obeying the formal rules of the institution, there are also informal rules and norms that are part of the unwritten but essential institutional and inmate culture and code that, at some level, must be abided. For some prisoners this means defending against the dangerousness and deprivations of the surrounding environment by embracing all of its informal norms, including some of the most exploitative and extreme values of prison life. Note that prisoners typically are given no alternative culture to which to ascribe or in which to participate. In many institutions the lack of meaningful programming has deprived them of pro-social or positive activities in which to engage while incarcerated. Few prisoners are given access to gainful employment where they can obtain meaningful job skills and earn adequate compensation; those who do work are assigned to menial tasks that they perform for only a few hours a day. With rare exceptions – those very few states that permit highly regulated and infrequent conjugal visits – they are prohibited from sexual contact of any kind. Attempts to address many of the basic needs and desires that are the focus of normal day-to-day existence in the free world – to recreate, to work, to love – necessarily draws them closer to an illicit prisoner culture that for many represents the only apparent and meaningful way of being.

However, as I noted earlier, prisoner culture frowns on any sign of weakness and vulnerability, and discourages the expression of candid emotions or intimacy. And some prisoners embrace it in a way that promotes a heightened investment in one's reputation for toughness, and encourages a stance towards others in which even seemingly insignificant insults, affronts, or physical violations must be responded to quickly and instinctively, sometimes with decisive force. In extreme cases, the failure to exploit weakness is itself a sign of weakness and seen as an invitation for exploitation. In men's prisons it may promote a kind of hyper masculinity in which force and domination are glorified as essential components of personal identity. In an environment characterized by enforced powerlessness and deprivation, men and women prisoners confront distorted norms of sexuality in which dominance and submission become entangled with and mistaken for the basis of intimate relations.

Of course, embracing these values too fully can create enormous barriers to meaningful interpersonal contact in the free world, preclude seeking appropriate help for one's problems, and a generalized unwillingness to trust others out of fear of exploitation. It can also lead to what appears to be impulsive overreaction, striking out at people in response to minimal provocation that occurs particularly with persons who have not been socialized into the norms of inmate culture in which the maintenance of interpersonal respect and personal space are so inviolate. Yet these things are often as much a part of the process of prisonization as adapting to the formal rules that are imposed in the institution, and they are as difficult to relinquish upon release.

F. Diminished sense of self-worth and personal value.

Prisoners typically are denied their basic privacy rights, and lose control over mundane aspects of their existence that most citizens have long taken for granted. They live in small, sometimes extremely cramped and deteriorating spaces (a 60 square foot cell is roughly the size of king-size bed), have little or no control over the identity of the person with whom they must share that space (and the intimate contact it requires), often have no choice over when they must get up or go to bed, when or what they may eat, and on and on. Some feel infantilized and that the degraded conditions under which they live serve to repeatedly remind them of their compromised social status and stigmatized social role as prisoners. A diminished sense of self-worth and personal value may result. In extreme cases of institutionalization, the symbolic meaning that can be inferred from this externally imposed substandard treatment and circumstances is internalized; that is, prisoners may come to think of themselves as "the kind of person" who deserves only the degradation and stigma to which they have been subjected while incarcerated.

G. Post-traumatic stress reactions to the pains of imprisonment.

For some prisoners, incarceration is so stark and psychologically painful that it represents a form of traumatic stress severe enough to produce post-traumatic stress reactions once released. Moreover, we now understand that there are certain basic commonalities that characterize the lives of many of the persons who have been convicted of crime in our society. A "risk factors" model helps to explain the complex interplay of traumatic childhood events (like poverty, abusive and neglectful mistreatment, and other forms of victimization) in the social histories of many criminal offenders. As Masten and Garmezy have noted, the presence of these background risk factors and traumas in childhood increases the probability that one will encounter a whole range of problems later in life, including delinquency and criminality. The fact that a high percentage of persons presently incarcerated have experienced childhood trauma means, among other things, that the harsh, punitive, and uncaring nature of prison life may represent a kind of "re-traumatization" experience for many of them. That is, some prisoners find exposure to the rigid and unyielding discipline of prison, the unwanted proximity to violent encounters and the possibility or reality of being victimized by physical and/or sexual assaults, the need to negotiate the dominating intentions of others, the absence of genuine respect and regard for their wellbeing in the surrounding environment, and so on all too familiar. Time spent in prison may rekindle not only the memories but the disabling psychological reactions and consequences of these earlier damaging experiences.

The dysfunctional consequences of institutionalization are not always immediately obvious once the institutional structure and procedural imperatives have been removed. This is especially true in cases where persons retain a minimum of structure wherever they re-enter free society. Moreover, the most negative consequences of institutionalization may first occur in the form of internal chaos, disorganization, stress, and fear. Yet, institutionalization has taught most people to cover their internal states, and not to openly or easily reveal intimate feelings or reactions. So, the outward appearance of normality and adjustment may mask a range of serious problems in adapting to the free world.

This is particularly true of persons who return to the free world lacking a network of close, personal contacts with people who know them well enough to sense that something may be wrong. Eventually, however, when severely institutionalized persons confront complicated problems or conflicts, especially in the form of unexpected events that cannot be planned for in advance, the myriad of challenges that the non-institutionalized confront in their everyday lives outside the institution may become overwhelming. The facade of normality begins to deteriorate, and persons may behave in dysfunctional or even destructive ways because all of the external structure and supports upon which they relied to keep themselves controlled, directed, and balanced have been removed.

III. Special Populations and Pains of Prison Life

Although everyone who enters prison is subjected to many of the above-stated pressures of institutionalization, and prisoners respond in various ways with varying degrees of psychological change associated with their adaptations, it is important to note that there are some prisoners who are much more vulnerable to these pressures and the overall pains of imprisonment than others. Either because of their personal characteristics – in the case of "special needs" prisoners whose special problems are inadequately addressed by current prison policies – or because of the especially harsh conditions of confinement to which they are subjected – in the case of increasing numbers of "supermax" or solitary confinement prisoners – they are at risk of making the transition from prison to home with a more significant set of psychological problems and challenges to overcome. The plight of several of these special populations of prisoners is briefly discussed below.

A. Mentally Ill and Developmentally Disabled Prisoners

Perhaps not surprisingly, mental illness and developmental disability represent the largest number of disabilities among prisoners. For example, a national survey of prison inmates with disabilities conducted in 1987 indicated that although less than 1% suffered from visual, mobility/orthopedic, hearing, or speech deficits, much higher percentages suffered from cognitive and psychological disabilities. A more recent follow-up study by two of the same authors obtained similar results: although less than 1% of the prison population suffered visual, mobility, speech, or hearing deficits, 4.2% were developmentally disabled, 7.2% suffered psychotic disorders, and 12% reported "other psychological disorders." It is probably safe to estimate, then, based on this and other studies, that upwards of as many as 20% of the current prisoner population nationally suffers from either some sort of significant mental or psychological disorder or developmental disability.

As my earlier comments about the process of institutionalization implied, the task of negotiating key features of the social environment of imprisonment is far more challenging than it appears at first. And it is surely far more difficult for vulnerable, mentally-ill and developmentally-disabled prisoners to accomplish. Incarceration presents particularly difficult adjustment problems that make prison an especially confusing and sometimes dangerous situation for them. For mentally-ill and developmentally-disabled inmates, part of whose defining (but often undiagnosed) disability includes difficulties in maintaining close contact with reality, controlling and conforming one's emotional and behavioral reactions, and generally impaired comprehension and learning, the rule-bound nature of institutional life may have especially disastrous consequences. Yet, both groups are too often left to their own devices to somehow survive in prison and leave without having had any of their unique needs addressed.

Combined with the de-emphasis on treatment that now characterizes our nation's correctional facilities, these behavior patterns can significantly impact the institutional history of vulnerable or special needs inmates. One commentator has described the vicious cycle into which mentally-ill and developmentally-disabled prisoners can fall:

- The lack of mental health care for the seriously mentally ill who end up in segregation units has worsened the condition of many prisoner's incapable of understanding their condition. This is especially true in cases where prisoners are placed in levels of mental health care that are not intense enough, and begin to refuse taking their medication. They then enter a vicious cycle in which their mental disease takes over, often causing hostile and aggressive behavior to the point that they break prison rules and end up in segregation units as management problems. Once in punitive housing, this regression can go undetected for considerable periods of time before they again receive more closely monitored mental health care. This cycle can, and often does, repeat.

B. Prisoners in "Super max" or Solitary Confinement

In addition, there are an increasing number of prisoners who are subjected to the unique and more destructive experience of punitive isolation, in so-called "super max" facilities, where they are kept under conditions of unprecedented levels of social deprivation for unprecedented lengths of time. This kind of confinement creates its own set of psychological pressures that, in some instances, uniquely disable prisoners for free world reintegration. Indeed, there are few if any forms of imprisonment that produce so many indices of psychological trauma and symptoms of psychopathology in those persons subjected to it. My own review of the literature suggested these documented negative psychological consequences of long-term solitary-like confinement include: an impaired sense of identity; hypersensitivity to stimuli; cognitive dysfunction (confusion, memory loss, ruminations); irritability, anger, aggression, and/or rage; other-directed violence, such as stabbings, attacks on staff, property destruction, and collective violence; lethargy, helplessness and hopelessness; chronic depression; self-mutilation and/or suicidal ideation, impulses, and behavior; anxiety and panic attacks; emotional breakdowns; and/or loss of control; hallucinations, psychosis and/or paranoia; overall deterioration of mental and physical health.

Human Rights Watch has suggested that there are approximately 20,000 prisoners confined to super max-type units in the United States. Most experts agree that the number of such units is increasing. In many states the majority of prisoners in these units are serving "indeterminate" solitary confinement terms, which means that their entire prison sentence will be served in isolation (unless they "debrief" by providing incriminating information about other prisoners). Few states provide any meaningful or effective "decompression" program for prisoners, which means that many prisoners who have been confined in these super max units – some for considerable periods of time

– are released directly into the community from these extreme conditions of confinement.

IV. Implications for the Transition From Prison to Home

The psychological consequences of incarceration may represent significant impediments to post-prison adjustment. They may interfere with the transition from prison to home, impede an ex-convict's successful re-integration into a social network and employment setting, and may compromise an incarcerated parent's ability to resume his or her role with family and children. The range of effects includes the sometimes subtle but nonetheless broad-based and potentially disabling effects of institutionalization prisonization, the persistent effects of untreated or exacerbated mental illness, the long-term legacies of developmental disabilities that were improperly addressed, or the pathological consequences of super max confinement experienced by a small but growing number of prisoners who are released directly from long-term isolation into free world communities. There is little or no evidence that prison systems across the country have responded in a meaningful way to these psychological issues, either in the course of confinement or at the time of release. Over the next decade, the impact of unprecedented levels of incarceration will be felt in communities that will be expected to receive massive numbers of ex-convicts who will complete their sentences and return home but also to absorb the high level of psychological trauma and disorder that many will bring with them.

The implications of these psychological effects for parenting and family life can be profound. Parents who return from periods of incarceration still dependent on institutional structures and routines cannot be expected to effectively organize the lives of their children or exercise the initiative and autonomous decision making that parenting requires. Those who still suffer the negative effects of a distrusting and hypervigilant adaptation to prison life will find it difficult to promote trust and authenticity within their children. Those who remain emotionally over-controlled and alienated from others will experience problems being psychologically available and nurturing. Tendencies to socially withdraw, remain aloof or seek social invisibility could not be more dysfunctional in family settings where closeness and interdependency is needed. The continued embrace of many of the most negative aspects of exploitative prisoner culture is likely to doom most social and intimate relations, as will an inability to overcome the diminished sense of self-worth that prison too often instills. Clearly, the residual effects of the post-traumatic stress of imprisonment and the traumatization experiences that the nature of prison life may incur can jeopardize the mental health of persons attempting to reintegrate back into the free world communities from which they came. Indeed, there is evidence that incarcerated parents not only themselves continue to be adversely affected by traumatizing risk factors to which they have been exposed, but also that the experience of imprisonment has done little or nothing to provide them with the tools to safeguard their children from the same potentially destructive experiences.

The excessive and disproportionate use of imprisonment over the last several decades also means that these problems will not only be large but concentrated primarily in certain communities whose residents were selectively targeted for criminal justice system intervention. Our society is about to absorb the consequences not only of the "rage to punish" that was so fully indulged in the last quarter of the 20th century but also of the "malign neglect" that led us to concentrate this rage so heavily on African American men. Remarkably, as the present decade began, there were more young Black men (between the ages of 20-29) under the control of the nation's criminal justice system (including probation and parole supervision) than the total number in college. Thus, whatever the psychological consequences of imprisonment and their implications for reintegration back into the communities from which prisoners have come, we know that those consequences and implications are about to be felt in unprecedented ways in these communities, by these families, and for these children, like no others. Not surprisingly, then, one scholar has predicted that "imprisonment will become the most significant factor contributing to the dissolution and breakdown of African American families during the decade of the 1990s"(29) and another has concluded that "[c]rime control policies are a major contributor to the disruption of the family, the prevalence of single parent families, and children raised without a father in the ghetto, and the 'inability of people to get the jobs still available'."

V. Policy and Programmatic Responses to the Adverse Effects of Incarceration

An intelligent, humane response to these facts about the implications of contemporary prison life must occur on at least two levels. We must simultaneously address the adverse prison policies and conditions of confinement that have created these special problems, and at the same time provide psychological resources and social services for persons who have been adversely affected by them. Both things must occur if the successful transition from prison to home is to occur on a consistent and effective basis.

There are three areas in which policy interventions must be concentrated in order to address these two levels of concern:

Prison Conditions, Policies, and Procedures

No significant amount of progress can be made in easing the transition from prison to home until and unless significant changes are made in the normative structure of American prisons. Specifically:

- The goal of penal harm must give way to a clear emphasis on prisoner-oriented rehabilitative services.
- The adverse effects of institutionalization must be minimized by structuring prison life to replicate, as much as possible, life in the world outside prison. A useful heuristic to follow is a simple one: "the less like a prison, and the more like the free world, the better."
- Prisons that give inmates opportunities to exercise pockets of autonomy and personal initiative must be created.
- Safe correctional environments that remove the need for hyper vigilance and pervasive distrust must be maintained, ones where prisoners can establish authentic selves, and learn the norms of interdependence and cooperative trust.
- A clear and consistent emphasis on maximizing visitation and supporting contact with the outside world must be implemented, both to minimize the division between the norms of prison and those of the free world, and to discourage dysfunctional social withdrawal that is difficult to reverse upon release.
- Program rich institutions must be established that give prisoners genuine alternative to exploitative

prisoner culture in which to participate and invest, and the degraded, stigmatized status of prisoner transcended. Prisoners must be given opportunities to engage in meaningful activities, to work, and to love while incarcerated.

- Adequate therapeutic and facilitative resources must be provided to address the needs of the large numbers of mentally ill and developmentally disabled prisoners who are now incarcerated.

- The increased use of super max and other forms of extremely harsh and psychologically damaging confinement must be reversed. Strict time limits must be placed on the use of punitive isolation that approximate the much briefer periods of such confinement that once characterized American corrections, prisoners must be screened for special vulnerability to isolation, and carefully monitored so that they can be removed upon the first sign of adverse reactions.

B. Transitional Services to Prepare Prisoners for Community Release

No significant amount of progress can be made in easing the transition from prison to home until and unless significant changes are made in the way prisoners are prepared to leave prison and reenter the free world communities from which they came. Specifically:

Prison systems must begin to take the pains of imprisonment and the nature of institutionalization seriously, and provide all prisoners with effective decompression programs in which they are re-acclimated to the nature and norms of the free world. Prisoners must be given some insight into the changes brought about by their adaptation to prison life. They must be given some understanding of the ways in which prison may have changed them, the tools with which to respond to the challenge of adjustment to the free world.

The process must begin well in advance of a prisoner's release, and take into account all aspects of the transition he or she will be expected to make. This means, among other things, that all prisoners will need occupational and vocational training and pre-release assistance in finding gainful employment. It also means that prisoners who are expected to resume their roles as parents will need pre-release assistance in establishing, strengthening, and/or maintaining ties with their families and children, and whatever other assistance will be essential for them to function effectively in this role (such as parenting classes and the like).

Prisoners who have manifested signs or symptoms of mental illness or developmental disability while incarcerated will need specialized transitional services to facilitate their reintegration into the free world. These would include, where appropriate, pre-release outpatient treatment and habilitation plans.

No prisoner should be released directly out of super max or solitary confinement back into the free world. Super max prisons must provide long periods of decompression, with adequate time for prisoners to be treated for the adverse effects of long-term isolation and reacquaint themselves with the social norms of the world to which they will return.

C. Community-Based Services to Facilitate and Maintain Reintegration

No significant amount of progress can be made in easing the transition from prison to home until and unless significant changes are made in the way ex-convicts are treated to in the free world communities from which they came. Specifically:

- Clear recognition must be given to the proposition that persons who return home from prison face significant personal, social, and structural challenges that they have neither the ability nor resources to overcome entirely on their own. Post-release success often depends of the nature and quality of services and support provided in the community, and here is where the least amount of societal attention and resources are typically directed. This tendency must be reversed.
- Gainful employment is perhaps the most critical aspect of post-prison adjustment. The stigma of incarceration and the psychological residue of institutionalization require active and prolonged agency intervention to transcend. Job training, employment counselling, and employment placement programs must all be seen as essential parts of an effective reintegration plan.
- A broadly conceived family systems approach to counselling for ex-convicts and their families and children must be implemented in which the long-term problematic consequences of "normal" adaptations to prison life are the focus of discussion, rather than traditional models of psychotherapy.
- Parole and probation services and agencies need to be restored to their original role of assisting with reintegration. Here too the complexity of the transition from prison to home needs to be fully appreciated, and parole revocation should only occur after every possible community-based resource and approach has been tried.

CHAPTER 18
WORKING OUT: THE SECRETS

Just about everyone has heard the old adage "survival of the fittest." Well, that statement could never be more fitting than it is for describing life in the devil's playground. Not only is it extremely important to stay physically fit for physical health reasons, but for mental health and safety reasons as well.

It's true that your body is your temple. And in prison, unless you're on death row, the "authorities" can take just about everything from you *but* your temple. They can take all your personal property if they want to – justified or not. They can put you in the hole somewhere, by yourself, and even take your state-issued clothing, mattress, etc.; leaving you in a dark, cold cell with absolutely nothing. Trust me, I know; I've been through it.

So, being that they can't take your temple and, in the end, *you* are all you *really* have, no investment is as important as the one you invest into yourself.

Furthermore, prison is an extremely dangerous place; it is ruled by violence. Prison is full of brutes, beasts and bullies, who often want to prove themselves as the strongest, toughest, and most savage. If you want to increase your odds of surviving among such men, then you need to be in the best physical shape you can be in. You can bet that the prisoners around you are exercising and building their bodies as much as they can, so if you aren't, what are the odds you will be able to hold your own if and when it comes to it?

Prisoners are known for having a particular build (often referred to as a "prison build") – big on top with skinny legs. A lot of prisoners focus on upper-body workouts because, in prison, we often have our shirts off, and guys want to look as big and buff as possible. It is also a defense mechanism – the bigger you are, the more intimidating you look; the more intimidating you look, the less people will want to challenge you. I know plenty of big boys who are pussies; however, not too many people want to take the chance of finding out for themselves.

Working towards achieving the "prison build" is an unintelligent way to work out. In order to work out properly, you *must* work your legs as well; they are your foundation. If you're top-heavy with the itty-bitty broomstick legs, you leave yourself open for a smart fighter – one who may even be smaller than you – to sweep them out from under you. And unless you're a trained MMA fighter or something, once you're on the ground, it will be easy for even a small guy to take advantage of your vulnerable position.

Working out / exercising / body building is not something you can master by reading a chapter or two out of a book – or even by reading a book or two, for that matter. The art and science of "body building" is something that takes years and years of practice and study in order to really learn and master. Furthermore, I have read many muscle magazines over the years, and each one has had a different philosophy regarding what will get you the "best" results.

In the end, what it boils down to is that everybody is different, and you need to learn what works best for *you* and *your* body type. What works for one man may not work very well for you, and, on the flip side, what one man may think is ineffective may be what gets you your *best* results.

However, to get you started on becoming the man-beast you're meant to be – or better learn to be if you intend on surviving prison – I'm going to explain to you some of the more popular prisoner muscle-building exercises, as well as some techniques you are not likely to see the average prisoner doing on the yard, because they are the secrets told to me by some of the biggest, most beastly prisoners I've ever met.

Not all prisons have "weights" these days. Therefore, most of the exercises I'm going to explain to you are ones you can do without weights; however, I'm also going to explain to you how we make our own weights in prison.

Here are some great exercises that will help you get in tip-top shape.

Biceps:

If you want to turn your biceps into solid rocks, you're going to have to do a lot of curls. In order to do a lot of curls, you're going to need something to curl, right? Well, since prison doesn't typically provide dumbbells, you're going to have to make your own.

Mattress Dumbbell

More than likely you have one of those 3-4-inch thick mattresses that are hard as hell and weigh about 30 pounds. And while it's a worthless provider of a good night's rest, it can easily be turned into a 30-pound dumbbell.

It is simple to make a curling weight out of your mattress. First, take your sheet, roll it up so that it forms a long strip, and lay it in the center of your floor. Then, roll your mattress up as tight as you can. Once your mattress is rolled into a tight roll, set it in the middle of your sheet "strip," and tie your sheet strip around your mattress so that it remains tightly rolled.

Once you have tied your sheet around your mattress, you will be able to grab the excess sheet strip and use it as a handle (for curling).

If curling your mattress is something you plan to do regularly, and you don't want to use your entire sheet, you can make "customized" ties by braiding 3-inch-thick strips of sheet together, and instead of tying one strip around the middle, some prisoners prefer to use two ties and tie *both* ends of the rolled-up mattress. They then take an additional strip and tie it *across* the mattress, from one end-tie to the other, and use *that* as a handle. This gives it more of a dumbbell feel, and it also makes it easier to balance.

Once you have your mattress dumbbell, you are officially ready to start curling. You can do one-arm curls for your "bulk weight" sets and two-arm curls for your burnouts. You can also do hammer curls and reverse curls for a more thorough arm workout.

I've explained to you how to make a dumbbell out of your mattress and sheet because those are items you will usually have access to. They're items provided to us and, unless you're on some kind of discipline status where your stuff has been taken from you, you will always be able to utilize this method. However, there are many other ways prisoners make dumbbells when the materials are available, including ones that are much heavier.

Water Bag

When the materials are available, a lot of prisoners would rather curl a water bag than their mattress; curling a water bag is a lot less awkward. Furthermore, it's easier to customize the weight of a water bag so that it suits you best.

To make a water bag, you will need a large, thick trash bag. (Usually you can get one from the building porter(s).) Fill the trash bag with the amount of water that will give you the weight you want. Once you have put the amount of water you want into your bag, squeeze all the air out of your bag and tie the top into a knot by twisting the excess bag, looping it around itself and pulling it through.

Once you have made your water weight, get an old T-shirt and tie off the bottom. Then, put your water weight inside of the T-shirt, and take the sleeves of your T-shirt and tie them together as tight as you can.

Now that your shirt sleeves are tied together, you can use them as your handle. Or, if you want, you can put a separate piece of sheet or towel through the tied sleeves and use *that* for a handle. You can do one-arm, two-arm, hammer, and reverse curls, and the shirt well prevent the bag from busting open.

Weight Bag

No access to a large, thick trash bag? OK, well, you can always make a weight bag out of magazines. All you need to do is stack up about 8 inches of magazines and tie them together real tight with a shoestring or sheet strip – so that you have a "block" of magazines. You can make a few of these block weights, put them inside of a T-shirt, and do the same thing you'd do with a water bag. Block weights are a little more awkward to curl than a water bag, but they still work extremely well.

Note: Guards usually confiscate water and weight bags. However, if they find yours, just make another one; it's nothing.

Sometimes, especially when you are in the hole, you will have to find other ways to work your biceps. When you don't have the materials to build a bag and you don't feel like curling your mattress, or your mattress isn't heavy enough, you may want to try this next exercise.

Body Weight Curls

Do you have a top bunk in your cell? If so, is there a space between the bunk and the wall (somewhere)? If there is, you can always wrap your sheet around the part of the bunk that's bolted or welded to the wall (usually the corner of the bunk), hold onto the sheet, lean back as far as you can, and then curl your own body weight. This method also allows you to do a variety of curling exercises – one-arm, two-arm, hammers, reverse, etc., and you can make your weight more difficult to curl by leaning further back.

TRICEPS

Tired of having noodle arms as skinny as your dick? Well, then you're going to have to put a lot of work into building your triceps – also known as back-arms. Triceps make up 2/3 of your arm size; a tricep is a much bigger muscle than a bicep.
There are several ways for you to work your triceps, and here are a few of the more popular ways prisoners do it without the use of weights...

Nose-breakers

Nose-breakers can be done just about anywhere. All you have to do is grab the edge of your table, sink, toilet, etc., with an overhand grip, and take a step or two back. Once you are in position, lower your nose down to the edge of whatever it is you're grabbing, and using only your arms, push yourself back up. Repeat the up and down process until you fall forward and break your nose.
     Depending on what you're grabbing, you can adjust your grip from narrow to wide. And you can adjust your weight by stepping farther back to make it more difficult.

Modified handstand tricep push-ups

Another great way you can work out your triceps is by doing modified handstand tricep push-ups. These, too, can be done in just about any prison cell, and they are a bit more difficult than nose-breakers.

To do a modified handstand tricep push-up, place your hands on the floor (palms down) so your index fingers and thumbs make a triangle. Then, plant your feet on your toilet or stool behind you, push your hips up high, and bend your knees slightly. Lower your body straight down until the top of your head touches the floor. Keeping your back aligned, push back up; repeat the up and down process as many times as you can.

Note: You should brace your abs throughout this move.

Plank tricep extensions

Get into a plank position with your forearms on the floor – basically a push-up position with your palms and forearms flat on the ground. Your elbows should be directly below your shoulders. Push through your palms to straighten your arms, keeping your abs tight throughout.

"Bench" tricep extensions

This exercise is similar to a nose-breaker, but it will give you a slightly different stretch, and it is a little more difficult.

Get into a push-up position with your hands gripping the edge of your toilet, stool or desk. Bend your elbows and drop your head down until it's slightly under what it is you decide to grab. Push yourself back up, and then repeat the up and down process. This is good because the triceps respond well to exercises that overload the stretch portion of the movement.

Incorporate these tricep exercises into your workout plan and you should do all right. And remember, some of the other exercises you do, such as push-ups and dips, will also work your triceps.

CHEST

Now it's time to pump your chest up a little bit. Nobody in prison is going to take you seriously if you're walking around with *negative* chest – the kind that is not even flat, it goes in.
Here are some of the more popular ways prisoners bulk their chest up...

Push-ups

Hopefully you already know *how* to do a push-up and *can* actually do one (and I don't mean on your knees, sissy). If you can't do a push-up then you're in serious trouble, and there isn't anything me or any book you read will be able to do to help you. In such a case, your best bet would be to learn how to make a really good knife.

So, assuming you already know how to do a push-up, the best advice I can give you is to do all variations of them: wide for your outer chest, shoulder-width for the middle portion of your chest, and diamonds for your inner chest.

You can also work the top portion of your chest by elevating your feet on your toilet, stool, or desk. This is equivalent to an incline bench press, and the higher you elevate your feet, the more weight it will put on your upper chest (and shoulders).

Many prisoners like to add weight to their push-ups by having their cellmate sit or lean against their back. For example, get into a push-up position. Then, your cellmate can put his butt and back up against your butt and back and lean his weight on you while you do your push-ups.

Note: It might seem a little strange to have your cellmate's butt up against yours; however, I assure you butt to butt is much better than nuts to butt... understand?

Fly Push-up

Fly push-ups will also get you great results; it is equivalent to a fly press.

To do a fly push-up, fold two towels up and place one under each hand while you kneel on your floor with your hands under your shoulders – like a push-up position, but on your knees. Spread your hands apart and lower your chest to the floor, bending your elbows. (It should look like the down position of a wide-grip push-up). Push yourself back up while also pulling your hands together in a fly motion.

Note: This works best if your cell floor is waxed; it will help the towels slide easier. If necessary, you can also try soaping up the area of the floor where the towels will be sliding.

Scorpion Push-up

Get into a push-up position and squeeze your butt cheeks (no homo). As you descend, rotate your upper body to your left while swinging your left leg across your right leg. Your left foot should touch the floor somewhere between your right foot and right hand (looking like a scorpion's tail). Push yourself back up and return the leg.

Dips

Dips are a great exercise that work a variety of muscles including your chest, triceps, and abs. Most prison yards have dip bars, so the opportunity to do dips is usually available.

If your yard doesn't have dip bars available, if you are on lockdown and don't have access to the yard, or if you'd rather just do them in your cell, there's usually a way that you can – depending on how your cell is designed.

Sometimes you can do dips between the top bunk and top locker. If one is a little higher than the other, you may need to place a book under the hand that is lower.

Some cells provide a place to do dips between your bottom locker and desk. However, if neither of these two ways are available, you can also do dips on a high, flat surface, such as a top bunk. All you have to do is balance yourself on the palms of your hands by leaning slightly forward, lower yourself down until your chest touches the bunk, and then push yourself back up. The stretch won't be as good as if dipping between two objects, but it still works.

ABS

Many prisoners like having ripped abs. The more defined your stomach is, the bigger your chest, shoulders, and arms look. Furthermore, if you are one of the lucky prisoners that will be getting out someday, the ladies will love it.

Crunches

Lie on your back with your legs bent and your heals close to your butt; put your chin on your chest and your hands behind your head. Then, raise your head up crunching your abs hard (you should only go about 1/3 of the way as compared to traditional sit-ups), lower, and repeat the movement as many times as you can.

Punch Plank

Get into a push-up position, balancing on your first two knuckles (of each hand), and with your feet no wider than shoulder width, lift one hand near your chin, resisting the urge to rotate your shoulders. Squeeze your pec on the side that's balancing and shift your weight on the opposite foot; hold it for as long as you can.

This exercise works your oblique's really well. It also teaches you to bring your body's full strength together for things like push-ups and punching.

Full-contact Plank

Get into plank position. Have your cellmate shove your midsection or kick your thighs and soles of your feet to increase the challenge. Keep your body completely straight and resist any kind of motion.

Drop Plank

Get into a push-up position and lock your elbows. Push your palms into the floor so your shoulder blades flare out and your chest caves in closer to the floor. Tighten your body. Have your cellmate pick up both of your feet and then release one of them without warning. Now, prevent your leg from falling to the floor.

Note: When doing this exercise, always keep your shoulders parallel to the floor and look straight down.

Crunch Chin-up

Hang from a chin-up bar, and keeping your body rigid, pull yourself up. As you near the top, raise your knees to your chest, balling yourself up. Finish each rep by pausing for a moment in the up position.

BACK/LATS

Now it's time for you to learn how most prisoners build a big, strong, powerful back...

Pull-Ups

The best way for you to work your back and lats in prison is by doing pull-ups. Doing pull-ups will make you a lot stronger while adding bulk to your back and building your lats so that you get that nice "V" shape.

To do a pull-up properly, grab the pull-up bar with an underhand grip and hang down getting a good stretch in your lats. Then, pull yourself up until your chest hits the bar, lower yourself back down, and repeat as many times as you can.

Note: The concept of pull-ups is fairly simple, but actually doing them isn't that easy until you build yourself up. When you first begin, if you need some assistance, bend your knees, cross your ankles, and have your cellmate or workout partner hold your feet.

Do pull-ups with several grip widths. The wider you go, the harder it will be. You will also notice that pull-ups work your arms out as well.

Overhand Grip Pull-up

These are done the same way as a standard pull-up but with your palms facing out (you should see the backs of your hands).

Overhand grip pull-ups should also be done in a variety of widths, and you should notice that when you put your hands together, it will work your forearms and biceps really well. When you grip the bar as wide as you can, the pull-up will be harder, but doing so is how you stretch your body wide and get the wings most prisoners want.

Behind the head pull-up

Once you strengthen your back, shoulders and arms, you can do behind the head pull-ups. To do this exercise, grab the bar as wide as you can with an overhand grip and pull up, but, instead of touching your chest with the bar, tuck your head down and touch the back of your neck or top of your shoulders with the bar. This exercise will put a lot more strain on your back and shoulders than a standard pull-up.

Hyper-extensions

It's important to have a strong lower back; not only so you have strong core muscles, but also because it will help you prevent back pain. And considering all the pain you're going to have anyway from sleeping on that hard-ass prison mattress, you're going to need all the back pain prevention you can get.

The best way to strengthen your lower back in prison is by doing hyper-extensions. In order to do these, however, your prison yard will need to have long, parallel dip bars.

To do hyper-extensions, get in between the two bars, facing one. Grab the bar in front of you and push yourself up. Rest your lower stomach on the bar and lean forward, hooking your legs on the bar behind you to keep your body from flipping all the way over. Let go of the bar you're holding and place your hands behind your head. Then, bend forward at the waist as fast as you can, raise back up until your back is straight, and repeat the down-up motion as many times as you can.

SHOULDERS

If you're interested in filling up your prison shirt or having the ability to throw rock-solid punches to an opponent's mandible, you're going to need to have big, strong shoulders.

Handstand push-ups

Pull-ups will work your shoulders, but only to a certain extent. If you really want to have big, strong, bulky shoulders, you will need to do handstand push-ups.

To do a handstand push-up, get into a handstand next to your cell wall or door, and put your toes or heals – depending on which way you're facing – against the wall or door for balance. Once you are in a stable position, lower yourself until the top of your head touches the ground, push yourself back up, and repeat as many times as you can.

This is a difficult exercise for most people, so it may take a little bit for you to build up the strength in order to be able to do these. When you first start, ask your celly to hold your ankles to prevent you from falling forward. Falling forward in a little tiny cell isn't fun when there's metal bunks, toilets, and lockers to fall into.

LEGS

As I mentioned earlier in this section, in order to build your body properly, you must work out your legs. Your legs are your foundation; your foundation needs to be strong and rock solid. What good is a big, buff chest, if you get into a fight and your opponent sweeps your skinny, weak legs out from under you and you fall to the ground? That will put you in a vulnerable and dangerous position – especially if he has a knife.

Here are some of the popular leg exercises many prisoners do.

Squats

Squats work real well for building power and endurance in your thighs. To do a squat, stand with your legs about shoulder width apart. Stick your arms straight out in front of you for balance, and while looking up, slowly bend your knees and lower yourself until your butt is just about touching the floor. Using only your legs to lift you, slowly stand back up as straight as you can (keep your heels on the floor). Repeat the up and down squat process as many times as you can, and for variation you can place your feet wider apart or closer together.

Note: Once you build up your leg strength and you're ready to step it up a notch, you can do squats with your cellmate or workout partner on your shoulders. If you do this, do it under a pull-up bar so the person on your shoulders can hold on to the pull-up bar for balance, and when you're first beginning this exercise, can even pull himself up slightly to make it easier on you.

Harbor Steps

While they're typically called harbor steps, obviously nobody in prison is doing them on a harbor. Instead, we do them on our toilet or stool.

Harbor steps are good for working your thighs and calves, and they can be done in any cell.

216

To do a harbor step, place your left foot onto the edge of your toilet or stool, and using only the muscles of your left leg, stand all the way up straight. Lower yourself down, step off the toilet, and repeat with your right leg. Do as many as you can.

Note: If you really want a high step, try doing these on your desk. The higher you step, the harder it is.

Lunges

Lunges are also a great leg exercise you can do anytime, anywhere, and they work just about every part of your leg.
To do a lunge, start in a standing position with your hands on your hips. Then, with your left leg, step forward as far as you can, keeping your back straight in an up position, and touching your right knee to the ground. Without moving your right foot from its spot, step your left foot back so that it's side-by-side with your right and your body is standing back up completely straight. Do as many as you can, alternating between your left and right legs.

Calf Raises

Calf raises will build and strengthen your calves. You should do them on the edge of your toilet, and hold on to the wall for balance. While standing on the edge of your toilet, lower your heals to get a good stretch, then raise up on your toes as high as you can. Lower yourself back down and repeat the process as many times as you can.

Note: You can do these on the floor but you won't get the same stretch. However, when doing them on the floor, you can do different variations by pointing your toes in or out. Doing so will ensure you work all sides of your calf muscle.

SECRETS

Now that I've explained to you the most popular and effective exercises done by prisoners, it's time to let you in on a few secrets on how to maximize your gain from doing them. If you ever wonder why these exercises seem to work better for some prisoners than others, it is because they are utilizing the following techniques:

Work to failure

This first technique is to just do the exercises in their traditional manner, but instead of doing a specific amount of reps during your sets, do each exercise until you no longer can. Doing this might not get you a lot size, but it will definitely build up your endurance, and endurance is extremely important for later, heavier workouts, as well as in battle.

Flex hard and hold it

Flex the muscle(s) you are about to work as hard as you can and hold it for 10 seconds, thus, pre-fatiguing them. For example, flex your triceps and chest muscles as hard as you can and then do a set of push-ups. This makes doing something as basic as push-ups much more difficult and produces much better results.

Reduce rest time between sets

Another technique is to reduce the rest time between sets. Start with resting for 60 seconds, then 50, 40, 30, 20, 10, etc. If you do a set of pull-ups and go until your muscles are really tired or even to failure, wait only a few seconds then do another set. How many reps were you able to do in your second set? Only 4 or 5, right? That's about what you'd do if you were doing some heavy pull-downs.

Supersets

This is one of my favourite techniques. It's what gets me a real good pump.

To do a superset, alternate exercises between two "opposite" muscles – biceps/triceps, chest/back, etc. For example, do a set of curls and then, without resting, do a set of nose-breakers. Going back and forth between these two exercises will have all the blood rushing to both your biceps and triceps and give you a great pump; your arms will feel like they're going to explode!

Slow motion reps

Slow motion reps are really good, especially when you don't have weights. To do these, try taking a full 12 seconds for the positive phase and 6 seconds for the negative phase of each rep. Don't lock out in the top position and don't rest in the bottom position – transition smoothly from the positive to the negative. Using slow continuous tension will make your exercise *much* more intense.

Flex while doing your reps

For this last technique, try flexing your muscles as hard as you can *while* doing your exercise. For example, flex your pectorals, shoulders, triceps, biceps, and lats as hard as you can while doing very slow push-ups. Or, when doing pull-ups, flex your lats, shoulders, biceps, triceps, chest, and forearms as hard as you can.

219

Keep the tension hard and steady when using this technique. It may take some practice to get it down, but the incredible pump and muscle growth you will get from it will be well worth it.

CHAPTER 19

CHESS: THE STRATEGIES

One of the most important things – if not *the* most important thing – for you to learn in order to survive prison, is how to defend yourself in times of challenge; not only physically, but mentally. And sometimes the best defense is offense, so in order to increase your chances of survival; you must learn to play both positions well.

Mental

Most victories are achieved through proper preparation, mental strategy, and the mind frame of the soldier or army – long before any actual physical combat takes place. You must learn how to mentally outwit your opponent(s), so that if the situation comes to physical battle, you start out with the upper hand.

Think of prison like a real-life game of Big Brother; everybody is plotting, planning, scheming, and scamming. 99.9% of the moves your fellow prisoners make will be because of some kind of ulterior motive, and be done in an effort to somehow further themselves in the game. Therefore, it is not what you see prisoners do directly that you have to worry about, it is what they are doing indirectly that you must learn to spot and be careful of.

Prisoners can be extremely devious and deceptive. In fact, many even study books relevant to war strategy, psychology, and manipulation techniques, specifically for the purpose of becoming as strategic and psychologically manipulative as possible.

Typically, the first move a prisoner will make when seeking out a victim will be a *mental* jab or test of some sort. If your response is one that makes the predator feel he is intellectually superior to you, he will see you as weak, and may decide to put you in his category of potential victims.

Educate yourself so that you are not naive to the manipulative ways of your fellow prisoners. Study the same material that they do, so that you are familiar with the techniques they use and can spot them before you become a victim.

Always assume you are at war; never get comfortable. You must never trust, let your guard down, or get tired, because as soon as you do, your enemy will strike; that is what he is waiting for.

Study the game of chess, as it is virtually the same "game" as prison. Chess is a great exercise to help you learn how to think several moves ahead in both setting up a defense and an attack.

It is important that you never, *ever* let anyone know what you are truly thinking. In prison, letting people know what you truly think is like showing your hand in a game of poker; you'll never win doing it.

Seem to give out information freely so that your fellow prisoners think you're open rather than secretive or sneaky. However, make sure that it is information unimportant to your true objectives and goals.

Pay very close attention to the details of what your fellow prisoners say. More than likely they will speak about the situation again, and if the details do not match what you were told the first time, you will know they are most likely lying.

While many prisoners are devious, deceptive, and skilled manipulators, most think they're manipulative masterminds and that they are far smarter than they actually are. Learn to use their arrogance against them.

Let people think they are smarter than you. If they think they've already got you beat mentally, they will think they don't have to try as hard to manipulate you, and it will be easier for you to spot their true intentions. Just remember that, if they think they are intellectually superior to you, they will most likely try to manipulate you in some way (eventually); however, you will be fully aware of what they are doing and can set up your defense.

Never let a manipulator know you are on to him. Instead, learn to manipulate manipulators by spotting their manipulations ahead of time and using them to your advantage. If you spot a manipulation and the person seeking to manipulate you does not know; you will be able to guide *his* manipulation(s) into benefiting *you*.

Perception is reality, and in prison, nothing is as it seems. Therefore, you will increase your chances of surviving if you master the art of illusion. What you have the ability to make people believe is often far more important than the truth.

Now, while it is a good strategy to seem less intelligent than you are so that your opponent will be lazier in his mental attack, it is to your benefit to make your fellow prisoners think you are more physically powerful and dangerous than you really are, because doing so will make them far less likely to want to physically battle you. Even if they are physically stronger and more dangerous than you, if you can make them *think* you physically have the upper hand, you will have 80% of the battle won should it ever become physical.

However, in order for that strategy to be successful, while your opponent has doubts about his own strengths when compared with yours, you must be confident about your own abilities, and learn how to use any fear that you may have to your benefit. Remember, it is OK to have fear; fear will keep you safe. But you must never let your fear turn you into a coward, or you will be defeated.

Physical

Prisoners are kept in check by the constant possibility of being physically harmed. Therefore, when there is a dispute of some sort among prisoners, it is usually handled with some type of physical combat – fist fights, "jumpings," slashings, stabbings, etc.

The best way to ensure your safety is to learn to foresee problems before they happen, so you can change the direction the situation is going in before it becomes physical. Learning to avoid a battle is one of the most valuable warfare techniques you can learn.

However, sometimes things are beyond your control, and no matter what you do, they're just going to happen how they're going to happen. Remember: prison's culture was established long before you got here, it's going to be what it is while you're here, and it's going to be what it is long after you're gone; your control is limited.

Different prisons have different levels of violence and danger. In some prisons people are trying to program and go home, so the farthest they want to take a conflict to is a one-on-one fist fight. However, other prisons are far more violent and dangerous, and to deal with a conflict that has become physical by doing anything less than stabbing your enemy is considered weak and looked down upon.

Regardless of the level of violence that takes place on your prison yard, it is wise to be prepared for the worst-case scenario. When your safety/life is at stake, it is much better to be over prepared than underprepared.

Here are a few basic tips you should follow in order to increase your chances of survival...

Be aware – pay attention to details

You need to be aware of your surrounding at all times. In many instances, if something is about to happen, and you are paying attention, you will notice a change in energy or behavior in the person or people planning an attack. Prisoners who are planning to attack will do their best to do so by surprise, and many are devious and deceptive, but if you pay close enough attention, you will *still* usually see some type of sign that something is wrong and you can prepare yourself.

The signs that you may pick up on can vary. Sometimes if a prisoner is planning an attack, he will associate with you less or seem a bit standoffish – maybe without even realizing his change in behavior.

Sometimes, however, maybe even more often than not, a prisoner may become even *more* friendly, as an attempt to make you feel *more* comfortable, so that you will let your guard down and he can attack. While some prisoners are extremely good at playing this game, many will overdue friendliness in an attempt to hide their true intentions. You should be very cautious of a prisoner who becomes overfriendly with you "all of a sudden," because he most likely has an ulterior motive, and that ulterior motive could be to lure you into a position where you are open for attack.

It is extremely important that you pay very close attention to the details of things going on around you, because doing so will allow you to foresee an attack before it happens; foreseeing an attack before it happens is critical because it will allow you to prepare for the situation.

If you do foresee an attack, however, make sure that you do not alert the attacker that you are on to him. Instead, turn the tables by acting as if you are unaware of what he is doing so he feels comfortable (in his plan), and then you will be able to either set up your defense, or catch the attacker by surprise by thwarting his plans.

Make sure that you always pay attention to how people position themselves around you. If someone is planning an attack and they are right-handed, they will likely stand with you at their left side so they can get a good swing in with their right hand. And if a group of people are planning to attack you they will likely take their positions sometime before the attack, so if you notice awkward positioning going on around you, you should quickly try to change your position and prepare yourself for the possibility of an attack.

When prisoners approach you, pay attention to their hands. Always glance at an approaching prisoner's hands to make sure he does not have a weapon of some sort.

Being adequately aware consists of more than just what you see; you must also pay very close attention to what you hear and smell. Prisoners like to talk, so let them. The more they talk, the more information they will reveal. Pay attention to any and all conversations going on around you, as the information you learn may end up saving your life.

Be aware of banging and scraping sounds going on in nearby cells, as those are the sounds of knife-making. And if you smell burning plastic, it is likely that somebody is making a plastic shank, or a plastic handle for a metal knife.

Stay ready

Stay ready for any possibility at all times – even in the shower. When you take a shower, make sure you have somebody you trust to have your back close by in case somebody tries to make a move on you.

Also, don't get caught slipping walking around in your shower shoes. Always wear your boots or sneakers when not in the shower or bed.

Remember: If you stay ready, you ain't gotta get ready, because you'll always be ready; understand?

Stay physically fit

The majority of prisoners – especially on the most violent and dangerous yards – work out. Therefore, you need to become as physically fit and strong as you possibly can. And don't just work your upper body, work your *entire* body – arms, chest, shoulders, back, stomach, and legs.

Build yourself into the strongest man-beast you can possibly be. For workout information, see the chapter titled "Working Out: The Secrets"

Note: Playing sports like handball and basketball will not only help you get in great shape, but also improve your hand-eye coordination!

Fist fight

Fist fights are a daily activity in the concrete warzone, and chances are you will have your share of fist fights during your tour of duty.

Hopefully by now you understand the importance of staying very aware of your surroundings, because if a prisoner wants to fist fight with you, he is most likely going to try to hit you first and without you seeing it coming. If you slip and do not see him coming, there is a good chance he will win the fight. However, if you do see him coming, you will be able to prepare your defense

If you are confronted by a prisoner about an issue, pay very close attention to his body language. If he is shaking, breathing heavily, tense, anxious, or showing hostility in any way, there is a good possibility he is working up the nerve to fight you.

You obviously want to do everything you can to *not* be attacked. However, if you are, the first thing you should do is check your attacker's hands to make sure it's just a fist fight and he doesn't have a weapon. You can be stabbed with a knife or sliced with a razor blade and not even realize it until you notice you're covered in blood. Whether your attacker has a weapon or not will determine how you should handle the situation.

If you determine that all it is a fist fight, analyze the situation and defend yourself accordingly. Hopefully you have been getting yourself in tip-top physical shape so that you have both strength and stamina.

It would be great if you could get some books or information on physical combat training and techniques, but most prisons won't let that type of information into the institution. However, if you have a TV in you cell, you can learn many beneficial moves by watching UFC, MMA, and boxing matches. Study how the moves are done, and then practice them in your cell until they come natural.

While I cannot possibly teach you everything there is to know about self-defence, there are two basic techniques that every fighter should know:

Move along a triangle (a bit of theory)...

There is one tip about self-defense that is so important that entire martial arts systems are based upon it. The tip? Don't get hit! I mention that, because moving along a triangle goes a long way toward achieving the goal of not getting hit.

One of the most dangerous mistakes the average person makes during a fight is to move in straight lines. They will move in a straight line, either forward or backward, or side to side.

Imagine a vertical dividing line along your body, dividing your body into left and right halves. Your attacker is *probably* going to attack some point along or around that line: your face, your throat, your heart, or your nuts. Moving in a straight line backward or forward will change the *distance* you are from your attacker, but it does not move your center-line out the attack path. And moving laterally (left or right) will change the location of your center-line, but it does not change the *distance* between you and your attacker.

Your attacker has mentally committed to striking at a particular target. His brain has sent the signal to his fist that your face, throat, heart, or nuts (the target he intends to hit) is located at a particular distance and in a particular direction. When you change the target's coordinates, it spoils the effectiveness of the attack.

Your goal is to move that line of your body out the path of attack and change the distance of the target from your attacker. Your attacker may be able to recover from a change in target location or a change in target distance alone, but changing *both* factors will make it extremely difficult. Furthermore, even if your attacker does connect, the strength of the attack will be greatly diminished.

So, why move along an imaginary triangle? Because doing so changes both the distance *and* location.

Imagine standing with both feet on the pointed end of a triangle and facing your attacker. The other two points of the triangle can either be in front of you or behind you.

Each of the other triangle points are only about one medium-large step away from where you are now. One point is found one step forward and to the left. Then there's another point one step forward and to the right. Behind you, one point of the triangle is one step backward and to the left, and the other point is one step backward and to the right. Are you following me?

Now, all you have to do is step one foot onto either of the two available triangle points in front of you or behind you. Doing so will change both the direction and distance of the attacker's original target; simply bring your other foot up, and you will be at the starting point of another triangle.

Use this concept every time you move and you will continue to confuse your attacker.

Always advance when you should retreat...

During a fight, as during a game of chess, the experienced fighter/player is already planning the second or third move before the first one is ever completed. In fact, many of the experienced fighters'/players' moves are used solely to get the opponent to react in a predetermined manner.

If you are attacked by another prisoner, do not follow your instinct and back up – your instinct is wrong. If a prisoner rushes you, he is expecting you to backpedal in order to escape the attack. So instead of playing into the attacker's expectations, surprise and confuse him by stepping forward (along your trusty triangle). That will turn the table on your attacker and while he is trying to adjust his thinking to handle your unexpected move, he will leave himself open for you to attack.

Surviving a group attack

Prisoners often attack in groups – two-on-one, three-on-one, etc. You can call it what you want, but in prison, there are no rules. It's all about hurting your enemy as bad as you can in the little bit of time you have to do it before the Guards come.

With that said, don't be surprised if you get "jumped" after having a dispute with one individual. You should expect the possibility of at least the individual's cellmate assisting him with his attack.

Like a one-on-one fight, if you are jumped, the first thing you should do is make sure that none of the attackers have weapons. Once you have determined that weapons are not involved, defend yourself according to how the situation plays out.

Do your best to keep both attackers in front of you and fight like your life depends on it. And, even if you have to accept the punches from one attacker, you should single one of them out and try to hurt him as bad as you can.

Note: While I am writing this book from the perspective of you being your own one-man army, it is wise to associate or align yourself with a solid group of prisoners. That way, if a situation arises where you are outnumbered, or that is just simply too heavy for you, they will be there to assist you in battle.

Surviving a riot

If you are attacked by a group of prisoners and your crew jumps in, there is a good chance that more members from the attacking group's crew will jump in, and as a result, more people from your crew will jump in as well. In that case, it becomes a full-fledged riot.

Riots are dangerous because they are chaotic. Prisoners are running in from all directions, and you have to be aware of where everybody is at all times. And, not only do you have to watch out for yourself, you are *obligated* to make sure that members from your own crew are avoiding injury as well.

When a riot occurs, as in any combat situation, you need to make sure you remain calm. Never *panic*. You need to be able to think as the situation develops. As soon as the adrenaline kicks in everything will seem to happen in slow motion, and if you are calm and do not panic, your mind will process thoughts so rapidly that it will seem like you have several minutes to make a decision about how to react.

As always, the most important thing you need to watch for is weapons. And because of the chaotic nature of riots, prisoners are more likely to use a weapon because it's easier to get away with. With all the confusion going on, it's harder for the Guards to prove who actually used one.

Surviving a knife attack

Some prisoners won't handle their disputes any way other than with a knife. Prisoners who're willing to use a knife are typically more respected and feared, and some prisoners take that respect so seriously, that if they have a conflict that comes to physical battle, they will always use a knife.

Being attacked by a prisoner with a knife is always going to be a dangerous thing – even for an experienced fighter. And these days, the use of razor blades is extremely popular, and they slice so easily it's almost impossible to come out of an attack unharmed.

You should always try to avoid letting a prisoner get close to you with a knife in the first place; however, sometimes that just isn't possible. So if you find yourself in this situation, here are a few simple things you can do to make sure you get out of it without serious injury.

The first thing you must do is reduce the surface area of your body that your attacker has to aim at. You do this by turning side-on to your attacker, rather than facing him directly. This makes dodging an attack easier as well as reducing the area which you need to defend.

At the same time as turning side-on you should also bring your arms up to protect your head, neck, and heart. Stab wounds to these areas are most likely to be fatal, and so they are obviously the most important areas to protect. Your forearms should be crossed in the center and held in front of your face with the back of your hand and forearm facing outwards, as cuts as those sides of the arm are less likely to bleed heavily.

By adopting this position you are not only protecting vital areas of the body, but also limiting and controlling the options of your attacker. Holding your arms in a high guard position while standing side-on exposes a large target along the side of the abdomen while covering and protecting the rest of the body. In 90% of the cases your assailant will attack the unprotected area. This gives you the advantage of effectively knowing what your attacker is going to do even before they do. Controlling options like this means that you only need to know one highly effective martial arts technique to defend yourself, rather than having to learn a different technique for every possible attack.

Now, I will describe this technique shortly, but first you must also be aware that a crazed attacker may still try to get through your guard to attack the head, neck, or heart. If this happens, you have to be willing to sacrifice. Many martial arts teach complex techniques to defend against all kinds of knife attacks. But the problem is that, if a technique goes wrong in this situation you could end up dead, and that is an unacceptable risk. The simple fact that you must remember is that you can't get stabbed in the hand and the neck at the same time with the same knife. You need to have balls and actively push the back of your hand or arm onto the knife (parrying it to the side if possible), while using the other hand to strike as quickly and as hard as you can to your attacker's face (preferably his eye or nose), or, use both hands to grab the attacker's hand that the knife is in so that he cannot stab you. Sure, holding one of his hands with both of yours will allow him one open hand to strike you with, but you will just have to accept the punches – at least you won't be getting stabbed. Furthermore, he will likely be holding the knife with his stronger hand, and that will be the one which you are holding, so the punches you have to accept will be coming from his weaker arm and won't be so bad anyway. Remember: fights in prison usually only last about a minute or so before the guards put the yard down and do what they have to do to break up the fight. Therefore, if you can manage to hold off your attacker for that small period of time, you should come out OK.

If you're unable to grab the knife, or while you're waiting for an opportunity to do so, and your assailant tries to stab the open target on your side, here is what you should do:

Bend over double, pulling your abdomen back away from the blade. At the same time, bring both of your forearms downwards forcefully, keeping them crossed over. You should hit your attacker's arm with your arms at the point where they cross over; keep pushing down so that your hands are pointing down and your attacker's arm is trapped in the space between them. Now you can grab your attacker's wrist or hand. If they have attacked with their right hand (which will be on your left-hand side), you should grab a hold of it with your right hand and twist clockwise so the elbow is facing upwards. As they will have put their strength into the strike and will not be expecting this, there should be little resistance. Keeping hold with your right hand, you can now strike down onto the elbow joint with your left hand, breaking the arm and forcing him to drop the knife.

Once you break you assailant's arm and he drops the knife, you can back away from him as he will no longer pose much of a threat.

CHAPTER 20

THE BLACK PEOPLES' PRISON SURVIVAL GUIDE: HOW TO SURVIVE MENTALLY, PHYSICALLY, AND SPIRITUALLY WHILE INCARCERATED

By Abdullah

Preface

This book is written with the Black male in mind who is suffering the ordeal of incarceration. Although, it is intended for Black males, it may be read by Black females suffering the same predicament. Also, the information and insights contained in the following pages might be valued by any of our people living in this society.

Some will question the purpose of such a book. They will read its title and feel a sense of shame and embarrassment in that persons of our race might need a guide to prison survival. Let me state that I feel a sense of shame and embarrassment, too; however, such a book is sorely needed and some benefit may derive from its publication.

Many of us suffer the "Ostrich Syndrome". We continuously bury our heads in the sand choosing to ignore certain realities in hopes that they will go away. The majority of us know someone who is locked-up or who has been locked-up or who has a family member who is now locked-up. Going to prison has become a "common thing". Black people have been deeply affected by the American penal system. In society, we are a minority. In prisons we are the majority. America will continue to lock many of us up in the future. This country has succeeded in creating generations of Black prison class societies.

This is a self-help book. It is not just a textbook of practical jail-house wisdom. It is a survival guide to help the reader safeguard his or her mental, physical and spiritual well-being while in prison. If you find yourself Incarcerated this book may prove itself especially useful to you. Experience is the most qualified teacher, and I have been well-schooled by my past experience with prisons and people in them. For the past 15 years, I have been locked-up In Ohio prisons for a crime that admittedly, I did commit. Two days ago, at a parole hearing, I was given a five-year continuance for being "too intelligent". The parole board said that the education I received while incarcerated makes me more dangerous to society. That may very well be true, but not but not in any physical sense, because I am not a criminal.

This book is about change. Hopefully, in reading it you will change your thinking, your way of seeing things and change your way of life one word of caution. I recognize that we are limited in our education, but I will not write down to anyone. You will do well to get yourself a dictionary and keep it handy. Look up each word you don't understand. Never skip over words because you don't understand them. Find their meanings. Remember: Lazy reading is a crime, too. It robs us of valuable knowledge.

Part I

America's Penal Past

America has a long penal tradition. In fact, this country was colonized as a penal experiment. England emptied its jails of its murderers, rapists, prostitutes, and thieves, placed them aboard ships and sent them here to conquer the native people and colonize this land. America's first citizens were England's worst criminal outcasts.

With their criminality the founding fathers and mothers brought a host of deadly diseases to wreak havoc upon the native people. They waged a type of germ warfare that exterminated untold thousands of the native population. Diseases such as small pox, syphilis, and the "common" cold systematically reduced their numbers. Add this to the host of tricks they brought from England with them, and you will see that the unsuspecting natives never really stood a chance.

After the period of colonization was completed in this country, it was found that a spirit of lawlessness continued to prevail. Even after accomplishing the task of gaining a foothold in this land the founding fathers and mothers still continued to ply their illicit trades. Moral factions in the colonies decided that jails had to be built to punish offenders.

The first jail in America to house felons was the Walnut Street Jail in Philadelphia. It was built in 1790 by Quakers. During their imprisonment, prisoners received intensive religious Instruction and endured harsh physical labor to build their work ethic. They also observed complete silence. There was no socializing between prisoners, and often brutal disciplinary measures were used to ensure their silence. Later prisons were founded at Auburn, New York, in the 1820's and a reformatory at Elmira, New York in 1876. Like the Walnut Street Jail, these later prisons instituted religious instruction, rigorous labor, and absolute silence as part of their rehabilitative process. These early penal experiments failed, because of the high insanity rate resulting from the policy of enforced silence. Many of the prisoners went crazy from being given the "silent treatment".

Penology in this country has reached its apex development in the past 100 years. It is now a science. There are actually people who attend universities to major in this field of study. They eventually earn the title of "Penologist". We may logically conclude that penology has become very important. No major university would include useless courses of study in their curriculums. It has specific purpose. Penology is one of the basic Five P's now used to systematically control the unconscious masses (Philosophy, Psychology, Politics and Propaganda being the others). At this point, let me emphasize that there has always been a connection between penology and labor. It is this connection that continues to effect Black people today.

Past Victims

The connection between penology and labor extends back to those early prisons in the colonies. Remember that labor was an integral part of the strict disciplinary regimen in those days. In those early prisons, the products that the prisoners made were later sold in the market place, and the prisoners received a small percentage of the profits as pay. The wardens were the ones who benefited from inmate labor.

After the Civil War, this country entered into what was known as the reconstruction period. The war had caused great property damage throughout the south. Large plantations houses had been destroyed during the fighting. Crops had died and there were no seasonal plantings. The northern forces had looted and pillaged as they swept their way to victory. All that had been damaged needed "reconstruction". This reconstruction period lasted for nearly 15 years after the war.

It is well documented that the African slaves had built up the whole of the Western hemisphere. A society and economy with free labor as its principle base could easily be developed and maintained. Slavery in the colonies was the first large scale capitalist Venture, and the most successful up to that point. The African people had brought important skills with them from their lands. They weren't just cotton and tobacco pickers, as white historians and television would have us believe. They were the needed brick masons, carpenters, farmers, weavers, doctors, and "blacksmiths". If the Blacks were used to build up the south once, then they would surely be used again.

The newly freed slaves were as easily exploited by white Southerners as the native people were by the early settlers. Free but uncertain, fearful of venturing out beyond the plantations of their births, they were easy targets for further exploitation. The plantation owners held out promises of better treatment, improved working conditions, and future pay as enticements for the freed Blacks to stay on and continue working. When these ploys failed, threats of lynching by groups such as the KKK held Blacks in check. After the period of reconstruction, the south was thriving again.

We must keep in mind that this was a time of no industrialization. There were no machines to perform the work. Still the work had to be done. Cheap sources of labor were sorely needed to keep things running smoothly for the profiteers. Slavery took on another form; hence, we had its other version, the "chain gang". The majority of prisoners in the south who were sentenced to spend time on its chain gangs were Black men. The symbolic connection between the chain and slavery is obvious. The particular stigma attached to the chain gang itself denoted that not only was a man guilty of some offense, but that he was deserving of his bondage and punishment, i.e., "hard labor".

Herein, we can see the connection between penology, Black people, and labor exploitation. Across the south, those who benefited most from this updated form of forced Labor were the states and local plantation owners. Forests were cleared, roads were built, and levees were constructed, fields were plowed and cotton was picked by those early chain gangs. Many times, these gangs were leased-out to work for farmers in nearby communities. The chain gang became an extension of slavery.

Present Victims

There are a variety of causes for crime in this country. Over the years, studies have been conducted to determine the causes of crime. No one specific cause or any exact combination of causes has been pinpointed as the determining factors that lead to criminal behavior. Crime is hot topic and punishment has become a big business.

The average white American, with nothing better to do, sits at home each evening viewing television programs such as Hard Copy and A Current Affair. These shows exploit crime to get higher viewer ratings. The more sensational crime it covers, the higher the show's ratings and the more commercial revenues it generates. The television program Cops gives actual footage of middle-aged, White suburban thrill-seekers and weekend survivalists, guns drown, crashing in the doors of terrified poor folks in their efforts to solve the crack (Black) problem. America loves it!

When people constantly view crime as depicted on television, they build up an immunity to having compassionate feelings for the criminal. What circumstances played a part in causing another to commit a crime becomes less important. Consideration is given only to his or her punishment. The insensitive public cries for blood. "Lock them up forever!" and "Throw away the key!" and "They ought to be fried!" became the cries of the day. Being influenced to react (it can't be called thinking) this way, our people are caught up in the same kind of dumb emotionalism. They make the same dumb statements, until it's a nephew or little brother who's sitting on death row. Only then do they stop to question what caused the nephew or little brother to go wrong. And there are many answers.

The attitudes about criminal behavior differ widely, depending on what country is looked at. A good example is Japan. In Japan, when a person is convicted of a crime it is seen as a failure of their society to provide the proper nurturing environment to mold that person into being a productive human being. Upon incarceration, extensive steps are taken to foster the rehabilitation of that person. On the other hand, in this country it is seen as a shortcoming of the individual who commits a crime and years of punishment is the best answer. Society shares none of the blame, although it creates criminals. Let us imagine this. A police decoy staggers down a dark Street at night pretending to be drunk. He has a large wad of money sticking out of his pocket. Someone comes along, sees this, snatches the money, runs, and is arrested by the police. In criminal law, there is a defense called "entrapment". It could be said that the poor man who snatched the baited money was victimized by circumstances which were set up by the police; thus, he was "entrapped" into committing his crime. As In the case of the poor man who snatched the money, society has set up a host of circumstances in our environments which bring about criminality in some of our people. When drugs are made available, when there is a proliferation of guns in our communities and when our youths are programmed to be violent by music and television, then the entrapment defense has some validity too. We should be at least partially exonerated because of the host of circumstances society has set up against us. The United States locks-up more Black people than racist South Africa. It creates criminals and jails them, because keeping a large prison population is beneficial. One reason for keeping a large prison population is population control. Fewer Black men means fewer Black babies. Another reason is that prisons employ a lot of poor, uneducated White people who are otherwise unemployable. Yet, the single most important reason is that it is profitable to lock people up. People who are locked-up are easily exploited for their labor.

Today's modem prisons are industrialized. Top quality products are being manufactured in America's prisons on assembly lines. In many cases, gone are the days of just pressing license plates. Large corporations have cast their lots on the sides of prisons as being a cheap readily available source of labor. And the biggest advantage to these corporations is that there are no labor unions to deal with. Some of these corporations that have invested in prisons are TWA, AT MCI, and Best Western, to name several.

One good example of prisoner labor exploitation is Ohio Penal Industries (OPI). OPI maintains factories in nearly all of Ohio's twenty-seven prisons. It reaps astronomical profits from the products it sells to the public, because it pays prisoners slave wages. It operates under the guise of training prisoners for employment when they are released, while it does not assist them in finding jobs when they get out. There is no unionization, and there is no form of compensation if prisoners are injured while working. The average pay for an OPI worker is less than $50 a month for 40 hours work weeks. An entire volume could be devoted to the exploits of OPI, but let it suffice here to say that OPIs competitors complained that they could not compete with OPI's prices because OPI maintains an almost zero per cent labor cost.

Recently, there has developed a trend of states a company can present a low-cost analysis, It can own itself a prison (and the Black people in them). The advantage to these companies in running these private prisons is that they can profit from the inmate labor pool. They may in turn contract with outside companies to produce goods using inmate labor. Since the majority of people incarcerated are Black, we can make the connection between this form of labor exploitation and the chain gangs of the past.

A Scenario of Victimization

America's criminal justice system is not based upon justice or fair play. It is predicated on lies, trickery, and deceit. Whether one of us is innocent or guilty, we must recognize that when we enter the courtroom, we have entered a bloody arena, where the prize at stake is our lives. Anything goes. Rights violations, prosecutor misconduct, coercion, perjured testimony, falsified reports, and the list goes on. What the prosecutor seeks is that initial conviction, because he knows that the appeal process will drag on for years. While you rot behind bars, your appeal briefs will collect dust on some obscure judge's desk.

When we are indicted for our alleged wrongs, many times we are overcharged for the crime itself. They rack-up many related charges that stem from one offense. We are faced with staggering amounts of time and our minds reel at the thought of doing so much time. "A thousand years?! All I did was...", you ask and say. It is basic psychology. It is to ensure your full cooperation when you are offered the coveted "deal" that will allow you to spend less time behind bars. Actually, it is a ruse to frighten you into accepting a plea agreement for something that the prosecutor would be hard pressed to fairly prove against you anyway. Many codefendants are tricked this way into offering testimony in exchange for lighter sentences or in some cases even total immunity for crimes they helped commit.

One essential thing to understand is that the sincere looking White attorney who is supposed to defend and protect your rights is in fact a "sworn officer of the court." He is bound by some oath of judicial fealty of which you know absolutely nothing about. "Why, you'll never see the light of day! Take the deal! It's a good deal. With time off for good behavior you'll be back out in a few years", the smooth talking, reassuring White face says. The dockets are full. He is no more than an amateur actor with mediocre legal abilities. He plays his part again and again. It's his job to ensure that the wheels of injustice continue to spin smoothly. He is the golfing buddy of the judge, the cousin of the prosecutor. He may have been a prosecutor himself once. They lunch together every afternoon. Their children attend the same private schools. They belong to the same clubs, the same lodge, they may even swap wives. Their allegiances are only to each other and not to you. For those who refuse to take that coveted deal, there will be hell to pay for having the nerve to buck the accepted system of things. You won't be dealt with fairly because you are poor. You will not be afforded a jury of your peers. The legal terms they use are spoken in Latin, a dead (buried and thus hidden) language, only spoken (and kept alive) by priests at the Vatican. Witnesses are coached in what to say. The police intimidate your witnesses to not appear in court. Hand signals are given and passwords are spoken. Objections are overruled by the judge with a nod and a sly wink. You sit in the midst of some Masonic ritual taking place. Your silence is assured. You are threatened with exposure of your criminal past (if you have one) if you dare to speak in your own defense. The cards are well-stacked against you and chances are you will go to jail.

Many of us lack a fundamental belief in ourselves; therefore, we lack faith and confidence in the abilities of those professionals of our race to perform accurately when things count most, we feel somehow that their education and training isn't on an equal footing with their White counterparts. We have been brainwashed to assume that a Black attorney isn't capable of competently representing our interests in the Whiteman's court of law. "Now don't you go in there with no nigga' lawyer. Get you a good Jew Lawyer. You go down there with a nigga' lawyer and you'll end up with more time." That is standard advice. By such a notion of "slave wisdom" we fall easy prey into the clutches of the corrupt White attorneys. If we fully understood what we were up against, we would see that no one should represent us other than another Black person. There are many White attorneys who earn their livelihoods extracting pounds of Black flesh inside America's-halls of injustice. They continuously deal Black lives away by the deft strokes of their pens. They trade in Black bodies as their slave owning forefathers did in the days of old. These attorneys deal cases with the prosecutors and collect bribes when we have the ability to pay. To these White attorneys we are just unsuspecting victims.

Part II

Inside

Entering prison for the first time can be a frightening experienced the noise level is what strikes you and it is unlike any noise that you have ever heard before. Its human noise and clamor. That, coupled with the sight of those dreary bars, made me think, "Man, what have I gotten myself into here?!" When you have entered prison, you have entered a world all its own. Each prison is different. What applies to one prison certainly will not apply to another. Prisons are classified by security levels (Maximum, Close, Medium, and Minimum). You will have different rules and types of people according to what kind of prison you find yourself in.

Although each prison is different, there exists three basic groupings in all prisons. This social stratum consists of the administration, guards, and the prisoners themselves. Each group operates according to its own set of rules and values, while there exists an interplay between the three, and none being totally independent of the others.

The administrators of prisoners are usually people with years of devoted service in the penal system. Some are educated in the science of penology, but for the most part they are persons who came up through the ranks as guards. After taking a number of college courses, or gaining a degree in some social science, they were granted their positions and titles. At the higher levels of penal administration can be found a bit more educated persons who are more devoted to the penal system. These are the wanders and people who help make policy decisions. In this modern day, they are usually Black people. For those who understand the negative consequences of Incarceration, their appointments to those positions can be recognized for what it is, a divisive tactic. Normally, hey are no more than mere figureheads who do the system's bidding in oppressing other Black people.

Rules in prison are formulated to either antagonize or placate prisoners, but their main purpose is to control. The guards are the people who enforce the rules. They act as middle men between administrators and prisoners. As prisons and people in them differ, so do guards. Some are real professionals. They respect other human beings. They spend eight hours at their jobs and go home. Others are the worst types of people. Dirt poor and barely literate, they exist in a no man's land between welfare or prison for themselves. They deal in contraband and are capable of brutal acts (including murder) against prisoners. Most are former military people, ex-cops, or people who couldn't qualify for police departments. They thrive on having authority. Some hold memberships in racist organizations and Masonic orders whose roles are to suppress non-White people. Suffering psychological problems, their world view is negative, and that is how they generally view most prisoners.

The most difficult part about having contact with prison administrators and guards is that they usually operate from a set of preconceived notions about all prisoners. For them a textbook example of a prisoner is dumb, petty, passively or aggressively homosexual, scheming, and manipulative. Their manuals generally describe all prisoners this way. They tend to lump all prisoners into these categories. Accordingly, it would be safe to lump them all into one category as well. Expect them to be indifferent, authoritative, brutal and racist toward you. When you encounter an administrator or guard who is different, consider it a rarity.

Prisoners come from a variety of backgrounds. Prison is a confined place, packed with living bodies of every shape, color and size. You will find yourself closer to other human beings than you have ever been before, many of whom you won't like. When conditions are crowded, there is a natural tendency for people to band together for mutual protection as well as friendship. Most prisons are divided by groups. These divisions occur along racial, religious, and ideological lines, as well as gang affiliations. The administrators and guards usually know who's who, because they are kept abreast of the inside goings-on by their inmate informants. There exists a class of people who are "at home" inside prison. They were conditioned for prison life from childhood. Starting out in juvenile correctional facilities they later made the transition to youth reformatories and adult prisons. They are totally inept as criminals and have been incarcerated any number of times. They are institutionalized and would rather be in prison than out. By conditioning, prison's safe, controlled environment is best suited to them, a place where they are clothed, fed, and told what to do. Outside life is too difficult to grapple with for these Individuals.

For another class of people, prison is a kind of homeless shelter. They don't necessarily want to be in prison, but in a sense they are forced to be. Unskilled, homeless and destitute, they enter jails and prisons for an array of minor crimes to be fed and rested up. Prison gives them a needed break from homelessness and crack addiction. For them a six month to a year sentence is a heavenly blessing. They aren't criminals in the real sense but men and women who have been forced by economic and social conditions to take the easy way out time and time again.

For yet another class of people coming to prison is an occupational hazard. Crime is their vocation and they take coming to prison all in stride. It would be incorrect to type them as institutionalized, because they long for the free world. They make no excuses for what they did and openly discuss what they will do once back out on the streets. They intend to gang bang, rob and peddle dope. Their time inside prison is just an extension of their criminal lives on the outside. Many continue to profit from vices while in prison.

It has been difficult characterizing people in prisons. As previously stated, prisons differ and so people confined in them differ as well. No description of prison has ever been positive because it is a negative place filled with negative personalities who exhibit some abnormal behavior patterns. The variety of criminal offenses that you will find inside prisons are too numerous to list. One thing that usually all prisoners have in common is that they have suffered some kind of abuse in their lives whether it be physical, mental, drug or alcohol related. Penal facilities are in the same class as mental institutions; therefore, you will find persons with mental histories who are prescribed various types of powerful psychotropic medications. The one general rule is to never attempt to apply reason and logic to people or the situations you may encounter. If you look for logic and reason, you'll find that you're in the wrong place.

Associations

In everyday life, whether we find ourselves in jail or out, associations are important. We are often judged by who we associate ourselves with. The old saying, "Birds of a feather flock together" holds true. Because of the close proximity, you will be judged more harshly by your associations by others in prison. We are assumed to be of a particular character or to engage in certain activities by whom we associate ourselves with. Associations are of two types, positive and negative. If we reflect on our pasts, it will usually be seen that our lives took a term for the worst when we began to "hang with the wrong crowd", and it was in that group that we smoked our first reefers, hooked school and began to steal. All behavior is learned, and so was our criminal behavior. As easily as going along with the wrong crowd, we could have sat in the front row of the class with those "A" students who went on to college and later became professionals. Had we made the decision to have positive associations we would not have fallen prey to the negativity that eventually led us to being where we are?

The same choice continues to hold itself out to us daily. One of the first steps toward change and self-improvement is to begin to choose positive associations in our prison environment whose influences will benefit us in the long run. One good look around will tell you that there is very little actual thinking going on in our prison environments. The real thinkers are few, and that is what makes them noticeable. You will find these persons taking full advantage of the educational and vocational opportunities made available to them. They use their time wisely preparing themselves for their lives in the free world. These are the best associates, and we can usually benefit from their insights and accept their advice.

A word to the wise. There exists another set of thinkers as well. Because we see someone carrying an armful of books does not mean that their association can always be beneficial. There are individuals who are extremely intelligent but they utilize their energies foolishly in creating friction. Having had problems with authority all their lives, they love to antagonize authority with frivolous grievances and baseless legal claims. They will make themselves (and you by association) targets of official reprisals. The thing to recognize about prison is our vulnerability and so it is best to remain distant from smart people doing stupid things.

There are others who are leaders of gangs and various other factions inside prison. In love with a feeling of power over others, like actors, they play out roles in their own little Godfather movies. They control the drugs, gambling, extortion, and other vices inside prison. Their manipulative abilities are usually honed by years of jailhouse experience. They know all the right buttons to push, and they orchestrate others in doing their bidding. Needless to say, nothing positive may be gained from these associations.

As previously stated, the choices in our associations holds itself out to us daily. I recognize that peer pressure plays a part, also, especially in a close environment such as prison; however, when most people see a person take a definite stand to do something good, they will usually respect it. The same is true for ourselves. We must take that firm stand to take on associations that are right and in our own best interest.

Family

The importance of the family bond cannot be overemphasized. The connections between us and our family's needs to be strengthened. No matter what the given set of circumstances, family is what we are linked to, not only in name but spiritually as well. After our Creator, family should be our primary source of strength to draw from. If you look around all you see are sons and daughters, brothers and sisters, mothers and fathers. We are all linked to a family system, no matter how good or bad. Americas slave system was responsible for the destruction of the Black family. The destruction of our families was the first thing that the oppressors did to our people. They sold us off from one another. The same thing is done by the American penal system in this day and age. Prison sells us off from those that we love.

Time and distance plays havoc upon what ties of family that we may have. The reason why most prisons are located in rural areas is not only to provide jobs to impoverished people, but because they isolate (in most cases totally) inner city Blacks locked up in them from their loved ones. When a person is isolated, they are easier to control. No one is there to question what happens to that person. This allows the racist White authorities to basically have their way.

The State of Ohio is notorious for its program for the destruction of Black family ties. Practically all of Ohio's prisons are located in rural areas. Black prisoners are routinely sent to prisons hundreds of miles away from their homes to render them inaccessible to concerned family members. Limitations are placed on the number of persons who may visit.

Conjugal visits are nonexistent (promoting homosexuality and spreading AIDS). Prisoners are given added time to their sentences then they go up for parole. This causes less committed family members to desert their cause. This program of systematic destruction takes place while the State of Ohio hypocritically states that it encourages strong family ties.

Many people in prison have not had the benefit of loving home environments. All along, the State has acted as a surrogate parent. These people are what you would term as being "state raised" from early childhood on. I think it is these persons who make up the bulk of the prison population, at least in Ohio. It is a deliberate crime, and it is unfortunate that we live under a system that conditions people from childhood to be locked up, so that the system can maintain control.

If you have a family or anyone in the outside to support you in any way, then consider yourself very fortunate. Do all that you can to maintain and build upon those relationships? Communication is the key. Regular letters, telephone calls and visits will help. Always report the positive happenings in your life, admit past mistakes and let go of old resentments. Always show your appreciation and love for them, because they need that too. A strong support system can carry you a long way.

Time Utilization

In doing time in prison, time is the essential factor. Our physical lives are measured by seconds, minutes, hours, days, weeks, months and years. Time measures our physical lives; therefore, we should begin to measure time and become time-conscious. In this way we can utilize our time in prison and work it to our best advantage.

If you look around the prison you are in, you will see a lot of time being squandered. Valuable hours of each day are being wasted senselessly in useless pursuits. There is no harm in recreation, but when entire days are spent playing board games, cards, basketball, and watching television, then priorities have to be questioned.

An objective evaluation must be made of each and every activity that we engage in. We can determine if the activity is beneficial to us by its end results (what we actually benefit from it) and how much of our time is devoted to it. An hour game of cards or chess can be enjoyable and relaxing, but when these games last up to four or five hours, then it has become a waste of time. The same stands true of basketball. (Don't dribble your life away.) None of these recreational pursuits can change our lives or prepare us to be stronger men and women who can go out into the world to face life's challenges.

The most senseless use of time in prison has to be constant television watching. There are adult men in prison who watch cartoons and soap operas for hours each day. They know all the soaps' characters, plots, and can figure all the possible scenarios of upcoming episodes. They live through the tube. They call television the "Boob Tube" because it will make you dumb if you aren't already. Its shameless, naked images will poison your mind and spirit. Its fantasy will rob you of all original creative thinking abilities. Constant television watching develops the dangerous habit of always wanting to be entertained, which causes laziness.

Television is a powerful tool of propaganda also, which is one of the Five P's mentioned earlier. Television is dangerous to Black people (especially children), because it will distort one's self-concept with its endless parade of White intellect, beauty and White super heroes. You cannot find a better stamp of approval for the notion of White supremacy than television. For a thinking Black person, in general, television is a no no. Cut out television for one month and you will be surprised at what you can get accomplished in that time. Knowing how to manage time properly is important in everyday life. When we learn how to, get the most out of our days, we will come to know a real sense of satisfaction and accomplishment. There are only twenty-four hours in a day. The more you begin to actually do the clearer it becomes that there never is enough time to get things done. Then you will understand the value of time.

Here are some suggestions for successful time management: develop the habit of getting up early. This can be a plus. All that is needed is an alarm clock and a little will power. Think of getting up early as getting a jump on the competition. When the rest of the world is just waking, you'll be up, cleaned, groomed, dressed and already in full motion.

Begin to make daily schedules. Think of yourself as someone with a lot to do but limited time. At night before going to bed, list all you want to do the next day. Keep this list with you and check off things off as you do them during the day. Review the list at night to see what you didn't get done. Put what you didn't do on the list for the next day.

Set short-term and long-term goals. Goals are objectives and life doesn't have much purpose without them. In order to attain your goal, you must formulate a plan. For instance, your short-term goal may be to get a G.E.D. in six months. Your plan to obtain that goal would be to study for a couple of hours a day. Beyond this, your long term goal could be to earn an Associate's Degree in two years. As your plan, you would set a pace for your classes in that two-year period of time.

Our time in prison should not be wasted. It is time in our lives. This is the best time that we can possibly have to develop ourselves in all ways. We're being fed, clothed and housed (in my case "warehoused"). There are no bills to pay, no job to go to. To gain as much knowledge, awareness and skills as we can should be our primary objective. If the racist system has given you a lot of time, then you should leave prison with a college degree or several good skills. Get the best out of the situation and don't let the situation get the best out of you. This is how to "beat the system" and walk away ahead of things. You can do all of this by learning how to use time effectively.

Part III

Your Mental Health

Prison will destroy you mentally if you allow it to. Being in prison can be one of the most degrading experiences in life. It seems that degradation is the main purpose of prison. Dress codes, serial numbers, buzzers and bells, strip searches, inadequate privacy and lists of rules too long to remember are used as means to humiliate, tear you down and annihilate you psychologically.

Having a strong mind helps one to survive the rigors of prison. This calls for having a positive mental outlook in spite of the circumstances. Prison is a negative place. Probably some of the most negative thinking on the planet takes place inside of prisons. There are many broken people in prison who suffer from defeatism. They have failed in life because they never really try. When they see others attempting to make positive strides, they often criticize but never encourage.

Never count yourself amongst the losers. By keeping a positive outlook you will have the advantage in any situation. It can be quite difficult, but at some point, all things face opposition. As prison can be one of the worst possible situations there will be many obstructions to your progress. In developing and keeping a positive mental outlook, you will remove your first and greatest obstacle --yourself.

Having a strong belief in yourself is vitally important. You must believe in yourself, that you can change your condition, that you can be a better human being. Believe that you can get out of prison and be a good father or mother or husband or wife and be a productive part of your community. You must believe in yourself. Hardly anyone else will.

How you see yourself determines how you see the world and others. Having a strong and clear mental image plays an important part in self-development. How do you see yourself? What is your self-concept? If your conception of yourself isn't strong, do you at least have some notion of the kind of individual you wish to become? Consider these things.

Thoughts are powerful. They create and give new life and can cause death. Never allow fear, anxiety, anger and doubt to run riot in your life and exert ruler ship over you. Negative thinking will defeat you. Be filled with confidence and optimism that problems will be resolved to your benefit. Have thoughts of patience and fortitude. Clear thinking is the best thinking there is.

Worry is the most senseless use of mental energy. I have seen others worry themselves until they become so overwhelmed that they give up all hope. We should not worry over things we have no control over. A pending appeal, a woman, unruly children at home, are things we shouldn't worry about. We have to realize that what is to be will be. You don't want to end-up dependent on some drug like Thorazine for your peace of mind or having some medical problem due to worry. Save yourself a lot of grief. Place focus on the improvement of your mind.

Knowledge is power. There is a vast difference between a learned person and a fool. The more one comes to know the more sensible the person will act. Education is the key. Prison will bestow the precious gift of free time to allow you to obtain knowledge and useful skills. Sublimate your energies toward gaining education and skills that can be used once you are released from prison.

Reading is fundamental. It was once a crime to teach a Black person how to read. The slave holders knew that an educated Black wouldn't make a good slave. This law still exists in its unwritten form. When you look at the low reading levels of Black children and the general condition of mental slavery, we find ourselves in today, it becomes obvious. Valuable knowledge is contained in books. There are books written on every subject. When you desire to know about something, find it in a book. Books can open whole new worlds.

Reading can be a waste of time if you don't know what to read. Books are the plates on which mental food is served. Will you eat a nutritious, well-balanced meal or will it be Mac Donald's? Will you read a technical book or a comic book? Will you read The Destruction of Black Civilization by Chancellor Williams or Iceberg Slim? Like looking at a menu, the choice is ours as to what we feed ourselves mentally by what we read.

Education without culture will only make an educated slave. Find the truth of history contained in books. Historical reading is the most rewarding and has a profound effect upon the psyche. I recall that when I learned from reading that medicine, mathematics, building and the arts and sciences had their origins in Africa (Egypt), it increased my thirst for knowledge. After reading about it, I was able to relate it to myself. When I finally entered college, I wasn't fooled when the White professor claimed those advances for the Greeks.

Do a great deal of reading to cultivate your mind. Developing a reading program will help. If you're not a good reader, then keep reading and you will surely improve. Never be intimidated by the number of pages in a book. Start with short books and work your way up. A steady diet of two books a week can't help but improve you.

Your Physical Health

Prison will destroy you physically if you allow it to. It would seem that is its purpose, to make you grow old, run you down, and cause you to suffer from ill-health. Knowing some steps to take a protect your physical being will help you get through prison.

Prison is a dirty place. Most prisons are old. Some date as far back as the civil war period. The drab condition, of buildings overcrowding makes prison a fertile environment for pests, rodents and diseases transmitted by human contact. Physical cleanliness is essential. Always be clean and groomed. This is the first step in keeping yourself healthy while in prison. Personal cleanliness enhances self-esteem; plus, it makes a positive statement to others about you.

Concentrate on the total cleanliness of your immediate living environment (bed area, cell, etc.) Always keep dirt and dust to a minimum. Now I'm sure at some point in our lives most of us have had some contact with those "brown cousins" and prisons are full of them. But, learn to be intolerant of roaches. If you roll over and see one crawling up the wall at three in the morning, then get up and kill it! Along with rodents, they carry all kinds of diseases.

Physical contact is nearly impossible to avoid because of the close proximity of others. Probably one of the first things you will realize in prison is that everyone isn't clean. Some people are just downright funky. Besides filthy habits and bad personal odors, common diseases carried by others could range from TB to A.I.D.S. Watch what you touch and never drink or smoke after anyone. If you're in a cell with someone else, then keep a window cracked at all times to maintain an air flow. Avoid constant coughers.

Abstain from the use of cigarettes, coffee and all drugs. Those things are bad for us health-wise. Besides that, you don't want anything that is habit forming, something that you Just "gotta' have" the first thing each morning. The use of habitual things robs us of our Independence. We need to develop independent thinking for when we get out. Habits stifle growth toward independence.

Food is life. Most food in prison isn't food at all but what I call "filler". It has no real-life substance in it and is used to fill your belly and keep you quiet and complacent. It comes canned and dehydrated, then usually gets boiled beyond taste or fried. The meat is usually ground up because of its inferior quality. Lots of potatoes and plenty of pork. Pork is the worst meat for human consumption because it's full of parasites. You'll find that because of the food people in prison suffer from many stomach ailments. As a general rule, eat less and you will be better off.

Fresh air and sunlight is essential to life. If you have access to movement outdoors then stay outside as much as possible, even during the winter months. Get lots of sunshine and breathe in as much fresh air as you can. Also, it has been proven that the sun has a positive effect on human emotions and physical health. Physical exercise each day will keep you in good condition and help to relieve stress. One of the best things that we can do is stretch. Stretching keeps the body flexible. Some form of martial art would be beneficial. Prison can be an unpredictable place. Anything could happen, so it's best to keep yourself at ready.

Getting proper rest at night is important. Prison can preserve your youthful features, because you aren't constantly on the go as free persons are. You can walk out of prison not having aged much physically. Proper rest with regular exercise and a good diet will carry you through. Always get a good night's sleep.

Your Spiritual Health

Prison will destroy you spiritually if you allow it to. The experience of being locked-up can make you bitter beyond compassionate feelings for other human beings. You can easily lose what moral values you have in prison. The prevalence of evil and vice inside prison can rob you of your spiritual life if you are unaware. Man is composed of mind, body and spirit (or soul). The three are connected and form life as we know it. We know that mind exists because we think most of the time. We are certain of our bodies because we see it and have the sense of touch. But what about the spirit or soul? When we become better attuned to ourselves, we know of its existence, because we "feel" it.

The knowledge of the existence of a spirit or soul that exists after bodily death, to face a judgment was common to our African ancestors. The Africans of Egypt were one of the first known people to promulgate the belief in the soul and a judgment with heaven or hell as a reward for earthly deeds. These beliefs had at some point become common to most of humanity but was always central to African life.

A focal point in African life was the belief in one divine Creator of all things. In fact, the first known purely monotheistic religion had its origins in Egypt, that which today is known as Judaism. Some African nations worshipped many deities, but even then there was always one supreme god who stood head and shoulders above all the rest. Belief was the essential theme of our forefathers' lives and should remain as the main theme of ours as well. When we became so "logical" (or embittered) that we deny the existence of our Creator and our own souls, then we have lost touch with our natural selves and our humanity. A strong sense of belief in the Creator will help us face life's challenges.

Constant prayer is the essence of spiritual life. It is man's way of calling upon and giving praise to the one great force of all the worlds. Whatever name we choose to call Him, be it "Allah or "Yahweh" or "Jehovah", we must know that He is even above names. He is the Most High and He is One. Being consistent in supplication acts as a reminder and keeps us within the bounds of upright conduct. Prayer helps us to understand our relationship to our Creator and to other human beings. Prayer is the spiritual food that nourishes the human spirit.

Charity is a means of fulfilling our duties to our fellow human beings. If our Creator is one, then His creation is one as well; therefore, it becomes our duty to act in the welfare of others, to want for others what we wish for ourselves. If we desire peace, security and happiness, then we should always extend those things to others. It is better to give than to receive. There are blessings in giving and, when we give, we will always find that we still always have enough for ourselves. A smile, a kind word, encouragement and a helping hand are all forms of charity.

Fasting is way of purifying ourselves. By short periods of fasting, we can rid our systems of toxins, develop inner-discipline and focus our attention toward our spiritual selves. Fasting not only places us in contact with our spiritual essence but grants us at least a momentary mastery over the desire for food. It will also grant us an exact understanding of the deprivation that others in the world now suffer daily and evoke feelings of empathy within us.

Pilgrimage is form of spiritual migration. It is a way of transcending beyond the cell, the fences and walls, those man-made barriers which stand between us and physical freedom. To perform a spiritual migration each day is to know true freedom. We all need a spiritual link to something, be it a church, temple, mosque or a distant place. It would be helpful to have persons in those places who pray daily for our well-being. It is in those directions that we should place our attention and travel spiritually each day.

Each one of us has the right to believe as we choose. Let there be no compulsion in matters of religion. Religion is social. Its purpose is to bring people together before the Creator, but most often it divides them. On the other hand, spirituality is personal. It is how we relate to our Creator and how we live. Spirituality lies deep within.

In attempting to make this book as readable as possible, I have sought a way around the issue of religion because I wished to address spiritual well-being and not get into differences. It then occurred to me as I was writing that the reader could hold no religious beliefs whatsoever, therefore, the subject then became unavoidable to my way of thinking. So the remainder of this is devoted to religion' purely from my perspective, which condemns no one else.

Islam is a beautiful religion and a total way of life. The religion transformed me and molded me into being a better human being. I sought-out the truth for myself. I asked questions, read, studied and made comparisons.

Never in my life have I accepted anything without investigation. I encourage everyone else to do the same, especially when it comes to religion, because it is such a serious matter.

There are many reasons why I accepted Islam, and here are some of them. Its scripture (the Holy Quran) was easier for me to read than the Bible had been. The principles of the religion were simple. Islam teaches that we are not to worship things or men and that Allah (The Creator) is One. It places a heavy emphasis on moral and physical cleanliness with the Prophet Muhammad (Peace and blessings of Allah be upon him) and his Sunnah (way) as the best example.

Perhaps the biggest reason why myself and others choose Islam is it gives a sense of cultural identity that most Black people in this country seek. The continent of Africa is populated by Muslims, so it aligns me with Africa. Islam is the largest religion on the earth. There are nearly one billion Muslims of all nationalities and colors, and so I am now able to identify with them too. Islam has restored in me a human identity.

The religion of Islam is the most active force in the world today. It is the perfection of all religion, as the Holy Quran teaches. If you find yourself locked in a spiritual battle, trying to fight against weaknesses and addiction, then try Islam as a way of living. The best thing about Islam is that it is open to be investigated and tried by anyone! Its easy principles (belief, prayer, charity, pilgrimage and fasting) were basically expounded upon in this book for spiritual health and well-being.

Conclusion

As I read over the pages of this book, I find that much has been left out. There were things that didn't come to mind as I was writing, but let this effort suffice. In writing this book, it has been my sincere desire that it will help someone to better their life. No matter what the condition or circumstance, one can live a cleaner and fuller life and become a better human being. I hold myself out as my best example.

Over the years, prison has changed me, but little has changed about prison. There are the same sights, sounds and I hear the same voices. I see many of the same faces returning time and time again. Other faces have become much younger. What all the faces seem to share In common is a lack of hope written in them.

I generally have compassion for people, and so I have often pondered over what could do to motivate others. My attempts at sharing my insights have usually encountered strong resistance on a personal level. Writing this book has been my best answer.

We live in an era where our people are being locked-up in staggering numbers. It seems as if we are all under lock and key. In this process of genocide, we are losing our most valuable resource-- our youths. If reading this book makes a difference for one of us, then this humble endeavor has been realized, and I thank Allah. I hold a strong belief in change.

SUGGESTED READING

The Holy Quran, Pickthall Translation
Toward Understanding Islam, Aft. Maududdi
Blackman of the Nile, Yusef Ben Jochohanan
We the Black Jews, Yusef Ben Jochohanan
Destruction of Black Civilization, Chancellor Williams
African Origins of Civilization, Chell Anta Diop
Stolen Legacy, George James
Nature Knows No Color Line, LA. Rogers
100 Amazing Pacts About the Negro, J.A. Rogers
Developmental Psychology of the Black Child, Amos Wilson
Chains and Images of Psychological Slavery, Nairn Akbar
Elijah Muhammad on American Education, Elijah Muhammad
How Not to Eat Pork, Sharazad Ali
The Autobiography of Malcolm X, Alex Haley
Roots, Alex Haley
The Spook Who Sat by the Door, Sam Greenlee
One Hundred Years of Lynchings, Ginzberg
Native Son, Richard Wright
Soledad Brother, George Jackson
Light on Yoga, Iyengar
Home Cookin' With Mother Nature, Dick Gregory
Back to Eden, Kloos
How to Win Friends and Influence People, Dale Carnegie
Success Through a Positive Mental Attitude, Napolean Hill

CHAPTER 21

PAROLING FROM PRISON (MY 2 CENTS):

If this topic applies to you, you are extremely fortunate; it means that you will have a second chance at life, which is obviously a beautiful thing. Keep in mind that there are many prisoners this topic does not apply to....

I cannot say that I am an expert on paroling from prison, as I have never paroled. Furthermore, I do not go out of my way to research things relevant to paroling, as I have life in prison *without* the possibility of parole.

However, while I am not an expert on the topic of parole, I am a man with 2 eyes, a brain (that is not on drugs), and awareness, and I cannot help but see prisoners parole and often come right back. Personally, I find watching prisoners parole and return over and over again to be absolutely disgusting. It means they have not learned that prison is a terrible place to be and there is a lot more to life than *this* bullshit lifestyle, and that they are still taking their freedom/life for granted and not respecting/appreciating the blessing of another chance – something that lot of us are only left to *fantasize* about....

Now, while I cannot give you information from a perspective of a man who has paroled or is paroling, I *can* tell you what I *do* know – what I've learned from watching people leave and come back over and over again, and what my *common sense* tell me – in hopes that it helps *you* not come back; if for nothing else, so that you do not disgust me.

Planning and preparation

From the minute you get to prison you should start preparing for your parole. For you, prison is not your life;

it is merely an experience that will someday end. And when that day comes, you should be fully prepared.

What I mean by preparing for your parole is; making the necessary changes and learning the necessary information that will ensure you don't only *get* out, but *stay* out.

2 questions you need to ask-yourself/answer

The first thing you need to do is ask yourself and answer 2 very important questions: 1) how can I make it out of prison as soon as possible? 2) What do I need to do while I'm in prison to prepare myself for success when I get out so that I never return?

Priority # 1

Whatever answer you come up with for question #1 should be your primary focus; your main objective should be to make that date. Regardless of how you play the game or what image you try to promote, your focus needs to stay aimed at your date and what you need to do to get out of prison as soon as possible that should *always* remain priority #1.

Strategizing

Create and customize a plan/strategy that will allow you to reach your objective/priority #1. Keep in mind that your blessing required you to figure out a different strategy than a prisoner who will not parole; you have your opportunity of paroling to lose while a prisoner who will never parole doesn't even have to factor that into his decision-making.

For example, I have life without the possibility of parole plus two 25-to-life sentences, and since I've been in prison I've caught 2 DA referrals. However, none of them have been picked up – including one for an "attempted murder" that was caught on camera and where the victim snitched and said it was me.

The reason it was not picked up, though, is because I have too much time; it's not worth the money the state would have to spend to try the case. But for someone who *has* a date, the DA may pick up something as minor as getting caught with a $50 paper of heroin or a razor blade.

So, while I can sell drugs on the yard all day long or stab people who offend me (because I don't have the possibility of paroling anyway), if you *do* have the blessing of a second chance, then by all means necessary you need to stay away from problems or trouble of any kind – you should do your absolute best to remain discipline free; you should not risk doing *anything* that will keep you in prison for even *one* extra day.

Only you can decide what's best for you, and you obviously need to remain safe. (The overall priority #1), but throughout this book I explain several options for dealing with situations, and I suggest you pay close attention to the ones that are more suitable for your reality versus the ones more suitable for mine. Even if you're in a position to where you must "play the game," you can still move very carefully and slick.

Proof of Accomplishments

It would also be a good idea to take into consideration what you are in prison for, and if you have to impress the parole board or not in order to get out. If you do, I suggest you earn as many certificates as possible. For example, if drugs were involved in your case, it might be wise to take a drug class or 2 where you will earn a certificate you can take to board with you. Or if you have some kind of assault case, an anger management certificate might look good on your behalf.

In any case, if you will be going before the parole board, it's probably wisest to get as many (*any* and *all*) certificates as you can – parenting, anger management, drugs/alcoholics anonymous, trades, correspondence courses, etc. Doing so will allow you to *show* the board what you've learned – something more valuable than you just telling them.

Priority #2 (Prepare for it now)

Once you've figured out what you're going to do in order to get *out* of prison, you need to figure out what you should be doing now to prepare for when you *do* get out, so that you can be successful and *remain* out.

2 questions you need to ask-yourself/answer

From my experience, the majority of prisoners who parole come back for 2 major reasons: 1) they are unable to find work and make money/a-living legally. 2) They are forced to parole right back to the environment they came from, and they get caught back up in the same lifestyle – drugs, crime, and all-around negativity.

With that said, here are 2 very important questions that you need to ask yourself and find answers for: 1) What do I need to do now to ensure I have the ability to make money/a-living legally when I get out? 2) When I get out, how can I avoid from getting sucked right back into the environment/lifestyle I came from?

Strategizing – work/money

When strategizing how you are going to be financially successful when you get out, figure out what it is you want to do as a job/career, and what you need to study/learn in order to prepare yourself for that job/career.

For example, would it be beneficial for you to take correspondence courses and earn a degree or two, or would it be best for you to read specific books that specialize in your area(s) of interest? These are all things you should figure out early on in your prison stay and start working towards as soon as possible.

Whatever you do, even if you already have "connections" for work on the outside, never rely solely on *that*. Don't use *that* to just sit around and be lazy in prison. For 1) just sitting around would be a waste of very valuable time and for 2) you should *never* rely on anything or anyone other than, *yourself*. I don't care if your wife's brother has a friend whose dad's cousin owns his own construction company and will hook you up when you get out. If that's the case and it works out for you, great; but hardly rely on it. It is much wiser to rely on what *you* have and what *you* can do.

For more information and ideas in regards to this point, read/re-read chapter "use your time wisely." If you use your time wisely, all of this will already be included in your game plan.

Strategizing – around your old environment/life-style

Coming up with a strategy to avoid your old environment can be a bit difficult – for several reasons. For 1) parole will probably force you to parole to the county you caught your case in. For 2) most of your resources – wife, family, friends, etc. – probably live in the same exact place/neighbourhood they did before you came to prison. And for 3) sometimes they – your "resources" – are actually the same people you should be trying to avoid.

It is possible to get your parole transferred to another county/state if you have some kind of positive support there and can convince your parole agent to allow it. And, if you're open to it, transitional housing (halfway-home-type-programs) is always an option. These are things you will have to work on with your parole officer, should you decide they are in your best interest.

If you feel you really have little choice but to parole fight back to the environment – people, place, and things – that cultivated/influenced you to get caught up in the things that led you to prison in the first place, it might be more difficult to succeed with the various influences and temptations you are sure to be surrounded by, but it is definitely not impossible. I am certain that with enough dedication and determination, *anything* – and this includes remaining free – can be done.

In any case, while you do your time in prison, I suggest you to some heavy soul searching; get to know who you truly are, who you want to be, and *decide* if living your life in prison is really the way you want to like. Because in the end, what it all boils down to is that, it is *you* who will make *your* decisions.

For more valuable information regarding paroling from prison, get our book *Get Out, Stay Out!: The Secrets to Getting Out of Prison Early, and Staying Out for Good!* See details in the TCB Bookshop at the back of this book.

CHAPTER 22

OVERVIEW OF CALIFORNIA'S PAROLE CONSIDERATION PROCESS

Documentation Hearing

Lifers are provided with a Documentation Hearing within the first three years of their incarceration, in this hearing, a Deputy Commissioner from the Board of Parole Hearings (BPH) reviews the prisoner's file and makes recommendations regarding the kinds of activities the prisoner should pursue in order to demonstrate parole suitability whenever he or she becomes eligible.

Parole Consideration

Lifers have their Initial Parole Consideration Hearings scheduled thirteen months prior to their Minimum Eligible Parole Dates (MEPD). Legally, the presumption is that lifers will be granted parole at their initial hearings; however, this has happened only thirteen times in the past ten years or so.

Prisoners are entitled to attend their hearings in person, to have an attorney present, to ask questions, to receive all hearing documents at least ten days in advance, to have their cases individually considered, to receive an explanation of the reasons for denying parole and to receive a transcript of the hearing.

Parties attending parole hearings include the prisoner, his or her attorney, a Commissioner and Deputy Commissioner of the BPH, a representative from the District Attorney's office, two guards, and the victims and/or their next of kin or representatives. Prisoners are not permitted to call witnesses or to have their family members attend, unless those family members happen to also be victims of the offense.

The main topics discussed at parole hearings are the following: the commitment offense and the circumstances surrounding it, any prior juvenile or adult criminal history; conduct (both good and bad) in prison; recent psychological evaluations prepared for the BPH; and the prisoner's plans for release upon parole. The area where prisoners' families and supporters have the most influence is in the parole plans. Through their letters to the BPH, supporters can demonstrate where prisoners are invited to live once released, where they are offered employment, where they may participate in any necessary transitional program (e.g., drug or alcohol treatment), and any other financial, emotional or spiritual support they may need. (See UnCommon Law's Free Guide to Lifer Support Letters, at www.theuncommonlaw.com.)

When Parole is Denied

On average, the BPH's commissioners only grant parole in approximately 10% to 15% of the cases they hear, which is actually a much higher rate than it was just a year ago. Until Proposition 9 is overturned, prisoners denied parole at either an Initial Hearing or a Subsequent Hearing will have another hearing scheduled either three years, five years, seven years, ten years or fifteen years later. Like other aspects of the parole consideration process that have changed since Prop 9, the BPH is directed to consider the wishes of the victims and their representatives in determining when the next hearing should be.

When Parole is Granted

Even though the Board grants a prisoner parole, it does not mean he or she will be released right away. This is because, in addition to deciding that the person is not currently dangerous, the Board decides how much time the person should actually have to serve based solely on the specific details of the crime. In some cases, the prisoner has already served that much time, so he or she will be released as soon as the decision becomes final. In other cases, the prisoner still has some months (or perhaps years) to serve prior to release. The actual release date is calculated during the days and weeks following the parole hearing.

After the parole hearing, the case will be reviewed by the BPH's Decision Review Unit for 120 days. If they affirm the date, then the case proceeds to the Governor's office for 30 days of review there. By the end of the 30 days, the Governor may either reverse the parole grant, modify the release date, or let the decision stand, after which the prisoner will be released on the date established by the BPH.

In cases other than murder, the Governor cannot directly reverse a parole grant Instead, the most the Governor can do is request that the full Board conduct an en banc review and schedule a rescission hearing, at which the prisoner's grant may be taken away (rescinded). In these cases, the Governor's review must take place within 120 days following the parole hearing; no additional 30-day period applies.

If a parole grant is reversed by the Governor or rescinded by the Board, the prisoner is placed back into the regular rotation of parole consideration hearings unless and until he or she is granted parole again. Some prisoners are granted parole several times before they are finally released from prison.

When Commissioners Cannot Agree

If a hearing results in a split decision between the Commissioner and Deputy Commissioner (there are only two people on a hearing panel), the case goes to the full Board of BPH commissioners at a monthly executive meeting. This is called an en banc review, and a majority vote is required for a prisoner to be granted parole. Members of the public may attend this hearing and speak to the Board.

When Courts Get Involved

At any stage of the parole consideration process, a prisoner may ask a court to intervene and correct some unlawful conduct by the BPH. In cases against the Governor, courts might set aside his decision and allow the prisoner's release. In cases against the BPH's denial of parole, courts might order the BPH to conduct a new hearing and grant parole unless there is some new evidence demonstrating a prisoner's risk to public safety.

The lifer cases from recent years that have helped establish the legal limits on conduct by the BPH and the Governor are In re Rosenkrantz (2002) 29 Cal.0h 616, In re Dannenberg (2005) 34 Cal.4th 1061, In re Lawrence (2008) 44 Cal.4th 1181, In re Shaputis (2008)44 Cal.4th 1241, in re Scott (2005) 133 CaLApp.4th 573; In re Rico (2009) 171 Cal.App4th 659; McQuillion v. Duncan (9th Cit 2002) 306 F.3d 895; Sass v. Cal. Bd. of Prison Terms (9th Cir. 2006) 461 F.3d 1123, and Irons v. Carey (9th Cir. 2007) 505 F.3d 846.

Life on Parole

Most lifers who are released on parole must serve a minimum of five years or seven years on parole before they may be discharged from parole. However, these parolees face a maximum of a lifetime on parole if parole authorities find that there is good cause to believe they continue to require intense parole supervision. While on parole, they must abide by specific conditions supervised by a parole agent. A former life prisoner who is on parole faces the possibility of a new life sentence if he or she is returned to prison for even a minor violation of parole.

THE INFORMATION IN THIS OVERVIEW IS NOT INTENDED AS LEGAL ADVICE IN ANY INDIVIDUAL PRISONER'S CASE. THERE ARE MANY EXCEPTIONS AND VARIATIONS IN THE PAROLE CONSIDERATION PROCESS. READERS ARE ENCOURAGED TO CONSULT AN EXPERIENCED PAROLE ATTORNEY FOR SPECIFIC ADVICE.

CHAPTER 23
HOW TO PREPARE FOR PAROLE CONSIDERATION

Scheduling

A Lifer's Minimum Eligible Parole Dale (MBPD) is the earliest date you may become eligible for release on parole. In general, you become eligible for parole once you have served the minimum term ordered by the court, however, that minimum term is reduced by any goodtime/worktime credits you earn. The amount of credit (or time off the minimum term) you earn is based on the type of crime and the date it was committed. Some Lifers can reduce their minimum terms by up to 1/3, while most others can only reduce their minimum terms by 15% or so.

The first parole consideration hearing will be scheduled to take place roughly thirteen months prior to the MEPD; however, the MEPD may change if you lose credits because of a rule violation report. If parole is denied at that first bearing, a recent law now lets the Board of Parole Hearings put off the next hearing for rip to fifteen years at a time! The minimum period between hearings is now three years, but the Board can choose between three, five, seven, ten or fifteen years for scheduling the follow up hearing. This memo is intended to help you and your supporters understand what necessary to prepare for the first is hearing and, if parole is denied, to minimize the delay before the next hearing.

Parole Consideration

The Board will always consider your- disciplinary record in prison, the programs you have participated in and your plans for where you will live and work if released on parole. It is important to address all those issues in order to have a chance for parole. However, this memo focuses on some areas that have not received enough attention from Lifers, their supporters, or even the programs they participate in while in prison. You have to gain a clear understanding of the circumstances leading to the crime, about your background (including family relationships and prior criminal or juvenile record), and how you have resolved the circumstances that led up to the crime. These circumstances may include addiction, physical abuse, emotional difficulties, and other factors that contributed to the lifestyle in which the crime took place. (A person's ability to understand and discuss these factors determines whether or not the Board finds that he or she lacks "insight".) If you do not understand these factors, you will be denied parole— no matter how much time you have served and no matter how- spotless your disciplinary record is.

The Board's theory is that, unless you truly understand how you ended up in the place where such a crime could be committed, then you cannot show that it is unlikely to ever happen again. Set forth below are some specific areas you need to explore when approaching your parole hearing? As you will see, family members and friends can help you explore these areas. You will also find that these topics touch on areas that are very sensitive and can reach down to the very core of what shaped your decisions about how to live your life. Although some of this material may seem "touchy-feely," you will find that exploring these issues can have a very powerful impact on your relationships and on your ability to show the Board just how much you have learned and changed while incarcerated. There is also a very good chance that this material will uncover issues that you only feel comfortable discussing within the confidential relationship you have with the attorney who is going to represent you in your hearing. This is what we are here for so take full advantage. If an attorney is unwilling to explore these issues with you, you should re-consider whether that attorney is really helping you get ready for your parole hearing.

Psychological Evaluations

Roughly six months prior to the parole consideration hearing, the Board will send one of its psychologists to interview you, review your central file and write a report that tries to predict your risk of future violence. This report is perhaps the most important document in determining whether or not you will be granted parole. However, too many Lifers make the mistake of not hiring an attorney or working on the areas discussed in this memo until after the psychological report is already written. In many cases, it is too late by then to have a significant impact on the parole hearing. This is because the psychologist is really previewing the case for the Board. You should review your Probation Report, prior hearing transcripts and prior psychological evaluations before meeting the psychologist.

If the psychologist finds that you do not understand the factors that contributed to your crime or that you have not quite resolved some of those factors, the psychological report will conclude that you lack insight or need more time and therapy to work on those areas. This conclusion will almost guarantee a parole denial of at least three or five years. The denial will be longer if you also have recent rule violations. For these reasons, do not delay in contacting an attorney to start getting ready.

Topics to Explore

These topics are not intended to be tackled all in one sitting. Take the time to consider each topic and the various factors that have shaped your life.

1. What was your relationship like with your family as you grew up? Consider how well you got along with your siblings, whether your parents were divorced, abusive, addicts, incarcerated, deceased, etc., and what kinds of decisions you made about how you wanted to be (or not be) when you got older.

2. If you used drugs or alcohol at a young age (age 16 or younger), can you recall the circumstances surrounding your first time? Did your drug or alcohol use begin (or increase) because you were experiencing some other difficulty that you did not know how to deal with?

3. If you had a drug or alcohol problem at the time of the crime, write out a short "Relapse Prevention Plan" that identifies the following: (a) two or three potential triggers to relapse (feelings or thoughts, such as rejection, depression or low self-esteem) that may have been associated with using drugs or alcohol in the past; and (b) whom you would call (sponsor, mentor, spouse, parent, sibling) or where you would go (AA/NA or other 12-Step Meeting, church, etc.) to make sure you do not use drugs or alcohol.

4. If you associated with gangs or participated in any gang-like behavior, when did you start to gravitate in this direction? Were there feelings of rejection or isolation that you wanted to avoid by associating with gangs?

5. If you sold drugs or engaged in other crimes, consider when you started doing this and why. Was there something you wanted to prove? Did you become addicted to that lifestyle?

6. At the time of the crime, what was going through your mind to have you make the decisions that lead to committing the crime? Why did you not stop the crime from happening?

7. What types of feelings/emotions can you identify from your past that you tried to deal with by engaging in misconduct? How have you learned to deal with those feelings/emotions in a pro-social way since you have

been in prison, and what programs or activities have contributed to your new approach?

8. If you have had a negative disciplinary record in prison, explain what was going on in your life to have you engage in this misconduct, and explain what is different now.

9. What kind of relationships (with children, parents, siblings, significant others) have you either maintained or established, since you have been in prison? And what kind, of support system have you put in place to help you-succeed once you are released?

SUPPORT LETTERS FOR YOUR HEARING

Prior to the parole hearing, and preferably before the psychological evaluation discussed above, the people who are in favor of your release should write a short letter (usually only one page) to the Board that explains the writer's relationship to you and why you should be paroled. These letters should avoid discussing legal statutes or cases.

Parole Plan Letters

These letters are the most important ones for you to have. At least one letter should provide specific information on where you would live, identifying the address of the home, the number of rooms, who else would live there and what your living arrangements would be. At least one letter should also describe actual (not potential) employment, including duties and pay, and any other information about how you would support yourself The home and job should both be in the same county, but this does not have to be in the county of last legal residence or the county of conviction. The Board can approve, parole in any California county. The Board cart also approve parole out of state, but it is a little harder to accomplish. Letters offering placement in a Transitional

281

Program are the absolute best, especially for people with histories of drug or alcohol abuse.

If you had a drug or alcohol problem at the time of the offense, the letter should identify places nearby where treatment can be obtained. The websites for Alcoholics Anonymous (AA) and Narcotics Anonymous (NA) often provide listings of all the available 12-step meetings in whichever geographic location your supporters search for. This information is critical for showing where you would seek this type of support once out on parole. A closely related issue to address in the letter is a relapse prevention plan, which should explain how the writer would help you if ever the urge to relapse arises.

General Support Letters

The best support letters explain the writer's personal knowledge of how you have changed during incarceration, and why the writer believes you can safely be released. The writer can explain the kind of support he or she will provide to you, but that support should be as specific as possible. For example, it could identify a car that you could use, or an amount of money that could be provided to help you get on your feet A generic letter that simply says "we will help him in any way we can" is not useful because it does not paint a clear enough picture for the Board. Writers must always remember to sign and date their letters.

The worst support letters try to minimize the seriousness of the crime or your role in it. They should never do this (and neither should you). Never refer to the crime as an "accident" or a "mistake." Also, even though signing a petition may be a good way to show support from a lot of people at once, petitions are of very little value to the Board because they suggest that the people signing do not actually know you or your case personally. It is also a bad idea to have several people sign their individual names to "form" letters that all say the same thing, just with different signatures. It is better to have three individualized letters than to have 15 form letters.

When and Where to Send Letters

You should start gathering support letters at least eight months before your hearing is due, even if the hearing has not yet been scheduled. In the past, it has been acceptable to obtain letters two or three months before your hearing; since a psychologist will be evaluating you and your parole plans months before the Board actually does, these letters need to be in place even before the psychological evaluation.

The letters should be sent to you, to your attorney, and to the Board of Parole. However, under the best circumstances, when the process for gathering letters starts very early, rough drafts of the letters should be provided to the attorney so that any necessary changes should be made before they are sent to the Board. You should have copies of these letters in band (along with their certificates, chronos, etc.) when you go to see the psychologist.

CONCLUSION

The directions provided here are generic. They are intended to give you a general idea of the things to expect and the things to work on as your hearing approaches. Within this framework, we will work with you on an individual basis to help you identify specific areas you need to address. However, you should review the contents of this letter and consider how each factor applies to you before our next meeting, at which more specific information will be discussed.

THERE ARE MANY EXCEPTIONS AND VARIATIONS IN THE PAROLE CONSIDERATION PROCESS. YOU ARE ENCOURAGED TO CONSULT AN EXPERIENCED PAROLE ATTORNEY FOR SPECIFIC ADVICE IN YOUR CASE.

CHAPTER 24
GUIDE TO LIFER SUPPORT LETTERS

The Board often complains that prisoners' parole plans are lacking something. Usually, this is because the prisoner, attorney and other advocates have not coordinated their efforts to make sure that all the important grounds are covered. Although we cannot give legal advice for any specific prisoner's situation, this guide should give you the best chance to avoid this problem in the future.

A. What is a Support Letter?

This should be a short letter (usually only one page) that typically explains the writer's relationship to the prisoner and why he or she should be paroled. These letters should almost always avoid discussing legal statutes or cases. There are three main types of support letters: (1) Parole Plans; (2) General Support; and (3) Testimonial. Each type is discussed below.

1. Parole Plans

This letter is the most important for most lifers. It should provide specific information on where the prisoner would live, identifying the number of rooms and the prisoner's living arrangements. A letter should also describe actual (not potential) employment, including duties and pay, and any other information about how he or she would support himself or herself. The home and job should both be in the same county, but this does not have to be in the county of last legal residence or the county of conviction. The Board can approve parole in any California county.

If the prisoner had a drug or alcohol problem at the time of the offense, the letter should identify places nearby where treatment can be obtained. The websites for Alcoholics Anonymous (AA) and Narcotics Anonymous (NA) often provide listings of all the available 12-step meetings in whichever geographic location you search for. This information is critical for showing where the prisoner would seek this type of support once out on parole. A closely related issue to address in the letter is a relapse prevention plan, which should explain the steps to be taken when the urge to relapse arises. This plan should explain who the prisoner would call or meet with to support his or her continued sobriety.

2. General Support

This letter should explain the writer's personal knowledge of how the prisoner has changed during incarceration, and why the writer believes the prisoner deserves to be paroled. This letter should not try to minimize the seriousness of the crime or the prisoner's role in it (leave that to the lawyer at the hearing or in court). Focusing on such issues here would harm the writer's credibility with the Board. Also, "petitions" signed by people without personal knowledge of the case should generally be avoided because they have very little impact on the Board and can take up a lot of space in a hearing packet with-almost no benefit.

3. Testimonial Letters

The testimonial letter should come from someone familiar with the case over a long period of time, but this generally should not include family members and friends. Typical writers include the defense attorney, judge or prosecutor at the time of trial; investigating officers, jurors, etc. These writers (unlike those writing "general support letters") may be able to explain the prisoner's role in the offense without appearing overly biased in the prisoner's favor. Many times, the people involved at the time of trial did not expect the prisoner to remain in prison decades later, and many times they will explain why the prisoner has done enough time for his or her role. Since some of these writers will be from the same segment of the community (i.e., law enforcement) as the parole board members, their input may be very influential.

Testimonial writers may also come from within the prison community. Educational or vocational instructors, volunteers in self-help and therapy programs, and work supervisors offer some of the best current evidence of how a prisoner gets along with others and how he or she approaches his or her responsibilities. Many times, these people have had the opportunity to observe a particular prisoner over a long period of time and can either talk about positive changes they have observed, or discuss the prisoner's consistently positive conduct throughout a variety of situations. These letters can also help minimize the impact of negative information in the prison file, such as 115s or 128s, either by providing important background information or by explaining how the prisoner has changed in the period since those write-ups occurred.

4. When and Where Should You Send your Support Letters?

Prisoners should start gathering support letters as soon as they know when their hearings have been scheduled. In years past, most scheduled hearings ended up being postponed or cancelled for one reason or another. They were often held many months after the original due dates, and the Board would sometimes complain that the support letters were too old and needed to be updated.

Nowadays, the postponement rate is much lower than it used to be; however, prisoners still should not obtain letters until they are actually scheduled for a hearing. The safest approach is to have the letters arrive 2 1/2 to 3 months before the scheduled hearing. When that is not possible (because, for example, plans are still being put together), they should still be obtained as soon as possible after that period in order to increase the chances the letters will be included in the "Board Packet," which includes documents pulled together at the prison and sent out to the commissioners and attorneys roughly 60 days before the hearing.

No matter when the letters arrive, they should be sent (or faxed, where possible) to the Board of Parole Hearings Desk (lifer desk) at the prison, to the prisoner's correctional counselor, the prisoner and the prisoner's attorney. At the very least, the prisoner should keep a copy of all the letters because too often, for one reason or another, no one else has copies at the time of the hearing. Late letters that get to the prisoner or his/her attorney on the eve of the hearing (or even on the morning of the hearing) can also be provided to the panel at the time of the hearing, if it cannot be avoided.

CHAPTER 25
PAROLE DAY BREAKDOWN

Keep in mind what the main purpose of this hearing is. It is for The Board to determine whether you have identified the factors that contributed to your crime and whether you have taken appropriate steps while incarcerated to make sure those factors will not contribute to another crime in the future. When the time comes, you will also need to explain how you have gained valuable tools through self-help and therapy programs (and books or other materials) in prison to make sure these issues do not lead to future violence. To be clear, though, if the commissioners cannot write down a couple of words or phrases they bear from you (but not the generic ones explaining what experiences, thoughts, feelings, or fears from your background led to the crime, they will not grant you parole.

Here is a rundown of how the hearing process generally goes:

Most bearing days have two or three bearings scheduled, set to take place at 8:30, 10:30 and 1:30. Shorter heating days may have hearings scheduled for 1:00 and 3:00. However) the bearings rarely start on time. For a hearing scheduled for 8:30 a.m., they will probably bring you to the BPH area of the prison around 7:30 and 8:00 a.m. Counsel can meet with you around 8 or 8:15ln go over any last-minute issues before the heating starts. (At some prisons, this meeting is not confidential so don't wait until this last meeting-to discuss anything significant) The hearing would then probably start around 8:40 or 8:45 and last approximately three hours (but it is impossible to predict the length—they can range from two hours to six). Hearings scheduled later in the day could therefore be delayed by a few minutes or a few hours, depending on what happens in the earlier hearings. Clients should be sure-to eat breakfast and request a sack lunch, if possible.

There will often be a representative from the District Attorney's Office present for the hearing, and it is possible that a victim, next-of-kin or a representative might be present—either in person or participating through video conference. All of these people, along with the Commissioner and Deputy Commissioner, will already be seated when you and your attorney enter the room.

Once we are seated, the Commissioner will start by explaining that the hearing is being tape-recorded and that everyone will need to state their names (spelling their last names) and you will need to add your CDC number so that they can all be made a part of the record. After that, the Commissioner will give you a quick overview of how the hearing will go, identifying which areas of your case will be covered by the Commissioner and which areas will be covered by the Deputy Commissioner. He or she will also explain that the DA's representative will be allowed to ask clarifying questions of the panel (they are not supposed to directly question you, and your attorney should make sure they don't), and that your attorney will be able to ask you questions.

Early in the hearing, the Commissioner will ask you questions to find out whether you have any disabilities (walking, seeing, hearing, talking, sitting, etc.) that will need any special attention during the hearing. You have the right to request assistance and the Board has to provide it. In order to determine your ability to understand and participate in the hearing, the Commissioner will ask you questions about your education on the streets, including how far you went, whether you were in special education classes, and whether you have participated in the mental health program in prison (either CCCMS or EOP). Just tell the truth about any previous challenges with school and about any help you think you need. (Your correctional counselor usually documents any requests for assistance on a BPH Form 1073.)

The Commissioner will confirm that you met with your correctional counselor, who notified you of your rights in the hearing and gave you an opportunity to review your central file (Olson Review). The Commissioner will also confirm that you had a chance to meet with your attorney, who advised you of the hearing procedures and your rights.

The Commissioner will confirm with your attorney that she or he has reviewed all the information contained in the 65-Day Board Packet and the 10-Day this applies. These are the documents from you that were shared with the attorney prior to the hearing, which you should have already seen.

The Board will sometimes ask your attorney whether you will be speaking to them during the hearing, about the crime and all other issues. Counsel will probably say that you arc (unless there's a really good reason not to), after which they will ask you to raise your right hand and be sworn in. Nowadays, they often just swear you in without asking whether you will be talking to them. If this happens and you would prefer not to discuss the crime, your attorney will need to step in and assert your rights not to discuss the crime under Penal Code Section 5011 and Section 2236 of Title 15 of the Code of Regulations.

The Board will adopt the statement of facts in your case from the Probation Officer's Report or from the Court of Appeal Opinion affirming your conviction. They will also probably look at the Risk Assessment (written by their psychologist) or other statements you have made to determine whether you have stated the facts differently prior to the hearing. Sometimes they read these facts and statements into the record. Other times they just jump right in and start asking you questions after saying they are incorporating those documents "by reference."

Their first questions are usually about your family, your upbringing, school, violence, gangs, substance or alcohol abuse and divorce or separation between your parents. They want to get a sense of how you fit in with the family and how you got along with your parents and siblings prior to the crime. Some of this information will probably come from the first few pages of the Comprehensive Risk Assessment, which contains some background information about where you were born and about your family. They are usually trying to establish that you had an "unstable social history," but this is not really a problem as long as you are prepared to later discuss how you have maintained relationships with your family members over the years, especially if they visit, write or talk to you often.

They will also ask you about prior arrests or convictions, including any juvenile incidents. They may even ask you if you had ever committed crimes that you were never arrested for. It generally does not hurt to admit these things at this point, as long as they were not recent crimes that could potentially carry a lengthy sentence if convicted.

Some commissioners will then move right into reviewing your letters of support and documenting who is writing and what kind of support (residence, job, sobriety sponsorship, etc.) they are offering you, as opposed to general letters of support for your release. Most commissioners, however, will move into asking youth describe the circumstances surrounding the crime. Sometimes they just ask youth tell them what happened. Other times, they read some parts of it into the record and ask you specific questions about it whichever way they bring it up, be prepared to tell the story of what happened in your crime. It is also really helpful when you are telling what happened if you admit (without them asking) that you have lied in the past about certain aspects of the crime. Volunteering this kind of information before they ask you about past lies gives you better credibility with the Board and is a clear indication that you recognized the need to change your past behaviors and attitude.

After hearing what happened in the crime, the commissioners will try to nail down the specific causative factors for the crime. They will either ask you to identify those factors, or they will ask you to explain WHY the crime happened. Some commissioners will just ask for your "insight." Again, as I explained above, if they cannot write down a couple of short words or words they hear from you explaining what experiences, thoughts, feelings, or fears from your background led you to commit the crime, they will not grant you parole.

After they have asked all the questions they have about your background and the crime, the Deputy Commissioner will talk to you about all the positive and negative factors from your time in prison ("post-conviction factors"). He or she will discuss your work, educational and vocational assignments, your disciplinary record (asking-you to discuss all your incidents, including 128A counseling chromos) and your self-help and therapy programs. They will review the chromos and certificates they find in your Central File, but be sure to have your own copies because those documents are often missing from the meeting. In the best case, your correctional counselor will have already documented all of your achievements in his or her report, but counselors often miss at least a few things, and those reports will not include anything you have done within the month or so immediately before the hearing. Most prisons have stopped having correctional counselors do these reports at all, though the documents you give your counselor in advance of the hearing are supposed to be placed in the file.

When you are discussing your programming, try to avoid simply giving yes or no answers to their questions about the different programs, even if that is what they seem to be looking for. Remember-that this is YOUR HEARING, and you need to take the time to explain to them what you have gained through this programming, especially if there are a couple of programs or activities you have found to be especially helpful in your growth.

The next topic is usually the psychological evaluation, which will either has a Comprehensive Risk Assessment (CRA) or a Subsequent Risk Assessment (SRA) Both reports are written by psychologists employed by the Board of Parole Hearings. The CRA is longer, covers many aspects of your life, discusses how well you understand the causes for the crime and accept responsibility. The CRA also uses at least one risk assessment tool (the HCR-20, version 3) to produce a rating of either low, moderate or high risk of future violence. (Prisoners with convictions for sex offenses committed as an adult will probably receive the Static-99, which is a-test to measure the risk of future sexual violence.) The SRA focuses on insight and acceptance of responsibility, as well as everything that has changed since the last CRA. The SRA does not reach its own risk assessment of low, moderate or high, but it is supposed to explain what, if anything, makes you a higher or lower risk than was shown in the most recent CRA.

They will then move on and ask you about your parole plans. Specifically, they want to know where you will live, where you will work; and how you will continue with any beneficial self-help or therapy programs from the inside once you are released (especially AA or NA). If you do not have a firm job offer, be prepared to discuss some ways in which you might use some of the vocational skills you have obtained while in prison. While the Board generally prefers to see that you are paroling to a transitional program, this is not a requirement, especially if you have not been identified as being dependent on drugs or alcohol in the past. Even if you do have a transitional program offering residence, you should explain where you will live after the six months to a year you are in that program.

The Board will usually not read all the letters of support into the record, especially if there are a lot of them. But you need to make sure they mention all letters that offer the specific type of support discussed above. It is also a good idea to point out any special letters, even if they are considered "general" support as opposed to parole plans. These might include letters from prison staff or volunteers, elected officials, victims' family members, judges, attorneys, etc.

After all this material is covered, the Board will give the DA's representative an opportunity to ask questions. They are technically asking questions to the Board about things they want clarified for the record. Your answers are also supposed to be directed to the Board and not directly to the DA's representative. But here are a few words of caution: First, pause after the DA asks each question because the commissioners may either re-phrase the question, tell the DA they are not going to have you answer the question, or they may go ahead and answer the question themselves based on what they have react or on your earlier testimony in the hearing. Also, your attorney might object to the question, answer it himself herself, or tell the Board and the DA that you are not answering the question. As you can see, a lot can happen when the DA asks questions, so you need to wait to see whether a question is actually going to be put to you for sure. The best way to limit or eliminate the DA's questions is to admit that you lied about certain aspects of the crime in the past because you were deeply ashamed of what you did, you were in denial and you wanted to avoid responsibility. This often takes the wind out of their sails and does not really hurt you in a parole bearing —just about everyone lies to avoid responsibility in the beginning of their case.

Once the DA is finished asking questions, the Board will give your attorney an opportunity to ask questions. Attorneys use this time to come back to any questions that may have given you trouble earlier in the hearing and we need you to discuss further and better. Your attorney should also have a short list of issues they or need to discuss in order to demonstrate remorse, acceptance of responsibility and insight into the crime. If any of those issues have not yet been addressed, your attorney will ask about it at this time.

After questioning, the DA's representative gets to make a closing statement/argument. They almost always focus on the nature of the crime and your previous attempts to avoid responsibility. In addition, they will highlight a few statements found in the psychological evaluation in their effort to connect the historical factors surrounding the crime to some current evidence of dangerousness. Be sure not to react visibly or verbally to what the DA says in his or her closing. The more experienced ones know how to get you upset and their goal is to have the Board see this. Your attorney will then get a chance to make a closing statement/argument, and you will, too.

Your closing statement should be limited to expressing remorse for the harm you caused the victim and victim's family. It is normal for people to write it down and read it at this time because it helps them stay focused and speak clearly. Do not try to respond to or address anything the DA has said during his or her questions or closing. This is a trap that you need to avoid.

If the victim or a representative is present, he or she will be given an opportunity to talk to the Board about the impact of the crime and why they think you should remain in prison (unless they are actually supportive of your release). While you will technically not get a chance to say anything after they have finished speaking, your attorney will sometimes object if they make statements that are completely false, including wild accusations that have never been proven.

After all of this, the commissioners kick everyone else out of the room and they deliberate on whether to grant or deny parole. Their deliberation generally takes between 20 minutes and an hour, but it can sometimes take longer. (The length of the deliberation does not tell you anything about whether parole is being granted or denied.) When they call you back into the room, they will read their decision, after which they will give you a three-page printout of what their decision was. A full transcript from-the hearing will be sent to you in approximately 30 days.

In their decision, whether they say that you are suitable or unsuitable for parole, they will calculate a term of your confinement that they think matches the seriousness of the crime. If they are granting you parole, they will then subtract months from that term based on bow many years you have spent in prison avoiding rule violations and participating in programs since you started serving your life term. On average, they will give you four months of additional credit for each disciplinary-free year, but they could give you six or eight or even twelve months of additional credit for each year you did something outstanding, such as college degrees, specialized vocational training, saving someone's life or some other pro-social activity. Once they subtract those credits from the base term they set based on the crime, the result is your total term of confinement your actual release date is then calculated by adding that total term to the date you started serving your life term.

You and your attorney will have a chance to talk during any recesses that are called in the hearing (either for a restroom break, for deliberations or for any other reason), and you-two will have a few minutes after the hearing to discuss the next steps to be taken, whether the decision is to grant parole or to deny it. If your parole is denied, you may have to wait until you get the transcript in about 30 days before you can talk more about whet options are available to you.

Hopefully, this takes some of the mystery out of hearing day. Keep in mind; also, that you can ask for a brief recess during the hearing to either meet with your attorney or to use the restroom. Good luck!

CHAPTER 27
A GUIDE TO PREPARING FOR YOUTH OFFENDER PAROLE HEARINGS

Understanding the Parole Process

Before you can prepare for a parole hearing, you need to understand how the process works. The next few pages will give you some basic information, but the laws and regulations about parole are complicated, so not everything can be explained here. This is just a start. Also, please understand that this is not legal advice; it is information. There are many resources available to provide information about parole.

How does the Board decide whether or not to grant parole?

The law requires the Board to grant parole unless it finds "some evidence" that you would pose a danger to the community if released. The most common reasons that commissioners use to deny parole are:

Recent and/or violent disciplinary violations (115s and sometimes 128As);

Recent gang involvement;

Recent substance abuse;

Lack of credibility or lack of truthfulness;

Lack of remorse for your actions;

Lack of insight (failing to understand why the crime happened and its effect on others)

Lack of realistic parole plans and proof (documentation) for those plans; and

Information contained in confidential file.

What Is the Board looking for?

The easy answer is that the Board wants to make sure that it does not release someone who will commit another crime. This core determination is an assessment of your current dangerousness. In re Lawrence, 44 Cal. 4th 1181 (2008). But you cannot simply tell the Board that you do not want to come back to prison or that you will not commit another crime. Your words are not enough. You must show the Board that you will not commit crimes in the future. You can do that, in part, by:

Explaining why you committed the crime (you cannot do this if you deny the crime, minimize your role in the crime, or blame others); and

Showing, by your actions, how you have matured and developed into a different person today compared to when you committed the crime.

If you do not show with your actions that you are now a different person and demonstrate that you understand what led up to your involvement in the crime, the Board will not believe that you can prevent it from happening again.

What are the three key questions the Board wants answers to?

The Board is essentially looking for truthful answers to the following big questions:

1. Do you take full responsibility for your crime?

- Do you fully admit to your offense without excuses?
- Can you be truthful about all of your intentions and choices before, during and after the crime?
- Have you thought deeply about how your choices impacted others?

- Do you understand the effect your crime had on others (the victim, the victim's family and friends, the community, your family, and others)?
- If the Board determines your testimony at the hearing is not credible, you will probably be denied parole.

2. Have you explored and do you understand why you committed the crime(s) ("causative factors")?

- Have you thought deeply about the things that led you to commit the crime? It is important that you speak openly about the circumstances of your childhood so that the Board can give great weight to any youth factors.
- What kind of person were you at the time of the crime? What kind of lifestyle were you living?
- Can you describe the choices you made, the perspectives you had, the situations you put yourself in that led you to commit the crime?
- Have you faced the challenges and traumas in your life that may have influenced your choices or character?
- The Board is looking for explanations, but not excuses for any negatives: the crime(s), your prior lies about the crime, your prior lifestyle, or your negative behavior in prison.

3. What have you done to address the things in your life that led to you committing the crime?

- Have you sincerely faced the issues in your life that led to criminal behavior?
- How are you different today? How does the way you live your life now show that you have addressed and overcome the causative factors of the crime?

- Does your disciplinary history (115s and 128As) reflect who you are today?
- How do you make choices today? What values guide your choices?
- What are some specific lessons or skills that you have learned from programs that you've done in prison?
- How have you grown and matured? Part of maturity is understanding both our strengths and weaknesses – what are your biggest strengths and weaknesses of character?

You need to have answers to these questions for the Board. You cannot fake it at a parole hearing. Answering these questions is hard work and can lead you to spend time thinking about very sensitive or difficult issues in your life that you may have ignored up to now because it is uncomfortable, painful, or hard. These questions require you to reach down to the very core of what shaped your choices and how you lived your life at the time of the crime. Addressing these issues will increase your ability to show the Board how much you have learned, matured, and changed while incarcerated. These questions are often very difficult to answer and answering them requires a long process of self-reflection. To help with this process of reflection, you can start by thinking about the "Starter Questions" on page 21 of this guide.

One of the best ways to get started is to discuss the questions with another person. Choose someone you trust and who will give you honest feedback and support as you work through things, but beware of revealing incriminating information that someone could use against you later. If you do not have a "safe" person or place to discuss these topics, you can also write about them. Once you start working with an attorney, it will be important to discuss these issues with him or her.

What will happen at my Youth Offender Parole Hearing?

This section provides an overview of basics of the process so you know what to expect as you prepare for the hearing. It is just a starting point.

Will I have an attorney?

Yes. You can hire your own attorney or, if you cannot afford a private attorney, the Board will appoint one to your case. It is the Board's expectation that an appointed attorney will meet with you no later than 45 days prior to your hearing.

Who will be at my parole hearing?

- Commissioners: One Commissioner (sometimes two) and one Deputy Commissioner from the Board of Parole Hearings will run the hearing – they will review all of the paperwork in your case, ask most of the questions, and make a decision to grant or deny you parole.
- District Attorney: A district attorney from the county of commitment may attend the hearing (in person, by video, or by phone). He or she will have an opportunity to ask questions and make a closing statement. He or she may say things that are untrue.
- Your Attorney: Your attorney will have a chance to ask you questions to clarify any issues that might be unclear for the Commissioners. Your attorney can also make objections and a closing statement
- You: You will answer questions throughout the hearing. After your attorney has given a closing statement, you have the right to make a brief (about 5 minutes) closing statement if you wish.

- Victims: The victim(s) and/or the victim(s)'s family may be present (in person, by video, by phone). They are allowed to make a statement at the end of the hearing. If they are not present, a victim's representative may read letters from victims or victim's family.
- There will also be a Correctional Officer in the room and there may also be a few neutral observers in the room. None of these people speak at the hearing.

Do the same commissioners who conduct parole hearings conduct YOPHs?

Yes. The same commissioners will hear these cases, but they are trained on how to conduct the Youth Offender Parole Hearings and apply the "great weight" factors described above. In addition, the Board is required to draft regulations that will guide the commissioners in these hearings. At the time this guide was written, the regulations were not completed.

Is there a role for my family and friends?

Yes, there is a special role at the hearing for friends and family members. The Youth Offender Parole laws state that family members, friends, school personnel, faith leaders, and representatives from community-based organizations who have knowledge about the young person prior to the crime, or who can attest to his or her growth and maturity since the time of the crime, can submit letters to the Board. This is allowed in regular parole hearings also, but the fact that the Youth Offender law specifically includes this should make the commissioners pay extra attention to that support for Youth Offenders. The law does not, however, allow friends and family to come to the hearing. PC 3051(f)(2).

What information will the Board have about me?

The Board will read and consider everything in your C-file. This may include, but is not limited to:
- Case paperwork (police reports, trial transcripts, probation report, autopsy, appellate decision)
- All 115s, 128As, and 602s
- Psychological Evaluations (see below)
- Transcripts of prior Parole Hearings
- Certificates and Vocations
- Positive and Negative Chronos for Programs or from Staff
- Victim Statements
- Confidential Information (You and your attorney cannot review the confidential information, but you are entitled to receive a CDCR form 810 listing any documents contained in the confidential file. You should also receive a CDCR form 1030 summarizing any confidential information that the Board relies on in its decision at least 10 days prior to the hearing.)

You are entitled to review your entire C-file, except the confidential portions, once a year in an Olsen review.

The Board will also read and consider any documents you and your attorney submit to the Commissioners. These may include:
- Documentation of parole plans
- Letters of support from people in the community who know you
- Insight Statement (not required, but might help). This is something you write that includes deep and thoughtful discussion of your insight.

- Remorse Statement (not required, but might help). This is something you write that includes a description of your understanding of the harm you have caused and your feelings about that harm.
- Relapse Prevention Plan
- Book reports on self-help or other books

Psychological Evaluations (Comprehensive Risk Assessments)

For everyone appearing for parole consideration, the Board uses psychological evaluations, called "Comprehensive Risk Assessments," to predict whether you present a low, moderate or high risk of future violence. The reports also contain other information about whether you accept responsibility for your actions, whether you understand why your crime happened and whether you have participated in the right kind and number of programs to address the factors that contributed to the crime. When these risk assessments are prepared for youth offender hearings, they must also take into consideration the diminished culpability of youth as compared to that of adults, the hallmark features of youth, and any subsequent growth and increased maturity of the individual. PC 3051(f)(1). The Board's psychologists address this requirement by adding a section in their reports that directly discusses those factors. It is not yet clear whether this is enough to meet the requirements of the law.

Your evaluation will include a meeting with a Board psychologist, which will usually take place at least a couple of months before the scheduled parole hearing. This meeting is very important, and you should approach it as you would approach your Board hearing. The psychologist will be evaluating and considering the same factors that the Board considers, and the Board will rely on the conclusions of the psychologist. You will receive a written copy of the psychologist's report before your hearing. Plan to discuss the report with your attorney, and be sure to identify for the attorney anything in the report you think is inaccurate.

If you have done positive things like reading books, doing correspondence classes, making plans for parole, creating a relapse prevention plan, or getting support letters from your family, try to get documentation of this before your psychological evaluation. You can ask your counselor to put copies of this kind of documentation in your C-file before the evaluation. However, you should also make sure to bring your own copies of this documentation with you when you go to the evaluation. Then, the psychologist who is evaluating you can see all the good things you are doing before he or she writes the evaluation.

What will the Board ask me at my parole hearing?

There are four main areas the Board will ask you questions about at the hearing:

1. Commitment Offense

The Board will ask many questions about your commitment offense. Often, the Board will read facts into the record (from the appellate decision or the probation report), and then ask if you agree with those facts. If you do not agree, the Board will allow you to state your own version. It is important to remember the Board will not decide all over again whether you were guilty of your crime. However, it may be important to correct any inaccurate facts about the crime. What facts, if any, you should correct is something that you should decide with your attorney's help. The most important thing is that the Board expects you to be truthful about the crime and your role in it. And the Board will be listening to how you describe the crime and whether you appear to be making excuses for your behavior or downplaying the effect of your crime. The Board wants to see if you have insight into your commitment offense and remorse for the impact of your actions.

2. Social History

The Board will also discuss your life before your crime. This is often called "social history." The Board can ask questions about anything in your life prior to the commitment offense. They are likely to ask about your family life and upbringing, your neighborhood, your school, your friends and relationships. The Board wants to know about positive activities (like sports, jobs, school, hobbies) and things that may have hurt you in some way (like learning difficulties, physical or sexual abuse, neglect, exposure to violence in your home or neighborhood, gang involvement, drug and alcohol use, criminal history). The Board wants to understand the person you were and the things that may have led to your crime (causative factors). There is more information on page 18 about causative factors.

3. Post-Commitment Factors

The Board will also discuss what you have done since you were incarcerated. This is an important part of the hearing and allows you to show how you have changed. This is your chance to demonstrate your growth and maturity and positive change. The Board will discuss your (1) disciplinary history; (2) education, jobs, programming; (3) any positive chromos; and (4) your psychological evaluations. If you have a history of gang involvement in prison, the Board will most likely ask about that as well. The Board wants to see evidence that you are on a different path than you were at the time of the crime

4. Parole Plans

Finally, you must have realistic parole plans and provide documentation of those plans. Documentation is proof, and usually it is in the form of letters from the people offering you support when you get out. It is important to have very specific parole plans. In addition, you should have at least one back-up option in case your first choice does not work. Usually the Board wants you to have:

- a job offer or employment skills;
- a place to live (a transitional home is preferred);
- emotional and/or financial support from family or friends; and
- a relapse prevention plan if you have a history of drug or alcohol use.

The Board wants to know that if you are released you will have the plans and support necessary to succeed.

Will the hearing be recorded?

Yes, by law, the hearing must be recorded and there will be a transcript of everything that is said. You will be provided a copy of the transcript approximately 30 days after the hearing. If you do not receive your transcript, you can write to the Board of Parole Hearings to request one. The transcript will become part of your record and the Commissioners will consider all your statements at any future parole hearings. If you are denied, it is a good idea to read and review your transcripts so that you can better understand the Board's reasons for denying parole and address them at the next hearing.

What can I do to prepare for my parole hearing?

There are many things you can do to prepare for your parole hearing. Take every class or program you can. Read books and write book reports on each one. Join available groups at your prison that help you with personal growth or give you opportunities to help others. Stay or get in contact with healthy friends and family on the outside. Limit your contact with negative people on the inside. Think about who you are and who you want to be. Make sure you keep track of all of your positive work and behavior, so you can talk about it at your hearing.

When should I start preparing for my hearing?

"NOW!" The Board considers your entire time in prison in deciding whether to grant parole or not. Focus on the present and use the time in a way that will help you get ready to go home. It is never too early to start preparing, but it is also never too late. Even if you were not on the right track before, you can turn things around and show the Board you are ready to go home.

How can I start preparing for my parole hearing?

Here are some starter questions to help you begin thinking deeply about some of the issues the Board will want you to address. Take your time on these. Write or talk about them with a trusted person, then take time to reflect and go deeper into the issues. Start over with what you have written and go more in-depth.

Starter Questions

Commitment Offense

Ask yourself: What was going through my mind as I made the choices that led to my committing the crime?

Why did I not stop the crime from happening? How would I handle the same situation differently today?

Read the Interview with a murder victim family member in this guide. Ask yourself: How were my victim(s) hurt? What did they feel? How were their family members and friends affected at the time of the crime? How was the community affected? And, now, years later, what is the impact of what I did?

Social History

Ask yourself: How were my relationships with my family members? Who were my role models? What did they teach me (good and bad)? Prior to my crime did I experience violence, abuse (physical, sexual, verbal, and emotional), neglect, poverty, mental illness, drug use, gangs, or criminal activity in my family? How did that affect me (anger, denial, loneliness, low self-esteem)? What decisions did I make about who I wanted to be (or not be) when I got older? How did my experiences in my family and community impact my decisions? What is different now? How did I get from there to here?

If you used drugs or alcohol, ask yourself: Can I remember the first time? What was the situation? Did my drug or alcohol use begin (or increase) because I was experiencing some other difficulty that I did not know how to deal with? What is different now? How did I get from there to here?

If you associated with gangs or participated in any gang-like behavior, ask yourself: When did I start to get involved? What was I running from? What did I think gangs would give me that was missing in my life? What was my experience with gangs? What did I believe about gangs? How was my gang involvement related to things going on in my family, community, or school? What is different now? How did I get from there to here?

311

If you sold drugs or committed other crimes, ask yourself. When did I start doing this, and why? How did it make me feel? How was my criminal behavior related to things going on in my family, community, or school? What is different now?

Post-commitment

If you have had a negative disciplinary record in prison, ask yourself: What was going on in my life that I chose to do things that would get me in trouble in prison? What is different now? What types of programs have I participated in while in prison to better myself? What were one or two programs that really focused on addressing my specific needs? What specific tools have I gained from these programs? Have I gotten any disciplinary write-ups in prison (115s or 128As)? What led me to violate the rules of the prison? Do I take responsibility for those violations? How will I avoid violating rules if I am released?

I was granted parole. When will I be released? Does the Governor get a say? When will I be released?

The Board has up to 120 days to review and finalize the panel's decision to grant parole. You will be notified if the Board makes any changes to the decision that adversely affect you. If the Board does not change its mind after 120 days, then the decision goes to the Governor's office for review.

What Is the Governor's role?

The state constitution allows the Governor to affirm, modify, or reverse the Board's decision to grant parole in the following cases. Cal. Constitution Art. 5, Sec. 8(b).

If you have a life sentence for murder, the Governor can reverse the Board's decision to grant or deny parole. The Governor has up to 30 days to review the Board's decision. In non-murder cases, the Governor cannot reverse the Board's decision, but he can require the full Board to re-consider the decision and potentially change the decision.

If the Governor decides to take no action in your case, you will be released.

Do I have to serve my "Thompson" term?

Maybe not. If you have been convicted and sentenced for new crimes committed before age 26 (during your incarceration), often called "Thompson terms", you may not be required to serve the sentences for these crimes after you are found suitable for Youth Offender Parole.

In April 2017, the California Court of Appeal, First Appellate District, decided In re Trejo, 10 Cal. App. 5th 972 (2017), which held that PC 3051 (the Youth Offender Parole Law, requiring youth offenders to be released once they have reached their YPED and been found suitable) supersedes PC 1170.1 (requiring that an inmate sentenced to consecutive terms not be released on parole before completing all the terms of imprisonment imposed).

At this time, CDCR and BPH are requiring people to serve "Thompson terms" for offenses committed after age 25. Many people are challenging this interpretation of Trejo in court, and some people have won these cases. The outcome is still to be determined in court.

What if I have an immigration hold?

The Youth Offender Parole laws will not change any immigration consequences.

I was denied parole. Now what? When will my next hearing be held?

Your next hearing will be scheduled according to "Marsy's Law," which was enacted in 2008. At the end of the hearing, the Commissioners will decide whether your next parole hearing will be in 3, 5, 7, 10, or 15 years. In making that determination, the Youth Offender Parole laws require the Commissioners to consider that you were under the age of 26 at the time of the crime, the diminished culpability of youth as compared to that of adults, the hallmark features of youth, and any subsequent growth and increased maturity of the individual. PC 3051(g).

You may have heard about the "Gilman" case. In February 2014, a federal court held that "Marsy's Law" violates a life prisoner's constitutional rights if he or she committed an offense before November 4, 2008 because the law increases the length of time a lifer must wait before his/her next hearing. The court ordered that, for this group of prisoners, the BPH must set their next hearing one year later unless there is good cause to postpone the hearing for three years or (for murder cases) five years. However, the state has appealed the order and the order has been stayed; this means the order will have no effect unless and until it is affirmed on appeal.

Remember that laws change, and before relying on anything in this guide you should make sure you have the most up-to-date information.

I was denied parole, but I have a determinate sentence and my EPRD is before my next parole hearing.

You will be released at the Earliest Possible Release Date (EPRD) established on the determinate term. You do not have to wait until your next parole hearing.

Example: Justin has a sentence of 18 years. He had his Youth Offender Parole Hearing at 15 years but was denied parole. His next hearing was set for five years later. Because his EPRD is before the next hearing date, he will be released at his EPRD and will not need the hearing.

Is there any way to move up the date of my hearing so that it comes sooner?

It is possible to file a Petition to Advance with the Board in order to move up the date of your next hearing. You can only do this once every three years, so you should consult with an attorney who knows parole law and procedure and your situation to decide whether it would be a good idea to file a Petition to Advance. It is helpful in some cases, but not in all cases; if you are not ready to go before the Board, then you might receive a denial with a long setback period.

Spend the time before your next hearing to do everything that the Board recommended that you do (and more!).

I want to challenge my parole denial. How do I do that?

In the first 120 days after the decision, you can send a letter to the Board's Decision Review Board.

After 150 days, you can file a petition for a writ of habeas corpus asking a judge to review the Board's denial (or the Governor's reversal) of parole. If you would like more information on how to do this, write to the Prison Law Office, General Delivery, San Quentin, CA 94964.

CHAPTER 28
A FATHER'S POINT OF VIEW

Soccer season had ended, and seven-year-old Elijah was looking forward to getting his team trophy. His mother packed him and his 10-month-old brother, Adam, in the back seat of the family car and drove to the sports office at a local park. They picked up the trophy and signed Eli up for basketball season. Next stop that afternoon was a school fundraiser at a pizza parlor. It should have been a perfect day for a seven-year-old.

But as his mother buckled her sons back into their seats, three members of a local gang stormed into the park, intent on revenge for a shooting earlier in the day. They opened fire on a man; He ran and their bullets pierced the family's car. The boys' mother desperately tried to move the vehicle. When the shooting was over, she turned to look at her children: Still strapped into their seats, Eli was slumped over, motionless; his tee-shirt soaked with blood. The baby, Adam, was crying hysterically and had blood on his face. Eli had been struck three times and died instantly. Adam, hit in the face, had his left eye damaged by metal fragments, but he lived.

James was at work when his wife and sons were attacked. Nearly 16 years have passed. "There's not a day that goes by that we don't hurt," James says. "It was nothing short of devastating for our family and friends."

Why did you agree to be interviewed and share you family's story with people in prison?

James: I hope that by telling this painful story it will give people in prison a deeper understanding of what victims and their families have gone through. My message to people in prison is this: Developing compassion will lead to healing for yourself and others.

You worked to pass laws that give second chances to people who were young when they committed their crimes. You repeatedly took time off from work and away from family to go to Sacramento and urge lawmakers to pass these laws. Why did you work so hard to change laws that help people like those who killed your son?

James: I worked on these bills because I believe each person has a purpose in life. Your crime, what you did then, does not fully define who you are now. I am a person of faith, and I believe we were created to promote life and love in one another. I helped pass these laws because I understand the importance of every human being, even people who have committed serious crimes. We must help pull each other up. I help one person, then that person can help someone else. It is how we create peace and vitality in the world.

What did you feel when you first found out about your family being attacked?

James: I got a call. "There's been a shooting involving your family and you need to go to the park." I was in shock. I am almost always composed, able to handle any kind of difficulty, but this was so unbelievable. On the drive to the park I was feeling fear of the unknown, rage, confusion ... I couldn't fully comprehend what had happened. I was in a state of disbelief. I arrived at the park and saw our car with officers around it. I didn't see my family. The commanding officer came up to me and said, "They have gone to the hospital. Your wife and son are going to be Ok." I said, "I have two sons." The officer hesitated, and dropped his head. "How old was your oldest son?" I said, "He is seven." The officer struggled with his own emotions. "I'm sorry. He didn't make it." I felt my world crash into a pile of pieces. I was left in this pile, trying to navigate emotionally, mentally, spiritually. It was overwhelming. I immediately needed to be with my wife and other son. I realized I didn't really know what it meant when the officer said they were going to "be Ok."

Tell us something about who Elijah was.

James: 50 pounds, 50 inches, seven years old. Full of hope and aspirations. Full of spunk. He could entertain a toddler or have an intelligent conversation with a senior citizen, freely expressing his point of view on many subjects. He was a straight "A" student, reading books before entering kindergarten, winning numerous awards, including "Student of the Month" and twice placing 3rd in the annual science fair. He was the 1st grade representative for our regional Spelling Bee. He played soccer, basketball, and baseball, earning a "Good Sportsmanship" medal in soccer. He also played the piano for four years. He was most proud of becoming a big brother, or maybe, he was most proud of his baby brother! My wife and I feel Elijah's life is an example for us: To love God and be exhilarated about the life we've been given, to honor and love one another, to seek to give our best each day and express God's gifts in us.

Your son Adam survived. How was he affected?

James: He had many surgeries and other painful treatments for years. He has learned to adapt to the deficits in that eye. And, he was impacted in ways that we will never really know. At the time he was a 10-month-old, joy-filled baby. Before this happened, we always called him "Happy Baby." He's grown up into a very composed and serious young man, and I often look at him and wonder if he would have been different had this tragedy not happened. He's got a sense of humor, but overall, he's a serious person. He's very aware of hard things going on in the world, perhaps in a way that isn't typical for someone his age. He's in a different place than his peers. Part of this is what we have modeled for him, and what we believe as spiritual people. He has embraced a spiritual path on his own as he has come to see the power of God in his own life.

At first, as a young child, other kids would notice his eye, and ask questions, and he would share what happened. When he was a little older, kids began teasing him. He was made fun of, and at one-point kids started calling him "Shot-eye." It was very hard for him. I was appalled. I felt so badly for him. Again, I felt violated, with my child being further traumatized. After that, he became a more private person; for a long time, he would have close friends but not share what happened to him and his brother. When he was around 12 or 13 years old, I saw that he started sharing with people who were sensitive and willing to talk about difficult things, but choose not to share with others.

Recently in high school he had to write an essay about someone being resilient and surviving despite a difficult thing. He let my wife and I read it. He had written something like, "In my own life I have examples of people who are resilient, even heroic, and they are my mother and father," and he told our story. I am proud of who he has become, but I so wish he had not gone through this.

Almost 16 years have passed. You mentioned not a day goes by without hurt since this happened. Would you share what you mean?

James: In the early years after Elijah was taken from us, I felt such a sense of deep violation. Everything was colored by red, I saw red—blood—everywhere. Our lives had been shattered, and although shattered we still had to function. But life was changed. We had to figure out—reinvent how to live. When something like this type of violent crime happens, it changes you. You are one way one moment, and then in an instant, the moment of that violation, you are changed. You look the same, but everything about you is different. You have to look around and put everything into a different perspective given what has happened to you.

I struggled with finding pleasure in things. Even now, I'm not sure the word "happiness" is in my vocabulary. I had to look deep into myself and ask really hard questions about what I believe about life and God after something this terrible happens. I realized my faith was intact, but my humanity was shaken down to the foundation. My reaction to everything was different. If the simplest thing was not right, it would cause feelings to rise up in me about my son. Natural, every-day kind of stuff, like, someone cut in line ahead of me at a store, and it seemed like a racial thing. I would feel violated, I'd feel enraged ... I'd think to myself, "You don't know what happened to me and you're disrespecting me here, treating me less than yourself." Having my son murdered created such a deep wound, it made me reactive in a way I wasn't before. It's like the terrible wound created by my son's murder caused a vulnerability I carry with me all the time.

Even though this happened 16 years ago, it could have been 16 minutes ago. The pain isn't 16 years ago. It is now. The pain might be different at different times, but I think one of the things that people who have not gone through this don't understand is that you don't just "get over it." I have moved past a lot of the anger; God has healed me. But the pain is still there.

What do you think victims or surviving family members want to hear from a prisoner at a parole hearing?

James: I think the most important thing to remember is that victims and survivors don't all feel the same way. Each person responds differently to tragedy. There will be some victims/survivors who might say things like, "I just want to know why you did what you did." Or, "I want to know what you have done to turn your life around and make sure you never do this kind of thing again." Other victim/survivors might want to have a conversation with you, back and forth, to get a sense of who you are at the hearing. Others still may want to hear and believe that you truly, deeply feel sorry for what you did, and that you have thought a lot about all of the ways your actions have harmed their lives.

On the other hand, some victims/survivors may not want to know anything about you, what you think, or what you have done to rehabilitate yourself. They may want the opportunity to tell you and the commissioner about how they have been injured by your acts, and why you should not be paroled. And, while some people's perspective might change over time and someday agree you should be released, others will never change their feeling that you should be locked up. Remember, too, that some victims/survivors may be angered about opportunities you have had in prison, for example, to further your education or watch your children grow up, that they have been denied.

Each person is on their own path, trying to figure out how they can heal from the crime and its effects.

What questions would you suggest a prisoner ask him or herself to get a deeper understanding of the effect of their crimes?

James: Life is full of challenges and injustices and difficulties. I believe that often times when people offend it is because of something that has happened to them. One thing I'd ask you to think deeply about is this: Do you know why you committed your crime? I'd also suggest you ask yourself: Do you honestly know how your crimes have hurt others? It may be difficult for you to face the pain you have caused. Are you doing the hard work needed to really understand the effect of your actions? Do you know how your family was impacted? And how your community was impacted as well? Have you thought deeply about how your victims were affected? Perhaps you have read my story and thought to yourself, "Well, at least I didn't kill a child." Even if that is true, or even if you were not the shooter in your crime, or even if your crime was not murder, your victims were harmed. It may be uncomfortable or even painful for you to think about the fact that you have hurt others. Are you making yourself face the reality of your actions?

What is your hope for people in prison?

James: My hope is this: That you will see your own self-worth, and that you understand that, no matter what you have done, you are a person of value. I believe you can choose to live your life in such a way that it reflects the worthy person you really are. If you have committed a terrible crime, even if someone died because of your action or inaction: I urge you, do not let that person's death be in vain. Do your best to live your life in a way that honors the lives you have taken or damaged.

CHAPTER 29

ADVICE FROM PEOPLE WHO HAVE SUCCESSFULLY PAROLED

How to Choose the Right Path in Prison: Eight Different Perspectives

There is more than one path to changing your life and finding success. We asked people who paroled from California prisons what advice they have for you. What they have in common is that each committed a crime at a young age and spent a long time in California prisons. They are now living full, successful lives on the outside. These individuals offer up their insights to you. Here is who they are:

- J.A. was convicted of two murders. He had just turned 18 at the time of his crimes. He spent nearly 23 years in California prisons. J.A. is currently an intern for a nonprofit, and this fall he will start as a student at a Cal State University where he will study math and physics.
- S.B. was convicted of murder for a crime committed at age 16. S.B. served nearly 20 years in prison and was paroled in 2013. Currently in a transitional living home, S.B. hopes to work on human rights issues.
- N.C. was convicted of murder for a crime she committed at age 20. She was in prison for 18 years. When she paroled at age 40, her son was already an adult. She is employed at "Get on the Bus," working hard on behalf of those she left behind in prison by helping as many people as she can.
- T.D. was convicted of two murders. He was 22 years old when he committed his crimes and he spent almost 22 years in prison. He was paroled in July

2010 and since then has earned a B.S. and a J.D. degree, discharged from life parole, and is now a licensed California attorney practicing parole law and committed to protecting and advancing the rights of prisoners and parolees

- L.G. was 22 when convicted of assault with a deadly weapon and burglary. He had parole violations which resulted in further incarceration. He now works full-time as a program analyst in a public mental health agency. He started community college in prison, and since being paroled he earned undergraduate and master's degrees. He is working towards his goal of a doctorate.

- T.N. was convicted of murder for a crime that occurred when he was 16 years old. He spent 18 years in California state prisons. He now works full time but volunteers extensively. T.N. was recently recognized by a community group with its "Most Inspirational Volunteer" award, and by another group with its "Unsung Hero" award. He is engaged to be married and is helping to raise his fiancé's child. T.N. hopes to go to school to become a social worker.

- V.R. was convicted of murder and sentenced to 25-to-life plus 12 years. After a rocky start in prison, she turned things around and was paroled after 29 years. She is currently living in a transition house, loves riding her bike on the beach, and cherishes every day. She appreciates the simple act of walking freely among people who know nothing about her past. She hopes to own a kennel and dog training business.

- D.S. was 16 at the time of his crime. He is currently building a family with his fiancé and young daughter, and hoping to become involved with the conservation corp.

What do you think is the most important thing people can do to become suitable for parole?

JA: To be found suitable for parole you must show the board of Parole Hearings that you are ready to be an outstanding citizen that is 100% committed to giving back. Not 90% or 95% committed, but 100% committed!

S.B.: Re-define your character, and have who you are on the inside reflect who you are on the outside.
N.C.: Be able to talk about and present what you have learned in the groups you have attended.

T.D.: Live like a square. Do your work/educational/vocational assignment and go back to your cell. Involve yourself in as many self-help groups and programs as possible. Sign up and complete whatever they offer. Overdo what the Board requires you to do.

L.G.: Accept your circumstances. Recognize that no matter what got you in prison, it's up to you to take responsibility for how you live going forward, including while in prison. Educate yourself.

T.N.: Aim for a progressive path of rehabilitation records. The Board will want to see a consistent path of rehabilitation, not just here and there. Even if you were a troublemaker when you first entered prison or you have had recent 115s, a positive record going forward will show the Board that you are moving forward, changing, and improving yourself.

V.R.: Education.
DS: Think less and feel more, just sounding educated is not enough. How did you develop Insight Into your crime?

J.A.: I put myself in my victims' shoes. I thought about how they felt. I thought about their families and how family, friends, and neighborhoods were affected by what I did. I made myself think: What does their family feel now, even years later? How would my family feel if it happened to me, or someone we love?

S.B.: I removed myself from the personal feelings I had about my victim, and I got to the core of recognizing that he was a human being, a person, somebody's son.

N.C.: Being a mom and understanding that my son has issues as a result of things that happened in his life helped me understand things about my victim and what happened in his life. I also tried to listen compassionately to as many people as possible. Hearing their stories gave me compassion and understanding about how things can spiral out of control. Finally, seeing how grief and sadness can overwhelm someone, and thinking deeply about how I created this grief in another family gave me insight into the effect of my crime.

T.D.: I read my transcripts over and over again. I started out thinking my crime (DUI 2nd degree murder) was not "as bad" as other crimes. I thought to myself: I did not rob or deliberately shoot someone. But no matter how my victims died, car or gun, dead is dead. Reading my transcripts caused me to view my actions from an outside perspective and I realized that I was just as dangerous, if not more dangerous, than a madman running around in a crowded mall shooting off a gun. Once I realized how bad my actions were, I stopped trying to minimize them. I was the worst of the worst. Why not admit it? I'm already tried and convicted. That was my key to gaining insight. Putting myself in another's shoes and looking at myself.

L.G.: I started by accepting my actions. I chose to not become bitter towards the justice system. And crucially: I developed self-awareness that I had a problem with alcohol.

T.N.: I asked myself: How did I become the person that landed me in prison? Am I really dealing with the problems that caused me to get in trouble in the first place? I looked back at the time of my crime (and earlier!) and listed the harms, damage, and pain I caused, and then I carefully listed out all the ways I could have avoided those things then and how I could avoid similar things now.

VR.: Three things that helped me develop insight to my crime were: 1. One-on-one counseling; 2. Self-help and self-discovery groups; and 3. Victim-awareness groups.

DS: I wrote out my whole life story as I remembered it. It was one of the hardest things I've ever done. Some parts of my life were very painful to write about, and that pain brought old feelings back. Some of these feelings were the feelings that created my negative thinking and led to my crime. By making myself look at this, I figured out that I was a tired victim who became a victimizer. That understanding gave me insight and the strength to never commit a crime again.

If you could only give one small piece of advice to people on the Inside, what would that be?

JA: Be real, and truly abandon all gang activity. Stop all drug or alcohol use and stop all criminal activity! Live as a good citizen now in prison! Don't wait! Better yourself and reject the prison criminal culture.

S.B.: Learn how to be genuinely honest. Don't down play your responsibility. When it comes to 115s, 128s: Just be honest about how you felt at that moment, faced with a difficult situation. Be honest about what led to the incident; don't water down the truth.

N.C.: View your prison stay as a type of "school" and learn as much as you can on how to professionally, kindly, and confidently deal with people from ALL walks of life. Pretend every interaction in prison is one with your boss or co-workers. That will help you when you are in the work force out here.

T.D.: You are the most important person in your universe. Your friends and homies will eventually go home without you. You need to live for yourself and do what is best for yourself. Don't allow others to get you caught up in drama. The stakes are too high: With the Youth Offender Parole law you have a better chance of going home.

LG.: Be yourself. Understand the dynamics of prison but never let that change who you are.

T.N.: Focus on going home and remind yourself you need to sacrifice now in order to go home. Sacrifice means letting go of the temporary temptations in prison. Tell yourself: Prison is temporary and won't last forever. I am going to focus on what's important: making myself eligible for parole.

V.R.: Accept total responsibility for your actions and your inactions.

DS: Practice doing good. We all practiced doing wrong until we ended up in prison. So, try practicing doing good and see where you end up.

Where did you draw strength from when faced with difficult situations in prison?

JA I drew strength by remembering my most shameful moments. I would think back to the night that put me in prison. That night, I went along with the crowd around me. Everyone wanted revenge and chose the way of aggression and violence. I did not think for myself; I did not stand up for doing the right thing. I caved into peer pressure and my own thoughts of revenge. Years later in prison I was faced with similar situations. I decided to not give in to my feelings or to the pressure from people around me. I made a vow to myself to never hurt another person. I drew strength from the thought that this time around I would not hurt anyone, no matter what the situation, and no matter what the pressure. I would make the right decision when given the chance, and I was given the chance many times.

S.B.: My strength developed over time. I had 20 115s when I went to Board. I entered prison defiant and angry. I couldn't understand the consequences of my actions. I was impulsive; my emotions led me, not logic. But you can change. Each time you make a good decision and walk away, it develops a pattern in your brain. Just start small. To change my patterns, I did this small thing: I would buy a chocolate bar (I love chocolate...) I'd put it in my drawer, and make a decision to be disciplined and not eat it. I'd look at it but not let myself eat it ... for months. That little step was one step toward being in control of my life. I also found a sense of perseverance to overcome obstacles by relying on my experience running track in high school. With sports, you have the competition, fear, apprehension, but you find some strength within yourself to push a little further to try to win. You might fail, but you start again.

N.C.: I practiced self-talk, telling myself, "don't get in the mud with the pigs." And I practiced 'healthy detachment' and would picture my son standing beside me and think how I would react if he were there.

T.D.: I drew (and still draw) strength from God. Behind those walls we have no one we can really trust or to turn to but God. I talked to God all the time in my heart and my head. God gave me the strength to go on. After six parole denials and untold habeas denials, God came through for me and opened the door with a release date.

LG.: I played by the rules. I did not lose my sense of identity of who I was as a person. A wise old convict once told me, "Be yourself and that will keep you from getting caught up."

T.N.: I focused my mind continually on GOING HOME. That made it clear to me that everything happening in prison is temporary, including having to "man up" or save face. Try to be straight up and let everyone know you ain't into it anymore, and you're doing your best to go home.

V.R.: I became involved in something more important than myself (for me it was the dog program) and any time I faced conflict I had to decide if it was worth losing involvement with that program.

D.S.: I remembered Jesus was tempted and how he handled himself. Pride is every man's downfall. Everyone needs to choose a first step. What was your first step?

J.A.: I thought a lot about when and why I started using drugs and alcohol, and when and why I joined a gang. Then I thought about when and why I stopped doing these things. And, last, but most importantly, I thought about what would keep me from turning to drugs, alcohol, and gang participation in the future.

S.B.: I began believing that I was worthy of changing. I don't know when it happened, but at some point I knew that I was a valid individual even though I didn't get that validation from family or peers. At random points I would get some validation—even a little thing, like a corrections officer saying something small or my having some success in school. I realized I didn't have to live up to the person the court said I was. I could be someone different.

T.D.: My first step was to enroll in an NA meeting. Second step was to sign up for a vocational trade. The Board requires both. PIA and paid jobs could wait. Get the requirements out the way first.

LA: I started by accepting my reality. Then, I took advantage of anything I could to improve my life. I earned my H.S. diploma while in jail. Since being paroled I graduated from college, earned a Master's degree, and am working on my doctorate. That could be you, too. If you are a high school drop-out, get your GED or diploma. Look at what's in front of you and grab any opportunity to learn to be a better person.

T.N.: I started by promising myself that I would do everything possible to stay away from trouble. Then, I figured out what I needed to do for my own rehabilitation. What are your main problems? (Drugs, alcohol, anger...?) Take a step, even a small one, to deal with those problems. Then keep dealing with them, whether with AA/NA programs or whatever. And, don't ever stop. Take any self-help programs and therapy you can!

V.R.: My first step was to stop getting 115s and 128s. My second step was to begin attending self-help groups.

D.S.: My first step was accepting life as it was. I decided that there was no need to resist life, I just needed to just do my best with the way things are. Next, I worked on my thought process. I believe you have to change your mind and your way of thinking to really change your actions.

Any last words of advice to those on the inside?

J.A.: Even though you are in prison, find ways to give back to your community. You can do this by programming positively, by improving yourself, and by living a good, clean life. Help others around you. Never give in to negative people. Don't give into despair. Your life has value right now.

S.B.: Don't let others define who you are. You have the power of choice. You can choose how to respond and who to be, even in the place you are right now. You do not have to die in prison.

N.C.: It is possible! Work on yourself, and aim to parole being your best self, physically, spiritually, and emotionally. Come to terms with what you do when the going gets tough: Is it productive? Finally, if you are using drugs then go back to the drawing board and figure something else out because that will be what defines you.

T.D.: The Board and the Governor are powerful, but they do not control destiny. No matter how many times you have been denied parole or if this is your first time going to the Board, you have to keep your eyes on the road ahead. A personal example: Who would have thought that an ex-lifer who was denied parole six times would become an attorney helping lifers? The future is wide open for you. Stay focused on it.

L.G.: Do not ever give up on yourself. Learn to forgive yourself. Hold on to hope.

T.N.: I used to think I will grow up, grow old, and die in prison. I thought none of my rehabs matter and the Board will just shut me down. Finally, I became tired of the excuses I was making to myself. I challenged myself to beat the odds. It happened! You can do it, too. You now have a law in your favor that will help. Pick yourself up and do everything you can to make sure you walk out that gate.

V.R.: At 23 I faced the death penalty. I received 25-to-life plus 12 years, and I really did not give a damn. Continuing to be active in my addiction resulted in my getting about 10 115s and 30 128s. Then I just got tired of it all. I had a lot of inner demons to conquer, and I tackled them one by one. I was found suitable and released after serving 29 years. You can be found suitable for parole, too, even if you have racked up a lot of 115s. Make the decision to turn things around today.

P.S.: Change requires action. You can't think your way into a new way of living, but you can live your way into a new way of thinking. Just start with every single small act and do the right thing. When you sit, sit. When you stand, stand. Whatever you do, don't wobble.

CHAPTER 30

LIFE AFTER LIFE (A SUCCESSFUL RETURN TO SOCIETY)
By Kunta Kenyatta (A Former Ohio Prisoner)

Looking back on when this journey all began it almost doesn't seem real. The Cuyahoga County Jail, with its concrete slabs for beds in closet size cells was where I got my wake-up call. I was 18 years old with a 30-year prison sentence; my out date was in October of 2016. I thought I would never see the streets again; and I did my prison time accordingly. In fact, once I got settled into doing my bit, I did not even think about ever going home again. That is, until about eight years later in 1994, when I received some clemency papers in the mail from the governor's office. I didn't know anything about clemency, had not even thought about it. Plus this was only about a year after the Lucasville Riot, and I was in the hole in Lucasville on an extremely violent case. So clemency was a long shot, to say the least, but I gave it a shot anyway by filling out the paperwork and sending it in. Needless to say, my request for clemency was denied, but along with that denial, I was informed that I would be receiving a parole hearing in October of 1998, which was much more reasonable than my maximum out date. Knowing about that date gave me a little something to hope for, even though the parole board at that time was giving out what became known as "super flops", so, I had to switch gears and try to stay out of the way.

As it turns out, staying out of the way was too much of a task for me. You see, by now I was a marked man. After the Lucasville Riot the state of Ohio had decided that they were going to build a 500-bed super maximum security prison, whether they had 500 super maximum prisoners in the state of Ohio or not, and there was never any doubt that I was going. And in Ohio you cannot be paroled from maximum security, let alone super maximum security, so I had to think of another way. Ohio's super maximum prison in Youngstown did not open up until May 1998, but the majority of those who the Department of Rehabilitation and Corrections had planned to send there were kept in isolation until that time, including myself; and because I was scheduled to see the parole board that same year I was not transferred to Youngstown until after my parole hearing. I tried to prepare for my parole hearing as best as I could. Being in handcuffs and shackles didn't help my cause at all. But, anyway, I was told to do another 39 months with no conduct reports and I would be released in January of 2002. However, this was an empty promise, because in Ohio's prison system a prisoner's security status overrides the parole board's decision and there was no certain way of working your way out of the super maximum prison at that time. They had every intention of keeping me there until 2016.

The Ohio State Penitentiary (OSP) in Youngstown was indeed a brand-new facility, the first new prison I had been in. You had your typical concrete slab for a bed, stainless steel sink and toilet, plus desk and stool that most cells had but this institution had a new space saver design that gave you much more open space to pace. Some prisoners took being in OSP pretty hard. There were three suicides in the first 18 months of it opening. That's an average of one suicide every six months in an institution that was only designed to hold 500 prisoners, and it had not yet been fully filled. Some prisoners would smear feces all over their body, while others would be screaming in their cells at the top of their lungs and banging their heads up against their cell doors. This 23-hours-a-day isolation had its effects on everybody in some way or another. Except for me that is, or at least I thought; until I got released and to this very day I have a real hard time having people around me.

I knew that in order for me to come out of this one it was going to take a lawsuit, and a pretty damn good one. So, before I even arrived here I wrote a pamphlet titled "Kunta Kenyatta vs The State of Ohio", to generate some outside support for the cause. But, ultimately it was the three suicides that got the attention of the ACLU. By the time lawyers form the outside got involved I had already had my paperwork done. Because of the Prison Litigation Reform Act, a prisoner has to exhaust his institutional remedies before a lawyer can take up the case. But, the ACLU wanted to make this a class action lawsuit, which is understandable; so, I had to wait for enough of the other prisoners there to do the same. In the meantime, the clock was ticking, and I had a January 2002 projected release date from the parole board that I had to meet. The lawsuit was filed in January 2001 and it was due to go to trial in January 2002. I was released from OSP and sent back to Lucasville in October 2001. Being back in Lucasville was actually worse than being in the super maximum prison. The cultural differences between the prison staff down here in the Southern tip of Ohio and the prisoners who came mostly from the inner cities up North was just too much to overcome, but this was part of the process that we had to go through at that time.

A month after being back in Lucasville I was taken back up in front of the parole board, this time minus the handcuffs and shackles (however, this time they didn't show up in person but on a TV screen), and the first thing they wanted to know is what did I do to get back in maximum security. I thought it was strange that they did not realize that I had never left maximum security, except to go to high maximum security, that is, so my response was, "I didn't do nothing." Being that I have not had a conduct report since the last time I had seen them (and in fact I hadn't had a legitimate conduct report in nine years, by this time), this was a true statement, but if they didn't know that I had been in high maximum security for the past three years, I sure as hell was not going to tell them. However, I was given another year and told to be out of maximum security in that year if I wanted to go home. That was fine except for the fact that I don't have a say-so as to where I'm housed at in this prison system. According to the policy a prisoner was supposed to have their security status reviewed at least once a year, and if they didn't have any conduct reports in that year, their security level should go down. Well, it has not worked that way for me in almost a decade now.

The lawsuit turned out to be my ace in the hole. Once the lawsuit went to trial all of those who were named in the suit were pushed out of OSP and out of the system, except for those on death row, so this seemed like my best shot yet. And sure enough, when I went up for a status review, the reviewing committee recommended that I be transferred out of maximum security to Trumbull County Correctional institution (TCI). This was both a good thing and a bad thing. On the one hand I was glad to be getting transferred out of maximum security after 16 years. But on the other, I was hoping to be sent anywhere other than TCI. Throughout my incarceration I have been an outspoken prisoner's rights activist which was the source of the majority of my problems with the prison administration. Since 1995, I accumulated over one hundred published writings, all of which was banned from TCI. Back in 1996 I even received a letter from the warden of TCI telling me that she did not want me corresponding with inmates in her institution. So I didn't know how I was to take this transfer to TCI; but, of course, I was going. On my 34th birthday, July 9, 2002, I was transferred out of the Southern Ohio Correctional Facility (Lucasville) to Trumbull Correctional Institution. For the first time during this whole ordeal I was out of maximum security, on the bus ride to TCI I still could not believe they were actually going to go through with this. Upon my arrival at TUI, I was immediately placed in the hole and told "happy birthday and welcome to TCI" This was done I was told, because they did not have any cells available in the general population and I would be out as soon as a bed came open, but it still took everything I had in me to keep from going ballistic. The next night I was let out of the hole and placed in population, and surprisingly I didn't have any more problems at this institution other than trying to adjust to this new environment, this was no doubt a major change from what I was used to.

In TCI they didn't have cell blocks, they had pods. Prisoners in TCI were able to hang out in their pods all day. Each pod had a TV room, a library, a ping pong table, exercise equipment, microwave oven, ironing board, ice machine and general seating area. There were some prisoners at TCI who never left the pod, but what amazed me most was that, at TCI, you could have a room full of prisoners watching the TV and another prisoner would walk into the TV room, and without saying a word change the channel. In Lucasville, back before the riot when they had day rooms with TV's in them, you could not pay nobody to touch the TV, it was a guaranteed instant death sentence. But my mission at TCI was to stay out of the way for four months, then I was out of there – home sweet home. I also had a cousin at TCI who I had not seen in 20 years. Eventually we were allowed to cell together until he was transferred to North Central Correctional Institution in Marion, about a month before I was scheduled to leave.

The parole board always comes two months before the actual time you are eligible for parole, because if you are granted a parole it would usually become effective two months after it was granted; which gives them time to do their pre-parole investigation. So, I went back to the parole board in September of 2002. This time when I went to the parole board there was only one parole board member on the TV screen, the newest parole board member at that time, but by no means new to me or

Ohio's prison system. Peter Davis was the ex-head of the Correctional Institution Inspection Committee, the state senate committee that was responsible for over-sight of all Ohio's prisons; the same committee that most of my complaints against the prison system over the years would end up with, now he was presiding over my parole hearing. Peter Davis had me worried for a minute there. Whenever the board shows upon TV, instead of in person, that alone is a bad sign, but after a few tense moments I was granted a parole to become effective on November 26, 2002.

Being granted a parole was, without question, a major accomplishment for me, but I still had two more months of walking on eggshells before I was home free, because, any conduct report at this time, not only would that parole be gone, it would more than likely take me many years before I could get myself back to this point. So, the main thing was to be very careful as to who I let know that I did have a parole (officer or inmate). This was by far the hardest part of my whole bit. I'm not used to letting people run over top of me and a few times I almost lost focus. Plus, the closer I got to that date, the more anxious I would get. I just couldn't sit still. It seemed like everything was coming my way, including advances from TCI female staff, and I had to keep reminding myself that I didn't come all this far to mess this up now. But what kept me on course more than anything else was the fact that if something did happen to cause me to lose my parole, I didn't know how I would have been able to explain it to my family; they just would not have been able to understand it.

I was released on parole from Trumbull Correctional Institution November 26, 2002. After signing all the necessary paperwork and collecting the little funds I had on my account, I was taken in a van to the Greyhound bus station in Downtown Warren. This is the first time that I had been in a motor vehicle without being handcuffed, shackled and belly chained in a long time. The Greyhound bus station in Warren is nothing more than a hole in the wall. If I wasn't dropped off right in front of it, would never have noticed it. And, when I bought my ticket, I was told that the buses only come through Warren every ten hours, and there would not be another one until just after 5:00pm (which was seven hours away). So I got on the pay phone to call my family, who was waiting to hear from me, so they could come and pick me up. After messing with the phone for a while, I soon realized that this phone was not like the phones in prison, or like the pay phones that I remember using before my incarceration, nor did I have a clue as to how to use it. That left me with only one choice, so I just hung out in Warren for the next seven hours, and I did manage to find a clothing store that wasn't too costly so I could get out of my prison clothes, and a fast food spot so I could have my first literal taste of freedom. But Warren was like a ghost town and it didn't take long for me to get bored with it. I couldn't help but think how lucky I was that I wasn't paroled to this city. If I was I would probably catch an escape case.

When I finally arrived at the Greyhound bus station in Cleveland it was a stark contrast. There were people everywhere, too many people, and I had to get away from around there as soon as possible. By the time I got to my mother's house, where I was paroled to, it was late in the day and everybody had been expecting to hear from me early that morning; so they were starting to get worried, but once I came in the house it was all good. I was lucky to have family after doing so many years (a lot of former prisoners did not have this luxury), but they could not afford to take care of me. My first day home was for family, the next day it was time to get down to business. Being on parole I had to report to my parole officer the very next morning, plus there was some lawyers in downtown Cleveland that had some money of mine. When you've been in the system as long as I have, you are going to run into a lot of familiar faces down at the state building, and it's a good thing that they know the routine because I sure has hell didn't, so I was glad to see them, too. When I told them who my parole officer was, they all said that I've got the worse one, but that don't surprise me at all, I wouldn't expect anything else. The first task my parole officer had for me was to go get a piss test, and between him and applying for jobs, I would piss test an average of once every three days for the next 90 days. Of course, this was a waste of time because I knew full well that, if I was going to make it in this society, getting drunk or high was not an option that I had at my disposal.

At the time I was taken off the streets I was in the middle of a lawsuit settlement that involved a car accident. By the time the money came to pay for the damage to my car I was already in the County Jail. So I told the lawyers handling the case to put the money in an interest baring account for me. As soon as I finished my business with my parole officer, this is where I was headed. By now that original $1300 should have built up to quite a bit of change, and if everything went right I would be right back on track. But, of course, this would not be the case. The lawyers were more than a little surprised to see me. In fact, they were so sure that they would not see me again in life that they split that money up between themselves a long time ago. I don't know how long they had planned on giving me the run around, telling me that they were having trouble locating my money in their escrow account, but after about a month or so I got tired of playing games with them and under the threat of violence, at the risk of violating my parole, they gave me back my original $1300, without any of the interest my money should have been earning. But in the meantime I had no money, no job and no real prospects for the future.

I got my driver's license four days after my release, which was excellent progress when I consider how long other former prisoners struggle with this small-but-necessary step towards re-establishing one's self back into society. The day after Thanksgiving my brother offered to drive me to take the written test for my temporary license, which is no longer written test, but a touch screen computer test. After passing that I wanted to schedule the driving test about a week away, to give myself time to practice, but I was told that the only opening was for the following morning, so I took it. It was my sister who took me to this test and, surprisingly enough, I passed it without having driven in 6 years. At that time my simple strategy was to put in at least 100 job applications a month. That way the odds would be in my favor. After all, my luck cannot be that bad. But all I got out of that was a few odd jobs here and there from people who knew me, so I had to come up with another strategy or I was going to be in trouble, because freedom in America is not free; it costs money, and lots of it.

By this time, I was receiving letters from prisoners with all types of requests, because I had made an announcement in a newsletter that circulated to prisoners nationally that I had been paroled and included my mailing address; they had no way of contemplating the fact that I didn't even have bus fare to get myself to the places I needed to be. On top of that, parolees now had to pay $20 a month for their parole, or my parole would be extended (keeping those 14 years I had left on my sentence over my head longer), plus my parole officer required me to find a job, in the poorest city in the nation (Cleveland) as a condition of my parole. Not all parole officers enforce these conditions on those under their supervision. Some parolees don't have to be bothered with their parole officers at all. But again, I had "the worst one."

One day, not too long after my release, I was at home in my room in the attic of my mother's house catching up

341

on some reading and my parole officer came by. So, after answering the door my mother let him know that I was there and she would go and get me, but instead of him letting her come get me he wanted to come up there himself so he could see what I was doing. However, instead of him catching me off guard he was the one who was caught off guard, because he could not believe that after doing 16 years in prison, I would get out here to all this freedom and be sitting at home in my room reading a book; so, he ordered a psyche evaluation on me.

November of 2002 was a good month for me, because of my release, and the little bit of progress I was able to make in the last few days of that month, by getting my license. But December was a different story. The holidays are always a good time to be home with your family, but it's hard to get your foot in the door when all the business doors are closed until after the holidays, so the only thing I could do was wait. Some people are alright with being totally dependent on others, but me, I have a real problem with it, and during that month of December I tried everything from going to town hall meetings with the mayor, to signing up with local job match programs. At the town hall meeting the mayor promised, in front of the cameras, that they would be doing something to help me; but, of course, once those cameras were gone, her and her whole team was missing in action. And the job match program told me that their classes would start after the holidays, so if it were not for my nephews, who had all out-grown me during my incarceration, giving me their hand-me-downs, I would not even have had clothes to wear at this point.

The New Year came without my participation in any of the festivities. Wasn't no need me being out there in somebody's way. But once it was over, I was on the move attending classes and putting in applications. There were quite a few jobs that turned me down because I did not have my own transportation, which is ultimately what forced my hand with these lawyers who had my money, but once I got that little bit of money I was in for a rude awakening. In the 1980's, $1300 could have got me just about any used car I wanted, but in 2003 it couldn't get anything worth having. However, if it was not having a car that was stopping me from getting over the hump, then I was determined to have one. At the very first car dealership I went to, I was told that having no credit. was worse than having bad credit, I thought that this was just a car salesman trying to get me to admit to having bad credit, but I learned the hard way that when you are in your mid 30's and you have never used a credit card, paid a bill or taxes, to the creditors you don't exist. There is no way for you to explain to them that you have spent your entire adult life in prison.

It was one of my nephews who told me about the auto auction where I might be able to get a good deal on a car. This auction (although called ADESA Cleveland) was all the way down in an Akron suburb, but I was able to make arrangements for my sister to take me down there. ADESA (Auto Dealers Exchange Serving America) is primarily a dealer's auction with at least 53 auctions throughout the United States and Canada, but they do let the public bid on the repossessed cars, and ADESA Cleveland held their auction on Thursdays. In order for me to be at the auction on Thursday I was going to have to break up my routine of job hunting and miss my job match class. And attendance was very important to those running this government funded program, but I went on and took off January 9th to go get me a car. As it turns out, I wasn't prepared for the auction. It was more like being in a gambling casino than trying to buy a car, and as fast as the auctioneers were talking, I needed a lawyer to keep up with them. I also did not have a big enough bankroll to compete with the dealer's that were there. Needless to say, I did not come away from there with a car, but I did leave from there with a job —on the only day since my return home that I wasn't looking for a job.

Now that I had a job, that was 34 miles away from where I stay, I really needed a car in a bad way. I had heard enough about the buy-here-pay-here car lots to not want to be bothered with them, but now I was running out of options fast, so I gave it a shot. The first car I bought since returning to society was a 1989 Nissan Maxima. It was the cleanest car on the lot. After I finished paying for it, I would have spent $3900 on it, by far the most I had every spent on a car, and it stayed on the road a frill 20 minutes before it died out. I wasn't about to play no games with these people who sold me this car and I didn't care nothing about their sold 'as is' policy. I gave them an ultimatum and they fixed the car for free, plus gave me a check for the tow. Now that I had transportation to get back and forth to my new job, I still had one more obstacle to clear before I could rest easy; my parole officer had to approve of me having a job that was in a different city from that which I was paroled to. Well, he didn't like it, but as long as I came right back to Cleveland after work every day, he said it would be okay, and of course he was going to be checking on me and the job. Perhaps I should mention that ADESA is not in the practice of hiring ex-felons. It just so happens that on their application the question was, have you been convicted of a felony within the last seven years? And of course, my conviction had been long before that, so my answer was "no" and their background check only went back ten years, so I slipped in on a technicality that was discovered too late.

January 2003 ended with me having a job, a car, and because of my participation in the job match program, I would also be receiving a check from the program every month that I kept my job for up to a year. Then, while on my way to work, early in the morning on February 7th 2003, I was caught in a snowstorm. Visibility was very bad so I moved to the left lane of the highway. I knew that traffic was not merging on and off the highway from this side, and there was a football-field-size divider between me going Southbound and the Northbound traffic. Next thing I know, I caught a glimpse of a shadow approaching from the left. I did manage to react to it but I still ended up under an Ohio Department of Transportation salt truck that had crossed all the way over from the Northbound lanes into the Southbound traffic. Miraculously I escaped without injury, but my car was demolished. However, this would turn out to be my lucky break, if you can consider getting run over by a salt truck lucky. But when you have buzzards' luck like I do, you have to take what you can get and this was going to be the fifth time that I would be filing suit against the state of Ohio.

It would take the state of Ohio nine months to pay me for this failed assassination attempt, so in the meantime, I was back to roughing it without my own transportation. I did have some fellow workers who were willing to give me a ride back and forth to work and I also managed to get my cab license with Ace Taxi, so I was able to lease a cab, any time, day or night, and make some extra money doing that. When people used to ask me wasn't it dangerous for me to be driving a cab at night I would say, "Yeah, it is, but I usually won't bother people without being provoked." Then, in March 2003, I received a call from my aunt asking me to come and get my cousins' truck. My cousin was in one of Ohio's prisons doing a year. His truck was in his mother's name, but she didn't drive and somebody had broken into it and stolen the sound system. So, I went over to her house and got the truck. This was a 1993 Eddie Bauer edition Ford Bronco, I put it back together and kept it for him until he got out in September. By that time, I had gotten used to it, and so I bought me a 1995 Eddie Bauer edition Ford Bronco. My work with cars goes all the way back to learning how to steal them in 1980 when I was just 12 years old, long before I actually knew how to drive them without tearing them up; now I was detailing them out at the auction.

Up until this point I had been on the constant grind. I did no going out or kicking it trying to have a good time. Then on March 14th my pen pal from England came to visit me. My pen pal had been writing me for two years prior to my release and a while ago she had expressed to me that she wanted to have a more personal relationship with me. I told her that I had never been involved with a white woman before, but if she was still corresponding with me by the time, I got out of prison I would be willing to give it a try. But I could not understand why a beautiful woman, with money, living in England would be looking for love in a high maximum-security prison in Ohio. When she came, she came with one of her friends, who was a black woman that was scared to death of black people; both of them were scared to death of Cleveland. The first thing they decided was that my cousins' truck wasn't good enough for them to be riding in, so they went out and rented a brand-new car, which was fine with me. Everywhere we went people were curious about them because they were spending big money and talking with an accent. This caused a lot of people to approach us which only added to their fear. One day, while we were having lunch in a Downtown restaurant, an elderly man came over to talk to us out of curiosity, and as he was talking, he slightly touched my pen pal on her shoulder and she fell out like he had assaulted her. I had to escort the old dude out of there. Before she left, she told me that if we were going to be together, I was going to have to move to England because she could not be around these types of people. I told her we don't have to worry about that because I'm just about sick of her anyway. But when she got back home, she did call me and thank me for looking out for her and her friend, plus she apologized for being so fussy, so I promised her I would come to England and see her as soon as I got off parole. England would end up being my first trip abroad.

Once my pen pal was back in England, it was back to the old grind for me. My cousin's truck required a lot of repairs to keep it on the road, plus the gas needle did not work and it ran out of gas on me one time before, so I would go to the gas station every morning before I headed off to work. At the gas stations at 4:30 in the morning is where I would see a lot of former prisoners, some of whom who were kingpins and legends in the penitentiary. They were now out here pan handling and begging people for spare change at gas stations. "Go do a robbery or a burglary or something, have some dignity," is what I used to tell them. But for those former prisoners who I came across that were trying to establish themselves out here in society, I would direct them to the job match program that I went to, plus I would show them how to go about getting their cab license and other resources that were available to us, while steering them away from the shams that were out here. This was the most that I was able to do at that time, because I had not yet established myself out here in society. Some followed up on the information I was able to provide, others had to find out the hard way that there is more honor in prison amongst thieves than out here in society. It was around this time that I ran into Muhammad (aka Polo). Muhammad was released from prison in December of 2002 after serving 18 years and we were close friends during the beginning of my journey through Ohio's prison system. I had not seen him since I left the Ohio State Reformatory in Mansfield back in 1990. Muhammad was living in a house that rented to people just getting out of prison off 105th street, a couple of blocks from my mother's house. He shared this single-family house with two other people, which is not the ideal conditions for someone coming out of prison after doing so many years, but neither is trying to get by on SSI. So, I showed Muhammad all the resources I had used to help me get on my feet, including job match and places where you can get free groceries once a month just

347

for living in the neighborhood, which was one of Cleveland's empowerment zones. Muhammad followed up on all of the information that I gave him, so I felt that he had a good chance of making it. The only thing he was having problems with was his driver's license.

Then, one day, Muhammad told me that he had met this woman that he wanted to go see, but she lived in Elyria and he didn't have no way of getting there. I told him that I would take him. When we started off for Elyria, Muhammad called his friend on the phone to let her know that he was on his way and that one of his partners was bringing him, so she told him that she had a friend and would he ask me if I would be interested in going on a double date. I agreed to this thinking that even if she is not my type, I could play wing man for just one night. It wasn't until we got to his friend's house that I found out that she was a 20 year old white girl (Muhammad was 38 years old at the time), and the friend she had for me to go out with was a 19 year old white girl with a 35 year old mother (I was 35 years old at the time). Muhammad's friend was living with her father and he wasn't none too happy about us being over there to see his daughter and she had to tell him a lie to get out of the house. So, when we got to her friend's house I wasn't about to go in the house. Both of these girls were still in high school, so I told her to call her friend and have her come out to the truck.

After hanging out in Elyria and Lorain with these girls for a little while, they decided that they wanted to go to Cleveland and hang out. I said as long as they could arrange for a ride back, I would take them, because I wasn't bringing them back to Elyria. They said that they would stay with their cousin overnight and she would bring them back in the morning. On the way to Cleveland, a police car rode past us with its sirens sounding. The first thing these girls did is take some weed off their person and throw it down on the floor of the truck. Both Muhammad and are on parole with big time hanging over our head, but the police were after somebody else. When we arrived in Cleveland these girls did not know where their cousin lived, nor were they able to contact her on the phone, so they had to spend the night with Muhammad and the rest of the people who stayed at this house. I wasn't taking them nowhere near my mother's house.

Before the night was over Muhammad was yelling at these girls saying, "How could y'all be so stupid." I had to remind him that these girls were teenagers. One was 19 and the other one had just turned 20 and that's what teenagers do, "dumb shit". We were the adults and it was us who should have known better. We didn't have no business letting these girls hang out with us and Muhammad would end up paying the price for it. One of the girls ended up getting into it with one of Muhammad's housemates, so Muhammad stood up for her. The police were called and Muhammad's parole was violated. He did get back out, but his dreadlocks were cut off as he was processed through reception because parole violators go straight back to prison from the county jail. Some lessons come hard but Muhammad did manage to get him another apartment. He also gave up his SSI for a job at H.H. Greg, plus he gave up young girls for women his age.

Then in April 2003, the American Friends Service Committee (AFSC) criminal justice program here in Ohio asked me to come and be a speaker at their Prison Activist Conference on Ohio State University's campus in Columbus. I had worked with the AFSC a lot in the past so I agreed as long as they arranged for me to have a ride down there. I didn't trust my cousin's truck to be going that far and I didn't know my way around Columbus at that time. When I got to the conference, they were selling copies of the very first pamphlet I had published, Criminals + Confinement = Conniption. This pamphlet was writing in support of the AFSC National

Campaign to End Control Units in 1995. This was also an award-winning pamphlet that kicked off my reputation as a writer. At this conference, attorney Alice Lynd and I were to speak about the conditions at the super maximum prison in Youngstown and the lawsuit against it. There were also a lot of other prison reform advocates and groups at this conference that would be covering other prison related issues. The majority of those who were involved in these types of issues in Ohio were already familiar with me through my writings. Some of them had even corresponded with me while I was incarcerated, but other than Staughton and Alice Lynd, who came to visit me while I was at OSP, none of them had seen me before.

As I move about the crowd, I soon realize that these people didn't realize that I'm Kunta Kenyatta. I could be standing right next to somebody and they would say, "I hear that Kunta Kenyatta is supposed to be speaking here, which ought to be interesting." I don't know if it was because of my black militant writing or my violent prison record, but people had developed a mental image of me being a 6'5" 250 lb monster with a pitch-black complexion. When it was time for me to go up on the podium, it blew their minds, and when I went amongst them afterwards they were saying things like: "you look so young, I was expecting a much older guy," "you are just a little guy, that was you causing all that trouble in there?" Some of the people there wanted me to stay in Columbus, host a little radio show that they were trying to put together and all type of stuff; but this I had to decline. Before I was going to be able to help somebody else, I was going to have to first establish myself. I didn't even have my own reliable transportation to get to Columbus, they had to arrange for somebody else to bring me here. Plus, I was on parole, and if my parole officer had known that I was down here speaking at this conference, I would have been violated.

My parole officer even gave me a hard time about going to my family reunion in Philadelphia. I asked because I felt that it was a reasonable enough request, but he was skeptical about this. I understood that the parole board assigned to him the cases that they felt were going to be a problem, but they did not explain to him the reason why they felt I was going to be a problem, so he didn't know how to take me or what to be looking out for. He was dealing with a highly disciplined soldier. The traps that he would normally have so much success with was not going to be even a temptation for me. He told me that he didn't want me to have a cell phone while I was under his supervision because he didn't want me using it to deal in drugs. Even the prison officials knew when they were running drug raids, drug tests and drug investigations that it would be a waste of their time to involve me in that mess. The prison officials didn't tell him that they considered me to be a radical agitator, organizer and activist. But I never missed an appointment, payment or anything else while I was on parole, so after my year was up, he had no choice but to let me off papers. So, 2003 ended pretty well for me. In October, I got my own truck which was much more dependable than my cousins, and in December I was off paper. Now was much more independent and I could finally move out of my mother's house, because that was something that my parole officer just wasn't going for. But first I was going to be flying to England, and the first thing I had to do was get a passport. You can apply for these at the main post office in any city. I applied for mine at the Beachwood Post Office. At the time it was $75, but the price is going up every year. The next thing I had to do was book me a flight and I found on the World Wide Web a round-trip e-ticket for $500. I'm still trying to get used to all this computer technology. But, on March 17th 2004 (St. Patrick's Day), I was on my way to England. This was my first time flying. I'm not too particular about heights, but this wasn't too bad. To make the trip I had to fly from Cleveland to Chicago and from Chicago to London. It was a nine-hour flight and I arrived in London in the middle of the night. Eastern Time USA is five hours behind England's time, but I got plenty of sleep on the plane, so jet lag was not going to be a problem for me. However, as I walked for miles to baggage claim, then more miles to customs, I could not help but think that this was a bit excessive for an airport.

My pen pal lived in the West Midlands of England. This was near Birmingham and about a three-hour drive from London, but my pen pal was there to pick me up at the airport. This was not long after the Madrid, Spain train bombings and the follow up investigation that discovered that those who funded these attacks were in England seeking political asylum, and this is what stayed in the news during the time I was there. England has a lot of immigrants; they have a negative stereotype for every category of immigrants. Those from the Middle East and India were called asylum seekers who were living off the British tax payers while plotting terrorist attacks around the world, and all the West Indians were either drug dealers or prostitutes. They were convinced that I was a Jamaican gigolo going in out of this woman's condominium. When I was eating my McDonald's with my hands, everybody in the restaurant was looking at me like I was a heathen; in England they eat everything with a knife and fork, including burgers and fries, which was a bit too much for me. Their money was worth twice as much as the U. S. dollar so anytime I used my bank card, I was getting charged double for it. My leather trench coat cost 225 British pounds – the same as 450 American dollars. But I did have a real good time while I was over there, up until it was time to go. When I flew in to London my flight was the only flight that was arriving at that time of the night, but I was leaving on a noon flight. Now I see why the airport was as big as it was, and I don't ever want to be around that many people at one time again in life. I stood in line for four hours. There were millions of people packed into this airport and I was mad as hell.

Vacations are a very necessary part of life for me, and each time I go on one it gets harder and harder to come back. But this was just my first one and I came back revitalized. Now it was time to get back to business and the next step for me was getting my own place. The housing situation in Cleveland is ridiculous, but at this time I didn't have anything else to compare it to, so I didn't know just how ridiculous it was, and I began my search here first. At the prices they were asking for rent in Cleveland, I might as well be paying a mortgage, so I teamed up with my ex-girlfriend from 20 years ago, who was on section 8. I was going to get a house in my name and she was going to move in and let her section 8 help me pay the mortgage. But, because of my lack of credit, the banks wanted me to attend a first-time homebuyer's class, have my job for three years, a cosigner and at least $3000 down. I didn't feel like jumping through all these hoops but I didn't see any other option at the time so I got in the Key Bank First-Time Home Owners class and kept my eyes open for something better. From visiting some of my coworkers in Akron, which I was able to do now that I was off parole, I noticed that the rent was a lot more reasonable than what they were talking about in Cleveland, and this was a lot closer to my job, so I was seriously considering making that move to Akron.

In the meantime, I had to make a trip to Cincinnati. I was supposed to go down there in January and speak to this local group that was involved in the rallies against the police murders that had been taking place there, but there was a snow storm which put that on hold. Cincinnati was the city that gave me the most support during my incarceration. This was probably because my writings used to appear regularly in the "Street Vibe", which is a newspaper that advocates for the homeless and has a wide grassroots circulation, so I committed my July

4, 2004 weekend to Cincinnati. I arrived in Cincinnati on Friday and parked my truck in a field in the Over-The-Rhine neighborhood. Local activist Sunny Williams and former prisoner Black Tone came down to meet me. Sunny gave me a tour of the "Street Vibe" publishing office, the Drop in Center, and the shower houses for the homeless. Tone was saying: "Damn, I live here and I didn't know they had all this down here," and they did have some damn good facilities for the homeless in Cincinnati. At the Drop In Center, the first floor was a dorm area that let anybody who needed a bed drop in. For those who wanted to participate in the program, they could work their way up to a more private room on one of the higher floors, and for those who went on to get a job they could move into their own apartments across the street for $100 a month; then they could go to the shower houses and get fresh clothes plus get the clothes, they had, washed. Tone said "Damn, I need one of those apartments, I wish my rent was $100 a month."

While I was in Cincinnati, I was going to be staying at Tone's apartment. Tone had spent quite a bit of time in prison himself and was in the super maximum prison during the time I was there, so after my tour I spoke with Sunny a little while longer, then he went on his way. Tone was saying that his apartment was a mess and he was going to get a maid to clean the place up. I asked, "Where are you going to get a maid from," so he said: "We have maids down here in Cincinnati and all you need to get one is to have a place for them to stay. My dude Veil already has one and I'll just go and borrow his." So, we headed over there, stopping on Dayton Street along the way. Tone wanted to show me his Pit Bull which he kept over at this ex-girlfriend's house. He said his ex-girlfriend used to look good before he went to prison, but now she was close to 400lbs. So he just wanted to be friends with her now, but she still wanted a relationship. When we got their Tone brought out his

354

dog. This was a big dog, and me and this dog didn't get along at all. Tone's ex also had one of her friends over at her house and she did look good. So, Tone introduced me to her and we made plans to go out before I left Cincinnati. Then we were off to see Veil about this maid. Veil was also a former Ohio prisoner who was recently released, but he hadn't been in none of the prisons I'd been in so I didn't know him personally. Veil was staying at his sister's place and she had one of those monitors on her ankle that would notify her probation officer if she left the house.

When we got their Veil's sister was having a fit about Veil having the maid over there and Veil leaving his son there for her to watch. Veil's sister was a real slim woman but she raises a whole lot of hell, so the maid had to go anyway. The maid was a young girl. I had guessed she was 32, but she was actually only 18. Her parents were on drugs so she was placed in foster care while she as under age but at 18 she was on her own. She had a lot of silk and polish for an 18 year old. She had a part-time job and she would clean houses in the neighborhood for a place to stay because she didn't want to stay in the shelters. So, off we were. Me, Tone, Veil and the maid went to Tone's apartment up on Mount Aubuim. When we got there, we dropped the maid off Tone let her know what she needed to do and we started on out the door. Then she stopped us asking what should she do if the phone rings? Being that Tone didn't have an answering machine or caller ID, he said, "Answer it, "but this is where all the trouble started. After we hung out for a while, we dropped Veil off and went back over on Dayton Street. When we got there, we ran into another former Ohio prisoner, Smoky, who was Tone's cell mate in Lebanon, Ohio, so now the three of us were standing out in front of Tone's ex's apartment talking. The next thing I know we start hearing screaming in a voice loud enough to shake the trees. "Nigga!" "Nigga!" "Nigga!" And I'm like, "What the hell is going on?" It was Tone's ex. She had called Tone's apartment and the maid answered the phone and now she was going nuts. She then kicked the dog out and was in the process of throwing all of Tone's belongings out of her apartment.

Tone went inside to try and get things worked out with his ex. Now it's just me, Smoky and this damn dog standing out here. The later it got the more people started coming around Dayton Street and it seems like they all wanted to get past where we were standing; but they was afraid of the dog, so I went to get the dog's collar so people could get by. The dog took off running from me so I chased him for a little bit, but then I said the hell with him. When I got back Smoky was gone, so now I'm just standing out there. As far as I knew, there was only a church sitting back behind the apartment. Later I would learn that there was an afterhours spot connected to the church, and people had a serious problem with me standing out there in front of this spot. Then the white T-shirt wearing boys got gathered up across the street from me showing me their guns. Now, I didn't want to have to leave Tone because he didn't have a ride home, nor did I want to get involved with his domestic issues, so I figured I would go Downtown for a little while then come back and get him. When I got Downtown, I met a woman who invited me over to her place to hang out. After being over there for a little while, I decided that it was time to go back and get Tone but this woman told me that I wasn't going nowhere; so, I had to wait for her to fall asleep in order to make my escape, and that was about 5:00am.

By the time I got back to Tone's apartment he was already there with the maid and the dog. So, I took the maid out to breakfast and asked her what had happened. She said, "Well, she just called there and went off on me saying "what you doing over there answering his phone?" and that she was on her way over." Then I asked "What you say to her?" She said, " I told her she wasn't gonna get in." After we got finished eating, I took her back to Tone's place. Then me and Tone went to get Veil; when we got back to Veil 's sister's place, she was going off again, because she didn't have no cigarettes and she couldn't go get none with that monitor on her ankle. So, she wanted Veil to go get some cigarettes for her. Veil told her, "Give me your car keys if you want me to go to the store for you, and don't worry, I'm going to bring your car back." She said, "I'm not worried about you bringing my car back because your friends are not going nowhere until you do get back." I said "Hold on, what I got to do with this?" I been in Cincinnati two days and I've already been held hostage once already.

We also went to see Cello up on College Hill. Cello had been in Lucasville and OSP with me. He was now doing pretty good, getting SSI and working under the table, because you have to work under the table to keep your SSI, which don't make no sense to me. SSI gives prisoners (who qualify) a $1500 check when they first get out, then $500 a month after that, as long as they don't get a job. But, nobody can live off of $500 a month, so why wouldn't they want those who get SSI to be paying taxes back into the system? With the little punk jobs that ex-felons get we need to have two sources of income anyway, and Cello had been able to put that together. Later that night, I went to River Boat Gambling in Indiana with the woman I had met over at Tone's ex's house. She seemed like a real nice woman, and she was until she got in that casino; that's when I saw that she had some serious issues. I had $40 that I was willing to spend in this casino, just as a night out and something to do, but if I didn't win anything by then, that was it. When I went to get her, she was already hundreds of dollars down, and when I tried to pull her away from the machine she said, "Get away from me." It was like once she heard those bells and whistles, she transformed into another individual and she didn't snap back to her senses until she had lost everything. Now, she was wondering what she was going to do. Well, I didn't know what she was going to do because I couldn't help her, so I took her on home and I went back to Tone's spot.

The next day after the maid made it her business to be up and out of there early in the morning, there was a knock at the door. Tone opened it and in come two women with high heel shoes, miniskirts and spike collars on; they were talking crazy, too. The one who was doing all the talking said, "I heard that you had one of your dudes from Cleveland down here and that you had went out with some other bitches last night, how you gone play us?" Tone said, "Where you hear that from?" She answered, "I called here, and where that tramp at that answered the phone?" Then she said, "We got some business to take care of right now but we gone be back tonight and we are going to go to Shakers to get our groove on, then we are coming back here to get our fuck on," and they left. I said, "God damn Tone, what the fuck be going on around here?" He said, "Man I been caught up in this madness since I've been out here." Then Tone got a call from a friend of his who had been placed in an insane asylum by his family, and he wanted Tone to come see him and I went with him. I was a little bit apprehensive about letting the doors of that asylum lock behind me as we went in there, but I tried to remain calm. The guy he went to see was also a former Ohio prisoner and was indeed insane, and we were visiting right in the general area where all those held there hang out. When it was time to leave, I was glad to be getting out of there, but on our way out the door, guess who we see? Smoky, the same guy that disappeared on me my first night here on Dayton Street, and he's talking about, "Sign me out of here." I asked him what he was doing in there, and he said, "They just came by and picked me up when we were standing out there on Dayton Street, and they brought me here." That was it for me, I was done, I got out of Cincinnati.

During the time I was in Cincinnati I received a call from a woman who used to work at my job through a temporary employment agency. She had stabbed the guy she was living with and she wanted me to bond her out of the Stark County Jail, so I had this to deal with as soon as I got back to North East Ohio. The Stark County Jail is in Canton, Ohio, right on state route 62, and about 70 miles away from where I was staying in Cleveland, with my job in the middle. Since I wasn't going to be able to do anything on the holiday I went home first, then went to work the next morning, and then to Canton when I got off work Her bond was originally set at $15,000 and I could have got her out for 10% of that, but by the time I got there the judge had raised her bond to $40,000, putting her well out of my reach. At first I didn't know why the judge had more than doubled her bond, but I should have known that racism was a factor. See, once the judge found out that she was a black woman who stabbed a white guy, her chances of coming out of this one with probation vanished. I tried to explain this to her, because I know this system all too well, but she felt that because she was defending herself that she would get a break, like other women do. If she would have stabbed me after I put my hands on her, she would have never went to jail; but she is an older black woman who stabbed a younger white dude. She is not only going to jail she is also going to prison; people with $40,000 bonds don't get probation.

Anyway, she gave me her keys so I could look after her house, plus keep her bills and rent paid until she went to court. This was something I could easily handle, plus it was going to give me a little refuge from Cleveland, so I agreed. Her rent for a whole month was only $400. This was unheard of in Cleveland. In Cleveland, you were looking at $1000.a month rent on a whole house off the top, and you couldn't get an efficiency apartment for $400. So now my search for my own home switched to Canton. While I was getting a little taste of being on my own, I knew now it would not be long. It was a cozy little house, completely furnished, cable TV, but junky. So I took a page out of my Cincinnati chapter and brought a woman from Cleveland, who was fresh out of jail and needing a place to stay, to Canton to keep the place clean. My maid worked well for a little. Making it out of Cleveland can be a breath of fresh air for anybody and living in Canton was like living in the suburbs compared to Cleveland, plus I was able to live on half of what it was costing me to live in Cleveland. So I was able to take care of her and myself without driving the cab on the side, as long as she continued to cook and clean. But the more we became involved sexually the less she felt she had to do until it got to the point where she would say to me, "I'm not use to having to do work, and all I have to do is look good." And this was a 40-year-old woman talking like this. You would think she'd know better by now, so I told her, "Okay with your bad self." Then one day when I came home from work to dirty dishes everywhere, no food cooked while she's out getting drunk with her friends, I just packed all her stuff up in the truck and waited for her to come home, then I took her back up to Cleveland and dropped her butt off. If a person wants to get out of prison and run the streets getting drunk or getting high, Cleveland is the place for them, the city will no doubt accommodate you; either there or Cincinnati. But I can only help those who at least attempt to help themselves.

Once the woman whose house I was staying in went to court and got sentenced to four years, it was time for me to move on. The original plan was for me to have her belongings put into storage, but I had found me a house by then. All I needed to do was find a way to get financed without any established credit. When I first spotted my house, I knew that this was the one I was going to somehow end up with. Out of all the houses that I looked at this was the only one that I didn't have to write down the address to remember (1834), because I went to prison when I was 18 and I got out when I was 34; there is no forgetting that. When I went to the open house to view it there was nobody there, so I called the real estate agent who came out, let me in and left, asking me to lock up when I leave. This house was built in 1965 which is relatively new for a house. It was ranch style with two bedrooms and a full finished basement, plus it was all electric, which means no gas bill, and that was the deciding factor. Working through my nephew, I was able to get a financer who was willing to finance the house after l had been on my job for two years, and by this time I had been working the same job for a year and a half, so I explained this to the real estate agent who said, "You don't have to wait for that, if you want the house I can get you in there." So, I did what was called a land contract, or rent- to-own, with my rent payments going toward down payment and my credit rating. The house would be signed over to my name in six months to a year. So instead of having to put my friend's stuff in storage, I was able to store it in my own basement which is only around the corner from where she was staying when she caught her case. This was a good year for me, I have to admit, and am my own harshest critic. But if I continue to progress at this rate it will soon be hard to believe that I walked out of prison just a few years ago without nothing but raw determination at my disposal.

I spent the New Year's Eve in Akron and as I was leaving the city my truck took two bullets in the passenger side. This was a bad omen for the year 2005, but again, I was determined to survive. After filing my taxes for the year I owed $1300 to the IRS and this almost put an end to my planned vacation for this year, but I know how important it is for me to take my breaks from the day-to-day grind in this dog-eat-dog society; and if I don't take a vacation I'll get burnt completely out. This year I was going to Jamaica and I used a travel agency right here in Canton to book this trip. It cost me around

$1000 for my round-trip flight and hotel stay for a week. I was to leave on March 14th 2005. I was going to be flying out of Cleveland so I drove up to my mother's house the night before. I left my truck in her garage and took a cab to the airport. This was a direct flight so I didn't have to go to no other American cities or change planes, which was a good thing because airports are very stressful places and I still have a problem being in those crowds.

When I flew out of Cleveland it was 38 degrees outside. Four hours later, when I arrived in Montego Bay it was 88 degrees outside. I knew that I didn't ever want to go back then. When I stepped off the plane they were asking, "You Rasta Man, why this your first time you come to Jamaica man?" As soon as I got to my hotel, I set my bags down and got out those hot clothes. I hit them streets, getting as far away from the resort area as soon as I possibly could; and it was on from ding to dong. By St. Patrick's Day I was all the way on the other end of the island in Kingston. Kingston was by far the most dangerous place I have ever been. By mid-March they had over 300 murders in the city that year. This qualified the city as a war zone, and they were walking around with AK-47s and M-16s over their shoulders. They needed their National Guard to protect armored cars when they were loading or unloading money. In Kingston there were two lines wrapped around the American Embassy, one for those who were picking up U.S. Visa's and the other for those applying for U.S. Visas. With a 45% unemployment rate in Jamaica all of this is understandable.

When I travel to foreign countries, I don't like to hang around no tourist spots. I like to kick it like I would in the hood. The key to not having problems is to not letting anybody know that you are from America. The best part of the trip was the fact that $100 U.S. was worth $6030 Jamaican dollars, and I spent one thousand dollars, which was around three quarters of a million Jamaican dollars, so I lived the life style of the rich and famous for a week. Coming back to the U.S. was the hard part, and I mean this literally. They did not want to let me come back through customs. I only had a few little bags but they searched me three times. They wanted to know where I worked, where I was born and all sorts of things like that. They figure that I was either trying to sneak into the country with a fake passport or I was smuggling drugs. I couldn't be just going over to Jamaica on a simple vacation. Maybe if I was from there or it was an occasion like a honeymoon or something, but not just a simple vacation.

Now that my fun was over, it was back to reality; which was, between the money I spent on vacation, paying the IRS and few other misfortunate mishaps, I was dead broke. And gas prices were sky high, so I couldn't even afford to be driving that long way back and forth to work. So June 2005 I took the other week of paid vacation I had at my regular job and worked temporary jobs through a temp agency down here in Canton. This is how I got back on my feet, getting paid by two jobs while working one; we have to do it that way sometimes. During this time my part time freelance activism involved finding out the whereabouts of the family members of some prisoners from Canton who had lost touch over the years. This issue becomes very important when they are getting close to seeing the parole board and need a place to parole to, but little did I know that I was about to be right back smack dab in the middle of this prison activist stuff. Around this time I received a letter from YSU journalism professor Daniel Sturm, who was going to write an article about the super maximum prison in Youngstown, and he wanted to interview me. I agreed to do the interview and it was to take place at my house on July 9, 2005, my 37th birthday.

Not such a big deal at the time because the O'Jays were in town for the weekend, having a street named after them, and I was going to celebrate by seeing them in concert; but, these things have a way of taking on a life of their own and you never know how one thing can lead to another and another and another, until you are knee deep in, all over again. But in the meantime, I was still doing my thing. It was hot out and that meant that almost every weekend I was on the road, and a couple of weeks after the interview, while in the area, I decided to drop in Steubenville. At that time Steubenville was one of the only two significant-sized cities in Ohio that I had never been to. Now, I've been everywhere from Zanesville to Painesville; from Lucasville to Steubenville; I've toured all of Ohio. If you were in the Youngstown area and want to travel to Steubenville, Ohio, state route 7 will take you there. But, while half of Youngstown is Cleveland Browns fans, the other half is Pittsburgh Steelers fans. Once you start getting close to Steubenville, you will start seeing the skull and cross bones signs saying, "No Browns fans beyond this point."

When I first arrived in Steubenville, I was in the wrong area. I had old ladies coming up to me asking me if they could touch my hair because they never seen anything like that before. So, I had to find out where the hood was at and I knew they had a hood because there are too many people in prison from Steubenville for them not to have a hood; so, I went to the downtown area. Downtown Steubenville is just a few streets this way, few streets that way and that's it. If you don't pay attention, you'll miss it, so I parked my truck and got out and walked. Downtown Steubenville sits right on the Ohio River, and if you cross one of those bridges going over the river you will be in Weirton, West Virginia. It's the same way that the Cuyahoga River separates the East and West side of Cleveland, but standing right there on the Ohio River you cannot help but notice the contrast between Ohio and the Mountain State of West Virginia. While I was walking, I met an elder lady by the name of

Ms. Shirley who offered to show me around, and it was her who introduced me to her daughter Laurie. Me and Laurie hit it off really well from the start and she gave me the rest of my tour of the city. The following week, Laurie came up to Canton to see me, which meant a lot to me and we have been together ever since.

Then, Daniel Sturm's article came out in the press. My name being in the article caused my mail load to increase with more prison mail. One of the main requests now was for me to help with bringing some publicity to these cases that stemmed from the Lucasville Riot, which have innocent people still locked up in OSP, and because these are people I know and have broken bread with over the years, I cannot say no. So, I began to make copies and send them to the different places that I think might be able to do something. Then, I made arrangements to personally take some of this information to the next CURE-Ohio meeting in Columbus to see what this organization that I was still a member of would be willing to do, since it had been awhile since I've been to one of these meetings.

I became a member of CURE-Ohio back in 1996, not long after its rebirth in Ohio. I was in the middle of pushing the African Name Change Drive when another prisoner sent me one of the CURE-Ohio's newsletters that was announcing that one of Ohio's senators had introduced a bill in the Ohio House of the Senate that would ban people in Ohio who had been convicted of a felony from being able to get their names legally changed, and CURE-Ohio was against the bill. So I joined CURE-Ohio at that time and immediately began pushing a CURE-Ohio membership drive along with the African Name Change Drive and the Reparations Education Drive, and my Community Petition for Release that I was pushing at that time. After that, CURE-Ohio went through some troubled times with prisoners because the then president, Paula Eyre (who was teaching college classes in one of Ohio's prisons in the Dayton area when she met and married an Ohio prisoner), had sabotaged a statewide prisoner work stoppage that was organized by prisoners in support of state senator Jeffrey Johnson's Senate Bill 182 (parole reform) in order to get her husband out of prison on parole. Prisoners were furious and I was one of those actively involved in calling for her expulsion from CURE-Ohio in 1998 for this betrayal. She continued to run the organization, but under fire from prisoners a Prisoner Advisory Board was created and I was selected to serve on this board in 1999.

Anyway, when Paula Eyre's husband did get out he left her and ran off with a younger woman, so she quit CURE-Ohio and wrote a nasty article in the newsletter that contradicted all the work she did in the last ten years. So now you had the three remaining members of the Board of Directors: Karen Thimmes, Ellen Kitchens, and Michelle Baker doing everything that they could just to hold this huge statewide organization of prisoners and their loved ones (out in society) together. When I got to CURE-Ohio's general membership meeting in November of 2005, on the agenda for the meeting was to fill vacancies on the board, and me and Beverly Seymour were nominated to serve on the Board of Directors. I spent that night in Columbus and I called Laurie and I let her know what it meant to be participating in this type of thing on this level (that our whole lives will be consumed by this), and she said that she thought that was good and that she thought I should go for it. So at the next CURE-Ohio meeting in January 2006 I was confirmed to serve on the Board of Directors as Prisoner Liaison, and from there it did not take long for my prediction to come true; I was right back in the thick of things. Also, at this meeting in January 2006 there was a discussion of cutting off the subscriptions of the newsletters to the prisoners who had not paid their dues, and this I was totally against because I know that when I was in prison that the state of Ohio's then Attorney General Betty Montgomery had found a way to rob all prisoners who had successfully sued the state of any funds on their account, and I was one of them. So, I said that they have grants for this type of work, and with CURE-Ohio's long history of non-profit work in the state, we are eligible for them, and I was willing to go and meet with a professional grant application writer in order to possibly acquire a grant. So, the following weekend I went to Youngstown to meet with Angela Jancius (the wife of Daniel Sturm) because she is an accomplished grant application writer. While in Youngstown, I got involved with organizing Youngstown Prison Forum Prison Conference that Angela and Daniel was a part of; I was also to be a speaker at this conference. Because of his article on the super maximum prison in Youngstown (which I gave an interview for), Daniel was also invited by the American Friends Service Committee to represent Ohio at their National Stop Max Campaign meeting in Chicago (from March 31st to April 2nd of 2006), but he was unable to attend so this invitation was offered to me and I accepted it.

However, it was vacation time once again for me and vacations always come first in my eyes, plus this year I was going to Brazil; so I was going to be in Chicago for half of that meeting, once I got back. When the head of CURE-National, Charlie Sullivan, got word that I was going to Brazil, he contacted me to ask me to put together a report on the prison conditions in Brazil for the National CURE Conference that will be held in Washington D.C. in the end of June 2006. I thought this was going to be an impossible task because I don't even speak the language that is used in Brazil, but Laurie learned enough Portuguese to interpret for me and put the report together, plus, we were able to get a DVD on the Carandiru prison massacre. Carandiru was a prison in Sao Paulo Brazil that had a riot after a prison soccer game in 1992. After the police surrounded the prison, the prisoners surrendered, but the police went in and shot everybody they could find whether they took part in it or not and when international human rights organizations started looking into the matter the prison was demolished to destroy the evidence. But my trip to Brazil was lovely. Laurie and I spent our first two days in Sao Paulo, the next two in Rio De Janeiro, then back to Sao Paulo for the last two days. In addition to our passports, which are good for ten years, we also had to have visas to go to Brazil, and these are good for the next five years so we may have to go back some day.

Our flight out of Sao Paulo, Brazil took us to Washington D.C. where we changed planes and continued on to Cleveland. In Cleveland I got Laurie into a cab to my mother's house and I had to jump on another plane to Chicago. The further West I got the colder the weather was and after coming out of the warm weather of Brazil, I wasn't enjoying the windy city of Chicago too much. There were a lot of big names in the prison reform movement there, and big-name prisoner advocates, but it was also a lot of people that I'd never heard of before in attendance. The main thing everybody was struggling with was how to get the people from the affected communities involved. I suggested that we make sure that people see the benefits to doing this type of work, because there are some benefits to doing this besides those who are getting paid $35,000 to $40,000 a year for doing what I do for free. I also should have mentioned going to the prisoners and asking them to pull together their personal supporters. I've been finding it surprising as to how many people there are doing this type of work that have absolutely no contact with prisoners.

The following weekend after the Stop Max meeting, I went to visit Siddique Abdullah Hasan in OSP (Ohio's High Max). Ohio's DRC started two new policies: one was to allow Ohio's prisoners to receive money from anybody who wanted to send it to them, and the other was to allow Ohio's prisoners to have up to 15 people on their visiting list without having to prove a relation to their visitors. Nobody seems to know what made the DRC do this now because this was one of those things that they were dead set against in the past. But in this policy (that was sent to me by my cousin Tony Harris from one of the prisons in Marion) they had no mention of whether ex-felons would still be banned from visiting, or if they would they continue to stop people from visiting more than one Ohio prisoner unless they were kin. Hasan was the ultimate test case for this policy. Not only was he on death row in the highest security prison in the state for being the "ring leader" of the Lucasville Riot, he was also in an institution that I had been in and sued, so all the prison officials there knew me. So, the theory was if they let me in to visit Hasan then anybody could visit any prisoner in Ohio. I have known Hasan since 1987, back on 3 southeasts in the old Ohio State Reformatory in Mansfield, where I did my first four years before being transferred to Lucasville. We were also in Lucasville and Youngstown together so it was good to get to see him again; and see that he is still holding up despite the situation (being on death row for not being able to control the violence that took place during the Lucasville Riot), and he was glad to see me, too.

Now that the first part of the test had passed and I was able to get in and visit with Hasan, it was now time for the second part of the test, which was to see if after letting me in to visit Hasan, if they were going to let me in another prison to visit another prisoner. So, I waited until the weekend of the Power Net Reentry Conference in Dayton, because I was going to be on that side of the state anyway to visit my cousin Tony Harris in Marion. It was harder to get in this medium security prison than it was to get into high max, but throughout my experience with the system, these lesser security prisons have always been pettier, and I did eventually get in. My cousin was also glad to see me. I had got to cell with him at TCI, briefly, before he was transferred to Marion and I was released. A lot of time has passed since then and a lot of things have happened, but it seems like it was only yesterday. After that visit was over, I headed on down state route 4 to Dayton.

The Dayton conference was by far the most elaborate conference I had ever been to. There was a lot of pump and pageantry involved, $40-a-plate meals, a host of celebrities and plenty of state officials. I had come there to help man the table for CURE-Ohio, but when we got into the workshop it was the people who had been to prison that they wanted to hear. And there were quite a few of us there with a story to tell: Gary Reece, served 25 years before being freed by DNA evidence; Walter Smith, served 11 years before being freed on DNA evidence; and Khalil Osiris, my comrade, who served 15 years and is now a professor at Write State University. It was at this conference that I saw the need for there to be a pamphlet such as this one, and as much as I hate writing, all this got started with me coming to the realization long ago that if I want to get something done, I have to do it myself, so here I go again.

The weekend after the Dayton conference I went back to visit again with Hasan. This time I was able to see both Hasan and Bomani Shakur (aka Keith Lamar). Bomani was also on death row because of the Lucasville Riot, and in his case people who admitted to committing murders during the riot was given lesser sentences and protective custody if they were willing to say that, "Keith Lamar made me do it," in court. And the list of people being held in high max on death row or doing double life goes on and on: Greg Curry, Derek Cannon, Eric Scales, Kweisi Mugabe (aka Derrick Mathews)...The state was able to get an average of seven murder convictions for each person killed during the riot when in fact, in most cases, only one or two people did each killing. But during that time, prosecutors were able to get a jury to do anything they wanted to a bunch of people who were already in prison anyway.

The Dayton Conference went a long way in preparing me for the upcoming Youngstown Conference. This one I played a part in organizing and I was hosting a workshop, which is a lot of work for grassroots organizers who do not have access to a large amount of funds. It's a good thing that I've been doing this for so long; not only can I host a workshop without having time to prepare, I also have a lot of old friends and comrades who I can count on for support. In order to rally some support for the conference, I gave an interview on a Cleveland radio station two days before the conference with Justin Hons (aka J. Uprising). Justin published my pamphlet "Kunta Kenyatta Vs the State of Ohio" when he was a college student at Kent State University, back in 1998/1999. He also re-published my first pamphlet "Criminals + Confinement = Corruption." He is still active within the community, and is now indeed a veteran activist and prisoners' advocate. The interview went well by all accounts that we received, and now it was on to the Youngstown Conference.

The turnout for the Youngstown Conference was not what we hoped it would be, but all the workshops were very good and the media was all over it so this conference was a greater success than any of us expected. Even my baby, Laurie, was on TV and I expect a lot to come out of our efforts. But in the meantime, I'll just keep on doing what I do; hopefully we'll get some more people to pick up the slack, too. Some prison reform workers ask me how can I go back in a prison to visit after being locked in one for so long, I tell them that they turned the old OSR in Mansfield into a haunted house and I even went there this past Halloween. They say they'll give anybody who can spend the night in there $100. If they were offering that during the four years, I did there, I would be doing alright by now. When your whole life has been like a horror movie, where you had as many close calls and pit falls as I have and still manage to come out of no worse for ware, there is not too much left to be afraid of. So being that I got drafted into this battle, I'm going to continue to give it my all and at the rate things are going, sooner or later something has got to give, and I'm willing to bet that it won't be me.

CHAPTER 31

STANDARD ON TREATMENT OF PRISONERS

ABA Criminal Justice Standards on Treatment of Prisoners

Standard 23-1.0 Definitions

Correctional agencies, facilities, staff and prisoners

a) The term "chief executive officer of the facility' means the correctional official with command authority over a particular correctional facility. In a prison, the chief executive officer is the person usually termed the warden: in a jail, the chief executive officer might be a sheriff or might have a title such as superintendent, jailer, or commander. The term includes the chief executive officer's emergency designee, if, for example, the chief executive officer is away or ill and has turned over command authority for a period of time.

b) The term "correctional administrator" means an individual with responsibility for system-wide operations and management.

c) The term "correctional agency" means an agency that operates correctional facilities for a jurisdiction or jurisdictions and sets system-wide policies or procedures, along with that agency's decision-makers.

d) The term "correctional authorities" means all correctional staff, officials, and administrators.

e) The term "correctional facility" means any place of adult criminal detention, including a prison, jail, or other facility operated by or on behalf of a correctional or law enforcement agency, without regard to whether such a facility is publicly or privately owned or operated. The term "correctional facility" does not include a facility that serves solely as an immigration detention facility, a juvenile detention facility, or a juvenile correctional facility.

f) The term "correctional official" means an individual with responsibility for facility-wide operations and management.

g) The term "correctional staff" or "staff" means employees who have direct contact with prisoners, including both security and non-security personnel, and employees of other governmental or private organizations who work within a correctional facility.

h) The term "governmental authorities" encompasses persons in all branches and levels of government whose conduct affects correctional policy or conditions, including members of the legislature, prosecutors, judges, governors, etc.

i) The term "jail" means a correctional facility holding primarily pretrial detainees and/or prisoners sentenced to a term of one year or less.

j) The term "prison" means a correctional facility holding primarily prisoners sentenced to a term of at least one year.

k) The term "prisoner" means any person incarcerated in a correctional facility.

Other defined terms

a) The term "counsel" means retained or prospectively retained attorneys, or others sponsored by an attorney such as paralegals, investigators, and law students.

b) The term "effective notice" means notice in a language understood by the prisoner who receives the notice; if that prisoner is unable to read, effective notice requires correctional staff to read and explain the relevant information, using an interpreter if necessary.

c) The term "health care" means the diagnosis and treatment of medical, dental, and mental health problems.

d) The term "long-term segregated housing" means segregated housing that is expected to extend or does extend for a period of time exceeding 30 days.

e) The term "qualified health care professional" means physicians, physician assistants, nurses, nurse practitioners, dentists, qualified mental health professionals, and others who by virtue of their education, credentials, and experience are permitted by law to evaluate and provide health care to patients.

f) The term "qualified mental health professional" means psychiatrists, psychologists, psychiatric social workers, licensed professional counselors, psychiatric nurses, or others who by virtue of their education, credentials, and experience are permitted by law to evaluate and provide mental health care to patients.

g) The term "segregated housing" means housing of a prisoner in conditions characterized by substantial isolation from other prisoners, whether pursuant to disciplinary, administrative, or classification action. "Segregated housing" includes restriction of a prisoner to the prisoner's assigned living quarters.

h) The term "serious mental illness" means a substantial disorder of thought or mood that significantly impairs judgment, behavior, and capacity to recognize reality or cope with the ordinary demands of life within the prison environment and is manifested by substantial pain or disability. It includes the status of being actively suicidal; severe cognitive disorders that result in significant functional impairment; and severe personality disorders that result in significant functional impairment and are marked by frequent episodes of psychosis, depression, or self-injurious behavior.

PART I: General Principles

Standard 23-1.1 General principles governing imprisonment

a) A correctional facility should be safe and orderly and should be run in a fair and lawful manner.

b) Imprisonment should prepare prisoners to live law-abiding lives upon release. Correctional authorities should facilitate prisoners' reintegration into free society by implementing appropriate conditions of confinement and by sustained planning for such reintegration.

c) A correctional facility should maintain order and should protect prisoners from harm from other prisoners and staff. Restrictions placed on prisoners should be necessary and proportionate to the legitimate objectives for which those restrictions are imposed.

d) Correctional authorities should respect the human rights and dignity of prisoners. No prisoner should be subjected to cruel, inhuman, or degrading treatment or conditions.

e) For a convicted prisoner, loss of liberty and separation from society should be the sole punishments imposed by imprisonment. For a prisoner not serving a sentence for a crime, the purpose of imprisonment should be to assure appearance of the prisoner at trial and to safeguard the public, not to punish.

f) A correctional facility should be appropriately staffed.

376

g) Correctional officials should implement internal processes for continually assessing and improving each correctional facility.
h) A correctional facility should be monitored and regularly inspected by independent government entities.
i) A lack of resources should not excuse treatment or conditions that violate prisoners' constitutional or statutory rights.
j) Governmental authorities should provide sufficient resources to implement these Standards.
k) If governmental authorities elect to furnish prisoners any services by contracting with private providers, those contracted services should comply with these Standards, and the correctional agency should monitor and ensure such compliance, and should be held accountable for doing so.

Standard 23-1.2 Treatment of prisoners

In order to effectuate these principles, correctional authorities should:
a) provide prisoners with:
  • humane and healthful living conditions;
  • safety from harm, including protection from punitive or excessive force and protection from abuse by other prisoners and staff;
  • necessary health care;
  • freedom from staff harassment and invidious discrimination;
  • freedom of religion and substantial freedom of expression;
  • conditions conducive to maintaining healthy relationships with their families;
  • to participate in constructive activity and rehabilitative programs; and

- comprehensive re-entry planning; and
b) implement effective policies and procedures for:
- investigation and resolution of complaints and problems:
- fair and rational decision-making: and
- internal and external oversight of correctional operations.

PART II: Intake and Classification

Standard 23-2.1 Intake screening

a) Correctional authorities should screen each prisoner as soon as possible upon the prisoner's admission to a correctional facility to identify the prisoner's immediate potential security risks, including vulnerability to physical or sexual abuse, and should closely supervise prisoners until screening and follow-up measures are conducted.
b) Correctional authorities should screen each prisoner as soon as possible upon the prisoner's admission to a correctional facility to identify issues requiring immediate assessment or attention, such as illness, communicable diseases, mental health problems, drug or alcohol intoxication or withdrawal, ongoing medical treatment, risk of suicide, or special education eligibility. Medical and mental health screening should:
- use a properly validated screening protocol, including if appropriate, special protocols for female prisoners, prisoners who have mental disabilities, and prisoners who are under the age of eighteen or geriatric:
- be performed either by a qualified health care professional or by specially trained correctional staff; and

- include an initial assessment whether the prisoner has any condition that makes the use of chemical agents or electronic weaponry against that prisoner particularly risky, in order to facilitate compliance with Standard 23-5.8(d).

c) Correctional authorities should take appropriate responsive measures without delay when intake screening identifies a need for immediate comprehensive assessment or for new or continuing medication or other treatment, suicide prevention measures, or housing that takes account of a prisoner's special needs.

Standard 23-2.2 Classification system

In order to implement appropriate classification, housing, and programming, correctional officials should:

a) implement an objective classification system that determines for each prisoner the proper level of security and control, assesses the prisoner's needs, and assists in making appropriate housing, work, cellmate and program assignments;

b) initially and periodically validate an objective classification instrument to ensure consistent and appropriate custody and other decisions for each correctional facility's population, including prisoners' assignments to multiple occupancy cells or dormitories; and

c) ensure that classification and housing decisions, including assignment to particular cells and cellmates, take account of a prisoner's gender, age, offense, criminal history, institutional behavior, escape history, vulnerability, mental health, and special needs, and whether the prisoner is a pretrial detainee.

Standard 23-2.3 Classification procedures

a) Initial classification of a prisoner should take place within [48 hours] of the prisoner's detention in a jail and within [30 days] of the prisoner's confinement in a prison.

b) Each classification decision should be in writing, and should set forth the considerations and factors that led to the decision; the written decision should be made available to the prisoner, and should be explained by an appropriate staff member if the prisoner is incapable of understanding it. Correctional authorities should be permitted to summarize or redact information provided to the prisoner if it was obtained under a promise of confidentiality or if its disclosure could harm the prisoner or others or would not serve the best treatment interests of the prisoner.

c) If a classification decision has an impact on a prisoner's release date or ability to participate in facility programs, correctional authorities should provide the prisoner an opportunity to request reconsideration and at least one level of appeal.

Correctional authorities should review the classification of a prisoner housed in a prison at least every [12 months], and the classification of a prisoner housed in a jail at least every [90 days].

Standard 23-2.4 Special classification issues

a) Classification and housing assignments should not segregate or discriminate based on race unless the consideration of race is narrowly tailored to serve a compelling governmental interest.

b) A prisoner should not be separated from the general population or denied programmatic opportunities based solely on the prisoner's offense or sentence, except that separate housing areas should be permissible for prisoners under sentence of death. If convicted capital offenders are separately housed based solely on their sentence, conditions should be comparable to those provided to the general population.

c) Correctional authorities should assign to single occupancy cells prisoners not safely or appropriately housed in multiple occupancy cells, and correctional and governmental authorities should maintain sufficient numbers of such single cells for the needs of a facility's particular prisoner population.

d) Correctional authorities should make individualized housing and custody decisions for prisoners who have undergone sex reassignment surgery or have had other surgical or hormonal treatment and present themselves and identify as having a gender different from their physical sex at birth. In deciding whether to assign such a prisoner to a facility for male or female prisoners and in making other housing and programming assignments, staff should consider on a case-by-case basis whether a placement would ensure the prisoner's health and safety, and whether the placement would present management or security problems. Placement and programming assignments for such a prisoner should be reassessed at least twice each year to review any threats to safety experienced by the prisoner. The prisoner's own views with respect to his or her own safety should be given serious consideration.

Standard 23-2.5 Health care assessment

Each prisoner should receive a comprehensive medical and mental health assessment by qualified medical and mental health professionals no later than [14 days] after admission to a correctional facility, and a comprehensive medical assessment periodically thereafter, which should include mental health screening. The frequency of periodic medical assessments should accord with community health standards, taking account of the age and health status of each prisoner. No new comprehensive medical and mental health assessment need occur for a prisoner transferred or readmitted to a correction facility who has received comprehensive health assessment within the prior year unless it is medically necessary, or the prisoner's medical records are not available. Unless a dental emergency requires more immediate attention, a dental examination by dentist or trained personnel directed by a dentist should be conducted within [90 days] of admission if the prisoner's confinement may exceed one year, and annually thereafter.

Standard 23-2.6 Rationales for segregated housing

a) Correctional authorities should not place prisoners in segregated housing except for reasons relating to: discipline, security, and ongoing investigation of misconduct or crime, protection from harm, medical care, or mental health care. Segregated housing should be for the briefest term and under the least restrictive conditions practicable and consistent with the rationale for placement and with the progress achieved by the prisoner. Segregation for health care needs should be in a location separate from disciplinary and long-term segregated housing. Policies relating to segregation for whatever reason should take account of the special developmental needs of prisoners under the age of eighteen.

b) If necessary, for an investigation or the reasonable needs of law enforcement or prosecuting authorities, correctional authorities should be permitted to confine a prisoner under investigation for possible criminal violations in segregated housing for a period no more than [30 days].

Standard 23-2.7 Rationales for long-term segregated housing

a) Correctional authorities should use long-term segregated housing sparingly and should not place or retain prisoners in such housing except for reasons relating to:
- discipline after a finding that the prisoner has committed a very severe disciplinary infraction, in which safety or security was seriously threatened:
- a credible continuing and serious threat to the security of others or to the prisoner's own safety; or
- prevention of airborne contagion.

(b) Correctional authorities should not place a prisoner in long-term segregated housing based on the security risk the prisoner poses to others unless less restrictive alternatives are unsuitable in light of a continuing and serious threat to the security of the facility, staff, other prisoners, or the public as a result of the prisoner's:
- history of serious violent behavior in correctional facilities;
- acts such as escapes or attempted escapes from secure correctional settings;
- acts or threats of violence likely to destabilize the institutional environment to such a degree that the order and security of the facility is threatened:
- membership in a security threat group accompanied by a finding based on specific and reliable information that the prisoner either has engaged in dangerous or threatening behavior directed by the group or directs the dangerous or threatening behavior of others; or
- incitement or threats to incite group disturbances in a correctional facility.

Standard 23-2.8 Segregated housing and mental health

a) No prisoner diagnosed with serious mental illness should be placed in long-term segregated housing.

b) No prisoner should be placed in segregated housing for more than [1 day] without a mental health screening, conducted in person by a qualified mental health professional, and a prompt comprehensive mental health assessment if clinically indicated. If the assessment indicates the presence of a serious mental illness, or a history of serious mental illness and decompensation in segregated settings, the prisoner should be placed in an environment where appropriate treatment can occur. Any prisoner in segregated housing who develops serious mental illness should be placed in an environment where appropriate treatment can occur.

c) The mental health of prisoners in long-term segregated housing should be monitored as follows:

- Daily, correctional staff should maintain a log documenting prisoners' behavior.

- Several times each week, a qualified mental health professional should observe each segregated housing unit, speaking to unit staff, reviewing the prisoner log, and observing and talking with prisoners who are receiving mental health treatment.

- Weekly, a qualified mental health professional should observe and seek to talk with each prisoner.

- Monthly. and more frequently if clinically indicated, a qualified mental health professional should see and treat each prisoner who is receiving mental health treatment. Absent an individualized finding that security would be compromised, such treatment should take place out of cell, in a setting in which security staff cannot overhear the conversation.

- At least every [90 days], a qualified mental health professional should perform a comprehensive mental health assessment of each prisoner in segregated housing unless a qualified mental health professional deems such assessment unnecessary in light of observations made pursuant to subdivisions (ii)-(iv).

Standard 23-2.9 Procedures for placement and retention in long-term segregated housing

a) A prisoner should be placed or retained in long-term segregated housing only after an individualized determination, by a preponderance of the evidence, that the substantive prerequisites set out in Standards 23-2.7 and 23-5.5 for such placement are met. In addition, if long-term segregation is being considered either because the prisoner poses a credible continuing and serious threat to the security of others or to the prisoner's own safety, the prisoner should be afforded, at a minimum, the following procedural protections:
- timely, written, and effective notice that such a placement is being considered, the facts upon which
- consideration is based, and the prisoner's rights under this Standard;
- decision-making by a specialized classification committee that includes a qualified mental health care professional;
- a hearing at which the prisoner may be heard in person and, absent an individualized determination of good cause, has a reasonable opportunity to present available witnesses and information;
- absent an individualized determination of good cause, opportunity for the prisoner to confront and cross-examine any witnesses or, if good cause to

limit such confrontation is found, to propound questions to be relayed to the witnesses;

- an interpreter, if necessary for the prisoner to understand or participate in the proceedings;
- if the classification committee determines that a prisoner is unable to prepare and present evidence and
- arguments effectively on his or her own behalf, counsel or some other appropriate advocate for the prisoner;
- an independent determination by the classification committee of the reliability and credibility of confidential
- informants if material allowing such determination is available to the correctional agency;
- a written statement setting forth the evidence relied on and the reasons for placement; and
- prompt review of the classification committee's decision by correctional administrators.

b) Within [30 days] of a prisoner's placement in long-term segregated housing based on a finding that the prisoner presents a continuing and serious threat to the security of others, correctional authorities should develop an individualized plan for the prisoner. The plan should include an assessment of the prisoner's needs, a strategy for correctional authorities to assist the prisoner in meeting those needs, and a statement of the expectations for the prisoner to progress toward fewer restrictions and lower levels of custody based on the prisoner's behavior. Correctional authorities should provide the plan or a summary of it to the prisoner, and explain it, so that the prisoner can understand such expectations.

c) At intervals not to exceed [30 days], correctional authorities should conduct and document an evaluation of each prisoner's progress under the individualized plan required by subdivision (b) of this Standard. The evaluation should also consider the state of the prisoner's mental health: address the extent to which the individual's behavior, measured against the plan, justifies the need to maintain, increase, or decrease the level of controls and restrictions in place at the time of the evaluation; and recommend a full classification review as described in subdivision (d) of this Standard when appropriate.

d) At intervals not to exceed [90 days], a full classification review involving a meeting of the prisoner and the specialized classification committee should occur to determine whether the prisoner's progress toward compliance with the individual plan required by subdivision (b) of this Standard or other circumstances warrant a reduction of restrictions, increased programming, or a return to a lower level of custody. If a prisoner has met the terms of the individual plan, there should be a presumption in favor of releasing the prisoner from segregated housing. A decision to retain a prisoner in segregated housing following consideration by the classification review committee should be reviewed by a correctional administrator, and approved, rejected, or modified as appropriate.

e) Consistent with such confidentiality as is required to prevent a significant risk of harm to other persons, a prisoner being evaluated for placement in long-term segregated housing for any reason should be permitted reasonable access to materials considered at both the initial and the periodic reviews, and should be allowed to meet with and submit written statements to persons reviewing the prisoner's classification.

f) Correctional officials should implement a system to facilitate the return to lower levels of custody of prisoners housed in long-term segregated housing. Except in compelling circumstances, a prisoner serving a sentence who would otherwise be released directly to the community from long-term segregated housing should be placed in a less restrictive setting for the final months of confinement.

PART III: Conditions of Confinement

Standard 23-3.1 Physical plant and environmental conditions

a) The physical plant of a correctional facility should be adequate to protect and promote the health and safety of prisoners and staff:

- (ii) be clean and well-maintained;
- (iii) include appropriate housing, laundry, health care, food service, visitation, recreation, education, and program space;
- (iv) have appropriate heating and ventilation systems;
- (v) not deprive prisoners or staff of natural light, of light sufficient to permit reading throughout prisoners' housing areas, or of reasonable darkness during the sleeping hours;
- (vi) be free from tobacco smoke and excessive noise;
- (vii) allow unrestricted access for prisoners to potable drinking water and to adequate, clean, reasonably private, and functioning toilets and washbasins: and
- (viii) comply with health, safety, and building codes, subject to regular inspection.

(b) Governmental authorities in all branches in a jurisdiction should take necessary steps to avoid crowding that exceeds a correctional facility's rated capacity or adversely affects the facility's delivery of core services at an adequate level, maintenance of its physical plant. or protection of prisoners from harm, including the spread of disease.

Standard 23-3.2 Conditions for special types of prisoners

a) Correctional agencies and facilities should provide housing options with conditions of confinement appropriate to meet the protection, programming, and treatment needs of special types of prisoners, including female prisoners, prisoners who have physical or mental disabilities or communicable diseases, and prisoners who are under the age of eighteen or geriatric.

b) No prisoner under the age of eighteen should be housed in an adult correctional facility. Where applicable law does not provide for all such prisoners to be transferred to the care and control of a juvenile justice agency, a correctional agency should provide specialized facilities and programs to meet the education, special education, and other needs of this population.

c) A correctional agency should be permitted to confine female prisoners in the same facility as male prisoners but should house female and male prisoners separately. Living conditions for a correctional agency's female prisoners should be essentially equal to those of the agency's male prisoners, as should security and programming. A facility that confines female prisoners should have on duty at all times adequate numbers of female staff to comply with Standard 23-7.10.

d) Correctional authorities should house and manage prisoners with physical disabilities, including temporary disabilities, in a manner that provides for their safety and security. If necessary, housing should be designed for use by prisoners with disabilities;

such housing should he in the most instated setting appropriate for such prisoners. Correctional authorities should safely accommodate prisoners who are particularly vulnerable to heat-related illness or infectious disease, or are otherwise medically vulnerable.

Standard 23-3.3 Housing areas

a) Correctional authorities should provide prisoners living quarters of adequate size. Single-occupancy cells should be the preferred form of prisoner housing. Facilities that must use dormitories or other multiple-prisoner living quarters should provide sufficient staffing, supervision, and personal space to ensure safety for prisoners and security for their belongings. All prisoner living quarters and personal hygiene areas should be designed to facilitate adequate and appropriate supervision of prisoners and to allow prisoners privacy consistent with their security classification.

b) Correctional authorities should provide each prisoner, at a minimum, with a bed and mattress off the floor, a writing area and seating, an individual secure storage compartment sufficient in size to hold personal belongings and legal papers, a source of natural light, and light sufficient to permit reading.

c) Correctional authorities should provide sufficient access to showers at an appropriate temperature to enable each prisoner to shower as frequently as necessary to maintain general hygiene.

Standard 23-3.4 Healthful food

a) Correctional authorities should provide each prisoner an adequate amount of nutritious, healthful, and palatable food, including at least one hot meal daily.

Food should be prepared, maintained, and served at the appropriate temperatures and under sanitary conditions.

b) Correctional authorities should make appropriate accommodations for prisoners with special dietary needs for reasons of health or age.

c) Correctional authorities should not withhold food or water from any prisoner. The standard menu should not be varied for any prisoner without the prisoner's consent, except that alternative food should be permitted for a limited period for a prisoner in segregated housing who has used food or food service equipment in a manner that is hazardous to the prisoner or others, provided that the food supplied is healthful, palatable, and meets basic nutritional requirements.

Standard 23-3.5 Provision of necessities

a) Correctional authorities should maintain living quarters and associated common areas in a sanitary condition. Correctional authorities should be permitted to require prisoners able to perform cleaning tasks to do so, with necessary materials and equipment provided to them regularly and without charge.

b) Correctional authorities should provide prisoners with clean, appropriately sized clothing suited to the season and facility temperature and to the prisoner's work assignment and gender, in quantities sufficient to allow for a daily change of clothing. Prisoners should receive opportunities to mend and machine launder their clothing if the facility does not provide these services. Correctional authorities should implement procedures to permit prisoners to wear street clothes when they appear in court before a jury.

c) Correctional authorities should provide prisoners, without charge, basic individual hygiene items appropriate for their gender, as well as towels and bedding, which should be exchanged or laundered at least weekly. Prisoners should also be permitted to purchase hygiene supplies in a commissary.

Standard 23-3.6 Recreation and out-of-cell time

a) To the extent practicable and consistent with prisoner and staff safety, correctional authorities should minimize the periods during the day in which prisoners are required to remain in their cells.

b) Correctional authorities should provide all prisoners daily opportunities for significant out-of-cell time and for recreation at appropriate hours that allows them to maintain physical health and, for prisoners not in segregated housing, to socialize with other prisoners. Each prisoner, including those in segregated housing, should be offered the opportunity for at least one hour per day of exercise, in the open air if the weather permits.

c) Correctional authorities should whenever practicably allow each prisoner not in segregated housing to eat in a congregate setting, whether that is a specialized room or a housing area dayroom, absent an individualized decision that a congregate setting is inappropriate for a particular prisoner. Prisoners should be allowed an adequate time to eat each meal.

Standard 23-3.7 Restrictions relating to programming and privileges

a) In no case should restrictions relating to a prisoner's programming or other privileges, whether imposed as a disciplinary sanction or otherwise, detrimentally alter a prisoner's:

- exposure to sufficient light to permit reading in the prisoner's housing area, and reasonable darkness during the sleeping hours;
- adequate ventilation:
- living area temperature;
- exposure to either unusual amounts of noise or to auditory isolation:
- opportunity to sleep:
- access to medication or medical devices or other health care;
- nutrition, except as permitted by Standard 23-3.4(c):
- access to water; and
- counsel or clergy visits, or written communication with family members, except as provided in subdivision of this Standard.

b) A prisoner should not he administered sedating or otherwise psychoactive drugs for purposes of discipline or convenience, or because of any decision relating to programming or privileges; such drugs should be used only to treat health conditions.

c) Restrictions relating to a prisoner's programming or other privileges, whether as a disciplinary sanction or otherwise, should be permitted to reduce, but not to eliminate, a prisoner's:

- access to items of personal care and hygiene:
- opportunities to take regular showers:
- personal visitation privileges, but suspension of such visits should he for no more than [30 days];
- opportunities for physical exercise;
- opportunities to speak with other persons;
- religious observance in accordance with Standard 23-7.3: and
- access to varied reading material.

d) Correctional authorities should be permitted to reasonably restrict, but not eliminate, counsel visits, clergy visits, and written communication if a prisoner has engaged in misconduct directly related to such visits or communications.

Standard 23-3.8 Segregated housing

a) Correctional authorities should be permitted to physically separate prisoners in segregated housing from other prisoners but should not deprive them of those items or services necessary for the maintenance of psychological and physical wellbeing.

b) Conditions of extreme isolation should not he allowed regardless of the reasons for a prisoner's separation from the general population. Conditions of extreme isolation generally include a combination of sensory deprivation, lack of contact with other persons, enforced idleness, minimal out-of-cell time, and lack of outdoor recreation.

c) All prisoners placed in segregated housing should be provided with meaningful forms of mental, physical, and social stimulation. Depending upon individual assessments of risks, needs, and the reasons for placement in the segregated setting, those forms of stimulation should include:

- in-cell programming, which should be developed for prisoners who are not permitted to leave their cells;
- additional out-of-cell time, taking into account the size of the prisoner's cell and the length of time the prisoner has been housed in this setting;
- opportunities to exercise in the presence of other prisoners, although, if necessary, separated by security barriers:
- daily face-to-face interaction with both uniformed and civilian staff; and
- access to radio or television for programming or mental stimulation, although such access should not substitute for human contact described in subdivisions (i) to (iv).

d) Prisoners placed in segregated housing for reasons other than discipline should be allowed as much out-of-cell time and programming participation as practicable, consistent with security.

e) No cell used to house prisoners in segregated housing should be smaller than 80 square feet, and cells should be designed to permit prisoners assigned to them to converse with and be observed by staff. Physical features that facilitate suicide attempts should be eliminated in all segregation cells. Except if required for security or safety reasons for a particular prisoner, segregation cells should be equipped in compliance with Standard 23-3.3(b).

f) Correctional staff should monitor and assess any health or safety concerns related to the refusal of a prisoner in segregated housing to eat or drink, or to participate in programming, recreation, or out-of-cell activity.

Standard 23-3.9 Conditions during lockdown

a) The term "lockdown" means a decision by correctional authorities to suspend activities in one or more housing areas of a correctional facility and to confine prisoners to their cells or housing areas.

b) A lockdown of more than one day should be imposed only to restore order; to address an imminent threat of violence, disorder, or serious contagion; or to conduct a comprehensive search of the facility.

c) During any lockdown, correctional authorities should not suspend medical services, food service, and provision of necessities, although necessary restrictions in these services should be permitted. Prisoners should continue to have unrestricted access to toilets, washbasins, and drinking water. Except in the event of an emergency lockdown oh' less than [72 hours] in which security necessitates denial of such access, prisoners should be afforded access to showers, correspondence, delivery of legal materials, and grievance procedures.

d) In the event of a lockdown of longer than [7 days], a qualified mental health professional should visit the affected housing units at least weekly to observe and talk with prisoners in order to assess their mental health and provide necessary services.

e) A lockdown should last no longer than necessary. As the situation improves, privileges and activities for the affected area should be progressively increased. Procedures should exist for identifying individual prisoners who did not participate in incidents that led to the lockdown and whose access to programs and movement within the facility may be safely restored prior to the termination of lockdown status. In the extraordinary situation that a lockdown lasts longer than [30 days], officials should mitigate the risks of mental and physical deterioration by increasing out-of-cell time and in-cell programming opportunities.

f) Correctional officials should not use a lockdown to substitute for disciplinary sanctions or for reclassification of prisoners

Part IV: Rules of Conduct and Discipline

Standard 23-4.1 Rules of conduct and informational handbook

a) Correctional administrators and officials should promulgate clear written rules for prisoner conduct, including specific definitions of disciplinary offenses, examples of conduct that constitute each type of offense, and a schedule indicating the minimum and maximum possible punishment for each offense.

b) Upon a prisoner's entry to a correctional facility, correctional authorities should provide the prisoner a personal copy of the rules for prisoner conduct and an informational handbook written in plain language. A written translation in a language the prisoner understands should be provided within a reasonable period of time to each literate prisoner who does not understand English. Copies of the rules and handbook in the languages a facility's prisoners understand should also be available in areas of the facility readily accessible to prisoners, including libraries. Staff should explain and read the rules and the handbook to any prisoner unable to read them by reason of illiteracy or disability.

c) The handbook should contain specific criteria and procedures for discipline and classification decisions, including decisions involving security status and work and housing assignments. In addition, the handbook should set forth the facility's policy forbidding staff sexual contact or exploitation of prisoners, and the procedures for making complaints, filing grievances, and appealing grievance denials, as well as describing any types of complaints deemed not properly the subject of the grievance procedures.

d) The handbook should specify the authorized means by which prisoners should seek information, make requests, obtain medical or mental health care, seek an accommodation relating to disability or religion, report an assault or threat, and seek protection.

e) Correctional officials and administrators should annually review and update facility and agency rules and regulations to ensure that they comport with current legal standards. Correctional officials should annually review and update the handbooks provided to prisoners to ensure that they comport with current legal standards, facility and agency rules, and practice.

Standard 23-4.2 Disciplinary hearing procedures

a) Correctional authorities should not se to impose a disciplinary sanction upon a prisoner for misconduct unless the misconduct is a criminal offense or the prisoner was given prior written and effective notice of the violated rule.

b) Informal resolution of minor disciplinary violations should be encouraged provided that prisoners have notice of the range of sanctions that may be imposed as a result of such an informal resolution, those sanctions are only minimally restrictive, and the imposition of a sanction is recorded and subject to prompt review by supervisory correctional staff, ordinarily on the same day.

c) Correctional authorities should be permitted to confine a prisoner in segregated housing pending the hearing required by subdivision (d) of this Standard, if necessary, for individual safety or institutional security. Such prehearing confinement should not exceed [3 days] unless necessitated by the prisoner's request for a continuance or by other demonstrated good cause. Prisoners should receive credit against any disciplinary sentence for time served in prehearing confinement if prehearing conditions were substantially similar to conditions in disciplinary segregation.

d) When the possible sanction for a disciplinary offense includes the delay of a release date, loss of sentencing credit for good conduct or good conduct time earning capability, or placement in disciplinary segregation, a prisoner should be found to have committed that offense only after an individualized determination, by a preponderance of the evidence. In addition, the prisoner should be afforded, at a minimum, the following procedural protections:

- at least 24 hours in advance of any hearing written and effective notice of the actions alleged to have been committed, the rule alleged to have been violated by those actions, and the prisoner's rights under this Standard:

- an impartial decision-maker;

- a hearing at which the prisoner may be heard in person and, absent an individualized determination of good cause, has a reasonable opportunity to present available witnesses and documentary and physical evidence;

- absent an individualized determination of good cause opportunity for the prisoner to confront and cross-examine any witnesses or if good cause to limit such confrontation is found, to propound questions to be relayed to the witnesses;

- an interpreter, if necessary, for the prisoner to understand or participate in the proceedings:

- if the decision-maker determines that a prisoner is unable to prepare and present evidence and arguments effectively on his or her own behalf, counsel or some other advocate for the prisoner, including a member of the correctional staff or another prisoner with suitable capabilities:

- an independent determination by the decision-maker of the reliability and credibility of any confidential informants:

- a written statement setting forth the evidence relied on and the reasons for the decision and the sanction imposed, rendered promptly but no later than [5 days] after conclusion of the hearing except in exceptional circumstances where good cause for the delay exists; and

- opportunity for the prisoner to appeal within [5 days] to the chief executive officer of the facility or higher administrative authority, who should issue a written decision within [10 days] either affirming or reversing the determination of misconduct and approving or modifying the punishment imposed.

a) If correctional officials conduct a disciplinary proceeding during the pendency of a criminal investigation or prosecution, correctional authorities should advise the prisoner of the right to remain silent during the proceeding, and should not use that silence against the prisoner.

b) A prisoner should be permitted to waive the right to a hearing if the prisoner so chooses after being informed of the disciplinary offense of which he or she is accused and the potential penalties and other consequences; such a waiver should be made in person to a designated correctional official who should accept it only if the prisoner understands the consequences.

Standard 23-4.3 Disciplinary sanctions

a) Correctional authorities should be permitted to impose a range of disciplinary sanctions to maintain order and ensure the safe custody of prisoners. Sanctions should be reasonable in light of the offense and the prisoner's circumstances, including disciplinary history and any mental illness or other cognitive impairment. In addition to the limitations itemized in Standard 233.7, sanctions should never include:

corporal punishment;

- conditions of extreme isolation as described in Standard 23-3.8(b);
- use of restraints, such as handcuffs, chains, irons, strait-jackets, or restraint chairs; or
- any other form of cruel, inhuman, or degrading treatment.

b) Only the most severe disciplinary offenses, in which safety or security are seriously threatened, ordinarily warrant a sanction that exceeds [30 days] placement in disciplinary housing, and no placement in disciplinary housing should exceed one year.

c) No disciplinary sanction should ever be administered by other prisoners, even under the direction of correctional authorities.

Part V: Personal Security

Standard 23-5.1 Personal security and protection from harm

a) Correctional authorities should protect prisoners from physical injury, corporal punishment, sexual assault, extortion, harassment, and personal abuse, among other harms,

b) Correctional authorities should exercise reasonable care with respect to property prisoners lawfully possess or have a right to reclaim. A remedy should be reasonably available to prisoners if correctional authorities negligently or intentionally destroy or lose such property.

Standard 23-5.2 Prevention and investigation of violence

a) Correctional and governmental authorities should take all practicable actions to reduce violence and the potential for violence in correctional facilities and during transport, including:

- using a validated objective classification system and instrument as provided in Standard 23-2.2;
- preventing crowding as provided in Standard 23-3.1(b);
- ensuring adequate and appropriate supervision of prisoners during transport and in all areas of the facility, preferably direct supervision in any congregate areas;
- training staff and volunteers appropriately as provided in Standard 23-10.3;
- preventing introduction of drugs and other contraband, and providing substance abuse treatment as provided in Standard 238.2(b);
- preventing opportunities for prisoners to exercise coercive authority or control over other prisoners, including through access to another prisoner's confidential information;
- preventing opportunities for gangs to gain any power;
- promptly separating prisoners when one may be in danger from another;
- preventing staff from tolerating, condoning, or implicitly or explicitly encouraging fighting, violence, bullying, or extortion;
- regularly assessing prisoners' level of fear of violence and responding accordingly to prisoners' concerns; and
- preventing idleness by providing constructive activities for all prisoners as provided in Standards 23-8.2 and 23-8.4.

Correctional officials should promptly and thoroughly investigate and make a record of all incidents involving violence, and should take appropriate remedial action.

Standard 23-5.3 Sexual abuse

a) Correctional authorities should protect all prisoners from sexual assault by other prisoners, as well as from pressure by other prisoners to engage in sexual acts. Correctional officials should strive to create an institutional culture in which sexual assault or sexual pressure is not tolerated, expected, or made the subject of humor by staff or prisoners. Correctional authorities should evaluate reports of sexual assault or threats of sexual assault without regard to a prisoner's sexual orientation, gender, or gender identity and should not be permitted to retaliate formally or informally against prisoners who make such reports. Correctional authorities should not presume that sexual activity among prisoners is consensual.

b) Correctional authorities should protect all prisoners from any sexual contact with or sexual exploitation by staff, including volunteers and employees of other governmental or private organizations who work in the correctional facility. States and the federal government should prohibit by statute and correctional agencies by policy any form of sexual contact between staff and prisoners.

c) Correctional officials should establish and publicize the means by which prisoners and others may easily and confidentially report to any staff member or appropriate outside entity a sexual assault or pressure to engage in sexual acts, sexual contact or exploitation involving a prisoner and staff, or the fear of such conduct. Correctional authorities should promptly relay any such report, or any other information they obtain regarding such conduct, to the chief executive officer of the facility. Correctional officials should implement a policy of prompt and thorough investigation of any credible allegation of the threat or commission of prisoner sexual assault or sexual contact with or sexual exploitation by staff. Correctional officials should establish criteria for forwarding such reports to a specialized unit trained in the appropriate investigation methods. Correctional authorities should take steps necessary to protect the prisoner from further sexual assaults, contacts, or exploitation. If a complaining prisoner and the subject of the complaint are separated during any such investigation, care should be taken to minimize conditions for the complaining prisoner that a reasonable person would experience as punitive.

d) Medical treatment and testing, and psychological counselling, should be immediately available to victims of sexual assault or of sexual contact with or sexual exploitation by staff. Correctional authorities, including health care staff, should be alert to identify and document signs of sexual assault and should implement a protocol for providing victims with a thorough forensic medical examination performed by an appropriately trained qualified medical professional.

e) Correctional authorities, including health care staff, should not reveal information about any incident of prisoner sexual abuse to any person, except to other staff or law enforcement personnel who need to know about the incident in order to make treatment, investigation, or other security or management decisions, or to appropriate external oversight officials or agencies.

Standard 23-5.4 Self-harm and suicide prevention

a) Correctional officials should implement procedures to identify prisoners at risk for suicide and to intervene to prevent suicides.

b) When the initial screening pursuant to Standard 23-2.1 or any subsequent observation identities a risk of suicide, the prisoner should be placed in a safe setting and promptly evaluated by a qualified mental health professional, who should determine the degree of risk, appropriate level of ongoing supervision, and appropriate course of mental health treatment.

c) Instead of isolating prisoners at risk of suicide, correctional authorities should ordinarily place such prisoners in housing areas that are designed to be suicide resistant and that allow staff a full and unobstructed view of the prisoners inside. A suicidal prisoner's clothing should be removed only if an individualized assessment finds such removal necessary, and the affected prisoner should be provided with suicide resistant garments that are sanitary, adequately modest, and appropriate for the temperature. Physical restraints should be used only as a last resort and their use should comply with the limitations in Standard 23-5.9.

d) At a minimum, prisoners presenting a serious risk of suicide should be housed within sight of staff and observed by staff, face-to-face, at irregular intervals of no more than 15 minutes. Prisoner's currently threatening or attempting suicide should be under continuous staff observation. Suicide observation should be documented, and prisoners under suicide observation should be evaluated by a qualified mental health professional prior to being removed from observation.

e) Correctional authorities should minimize the risk of suicide in housing areas and other spaces where prisoners may be unobserved by staff by eliminating, to the extent practicable, physical features that facilitate suicide attempts.

f) When staff observe a prisoner who appears to have attempted or committed suicide, they should administer appropriate first-aid measures immediately until medical personnel arrive and assess the situation. Cut-down tools should be readily available to security personnel, who should be trained in first aid and cardiopulmonary resuscitation, cut-down techniques, and emergency notification procedures.

Standard 23-5.5 Protection of vulnerable prisoners

a) The term "protective custody" means housing of a prisoner in segregated housing or under any other substantially greater restrictions than those applicable to the general population with which the prisoner would otherwise be housed, in order to protect the prisoner from harm.

b) Correctional officials should implement procedures for identifying those prisoners who are particularly vulnerable to physical or sexual abuse, manipulation, or psychologically harmful verbal abuse by other prisoners or by staff, and for protecting these and other prisoners who request and need protection.

c) Correctional authorities should minimize the extent to which vulnerable prisoners needing protection are subjected to rules and conditions a reasonable person would experience as punitive. Correctional authorities should not stigmatize prisoners who need protection. Such prisoners should not be housed with prisoners who have been identified as potential aggressors.

d) Correctional authorities should not assign a prisoner to involuntary protective custody for a period exceeding [30 days] unless there is a serious and credible threat to the prisoner's safety and staff are unable to adequately protect the prisoner either in the general population or by a transfer to another facility.

e) At intervals not to exceed three months, correctional authorities should afford a prisoner placed in protective custody a review to determine whether there is a continuing need for separation from the general population.

f) Consistent with such confidentiality as is required to prevent a significant risk of harm to other persons, a prisoner being evaluated for involuntary placement in protective custody should be permitted reasonable access to materials considered at both the initial and the periodic reviews, and should be allowed to meet with and submit written statements to persons reviewing the prisoner's classification.

g) If correctional authorities assign a prisoner to protective custody, such a prisoner should be:

- housed in the least restrictive environment practicable, in segregated housing only if necessary, and in no case in a setting that is used for disciplinary housing;

- allowed all of the items usually authorized for general population prisoners;

- provided opportunities to participate in programming and work as described in Standards 23-8.2 and 8.4; and

- provided the greatest practicable opportunities for out-of-cell time.

Standard 23-5.6 Use of force

a) "Force" means offensive or defensive physical contact with a prisoner, including blows, pushes, or defensive holds, whether or not involving batons or other instruments or weapons: discharge of chemical agents; discharge of electronic weaponry; and application of restraints such as handcuffs. chains, irons, strait-jackets, or restraint chairs. However, force does not include a firm hold, or use of hand or leg restraints, or fitting of a stun belt, on an unresisting prisoner.

b) Correctional authorities should use force against a prisoner only:

- to protect and ensure the safety of staff, prisoners, and others; to prevent serious property damage; or to prevent escape;
- if correctional authorities reasonably believe the benefits of force outweigh the risks to prisoners and staff; and
- as a last alternative after other reasonable efforts to resolve the situation have failed.

c) In no case should correctional authorities use force against a prisoner:

- to enforce an institutional rule or an order unless the disciplinary process is inadequate to address an immediate security need;
- to gratuitously inflict pain or suffering punish past or present conduct, deter future conduct, intimidate, or gain information; or
- after the risk that justified the use of force has passed.

d) A correctional agency should implement reasonable policies and procedures governing staff use of force against prisoners; these policies should establish a range of force options and explicitly prohibit the use of premature, unnecessary, or excessive force. Control techniques should be intended to minimize injuries to both prisoners and staff. Except in highly unusual circumstances in which a prisoner poses an imminent threat of serious bodily harm, staff should not use types of force that carry a high risk of injury, such as punches, kicks, or strikes to the head, neck, face, or groin.

e) Correctional authorities should not be assigned responsibilities potentially requiring the use of force unless they are appropriately trained for the anticipated type of force, and are initially and periodically evaluated as being physically and mentally fit for such hazardous and sensitive duties.

f) Except in an emergency, force should not he used unless authorized by a supervisory officer. Such an officer should be called to the scene whenever force is used, to direct and observe but ordinarily not to participate in the physical application of force, and should not leave the scene until the incident has come to an end. To the extent practicable, continually operating stationary video cameras should be used in areas in which uses of force are particularly likely, such as intake areas, segregation, and mental health units. Correctional authorities should video and audio record every planned or anticipated use of force from the initiation of the action, and should begin recording any other use of force incident as soon as practicable after the incident starts.

g) If practicable staff should seek intervention and advice from a qualified mental health professional prior to a planned or predictable use of force against a prisoner who has a history of mental illness or who is exhibiting behaviors commonly associated with mental illness.

h) Following any incident in which a prisoner is subjected to use of either chemical agents or any kind of weapon or is injured during a use of force, the prisoner should receive an immediate health care examination and appropriate treatment, including decontamination. Health care personnel should document any injuries sustained.

i) Correctional agency policies should strive to ensure full staff accountability for all uses of force. Correctional authorities should memorialize and facilitate review it's uses of force. Following any incident that involves a use of force against a prisoner, participants and witnesses should be interviewed or should file written statements. Correctional authorities should prepare a complete file for the chief executive officer of the facility, including a report, any recordings, and written statements and medical reports for both prisoners and staff. Correctional officials and administrators should review and retain the file for purposes of management, staff discipline, training, and the identification of trends.

j) A jurisdiction or correctional agency should establish criteria, based on the extent of prisoner injury and the type of force, for forwarding use of force reports to a person or office outside the relevant facility's chain of command for a more in-depth investigation. Such investigation should take place for every use of force incident that results in a death or major traumatic injury to a prisoner or to staff.

Standard 23-5.7 Use of deadly force

a) "Deadly force" means force that creates or is intended to create a substantial risk of death or serious bodily harm. The use of firearms should always be considered the use of deadly force.

b) Correctional agency policies and procedures should authorize the use of deadly force only by security personnel trained in the use of deadly force, and only in a situation when correctional authorities reasonably believe that deadly force is necessary to prevent imminent death or serious bodily harm or to prevent an escape from a secure correctional facility, subject to the qualification in subdivision (c) of this Standard.

c) Deadly force to prevent an escape should be permitted only when the prisoner is about to leave the secure perimeter of a correctional facility without authorization or, if the prisoner is permitted to be on the grounds outside the secure perimeter, the prisoner is about to leave the facility grounds without authorization. Before staff use a firearm to prevent an escape, they should shout a warning and, if time and circumstances allow, summon other staff to regain control without shooting. For purposes of this subdivision, a prisoner in custody for transit to or from a secure correctional facility is considered to be within the perimeter of such facility.

d) The location and storage of firearms should be strictly regulated. Correctional authorities carrying firearms should not be assigned to positions that are accessible to prisoners or in which they come into direct contact with prisoners, except during transport or supervision of prisoners outside the secure perimeter, or in emergency situations. In those situations, each staff member should also have available for use a weapon less likely to be lethal.

Standard 23-5.8 Use of chemical agents, electronic weaponry, and canines

a) Correctional administrators should develop and implement policies governing use of chemical agents and electronic weaponry. Such policies should:
- provide for testing and training;
- specify that, as with any use of force, chemical agents and electronic weaponry are to be used only as a last resort after the failure of other reasonable conflict resolution techniques;
- cover the medical and tactical circumstances in which use of such agents and weaponry is inappropriate or unsafe;

411

- forbid the use of such agents and weaponry directly on vital parts of the body, including genitals and, for electronic weaponry, eyes, mouth, and neck; and forbid the use of electronic weaponry in drive-stun or direct contact mode.

b) Correctional agency policy should prohibit use of electronic or chemical weaponry for the following purposes:

- as punishment;
- as a prod;
- to rouse an unconscious, impaired, or intoxicated prisoner;
- against any prisoner using passive resistance when there is no immediate threat of bodily harm; or to enforce an order after a prisoner has been immobilized or a threat has been neutralized.

c) Correctional officials should implement any appropriate facility-specific restrictions on use of chemical agents and electronic weaponry that are appropriate for the particular facility and its prisoner population, and should promulgate policy that sets forth in detail the circumstances in which such weapons may be used.

d) When practicable, before using either chemical agents or electronic weaponry against a prisoner, staff should determine whether the prisoner has any contraindicating medical conditions, including mental illness and intoxication, and make a contemporaneous record of this determination.

e) Correctional authorities should be permitted to use canines inside the secure perimeter of a correctional facility only for searches and, except in emergencies, only if prisoners have been moved away from the area to be searched. Canines should never be used for purposes of intimidation or control of a prisoner or prisoners.

Standard 23-5.9 Use of restraint mechanisms and techniques

Correctional authorities should not use restraint mechanisms such as handcuffs, leg irons, straitjackets, restraint chairs, and spit-masks as a form of punishment or retaliation. Subject to the remainder of this Standard, restraints should not be used except to control a prisoner who presents an immediate risk of self-injury or injury to others, to prevent serious property damage, for health care purposes, or when necessary as a security precaution during transfer or transport.

When restraints are necessary, correctional authorities should use the least restrictive forms of restraints that are appropriate and should use them only as long as the need exists, not for a pre-determined period of time. Policies relating to restraints should take account of the special needs of prisoners who have physical or mental disabilities, and of prisoners who are under the age of eighteen or are geriatric, as well as the limitations specified in Standard 23-6.9 for pregnant prisoners or those who have recently given birth. Correctional authorities should take care to prevent injury to restrained prisoners, and should not restrain a prisoner in any manner that causes unnecessary physical pain or extreme discomfort, or that restricts the prisoner's blood circulation or obstructs the prisoner's breathing or airways. Correctional authorities should not hog-tie prisoners or restrain them in a fetal or prone position.

a) Correctional authorities should prevent co-mingling of restrained and unrestrained prisoners either in a correctional facility or during transport.

b) Other than as allowed by subdivision of this Standard, correctional authorities should not use restraints in a prisoner's cell except immediately preceding an out-of-cell movement or for medical or mental health purposes as authorized by a qualified medical or mental health professional. Reasonable steps should be taken during movement to protect restrained prisoners from accidental injury.

c) If restraints are used for medical or mental health care purposes, the restrained prisoner should, if possible, be placed in a health care area of the correctional facility, and the decision to use, continue, and discontinue restraints should be made by a qualified health care professional, in accordance with applicable licensing regulations.

d) Four- or five-point restraints should be used only if a prisoner presents an immediate and extreme risk of serious self-injury or injury to others and only after less restrictive forms of restraint have been determined likely to be ineffective to control the prisoner's risky behavior. Whenever practicable, a qualified health care professional should participate in efforts to avoid using four- or five-point restraints.

e) If it is necessary for correctional authorities to apply four- or five-point restraints without participation of a qualified health care professional because the situation is an emergency and health care staff are not available, a qualified health care professional should review the situation as soon as possible and assess whether such restraints are appropriate. If correctional authorities have applied four- or five-point restraints without the participation of a qualified health care professional or if that professional disagrees with the application of the restraints, correctional authorities should notify the facility's chief executive office immediately on gaining control of the prisoner. The chief executive officer should decide promptly whether the use of such restraints should continue.

f) Whether restraints are used for health care or for custodial purposes, during the period that a prisoner is restrained in a four-or five-point position, staff should follow established guidelines for use of the restraint mechanism that take into account the prisoner's physical condition, including health problems and body weight, should provide adequate nutrition, hydration, and toileting, and should take the following precautions to ensure the prisoner's safety:

- for the entire period of restraint, the prisoner should be video- and audio-recorded;

- immediately, a qualified health care professional should conduct an in-person assessment of the prisoner's medical and mental health condition, and should advise whether the prisoner should be transferred to a medical or mental health unit or facility for emergency treatment;

- until the initial assessment by a qualified health care professional required by subdivision (ii), staff should continuously observe the prisoner, in person:

- after the initial medical assessment, at least every fifteen minutes medically trained staff should conduct visual observations and medical checks of the prisoner, log all checks, and evaluate the continued need for restraint;

- at least every two hours, qualified health care staff should check the prisoner's range of motion and review the medical checks performed under subdivision and at least every four hours, a qualified medical professional should conduct a complete in-person evaluation to determine the prisoner's need for either continued restraint or transfer to a medical or mental health facility.

PART VI: Health Care

Standard 23-6.1 General principles governing health care

a) Correctional authorities should ensure that:

- a qualified health care professional is designated the responsible health authority for each facility, to oversee and direct the provision of health care in that facility:
- prisoners are provided necessary health care, including preventive, routine, urgent, and emergency care;
- such care is consistent with community health care standards, including standards relating to privacy except as otherwise specified in these Standards;
- special health care protocols are used, when appropriate, for female prisoners, prisoners who have physical or mental disabilities, and prisoners who are under the age of eighteen or geriatric; and
- health care that is necessary during the period of imprisonment is provided regardless of a prisoner's ability to pay, the size of the correctional facility, or the duration of the prisoner's incarceration.
- Prisoners should not be charged fees for necessary health care. Dental care should be provided to treat prisoners' dental pain, eliminate dental pathology, and preserve and restore prisoners' ability to chew. Consistent with Standard 23-2.5, routine preventive dental care and education about oral health care should be provided to those prisoners whose confinement may exceed one year. Prisoners should be provided timely access to appropriately trained and licensed health care staff in a safe and sanitary setting designed and equipped for diagnosis or treatment.
- Health care should be based on the clinical judgments of qualified health care professionals, not on non-medical considerations such as cost and convenience. Clinical decisions should be the sole province of the responsible health care professionals,

and should not be countermanded by non-medical staff. Work assignments, housing placements, and diets for each prisoner should be consistent with any health care treatment plan developed for that prisoner.

b) Prisoners should be provided basic educational materials relating to disease prevention, good health, hygiene, and proper usage of medication.

Standard 23-6.2 Response to prisoner health care needs

a) Correctional authorities should implement a system that allows each prisoner, regardless of security classification, to communicate health care needs in a timely and confidential manner to qualified health care professionals, who should evaluate the situation and assess its urgency. Provision should be made for prisoners who face literacy, language, or other communication harriers to be able to communicate their health needs. No correctional staff member should impede or unreasonably delay a prisoner's access to health care staff or treatment.

b) A prisoner suffering from a serious or potentially life-threatening illness or injury, or from significant pain, should be referred immediately to a qualified medical professional in accordance with written guidelines. Complaints of dental pain should be referred to a qualified dental professional, and necessary treatment begun promptly.

c) When appropriate, health care complaints should be evaluated and treated by specialists. A prisoner who requires care not available in the correctional facility should be transferred to a hospital or other appropriate place for care.

Standard 23-6.3 Control and distribution of prescription drugs

A correctional facility should store all prescription drugs safely and under the control and supervision of the physician in charge of the facility's health care program. Prescription drugs should be distributed in a timely and confidential manner. Ordinarily, only health care staff should administer prescription drugs, except that health care staff should be permitted to authorize prisoners to hold and administer their own asthma inhalers, and to implement other reasonable "keep on person" drug policies. In an emergency, or when necessary, in a facility in which health care staff are available only part-time, medically trained correctional staff should be permitted to administer prescription drugs at the direction of qualified health care professionals. In no instance should a prisoner administer prescription drugs to another prisoner.

Standard 23-6.4 Qualified health care staff

a) Each correctional agency should employ or contract with a sufficient number of qualified medical, dental, and mental health professionals at each correctional facility to render preventive, routine, urgent and emergency health care in a timely manner consistent with accepted health care practice and standards.
b) Health care providers in a non-federal correctional facility should be fully licensed in the state in which the facility is located; health care providers in a federal correctional facility should he fully licensed in the United States. No health care provider should he permitted to practice in a correctional facility beyond the scope permissible for that individual provider outside of a correctional facility, given the provider's particular qualifications and licensing.

c) Regardless of any training a prisoner may have had, no prisoner should be allowed to provide health care evaluation or treatment to any other prisoner.

Standard 23-6.5 Continuity of care

a) A correctional agency should ensure each prisoner's continuity of care, including with respect to medication, upon entry into the correctional system, during confinement and transportation, during and after transfer between facilities, and upon release. A prisoner's health care records and medication should travel with the prisoner in the event of a transfer between facilities, including facilities operated by different agencies.

b) Prisoners who are determined to he lawfully taking prescription drugs or receiving health care treatment when they enter a correctional facility directly from the community, or when they are transferred between correctional facilities—including facilities operated by different agencies--should he maintained on that course of medication or treatment or its equivalent until a qualified health care professional directs otherwise upon individualized consideration.

Standard 23-6.6 Adequate facilities, equipment, and resources

a) Health care areas in a correctional facility should be safe and sanitary, should include appropriately private areas for examination and treatment, and should he designed so that prisoners can hold confidential discussions with health care personnel.

b) A correctional facility should have equipment necessary for routine health care and emergencies, and an adequately supplied pharmacy. Specialized equipment may be required in larger facilities and those serving prisoners with special medical needs. Smaller facilities should be permitted to provide for prisoners' health care needs by transferring them to other facilities or health care providers, but should have equipment that is reasonably necessary in light of its preexisting transfer arrangements.

c) Hospitals and infirmaries operated by or within correctional facilities should meet the licensing standards applicable to similar, non-prison hospitals or infirmaries.

d) Vehicles used to transport prisoners to and from medical facilities should be adequately equipped with emergency medical equipment and provisions for prisoners with special needs.

Standard 23-6.7 Quality improvement

A correctional health care system should include an ongoing evaluation process to assess and improve the health care provided to prisoners and to enable health care staff to institute corrective care or other action as needed. The evaluation process should include mechanisms by which prisoners can provide both positive and negative comments about their care.

Standard 23-6.8 Health care records and confidentiality

a) Prisoners' health care records should:
• be compiled, maintained, and retained in accordance with accepted health care practice and standards;
• not include criminal or disciplinary records unless a qualified health care professional finds such records

relevant to the prisoner's health care evaluation or treatment;

- be maintained in a confidential and secure manner, separately from non-health-care tiles:
- accompany a prisoner to every facility to which the prisoner is transferred; and
- be available to the prisoner who is the subject of the records, absent an individualized finding of good cause.

b) Information about a prisoner's health condition should not be disclosed to other prisoners. No prisoner should have access to any other prisoner's health care records.

c) Information about a prisoner's health condition should be shared with correctional staff only when necessary and permitted by law, and only to the extent required for:

- the health and safety of the prisoner or of other persons;
- the administration and maintenance of the facility or agency;
- quality improvement relating to health care; or
- law enforcement purposes.

d) Health care personnel or correctional authorities should provide information about a prisoner's health condition to that prisoner's family or other persons designated by the prisoner if the prisoner consents to such disclosure or, unless the prisoner has previously withheld consent, if the prisoner's condition renders the prisoner unable to consent or if the prisoner has died.

Standard 23-6.9 Pregnant prisoners and new mothers

a) A pregnant prisoner should receive necessary prenatal and postpartum care and treatment, including an adequate diet, clothing, appropriate accommodations relating to bed assignment and housing area temperature, and childbirth and infant care education. Any restraints used on a pregnant prisoner or one who has recently delivered a baby should be medically appropriate; correctional authorities should consult with health care staff to ensure that restraints do not compromise the pregnancy or the prisoner's health.

b) A prisoner in labor should be taken to an appropriate medical facility without delay. A prisoner should not be restrained while she is in labor, including during transport, except in extraordinary circumstances after an individualized finding that security requires restraint, in which event correctional and health care staff should cooperate to use the least restrictive restraints necessary for security, which should not interfere with the prisoner's labor.

c) Governmental authorities should facilitate access to abortion services for a prisoner who decides to exercise her right to an abortion, as that right is defined by state and federal law, through prompt scheduling of the procedure upon request and through the provision of transportation to a facility providing such services.

d) Governmental authorities should ensure that no birth certificate states that a child was horn in a correctional facility.

e) Governmental and correctional authorities should strive to meet the legitimate needs of prisoner mothers and their infants, including a prisoner's desire to breastfeed her child. Governmental authorities should ordinarily allow a prisoner who gives birth while in a correctional facility or who already has an infant at the time she is admitted to a correctional facility to keep the infant with her for a reasonable time, preferably on extended furlough or in an appropriate community facility or, if that is not practicable or reasonable, in a nursery at a correctional facility that is staffed by qualified persons. Governmental authorities should provide appropriate health care to children in such facilities.

f) If long-term imprisonment is anticipated, a prisoner with an infant should be helped to develop necessary plans for alternative care for the infant following the period described in subdivision (e) of this Standard, in coordination with social service agencies. A prisoner should be informed of the consequences for the prisoner's parental rights of any arrangements contemplated. When a prisoner and infant are separated, the prisoner should be provided with counseling and other mental health support.

Standard 23-6.10 Impairment-related aids

Prisoners whose health or institutional adjustment would otherwise be adversely affected should be provided with medical prosthetic devices or other impairment-related aids, such as eyeglasses, hearing aids, or wheelchairs, except when there has been an individualized finding that such an aid Would be inconsistent with security or safety. When the use of a specific aid believed reasonably necessary by a qualified medical professional is deemed inappropriate for security or safety reasons, correctional authorities should consider alternatives to meet the health needs of the prisoner.

Standard 23-6.11 Services for prisoners with mental disabilities

a) A correctional facility should provide appropriate and individualized mental health care treatment and habilitation services to prisoners with mental illness, mental retardation, or other cognitive impairments.

423

b) Correctional officials should implement a protocol for identifying and managing prisoners whose behavior is indicative of mental illness, mental retardation, or other cognitive impairments. In addition to implementing the mental health screening required in Standard 23-2.1 and mental health assessment required in Standard 23-2.5, this protocol should require that the signs and symptoms of mental illness or other cognitive impairments be documented and that a prisoner with such signs and symptoms be promptly referred to a qualified mental health professional for evaluation and treatment.

c) A correctional facility should provide prisoners diagnosed with mental illness, mental retardation, or other cognitive impairments appropriate housing assignments and programming opportunities in accordance with their diagnoses, vulnerabilities, functional impairments, and treatment or habilitation plans. A correctional agency should develop a range of housing options for such prisoners, including high security housing; residential housing with various privilege levels dependent upon treatment and security assessments; and transition housing to facilitate placement in general population or release from custody.

d) When appropriate for purposes of evaluation or treatment, correctional authorities should be permitted to separate from the general population prisoners diagnosed with mental illness, mental retardation, or other cognitive impairments who have difficulty conforming to the expectations of behavior for general population prisoners. However, prisoners diagnosed with serious mental illness should not be housed in settings that may exacerbate their mental illness or suicide risk, particularly in settings involving sensory deprivation or isolation.

Standard 23-6.12 Prisoners with chronic or communicable diseases

a) Correctional officials should provide for the voluntary medically appropriate testing of all prisoners for widespread chronic and serious communicable diseases and for appropriate treatment, without restricting the availability of treatment based on criteria not directly related to the prisoner's health.
b) Correctional authorities should not discriminate against a prisoner in housing, programs, or other activities or services because the prisoner has a chronic or communicable disease, including HIV or AIDS, unless the best available objective evidence indicates that participation of the prisoner poses a direct threat to the health or safety of others. When medically necessary, correctional authorities should be permitted to place a prisoner with a readily transmissible contagious disease in appropriate medical isolation or to restrict such a prisoner in other ways to prevent contagion of others.
c) Any accommodation made to address the special needs or risks of a prisoner with a communicable disease should not unnecessarily reveal that prisoner's health condition.

Standard 23-6.13 Prisoners with gender identity disorder

A prisoner diagnosed with gender identity disorder should be offered appropriate treatment. At a minimum, a prisoner who has begun or completed the medical process of gender reassignment prior to admission to a correctional facility should be offered treatment necessary to maintain the prisoner at the stage of transition reached at the time of admission, unless a qualified health care professional determines that such treatment is medically inadvisable for the prisoner.

Standard 23-6.14 Voluntary and informed consent to treatment

a) Correctional officials should implement a policy to require voluntary and informed consent prior to a prisoner's health care examination, testing, or treatment, except as provided in this Standard. A prisoner who lacks the capacity to make decisions consenting or withholding consent to care should have a surrogate decision-maker designated according to applicable law, although that decision-maker's consent should not substitute for the protections specified in Standard 23-6.15. A competent prisoner who refuses food should not be force-fed except pursuant to a court order.

b) Prisoners should be informed of the health care options available to them. If a prisoner refuses health care examination testing, or treatment, a qualified health care professional should discuss the matter with the prisoner and document in the prisoner's health care record both the discussion and the refusal; the health care professional should attempt to obtain the prisoner's signature attesting to the refusal. Any claim that a prisoner is refusing treatment for a serious medical or mental health condition should be investigated by a qualified health care professional to ensure that the refusal is informed and voluntary, and not the result of miscommunication or misunderstanding. If a prisoner refuses care in such a situation, health care staff should take steps to involve other trusted individuals, such as clergy or the prisoner's family members, to communicate to the prisoner the importance of the decision.

c) A prisoner who refuses testing or treatment for a serious communicable disease should be housed in a medically appropriate setting until a qualified health care professional can ascertain whether the prisoner is contagious. Involuntary testing or treatment should be permitted only if:
- there is a significant risk of the spread of disease;
- no less intrusive alternative is available: and
- involuntary testing or treatment would accord with applicable law for a non-prisoner.

Standard 23-6.15 Involuntary mental health treatment and transfer

a) Involuntary mental health treatment of a prisoner should be permitted only if the prisoner is suffering from a serious mental illness, non-treatment poses a significant risk of serious harm to the prisoner or others, and no less intrusive alternative is reasonably available.
b) Prior to long-term involuntary transfer of a prisoner with a serious mental illness to a dedicated mental health facility, the prisoner should be afforded, at a minimum, the following procedural protections:
- at least 3 days] in advance of the hearing, written, and effective notice of the fact that involuntary transfer is
- being proposed, the basis for the transfer, and the prisoner's rights under this Standard;
- decision-making by a judicial or administrative hearing officer independent of the correctional agency, or by
- an independent committee that does not include any health care professional responsible for treating or referring the prisoner for transfer or any other correctional staff but does include at least one qualified mental health professional;

427

- a hearing at which the prisoner may be heard in person and, absent an individualized determination of good
- cause, present testimony of available witnesses, including the prisoner's treating mental health professional, and documentary and physical evidence;
- absent an individualized determination of good cause, opportunity for the prisoner to confront and cross-examine witnesses or, if good cause to limit such confrontation is found, to propound questions to be relayed to the witnesses;
- an interpreter, if necessary, for the prisoner to understand or participate in the proceedings;
- counsel, or some other advocate with appropriate mental health care training;
- a written statement setting forth in detail the evidence relied on and the reasons for a decision to transfer;
- an opportunity for the prisoner to appeal to a mental health care review panel or to a judicial officer; and
- a de novo hearing held every [6 months], with the same procedural protections as here provided, to decide if involuntary placement in the mental health facility remains necessary.

c) In an emergency situation requiring the immediate involuntary transfer of a prisoner with serious mental illness to a dedicated mental health facility because of a serious and imminent risk to the safety of the prisoner or others, the chief executive of a correctional facility should be authorized to order such a transfer, but the procedural protections set out in subdivision (b) of this Standard should be provided within [7 days] after the transfer.

d) Prior to involuntary mental health treatment of a prisoner with a serious mental illness, the prisoner should be afforded, at a minimum, the procedural protections specified in subdivision (h) of this

Standard for involuntary mental health transfers, except that:

- (decision-making in the first instance and on appeal should be by a judicial or administrative hearing officer

- independent of the correctional agency, or by an neutral committee that includes at least one qualified mental health professional and that may include appropriate correctional agency staff, but does not include any health care professional responsible for treating or referring the prisoner for transfer;

- the notice should set forth the mental health staff's diagnosis and basis for the proposed treatment, a description of the proposed treatment—including, where relevant, the medication name and dosage— and the less-intrusive alternatives considered and rejected; and

- the de novo hearing held every [6 months] should decide whether to continue or modify any involuntary treatment, and in reaching that decision should consider, in addition to other relevant evidence, evidence of side effects.

e) In an emergency situation requiring the immediate involuntary medication of a prisoner with serious mental illness, an exception to the procedural requirements described in subdivision (d) of this Standard should he permitted, provided that the medication is administered by a qualified health care professional and that it is discontinued within 72 hours unless the requirements in subdivision (d) of this Standard are met.

f) Notwithstanding a finding pursuant to subdivision (d) of this Standard that involuntary treatment is appropriate, mental health care staff should continue attempting to elicit the prisoner's consent to treatment.

PART VII: Personal Dignity

Standard 23-7.1 Respect for prisoners

a) Correctional authorities should treat prisoners in a manner that respects their human dignity, and should not subject them to harassment, bullying, or disparaging language or treatment, or to invidious discrimination based on race, gender, sexual orientation, gender identity, religion, language, national origin, citizenship, age, or physical or mental disability.

b) Correctional authorities should implement policies and practices to prevent any such discrimination, harassment, or bullying of prisoners by other prisoners.

Standard 23-7.2 Prisoners with disabilities and other special needs

a) If a prisoner with a disability is otherwise qualified to use a correctional facility, program, service, or activity, correctional authorities should provide such a prisoner ready access to and use of the facility, program, service, or activity, and should make reasonable modifications to existing policies, procedures, and facilities if such modifications are necessary. Modifications are not required if they would pose an undue burden to the facility, cause a fundamental alteration to a program, or pose a direct threat of substantial harm to the health and safety of the prisoner or others. Disabled prisoners' access to facilities, programs, services, or activities should be provided in the most integrated setting appropriate.

b) To the extent practicable, a prisoner who does not have a disability but does have special needs that affect the prisoner's ability to participate in a prison program, service, or activity should receive programs, services, and activities comparable to those available to other prisoners. Correctional authorities should assess and make appropriate-accommodations in housing placement, medical services, work assignments, food services, and treatment, exercise, and rehabilitation programs for such a prisoner.

c) A prisoner has the right to refuse proffered accommodations related to a disability or other special needs, provided that the refusal does not pose a security or safety risk.

d) There should be no adverse consequences, such as loss of sentencing credit for good conduct, discipline, or denial of parole, for a prisoner who is unable to participate in employment, educational opportunities, or programming due to a disability or other special needs that cannot be accommodated. Such a prisoner should have the opportunity to earn an equal amount of good conduct time credit for participating in alternative activities.

e) Correctional authorities should communicate effectively with prisoners who have disabling speech, hearing, or vision impairments by providing, at a minimum:

- hearing and communication devices, or qualified sign language interpretation by a non-prisoner, or other communication services, as needed, including for disciplinary proceedings or other hearings, processes k' which a prisoner may make requests or lodge a complaint, and during provision of programming and health care;

- closed captioning on any televisions accessible to prisoners with hearing impairments;
- readers, taped texts, Braille or large print materials, or other necessary assistance for effective written communication between correctional authorities and prisoners with vision impairments, and when a prisoner with a vision impairment is permitted to review prison records, as in preparation for a disciplinary or other hearing: and
- fire alarms and other forms of emergency notification that communicate effectively with prisoners with hearing or vision impairments.
f) Correctional authorities should make reasonable attempts to communicate effectively with prisoners who do not read, speak, or understand English. This requirement includes:
- to the extent practicable, the translation of official documents typically provided to prisoners into a language understood by each prisoner who receives them;
- staff who can interpret at all times in any language understood by a significant number of non-English-speaking prisoners; and
- necessary interpretive services during disciplinary proceedings or other hearings, for processes by which a prisoner may lodge a complaint about staff misconduct or concerns about safety, and during provision of health care.

Standard 23-7.3 Religious freedom

a) Correctional authorities should recognize and respect prisoners' freedom of religion.
b) Correctional authorities should permit prisoners to pursue lawful religious practices consistent with their orderly confinement and the security of the facility. Correctional facility policies should not significantly

burden a prisoner's ability to engage in a practice motivated by a sincerely held religious belief, even by imposition of a facially neutral rule or policy, absent a compelling institutional interest and a determination that there are no less restrictive means of furthering that interest.

c) As required by subdivision (b) of this Standard, correctional authorities should provide prisoners with diets of nutritious food consistent with their sincerely held religious beliefs. Prisoners should be entitled to observe special religious practices, including fasting and special dining hours.

d) Correctional authorities should not require prisoners to engage in religious activities or programs. Prisoners should not receive as a direct result of their participation in a religious activity or program any financial or other significant benefit, including improved housing additional out-of-cell time, extra sentencing credit for good conduct, or improved chances for early release, unless prisoners not participating in religious activities or programs are afforded comparable opportunities for such benefits.

e) Correctional authorities should allow prisoners to follow religiously motivated modes of dress or appearance, including wearing religious clothing, headgear, jewelry, and other symbols, subject to the need to maintain security and to identify prisoners.

f) Correctional officials should, to the extent reasonable, make resources and facilities available for religious purposes to all religious groups and prisoners following sincerely held religious beliefs within a correctional facility, and should not show favoritism to any religion.

Standard 23-7.4 Prisoner organizations

Prisoners should be permitted to form or join organizations whose purposes are lawful and consistent with legitimate penological objectives. Correctional officials should allow reasonable participation by members of the general public in authorized meetings or activities of such organizations, provided the safety of the public or the security or safety of persons within the facility are not thereby jeopardized.

Standard 23-7.5 Communication and expression

Governmental authorities should allow prisoners to produce newspapers and other communications media for the dissemination of information, opinions, and other material of interest, and to distribute such media to the prisoner population and to the general public. To the extent practicable, funding, space, and institutional support should be provided for such efforts, and prisoners should be allowed to establish and operate independently-funded publications.

Correctional officials should be permitted to require that prior to publication of an internal newspaper all material be submitted for review by a designated official, and to prohibit the publication or dissemination of material that is obscene or that constitutes a substantial threat to institutional security or order or to the safety of any person. Correctional authorities should be permitted to censor material if it could be censored in publications sent to prisoners through the mail. Officials should provide a clear rationale in writing for any censorship decision, and should afford prisoners a timely opportunity to appeal the decision to a correctional administrator.

Subject to the restrictions in Standard 23-8.6, correctional authorities should allow prisoners to produce works of artistic expression and to submit for publication books, articles, creative writing, art, or other contributions to media outside the facility under their own names.

Correctional authorities should not subject prisoners to retaliation or disciplinary action based on their constitutionally protected communication and expression.

Standard 23-7.6 Personal appearance

Correctional authorities should allow prisoners a reasonable choice in the selection of their own hair styles and personal grooming, subject to the need to identify prisoners and to maintain security and appropriate hygienic standards.

Standard 23-7.7 Records and confidentiality

a) Where consistent with applicable law, correctional authorities should be permitted to release without a prisoner's consent basic identifying information about the prisoner and information about the prisoner's crime of conviction, sentence, place of incarceration, and release date. All other information should be disclosed only upon the prisoner's written consent unless:

- a government official specifies in writing the particular information desired, the official's agency is authorized by law to request that information, and the disclosure of the information is appropriately limited to protect the prisoner's privacy;

- the material is sought only for statistical, research, or reporting purposes and is not in a form containing the prisoner's name, number, symbol, or other information that might identify the prisoner;

- the disclosure is made pursuant to a valid court order or subpoena, or is otherwise required by law; or

- the prisoner is dead, and disclosure is authorized by the prisoner's next of kin or by the administrator of the prisoner's estate if one has been appointed.

b) A correctional agency should allow a prisoner to examine and copy information in the prisoner's file, challenge its accuracy, and request its amendment. Correctional officials should be permitted to withhold:

- information that constitutes diagnostic opinion that might disrupt the prisoner's rehabilitation:
- sources of information obtained upon a promise of confidentiality, including as much of the information itself as risks disclosing the source;
- information that, if disclosed, might result in harm, physical or otherwise, to any person; and
- any other information reasonably believed to jeopardize institutional security if disclosed.

c) Information given by a prisoner to any employee of the correctional authority in a designated counseling relationship under a representation of confidentiality should be privileged, except if the information concerns a contemplated crime or disclosure is required by law. Exceptions to confidentiality should be explained to a prisoner prior to any conversation or course of counseling in which confidentiality is promised, explicitly or implicitly.

Standard 23-7.8 Searches of facilities

a) Correctional authorities should conduct all searches of prisoner living quarters and belongings so as to minimize damage to or disorganization of prisoner property and unnecessary invasions of privacy. When practicable and consistent with security, a prisoner should be permitted to observe any search of personal property belonging to that prisoner. Correctional authorities should not conduct searches in order to harass or retaliate against prisoners individually or as a group.

b) When practicable, correctional authorities should prevent prisoners from observing searches and shakedowns of other prisoners' cells and property.

c) A record should be kept of all facility searches, including documentation of any contraband that is found. The record should identify the circumstances of the search, the persons conducting the search, any staff who are witnesses, and any confiscated materials. When any property is confiscated, the prisoner should be given written documentation of this information.

Standard 23-7.9 Searches of prisoners' bodies

a) In conducting a search of a prisoner's body, correctional authorities should strive to preserve the privacy and dignity of the prisoner. Correctional authorities should use the least intrusive appropriate means to search a prisoner. Searches of prisoners' bodies should follow a written protocol that implements this Standard.

b) Except in exigent situations, a search of a prisoner's body, including a pat-down search or a visual search of the prisoner's private bodily areas, should be conducted by correctional staff of the same gender as the prisoner.

c) Pat-down searches and other clothed body searches should be brief and avoid unnecessary force, embarrassment, and indignity to the prisoner.

d) Visual searches of a prisoner's private bodily areas, whether or not inspection includes the prisoner's body cavities, should:

437

- be conducted only by trained personnel in a private place out of the sight of other prisoners and of staff not involved in the search, except that a prisoner should be permitted to request that more than one staff member be present; and
- be permitted only upon individualized reasonable suspicion that the prisoner is carrying contraband, unless the prisoner has recently had an opportunity to obtain contraband, as upon admission to the facility, upon return from outside the facility or a work assignment in which the prisoner has had access to materials that could present a security risk to the facility, after a contact visit, or when the prisoner has otherwise had contact with a member of the general public provided that a strip search should not be permitted without individualized reasonable suspicion when the prisoner is an arrestee charged with a minor offense not involving drugs or violence and the proposed strip search is upon the prisoner's admission to a correctional facility or before the prisoner's placement in a housing unit.

e) Any examination of a transgender prisoner to determine that prisoner's genital status should he performed in private by a qualified medical professional, and only if the prisoner's genital status is unknown to the correctional agency.

f) Except as required by exigent circumstances, a digital or instrumental search of the anal or vaginal cavity of a prisoner should be conducted only pursuant to a court order. Any such search should be conducted by a trained health care professional who does not have a provider-patient relationship with the prisoner, and should be conducted in a private area devoted to the provision of medical care and out of the sight of others, except that a prisoner should be permitted to request that more than one staff member be present.

g) A record should be kept documenting any digital or instrumental anal or vaginal cavity search and any other body search in which property is confiscated. The record should identify the circumstances of the search, the persons who conducted the search, any staff who are witnesses, and any confiscated materials. The prisoner should be given written documentation of this information.

Standard 23-7.10 Cross-gender supervision

Correctional authorities should employ strategies and devices to allow correctional staff of the opposite gender to a prisoner to supervise the prisoner without observing the prisoner's private bodily areas. Any visual surveillance and supervision of a prisoner who is undergoing an intimate medical procedure should be conducted by guards of the same gender as the prisoner. At all times within a correctional facility or during transport, at least one staff member of the same gender as supervised prisoners should share control of the prisoners.

Standard 23-7.11 Prisoners as subjects of behavioral or biomedical research

a) Subject to the provisions of this Standard, prisoners should not be prohibited from participating in therapeutic behavioral or biomedical research if the potential benefits to prisoners outweigh the risks involved. For biomedical research that poses only a minimal risk to its participants or for behavioral research, prisoner participation should be allowed only if the research offers potential benefits to prisoners either individually or as a class. For biomedical research that poses more than a minimal risk to its participants, prisoner participation should be allowed only if the research offers potential benefits to its participants, and only if it has been determined to be safe for them. Except in unusual circumstances, such as a study of a condition that is solely or almost solely found among incarcerated populations, at least half the subjects involved in any behavioral or biomedical research in which prisoner participation is sought should be non-prisoners. No prisoner should receive preferential treatment, including improved living or work conditions or an improved likelihood of early release, in exchange for participation in behavioral or biomedical research, unless the purpose of the research is to evaluate the outcomes associated with such preferential treatment.

b) Adequate safeguards and oversight procedures should be established for behavioral or biomedical research involving prisoners, including:

- Prior to implementation, all aspects of the research program, including design, planning, and implementation, should be reviewed and approved, disapproved, or modified as necessary by an established institutional review board that complies with applicable law and that includes a medical ethicist and a prisoners' advocate.

- Research studies should not be the sole avenue for prisoners to receive standard treatment for any medical or mental health condition.

- The institutional review board should ensure that mechanisms exist to closely monitor the progress of the study to detect and address adverse events or unanticipated problems. Correctional staff, health care staff, and the researchers should promptly report all adverse events involving prisoner study subjects to the institutional review board's chair and the prisoners' advocate.

- Provision should be made for appropriate health care for adverse medical or mental health conditions or reactions resulting from participation.
- No prisoner should be allowed to participate in behavioral or biomedical research unless that prisoner has given voluntary and informed consent in writing in accordance with an approved protocol which requires that the prisoner be informed and express understanding of:

A. the likely risks, including possible side effects, of any procedure or medication:

B. the likelihood and degree of improvement, remission, control, or cure resulting from any procedure or medication;

C. the uncertainty of the benefits and hazards of any procedure or medication and the reasonable alternatives;

D. the fact that a decision to participate or to decline participation will not affect the conditions of the prisoner's confinement;

E. the ability to withdraw from the study at any time without adverse consequences unrelated to any physical or psychological results of such withdrawal; and

F. the contact information for a person to whom questions about the study can be posed and problems reported.

c) All consent forms should be reviewed and approved by the institutional review board before they are presented to the prisoner.

PART VIII: Rehabilitation and Reintegration

Standard 23-8.1 Location of facilities

Governmental authorities should strive to locate correctional facilities near the population centers from which the bulk of their prisoners are drawn, and in communities where there are resources to supplement treatment programs for prisoners and to provide staff for security, programming, and treatment.

Standard 23-8.2 Rehabilitative programs

a) For the duration of each prisoner's confinement, the prisoner — including a prisoner in long-term segregated housing or incarcerated for a term of life imprisonment —should be engaged in constructive activities that provide opportunities to develop social and technical skills, prevent idleness and mental deterioration, and prepare the prisoner for eventual release. Correctional authorities should begin to plan for each prisoner's eventual release and reintegration into the community from the time of that prisoner's admission into the correctional system and facility.

b) After consultation with each prisoner, correctional authorities should develop an individualized programming plan for the prisoner, in accordance with which correctional authorities should give each prisoner access to appropriate programs, including educational opportunities, mental health and substance abuse treatment and counseling, vocational and job readiness training, personal financial responsibility training, parenting skills, relationship skills, cognitive or behavioral programming, and other programs designed to promote good behavior in the facility and reduce recidivism.

c) Correctional authorities should afford every prisoner an opportunity to obtain a foundation in basic literacy, numeracy, and vocational skills. Correctional authorities should offer prisoners expected to be incarcerated for more than six months additional educational programs designed to meet those prisoners' individual needs. Correctional authorities should offer high school equivalency classes, post-secondary education, apprenticeships, and similar programs designed to facilitate re-entry into the workforce upon release. While on-site programs are preferred, correctional authorities without resources for on-site classes should offer access to correspondence courses, online educational opportunities, or programs conducted by outside agencies. Correctional authorities should actively encourage prisoner participation in appropriate educational programs.

d) A correctional facility should have or provide adequate access to a library for the use of all prisoners, adequately stocked with a wide range of both recreational and educational resources, books, current newspapers, and other periodicals. Prisoners should also have regular access to a variety of broadcast media to enable them to remain informed about public affairs.

e) Correctional officials should provide programming and activities appropriate for specific types of prisoners, including female prisoners, prisoners who face language or communication barriers or have physical or mental disabilities, prisoners who are under the age of eighteen or geriatric, and prisoners who are serving long sentences or are assigned to segregated housing for extended periods of time.

f) Correctional authorities should permit each prisoner to take full advantage of available opportunities to earn credit toward the prisoner's sentence through participation in work, education, treatment, and other programming.

Standard 23-8.3 Restorative justice

a. Governmental and correctional authorities should facilitate programs that allow crime victims to speak to groups of prisoners, and, at the request of a crime victim and with the consent of the prisoner, appropriate meetings or mediation between prisoners and their victims.

b. Consistent with security needs, correctional officials should provide opportunities for prisoners to contribute to the community through volunteer activities.

Standard 23-8.4 Work programs

a) Each sentenced prisoner should be employed substantially full-time unless there has been an individualized determination that no work assignment for that prisoner is consistent with security and safety. Substantial educational or rehabilitative programs can substitute for employment of the same duration. Whenever practicable, pretrial detainees should also be offered opportunities to work. Correctional authorities should be permitted to assign prisoners to community service; to jobs in prison industry programs; or to jobs useful for the operation of the facility, including cleaning, food service, maintenance, and agricultural programs. Prisoners' work assignments, including community service assignments, should teach vocational skills that will assist them in finding employment upon release, should instill a work ethic, and should respect prisoners' human dignity. To promote occupational training for prisoners, work release programs should be used when appropriate.

b) Prisoners' job assignments should not discriminate on the basis of race, national origin, ethnicity, religion, or disability. Correctional authorities should make reasonable accommodations for religion and disability with respect to job requirements and sites. Correctional authorities should provide female prisoners job opportunities reasonably similar in nature and scope to those provided male prisoners.

c) Prisoners should work under health and safety conditions substantially the same as those that prevail in similar types of employment in the free community, except to the extent that security requires otherwise. No prisoner should be shackled during a work assignment except after an individualized determination that security requires otherwise. Prisoners should not be required to work more than 40 hours each week, and should he afforded at least one rest day each week and sufficient time apart from work for education and other activities.

d) Prisoners employed by a correctional facility should be compensated in order to create incentives that encourage work habits and attitudes suitable for post-release employment.

e) Correctional officials should be permitted to contract with private enterprises to establish industrial and service programs to employ prisoners within a correctional facility, and goods and services produced should be permitted to freely enter interstate commerce. If such enterprises are for-profit firms, prisoners should he paid at least minimum wage for their work.

Standard 23-8.5 Visiting

a) To the extent practicable, a prisoner should be assigned to a facility located within a reasonable distance of the prisoner's family or usual residence in order to promote regular visitation by family members and to enhance the likelihood of successful reintegration.

b) Correctional officials should implement visitation policies that assist prisoners in maintaining and developing healthy family relationships by:

- providing sufficient and appropriate space and facilities for visiting;
- establishing reasonable visiting hours that are convenient and suitable for visitors, including time on weekends, evenings, and holidays; and
- implementing policies and programs that facilitate healthy interactions between prisoners and their families, including their minor children.

c) Correctional authorities should treat all visitors respectfully and should accommodate their visits to the extent practicable, especially when they have traveled a significant distance. Prisoners should be allowed to receive any visitor not excluded by correctional officials for good cause. Visitors should not be excluded solely because of 0 prior criminal conviction, although correctional authorities should be permitted to exclude a visitor if exclusion is reasonable in light of the conduct underlying the visitor's conviction. Correctional authorities should be permitted to subject all visitors to nonintrusive types of body searches such as pat-down and metal-detector-aided searches, and to search property visitors bring inside a correctional facility.

d) Visiting periods should be of adequate length. Visits with counsel and clergy should not be counted as visiting time, and ordinarily should be unlimited in frequency. Pretrial detainees should be allowed visiting opportunities beyond those afforded convicted prisoners, subject only to reasonable institutional restrictions and physical plant constraints.

e) For prisoners whose confinement extends more than [30 days], correctional authorities should allow contact visits between prisoners and their visitors, especially minor children, absent an individualized determination that a contact visit between a particular prisoner and a particular visitor poses a danger to a criminal investigation or trial, institutional security, or the safety of any person. If contact visits are precluded because of such an individualized determination, non-contact, in-person visiting opportunities should be allowed, absent an individualized determination that a non-contact visit between the prisoner and a particular visitor poses like dangers. Correctional officials should develop and promote other forms of communication between prisoners and their families, including video visitation, provided that such options are not a replacement for opportunities for in-person contact.

f) Correctional officials should facilitate and promote visiting by providing visitors travel guidance, directions, and information about visiting hours, attire, and other rules. If public transportation to a correctional facility is not available, correctional officials should work with transportation authorities to facilitate the provision of such transportation.

g) Governmental authorities should establish home furlough programs, giving due regard to institutional security and community safety, to enable prisoners to maintain and strengthen family and community ties. Correctional officials should allow a prisoner not receiving home furloughs to have extended visits with the prisoner's family in suitable settings, absent an individualized determination that such an extended visit would pose a threat to safety or security.

h) When practicable, giving due regard to security, public safety, and budgetary constraints, correctional officials should authorize prisoners to leave a correctional facility for compelling humanitarian reasons, such as a visit to a dying parent, spouse, or child, either under escort or alone.

Standard 23-8.6 Written communications

a) Correctional authorities should allow prisoners to communicate as frequently as practicable in writing with their families, friends, and representatives of outside organizations, including media organizations. Indigent prisoners should be provided a reasonable amount of stationery and free postage or some reasonable alternative that permits them to maintain contact with people and organizations in the community. Correctional policies regarding electronic communication by prisoners should consider public safety, institutional security, and prisoners' interest in ready communication.

b) Correctional authorities should allow prisoners to receive or access magazines, soft- or hard-cover books, newspapers, and other written materials, including documents printed from the Internet, subject to the restrictions in subdivisions (c) and (d) of this Standard.

c) Correctional authorities should be permitted to monitor and restrict both outgoing and incoming written communications and materials to the extent necessary for maintenance of institutional order, safety, and security; prevention of criminal offenses; continuing criminal investigations; and protection of victims of crime. Correctional officials should be permitted to impose reasonable page limits and limitations on receipt of bound materials from sources other than their publisher, but should not require that items be mailed using particular rates or particular means of payment. Correctional officials should set forth any applicable restrictions in a written policy.

d) Correctional authorities should be permitted to open and inspect an envelope, package, or container sent to or by a prisoner to determine if it contains contraband or other prohibited material, subject to the restrictions set forth in these Standards on inspection of mail to or from counsel.

e) A prisoner should be informed if correctional authorities deny the prisoner permission to send or receive any publication or piece of correspondence and should be told the basis for the denial and afforded an opportunity to appeal the denial to an impartial correctional administrator. If a publication or piece of correspondence contains material in violation of the facility's written guidelines, correctional authorities should make reasonable efforts to deny only those segregable portions of the publication or correspondence that present concerns.

Standard 23-8.7 Access to telephones

a) Correctional authorities should afford prisoners a reasonable opportunity to maintain telephonic communication with people and organizations in the community, and a correctional facility should offer telephone services with an appropriate range of options at the lowest possible rate, taking into account security needs. Commissions and other revenue from telephone service should not subsidize non-telephone prison programs or other public expenses.

b) Correctional authorities should provide prisoners with hearing or speech impairments ready access to telecommunications devices for the deaf or comparable equipment and to telephones with volume control, and should facilitate prisoners' telephonic communication with persons in the community who have such disabilities.

c) Correctional authorities should be permitted to monitor or record telephonic communications subject to the restrictions set forth in these Standards relating to communications with counsel and confidential communications with external monitoring agencies. Correctional authorities should inform prisoners that their conversations may be monitored, and should not monitor or record conversations for purposes of harassment or retaliation.

Standard 23-8.8 Fees and financial obligations

a) Unless a court orders otherwise in a situation in which a prisoner possesses substantial assets, correctional authorities should not charge prisoners fees for any non-commissary services provided them during the period of imprisonment, including their food or housing or incarceration itself, except that correctional authorities should be permitted to assess prisoners employed at or above minimum wage a reasonable portion of their wages in applicable fees.

b) In imposing and enforcing financial obligations on prisoners, governmental authorities, including courts, should consider both the interest served by the imposition of the obligation and the cumulative effect of financial obligations on a prisoner's successful and law-abiding re-entry.

Standard 23-8.9 Transition to the community

a) Governmental officials should ensure that each sentenced prisoner confined for more than [6 months] spends a reasonable part of the final portion of the term of imprisonment under conditions that afford the prisoner a reasonable opportunity to adjust to and prepare for re-entry into the community. A correctional agency should provide community-based transitional facilities to assist in this reintegration process.

b) In the months prior to anticipate release of a sentenced prisoner confined for more than [6 months], correctional authorities should develop an individualized re-entry plan for the prisoner, which should take into account the individualized programming plan developed pursuant to Standard 23-.2(h). In developing the re-entry plan, correctional authorities should involve any agency with supervisory authority over the prisoner in the community and, with the prisoner's permission, should invite involvement by the prisoner's family. Preparation for re-entry should include assistance in locating housing, identifying and finding job opportunities, developing a resume and learning interviewing skills, debt counseling, and developing or resuming healthy family relationships.

c) Correctional authorities should provide each prisoner released to the community with a written health care discharge plan that identifies medical and mental health services available to the prisoner in the community. The plan should describe the course of treatment provided the prisoner in the facility and any medical, dental, or mental health problems that may need follow-up attention in the community.

d) When a prisoner with ongoing medical or mental health care needs is released to the community, correctional authorities should make reasonable efforts to:

• identify and arrange for community-based health care services, including substance abuse treatment: and

451

- ensure that all health care treatment and medications provided to the prisoner during the term of imprisonment will continue uninterrupted, including, if necessary, providing prescription medication or medical equipment for a brief period reasonably necessary to obtain access to health care services in the community; providing initial medically necessary transportation from the correctional facility to a community health care facility for continuing treatment; or otherwise addressing the prisoner's serious immediate post-release health care needs.

e) Correctional authorities should provide each convicted prisoner being released to the community with:

- specific information about when and how to contact any agency having supervisory responsibility for the prisoner in the community;
- general information about the collateral sanctions and disqualifications that may apply because of the prisoner's conviction, and where to get more details; and
- general information about the process for obtaining relief from such sanctions and disqualifications, and contact information for government or nonprofit organizations, if any, offering assistance to individuals seeking such relief.

f) Whenever possible, prisoners should be released from a correctional facility at a reasonable time of day. Each prisoner should have or be provided with transportation to the prisoner's reasonable destination and with contact information for all relevant community service providers. Upon release, each prisoner who was confined for more than [3 months] should possess or be provided with:

- photographic identification sufficient to obtain lawful employment;

- clothing appropriate for the season
- sufficient money or its equivalent necessary for maintenance during a brief period immediately following release; and
- a voter registration card or general instructions on how to register to vote, if eligible to vote upon release.

g) When public safety and the interests of justice would not be compromised, governmental authorities should provide judicial and administrative mechanisms to accomplish the early release of prisoners in exceptional circumstances, such as terminal illness, permanent disability that substantially diminishes the ability of the prisoner to provide self-care within a correctional facility, or exigent family circumstances.

h) Governmental authorities should implement policies that allow government benefits, including health benefits, to be restored to prisoners immediately upon release, and correctional officials should ensure that correctional authorities or community service providers assist prisoners—especially prisoners with mental disabilities or significant health care needs— in preparing and submitting appropriate benefits applications sufficiently in advance of their anticipated release date to meet this objective and facilitate continuity of care.

PART IX: Grievances and Access to Courts

Standard 23-9.1 Grievance procedures

a) Correctional administrators and officials should authorize and encourage resolution of prisoners' complaints and requests on an informal basis whenever possible.

b) Correctional officials should provide prisoners opportunities to make suggestions to improve correctional programs and conditions.

c) Correctional administrators and officials should adopt a formal procedure for resolving specific prisoner grievances, including any complaint relating to the agency's or facility's policies, rules, practices, and procedures or the action of any correctional official or staff. Prisoners should be informed of this procedure pursuant to Standard 23-4.1, including any applicable timeframes or other bases for rejecting a grievance on procedural grounds.

d) Correctional officials should minimize technical requirements for grievances and should allow prisoners to initiate the grievance process by describing briefly the nature of the complaint and the remedy sought. Grievances should be rejected as procedurally improper only for a reason stated in the written grievance policy made available to prisoners. If correctional officials elect to require use of a particular grievance form, correctional authorities should make forms and writing implements readily available and should allow a grievant to proceed without using the designated form if it was not readily available to that prisoner.

e) A correctional agency's grievance procedure should he designed to instill the confidence of prisoners and correctional authorities in the effectiveness of the process, and its success in this regard should he periodically evaluated. Procedural protections for prisoners should include, at a minimum:

- access for all prisoners, with safeguards against reprisal;
- methods for confidential submission of grievances;
- reasonable filing and appeal deadlines;
- acceptance of grievances submitted or appealed outside the reasonable deadlines, if a prisoner has a

legitimate reason for delay and that delay has not significantly impaired the agency's ability to resolve the grievance;

- written responses to all grievances, including those deemed procedurally improper, stating the reasons for the decision, within prescribed, reasonable time limits;
- shortened time limits the responses to emergencies;
- an appeal process that allows no more than [70 days]. cumulatively, for official response(s) to all levels of appeal except if a correctional official extends the period upon an individualized finding of special circumstances;
- treatment of any grievance or appeal as denied, for purposes of the prisoner's subsequent appeal or review, if the prisoner is not provided a written response within the relevant time limit; and
- an appropriate individual and, when appropriate, systemic remedy if the grievance is determined to be well-founded.

Standard 23-9.2 Access to the judicial process

a) Governmental officials should assure prisoners full access to the judicial process.
b) Prisoners' access to the judicial process should not he restricted by the nature of the action or the relief sought, the phase of litigation involved, or the likelihood of success of the action, except if like restrictions, including filing fees, are imposed on non-prisoners. Prisoners should be entitled to present any judicially cognizable issue, including:
- challenges to the legality of their conviction, confinement, extradition, deportation. or removal;

- assertions of any rights protected by state or federal constitution, statute, administrative provision, treaty, or common law;
- civil legal problems, including those related to family law; and
- assertions of a defense to any action brought against them.

c) The handbook required by Standard 23-4.1 should advise prisoners about the potential legal consequences of a failure to use the institutional grievance procedures.

d) A prisoner who files a lawsuit with respect to prison conditions but has not exhausted administrative remedies at the time the lawsuit is filed should be permitted to pursue the claim through the grievance process, with the lawsuit stayed for up to [90 days] pending the administrative processing of the claim, after which a prisoner who filed a grievance during the period of the stay should be allowed to proceed with the lawsuit without any procedural bar.

e) Upon request by a court, correctional authorities should facilitate a prisoner's participation—in person or using telecommunications technology—in legal proceedings.

f) A prisoner should be allowed to prepare, receive, and send legal documents to courts, counsel, and public officials. Correctional officials should not unreasonably delay the delivery of these legal documents.

g) Courts should be permitted to implement rules to protect defendants and courts from vexatious litigation, but governmental authorities should not retaliate against a prisoner who brings an action in court or otherwise exercises a legal right.

Standard 23-9.3 Judicial review of prisoner complaints

a) Judicial procedures should be available to facilitate timely resolution of disputes involving the legality, duration, or conditions of confinement.
b) When determining whether a pleading or other court filing has stated a legally cognizable claim or complied with other requirements, courts should take into account the challenges faced by pro se prisoners.
c) Prisoners should not be required to demonstrate a physical injury in order to recover for mental or emotional injuries caused by cruel and unusual punishment or other illegal conduct.
d) Courts should have the same equitable authority in cases involving challenges to conditions of confinement as in other civil rights cases.

Standard 23-9.4 Access to legal and consular services

a) Correctional authorities should facilitate prisoners' access to counsel. The provisions of this Standard applicable to counsel apply equally to consular officials for prisoners who are not United States citizens.
b) A prisoner with a criminal charge or removal action pending should be housed in a correctional facility sufficiently near the courthouse where the case will be heard that the preparation of the prisoner's defense is not unreasonably impaired.
c) Correctional authorities should implement policies and practices to enable a prisoner's confidential contact and communication with counsel that incorporate the following provisions:
• For letters or other documents sent or passed between counsel and a prisoner:

A. correctional authorities should not read the letter or document, and should search only for physical contraband; and

B. correctional authorities should conduct such a search only in the presence of the prisoner to or from whom the letter or document is addressed.

- For meetings between counsel and a prisoner:

A. absent an individualized finding that security requires otherwise, counsel should be allowed to have direct contact with a prisoner who is a client, prospective client, or witness, and should not be required to communicate with such a prisoner through a glass or other barrier;

B. counsel should be allowed to meet with a prisoner in a setting where their conversation cannot be overheard by staff or other prisoners;

C. meetings or conversations between counsel and a prisoner should not be audio recorded by correctional authorities;

D. during a meeting with a prisoner, counsel should be allowed to pass previously searched papers to and from the prisoner without intermediate handling of those papers by correctional authorities;

E. correctional authorities should be allowed to search a prisoner before and after such a meeting for physical contraband, including by performing a visual search of a prisoner's private bodily areas that complies with Standard 23-7.9;

F. rules governing counsel visits should be as flexible as practicable in allowing counsel adequate time to meet with a prisoner who is a client, prospective client, or witness, including such a prisoner who is for any reason in a segregated housing area, and should allow meetings to occur at any reasonable time of day or day of the week; and

G. the time a prisoner spends meeting with counsel should not count as personal visiting time.

- telephonic contact between counsel and their clients
- correctional officials should implement procedures to enable confidential telephonic contact between counsel and a prisoner who is a client, prospective client, or witness, subject to reasonable regulations, and should not monitor or record properly placed telephone conversations between counsel and such a prisoner: and
- the time a prisoner spends speaking on the telephone with counsel should not count against any applicable maximum telephone time.

(d) The right of access to counsel described in subdivisions (a) and (c) of this Standard should apply in connection with all legal matters, regardless of the type or subject matter of the representation or whether litigation is pending or the representation has commenced.

(e) Governmental authorities should allow a prisoner to engage counsel of the prisoner's choice when the prisoner is able to do so.

(f) Rules governing attorney's fees and their recovery should be the same for prisoners as for non-prisoners

(g) Government legal services should be available to prisoners to the same extent they are available to non-prisoners. Government-funded legal services organizations should be permitted to provide legal services to prisoners without limitation as to the subject matter or the nature of the relief sought. The relationship between a prisoner and a person providing legal assistance under this subdivision should he governed by applicable ethical rules protecting the attorney-client relationship.

Standard 23-9.5 Access to legal materials and information

a) A correctional facility should provide prisoners reasonable access to updated legal research resources relevant to prisoners' common legal needs, including an appropriate collection of primary legal materials, secondary resources such as treatises and self-help manuals, applicable court rules, and legal forms. Access to these legal resources should be provided either in a law library or in electronic form, and should be available even to those prisoners who have access to legal services. Correctional authorities should be permitted to regulate the time, place, and manner of prisoners' access to these resources for purposes of facility security and scheduling, but prisoners should have regular and sufficient access, without interference with the prisoners' ability to eat meals, work, receive health care, receive visits, or attend required treatment or educational programming. Prisoners who are unable to access library resources because of housing restrictions, language or reading skills, or for other reasons, should have access to an effective alternative to such access, including the provision of counsel, or of prisoners or non-prisoners trained in the law.

b) Prison officials should provide programs for the education and training of prisoners who can help other prisoners with legal matters.

c) Correctional authorities should allow prisoners to purchase or, if they are indigent, to receive without charge materials to support their communications with court-attorneys, and public officials. These materials should include paper writing implements, envelopes, and stamps. Correctional authorities should provide access to copying services, for which a reasonable fee should be permitted, and should provide prisoners with access to typewriters or word processing equipment.

d) Correctional authorities should allow prisoners to acquire personal law books and other legal research material and to prepare and retain legal documents. Regulations relating to the storage of legal material in personal quarters or other areas should be only for purposes of safety or security and should not unreasonably interfere with access to or use of these materials.

e) Correctional authorities should not read, censor, alter, or destroy a prisoner's legal materials. Correctional authorities should be permitted to examine legal materials received or retained by a prisoner for physical contraband. If correctional authorities have a reasonable suspicion that a prisoner's legal materials contain non-legal material that violates written policy, they should be permitted to read the materials only to the extent necessary to determine whether they are legal in nature.

PART X: Administration and Staffing

Standard 23-10.1 Professionalism

a) A correctional agency should have a clear written statement of its mission and core values. Established professional standards should serve as the basis for an agency's operating policies and procedures.

b) Correctional administrators and officials should foster an institutional culture that helps maintain a safe and secure facility, is conducive to humane and respectful treatment of prisoners, supports adherence to professional standards, and encourages ethical conduct.

c) To effectuate rehabilitative goals, correctional staff members should have rehabilitative responsibilities in addition to custodial functions. In their interactions with prisoners, they should model fair, respectful, and constructive behavior; engage in preventive problem-solving; and rely upon effective communication.

d) If a correctional staff member discovers a breach of security; a threat to prisoner, staff, or public safety; or some other actual or threatened harm to a prisoner, staff, or the public, the correctional staff member should report that discovery promptly to a supervisor. A staff member should report any information relating to corrupt or criminal conduct by other staff directly to the chief executive officer of the facility or to an independent government official with responsibility to investigate correctional misconduct, and should provide any investigator with full and candid information about observed misconduct.

Standard 23-10.2 Personnel policy and practice

a. A correctional agency and facility should be appropriately staffed to promote safety for all staff and prisoners and allow the full operation of all programs and services and a reasonable work schedule for each staff member. Salaries and benefits should be sufficient to attract and retain qualified staff.

b. Correctional administrators and officials should implement recruitment and selection processes that will ensure that staff are professionally qualified, psychologically fit to work with prisoners, and certified or licensed as appropriate.

c. Correctional administrators and officials should strive to employ a work force at each correctional facility that reasonably reflects the racial and ethnic demographics of the prisoner population by engaging in outreach and recruiting efforts to increase the pool of qualified applicants from underrepresented groups

462

and by implementing appropriate retention policies. Each correctional facility should employ sufficient numbers of men and women to comply with Standard 23-7.10.

d. Correctional staff should be provided with safe and healthful working conditions. They should have opportunities to make suggestions and express concerns, develop innovative practices, and contribute to the agency's institutional planning process.

Standard 23-10.3 Training

a) For all staff, correctional administrators and officials should integrate training relating to the mission and core values of the correctional agency with technical training.

b) Correctional administrators should require staff to participate in a comprehensive pre-service training program, a regular program of in-service training, and specialized training when appropriate. Training programs should equip staff to:

- maintain order while treating prisoners with respect, and communicate effectively with prisoners;
- follow security requirements, conduct searches, and use technology appropriately;
- use non-force techniques for avoiding and resolving conflicts, and comply with the agency's policy on use of force;
- identify and respond to medical and mental health emergencies, recognize and report the signs and symptoms of mental disability and suicide risk, and secure appropriate medical and mental health services;

c) detect and respond to signs of threatened and actual physical and sexual assault and sexual pressure against prisoners;

- avoid inappropriate relationships, including sexual contact, with prisoners;
- understand the legal rights of prisoners relevant to their professional duties;
- facilitate prisoner use of the grievance process, and understand that process's benefits for correctional staff and facilities;
- maintain appropriate records, including clear and accurate reports; and
- perform the above functions in a way that promotes the health and safety of staff.

a) Correctional administrators and officials should provide specialized training to staff who work with specific types of prisoners to address the physical, social, and psychological needs of such prisoners, including female prisoners, prisoners who face language or communication barriers or have physical or mental disabilities, prisoners who are under the age of eighteen or geriatric, and prisoners who are serving long sentences or are assigned to segregated housing for extended periods of time.

b) Correctional administrators and officials should provide training to volunteers about how to avoid and report inappropriate conduct.

Standard 23-10.4 Accountability of staff

a) A correctional agency should have clear rules of conduct for staff and guidelines for disciplinary sanctions, including progressive sanctions for repeated misconduct involving prisoners. The chief executive of the facility or a higher-ranking correctional administrator should receive reports of all cases in which staff are found to have engaged in misconduct involving prisoners and should have final responsibility for determining the appropriate sanction.

b) If correctional officials determine that an allegation of serious misconduct involving a prisoner is credible, the staff member who is the subject of the allegation should be promptly removed from a position of trust and placed either on administrative leave or in a position that does not involve contact with prisoners or supervision of others who have contact with prisoners, pending resolution of the matter. A final determination of serious misconduct involving a prisoner should result in termination of the employment of the staff member and should be reported to relevant law enforcement and licensing agencies.

c) Correctional officials should require all correctional staff arrested or charged with a misdemeanor or felony to report that fact promptly.

Standard 23-10.5 Privately operated correctional facilities

a) Contracts with private corporations or other private entities for the operation of a secure correctional facility should be disfavored. Governmental authorities should make every effort to house all prisoners in need of secure confinement in publicly operated correctional facilities.

b) Governmental authorities should not enter into a contract with a private entity for the operation of any correctional facility, secure or not, unless it can be demonstrated that the contract will result either in improved performance or in substantial cost savings, considering both routine and emergency costs, with no diminution in performance.

c) A jurisdiction that enters into a contract with a private entity for the operation of a correctional facility should maintain the ability to house its prisoners in other facilities if termination of the contract for noncompliance proves necessary. Each jurisdiction should develop a comprehensive plan, in advance of entering into any contract, to ensure that this ability remains.

d) Laws, policies, administrative rules, standards, and reporting requirements applicable to publicly operated correctional facilities of similar security levels in the contracting jurisdiction, including those applicable to staff qualifications and training, freedom of information demands and disclosures, and external oversight, should apply in substance to a privately operated facility either as a matter of statutory law or as incorporated contract terms.

e) Core correctional functions of determining the length and location of a prisoner's confinement, including decisions relating to prisoner discipline, transfer, length of imprisonment, and temporary or permanent release, should never be delegated to a private entity.

f) Any contract by which a private entity operates a correctional facility should include terms that comport with the following restrictions:

g) (g) Any jurisdiction that enters into a contract with a private corporation or entity for the operation of a correctional facility should implement procedures to monitor compliance with that contract systematically, regularly, and using a variety of on- and off-site monitoring techniques, including reviewing files and records, physically inspecting the facility, and interviewing staff and prisoners.

h) (h) Except in an emergency, such as a natural disaster, no prisoner of a state or local correctional agency should be sent out of state to a private facility pursuant to a contract unless there has been an individualized determination that security of the system or the prisoner requires it, or that the prisoner and the prisoner's individualized programming plan and individualized re-entry plan will not be significantly adversely affected by the move. A contracting agency should make provision for on-site monitoring of each location to which prisoners are sent.

PART XI: Accountability and Oversight

Standard 23-11.1 Internal accountability

a) A correctional agency should establish an independent internal audit unit to conduct regular performance auditing and to advise correctional administrators on compliance with established performance indicators, standards, policies, and other internal controls.

b) A correctional agency should designate an internal unit, answerable to the head of the agency, to be responsible for investigating allegations of serious staff misconduct, including misconduct against prisoners, and for referring appropriate cases for administrative disciplinary measures or criminal prosecution.

c) If a correctional agency contracts for provision of any services or programs, it should ensure that the contract requires the provider to comply with these Standards, including Standard 23-9.1 governing grievances. The agency should implement a system to monitor compliance with the contract, and to hold the contracted provider accountable for any deficiencies.

d) Correctional administrators and officials should seek accreditation of their facilities and certification of staff from national organizations whose standards reflect best practices in corrections or in correctional sub-specialties.

e) Correctional administrators and officials should regularly review use of force reports, serious incident reports, and grievances, and take any necessary remedial action to address systemic problems.

f) Correctional administrators should routinely collect, analyze, and publish statistical information on agency operations including security incidents, sexual assaults, prisoner grievances, uses of force, health and safety, spending on programs and services, program participation and outcomes, staffing, and employee discipline.

g) Correctional administrators and officials should evaluate short and long-term outcomes of programs provided to prisoners and, where permitted by applicable law, should make the evaluations and any underlying aggregated data available upon request to researchers, investigators, and media representatives.

h) Correctional agencies should work together to develop uniform national definitions and methods of defining, collecting, and reporting accurate and complete data.

i) Governmental authorities should not exempt correctional agencies from their jurisdiction's Administrative Procedure Act, Freedom of Information Act, or Public Records Act.

Standard 23-11.2 External regulation and investigation

a) Independent governmental bodies responsible for such matters as fire safety, sanitation, environmental quality, food safety, education, and health should regulate, inspect, and enforce regulations in a correctional facility. A correctional facility should be subject to the same enforcement penalties and procedures, including abatement procedures for noncompliance, as are applicable to other institutions.

b) Governmental authorities should authorize and fund an official or officials independent of each correctional agency to investigate the acts of correctional authorities, allegations of mistreatment of prisoners, and complaints about conditions in correctional facilities, including complaints by prisoners, their families, and members of the community, and to refer appropriate cases for administrative disciplinary measures or criminal prosecutions.

c) When federal or state law authorizes a governmental or non-governmental agency or organization to conduct an investigation relating to a correctional facility, correctional officials should allow that agency or organization convenient and complete access to the facility and should cooperate fully in the investigation.

d) When a prisoner dies, correctional officials should promptly notify the jurisdiction's medical examiner of the death and its circumstances; the medical examiner should decide whether an autopsy should be conducted. Where authorized by law, a correctional official should also be permitted to order an autopsy.

e) Correctional officials should encourage and accommodate visits by judges and lawmakers and by members of faith-based groups, the business community, institutions of higher learning, and other groups interested in correctional issues.

Standard 23-11.3 External monitoring and inspection

a) Governmental authorities should authorize and fund a governmental agency independent of each jurisdiction's correctional agency to conduct regular monitoring and inspection of the correctional facilities in that jurisdiction and to issue timely public reports about conditions and practices in those facilities. This agency, which should be permitted to be the same entity responsible for investigations conducted pursuant to Standard 23-11.2(b), should anticipate and detect systemic problems affecting prisoners, monitor issues of continuing concern, identify best practices within facilities, and make recommendations for improvement.

b) Monitoring teams should possess expertise in a wide variety of disciplines relevant to correctional agencies. They should receive authority to:

- examine every part of every facility;
- visit without prior notice;
- conduct confidential interviews with prisoners and staff; and
- review all records, except that special procedures may be implemented for highly confidential information.

c) A correctional agency should he required to respond in a public document to the findings of the monitoring agency, to develop an action plan to address identified problems, and to periodically document compliance with recommendations or explain noncompliance: however, if security requires, the public document should be permitted to be supplemented by a confidential one.

d) The monitoring agency should continue to assess and report on previously identified problems and the progress made in resolving them until the problems are resolved.

Standard 23-11.4 Legislative oversight and accountability

a) Governmental authorities should enact legislation to implement and fund compliance with these Standards.
b) Legislative bodies should exercise vigorous oversight of corrections, including conducting regular hearings and visits. Correctional authorities should allow legislators who sit on correctional oversight committees to speak privately with staff and prisoners.
c) Each state legislature should establish an authority to promulgate and enforce standards applicable to jails and local detention facilities in the state.
d) Governmental authorities should prepare a financial and correctional impact statement to accompany any proposed criminal justice legislation that would affect the size, demographics, or requirements of the jurisdiction's prison and jail populations, and should periodically assess the extent to which criminal justice legislation is achieving positive results.

Standard 23-11.5 Media access to correctional facilities and prisoners

a) Correctional administrators should develop agency media access policies and make them readily available to the public in written form. Correctional authorities should generally accommodate professionally accredited journalists who request permission to visit a facility or a prisoner, and should provide a process for expeditious appeal if a request is denied.
b) Prisoners should have the right to refuse requests for interviews and should be notified of that right and

given an opportunity to consult with counsel, if they have counsel, prior to an interview.

c) Correctional authorities should allow professionally accredited journalists reasonable use of notebooks, writing implements, video and still cameras, and audio recorders.

d) The time, place, and manner of media visits should be reasonably regulated to preserve the privacy and dignity of prisoners and the security and order of the facility.

e) Correctional authorities should not retaliate against a prisoner for that prisoner's lawful communication with a member of the media.

Education! Money-Making Opportunities! Resources for Prison Writers, Poets, Artists! And much, much more! Anything you can think of doing from your prison cell, this book contains the resources to do it!

A GUIDE TO RELAPSE PREVENTION FOR PRISONERS, $15.00 & $5.00 S/H: This book provides the information and guidance that can make a real difference in the preparation of a comprehensive relapse prevention plan. Discover how to meet the parole board's expectation using these proven and practical principles. Included is a blank template and sample relapse prevention plan to assist in your preparation.

THEE ENEMY OF THE STATE (SPECIAL EDITION), $9.99 & $4.00 S/H: Experience the inspirational journey of a kid who was introduced to the art of rapping in 1993, struggled between his dream of becoming a professional rapper and the reality of the streets, and was finally offered a recording deal in 1999, only to be arrested minutes later and eventually sentenced to life in prison for murder... However, despite his harsh reality, he dedicated himself to hip-hop once again, and with resilience and determination, he sets out to prove he may just be one of the dopest rhyme writers/spitters ever .... At this point, it becomes deeper than rap .... Welcome to a preview of the greatest story you never heard.

LOST ANGELS: $15.00 & $5.00: David Rodrigo was a child who belonged to no world; rejected for his mixed heritage by most of his family and raised by an outcast uncle in the mean streets of East L.A. Chance cast him into a far darker and more devious pit of intrigue that stretched from the barest gutters to the halls of power in the great city. Now, to survive the clash of lethal forces arrayed about him, and to protect those he loves, he has only two allies; his quick wits, and the flashing blade that earned young David the street name, Viper.

LOYALTY AND BETRAYAL DELUXE EDITION, $19.99 & $7.00 S/H: Chunky was an associate of and soldier for the notorious Mexican Mafia – La Eme. That is, of course, until he was betrayed by those, he was most loyal to. Then he vowed to become their worst enemy. And though they've attempted to kill him numerous times, he still to this day is running around making a mockery of their organization .... This is the story of how it all began.

MONEY IZ THE MOTIVE: SPECIAL 2-IN-1 EDITION, $19.99 & $7.00 S/H: Like most kids growing up in the hood, Kano has a dream of going from rags to riches. But when his plan to get fast money by robbing the local "mom and pop" shop goes wrong, he quickly finds himself sentenced to serious prison time. Follow Kano as he is schooled to the ways of the game by some of the most respected OGs whoever did it; then is set free and given the resources to put his schooling into action and build the ultimate hood empire...

DEVILS & DEMONS: PART 1, $15.00 & $5.00 S/H: When Talton leaves the West Coast to set up shop in Florida he meets the female version of himself: A

475

drug dealing murderess with psychological issues. A whirlwind of sex, money and murder inevitably ensues and Talton finds himself on the run from the law with nowhere to turn to. When his team from home finds out he's in trouble, they get on a plane heading south...

DEVILS & DEMONS: PART 2, $15.00 & $5.00 S/H: The Game is bitter-sweet for Talton, aka Gangsta. The same West Coast Clique who came to his aid ended up putting bullets into the chest of the woman he had fallen in love with. After leaving his ride or die in a puddle of her own blood, Talton finds himself on a flight back to Oak Park, the neighborhood where it all started...

DEVILS & DEMONS: PART 3, $15.00 & $5.00 S/H: Talton is on the road to retribution for the murder of the love of his life. Dante and his crew of killers are on a path of no return. This urban classic is based on real-life West Coast underworld politics. See what happens when a group of YG's find themselves in the midst of real underworld demons...

DEVILS & DEMONS: PART 4, $15.00 & $5.00 S/H: After waking up from a coma, Alize has locked herself away from the rest of the world. When her sister Brittany and their friend finally take her on a girl's night out, she meets Luck – a drug dealing womanizer.

FREAKY TALES, $15.00 & $5.00 S/H: *Freaky Tales* is the first book in a brand-new erotic series. King Guru, author of the *Devils & Demons* books, has put together a collection of sexy short stories and memoirs. In true TCB fashion, all of the erotic tales included in this book have been loosely based on true accounts told to, or experienced by the author.

THE ART & POWER OF LETTER WRITING FOR PRISONERS: DELUXE EDITION $19.99 & $7.00 S/H: When locked inside a prison cell, being able to write well is the most powerful skill you can have! Learn how to increase your power by writing high-quality personal and formal letters! Includes letter templates, pen-pal website strategies, punctuation guide and more!

THE PRISON MANUAL: $24.99 & $7.00 S/H: *The Prison Manual* is your all-in-one book on how to not only survive the rough terrain of the American prison system, but use it to your advantage so you can THRIVE from it! How to Use Your Prison Time to YOUR Advantage; How to Write Letters that Will Give You Maximum Effectiveness; Workout and Physical Health Secrets that Will Keep You as FIT as Possible; The Psychological impact of incarceration and How to Maintain Your MAXIMUM Level of Mental Health; Prison Art Techniques; Fulfilling Food Recipes; Parole Preparation Strategies and much, MUCH more!

GET OUT, STAY OUT!, $16.95 & $5.00 S/H: This book should be in the hands of everyone in a prison cell. It reveals a challenging but clear course for overcoming the obstacles that stand between prisoners and their freedom. For those behind bars, one goal outshines all others: GETTING OUT! After being released, that goal then shifts to STAYING OUT! This book will help prisoners do both. It has been masterfully constructed into five parts that will help prisoners maximize focus while they strive to accomplish whichever goal is at hand.

MOB$TAR MONEY, $12.00 & $4.00 S/H: After Trey's mother is sent to prison for 75 years to life, he and his little brother are moved from their home in Sacramento, California, to his grandmother's house in Stockton, California where he is forced to find his way in life and become a man on his own in the city's grimy streets. One day, on his way home from the local corner store, Trey has a rough encounter with the neighborhood bully. Luckily, that's when Tyson, a member of the MOBTAR, a local "get money" gang comes to his aid. The two kids quickly become friends, and it doesn't take long before Trey is embraced into the notorious MOB$TAR money gang, which opens the door to an adventure full of sex, money, murder and mayhem that will change his life forever... You will never guess how this story ends!

BLOCK MONEY, $12.00 & $4.00 S/H: Beast, a young thug from the grimy streets of central Stockton, California lives The Block; breathes The Block; and has committed himself to bleed The Block for all it's worth until his very last breath. Then, one day, he meets Nadia; a stripper at the local club who piques his curiosity with her beauty, quick-witted intellect and rider qualities. The problem? She has a man – Esco – a local kingpin with money and power. It doesn't take long, however, before a devious plot is hatched to pull off a heist worth an indeterminable amount of money. Following the acts of treachery, deception and betrayal are twists and turns and a bloody war that will leave you speechless!

HOW TO HUSTLE & WIN: SEX, MONEY, MURDER EDITION $15.00 & $5.00 S/H: *How To Hu$tle & Win: Sex, Money, Murder Edition* is the grittiest, underground self-help manual for the 21st century street entrepreneur in print. Never has there been such a book written for today's gangsters, goons and go-getters. This self-help handbook is an absolute must-have for anyone who is actively connected to the streets.

RAW LAW: YOUR RIGHTS, & HOW TO SUE WHEN THEY ARE VIOLATED! $15.00 & $5.00 S/H: *Raw Law For Prisoners* is a clear and concise guide for prisoners and their advocates to understanding civil rights laws guaranteed to prisoners under the US Constitution, and how to successfully file a lawsuit when those rights have been violated! From initial complaint to trial, this book will take you through the entire process, step by step, in simple, easy-to-understand terms. Also included are several examples where prisoners have sued prison officials successfully, resulting in changes of unjust rules and regulations and recourse for rights violations, oftentimes resulting in rewards of thousands, even millions of dollars in damages! If you feel your rights have been violated, don't lash out at guards, which is usually ineffective and only makes matters worse. Instead, defend yourself successfully by using the legal system, and getting the power of the courts on your side!

HOW TO WRITE URBAN BOOKS FOR MONEY & FAME: $16.95 & $5.00 S/H: Inside this book you will learn the true story of how Mike Enemigo and King Guru have received money and fame from inside their prison cells by writing urban books; the secrets to writing hood classics so you, too, can be caked up and famous; proper punctuation using hood examples; and resources you can use to achieve your money motivated ambitions! If you're a prisoner who want to write urban novels for money and fame, this must-have manual will give you all the game!

PRETTY GIRLS LOVE BAD BOYS: AN INMATE'S GUIDE TO GETTING GIRLS: $15.00 & $5.00 S/H: Tired of the same, boring, cliché pen pal books that don't tell you what you really need to know? If so, this book is for you! Anything you need to know on the art of long and short distance seduction is included within these pages! Not only does it give you the science of attracting pen pals from websites, it also includes psychological profiles and instructions on how to seduce any woman you set your sights on! Includes interviews of women who have fallen in love with prisoners, bios for pen pal ads, pre-written love letters, romantic poems, love-song lyrics, jokes and much, much more! This book is the ultimate guide – a must-have for any prisoner who refuses to let prison walls affect their MAC'n.

THE LADIES WHO LOVE PRISONERS, $15.00 & $5.00 S/H: New Special Report reveals the secrets of real women who have fallen in love with prisoners, regardless of crime, sentence, or location. This info will give you a HUGE advantage in getting girls from prison.

THE MILLIONAIRE PRISONER: PART 1, $16.95 & $5.00 S/H

THE MILLIONAIRE PRISONER: PART 2, $16.95 & $5.00 S/H

THE MILLIONAIRE PRISONER: SPECIAL 2-IN-1 EDITION, $24.99 & $7.00 S/H: Why wait until you get out of prison to achieve your dreams? Here's a blueprint that you can use to become successful! *The Millionaire Prisoner* is your complete reference to overcoming any obstacle in prison. You won't be able to put it down! With this book you will discover the secrets to: Making money from your cell! Obtain FREE money for correspondence courses! Become an expert on any topic! Develop the habits of the rich! Network with celebrities! Set up your own website! Market your products, ideas and services! Successfully use prison pen pal websites! All of this and much, much more! This book has enabled thousands of prisoners to succeed and it will show you the way also!

THE MILLIONAIRE PRISONER 3: SUCCESS UNIVERSITY, $16.95 & $5 S/H: Why wait until you get out of prison to achieve your dreams? Here's a new-look blueprint that you can use to be successful! *The Millionaire Prisoner 3* contains advanced strategies to overcoming any obstacle in prison. You won't be able to put it down!

THE MILLIONAIRE PRISONER 4: PEN PAL MASTERY, $16.95 & $5.00 S/H: Tired of subpar results? Here's a master blueprint that you can use to get tons of pen pals! *TMP 4: Pen Pal Mastery* is your complete roadmap to finding your one true love. You won't be able to put it down! With this book you'll DISCOVER the SECRETS to: Get FREE pen pals & which sites are best to use; Successful tactics female prisoners can win with; Use astrology to find love; friendship & more; Build a winning social media presence; Playing phone tag & successful sex talk; Hidden benefits of foreign pen pals; Find your success mentors; Turning "hits" into friendships; Learn how to write letters/emails that get results. All of this and much more!

GET OUT, GET RICH: HOW TO GET PAID LEGALLY WHEN YOU GET OUT OF PRISON!, $16.95 & $5.00 S/H: Many of you are incarcerated for a money-motivated crime. But with today's tech and opportunities, not only is the crime-for-money risk/reward ratio not strategically wise, it's not even necessary. You can earn much more money by partaking in any one of the easy, legal hustles explained in this book, regardless of your record. Help yourself earn an honest income so you can not only make a lot of money, but say good-bye to penitentiary chances and prison forever! (Note: Many things in this book can even he done from inside prison.) (ALSO PUBLISHED AS *HOOD MILLIONAIRE: HOW TO HUSTLE AND WIN LEGALLY!*)

THE CEO MANUAL: HOW TO START A BUSINESS WHEN YOU GET OUT OF PRISON, $16.95 & $5.00 S/H: $16.95 & $5 S/H: This new book will teach you the simplest way to start your own business when you get out of prison. Includes: Start-up Steps! The Secrets to Pulling Money from Investors! How to Manage People Effectively! How To Legally Protect Your Assets from "them"! Hundreds of resources to get you started, including a list of "loan friendly" banks! (ALSO PUBLISHED AS *CEO MANUAL: START A BUSINESS, BE A BOSS!*)

THE MONEY MANUAL: UNDERGROUND CASH SECRETS EXPOSED! 16.95 & $5.00 S/H: Becoming a millionaire is equal parts what you make, and what you don't spend – AKA save. All Millionaires and Billionaires have mastered the art of not only making money, but keeping the money they make (remember Donald Trump's tax maneuvers?), as well as establishing credit so that they are loaned money by banks and trusted with money from investors: AKA OPM – other people's money. And did you know there are millionaires and billionaires just waiting to GIVE money away? It's true! These are all very-little known secrets "they" don't want YOU to know about, but that I'm exposing in my new book!

HOOD MILLIONAIRE; HOW TO HUSTLE & WIN LEGALLY, $16.95 & $5.00 S/H: Hustlin' is a way of life in the hood. We all have money motivated ambitions, not only because we gotta eat, but because status is oftentimes determined by one's own salary. To achieve what we consider financial success, we often invest our efforts into illicit activities – we take penitentiary chances. This leads to a life in and out of prison, sometimes death – both of which are counterproductive to gettin' money. But there's a solution to this, and I have it...

CEO MANUAL: START A BUSINESS BE A BOSS, $16.95 & $5.00 S/H: After the success of the urban-entrepreneur classic *Hood Millionaire: How To Hustle & Win Legally!*, self-made millionaires Mike Enemigo and Sav Hustle team back up to bring you the latest edition of the Hood Millionaire series – *CEO Manual: Start A Business, Be A Boss!* In this latest collection of game laying down the art of "hoodpreneurship", you will learn such things as: 5 Core Steps to Starting Your Own Business! 5 Common Launch Errors You Must Avoid! How To Write a Business Plan! How To Legally Protect Your Assets From "Them"! How To Make Your Business Fundable, Where to Get Money for Your Start-up Business, and even How to Start a Business With No Money! You will learn How to Drive Customers to Your Website, How to Maximize Marketing Dollars, Contract Secrets for the savvy boss, and much, much more! And as an added bonus, we have included over 200 Business Resources, from government agencies and small business development centers, to a secret list of small-business friendly banks that will help you get started!

PAID IN FULL: WELCOME TO DA GAME, $15.00 & $5.00 S/H. In 1983, the movie *Scarface* inspired many kids growing up in America's inner cities to turn their rags into riches by becoming cocaine kingpins. Harlem's Azie Faison was one of them. Faison would ultimately connect with Harlem's Rich Porter and Alpo Martinez, and the trio would go on to become certified street legends of the '80s and early '90s. Years later, Dame Dash and Roc-A-Fella Films would tell their story in the based-on-actual-events movie, *Paid in Full*. But now, we are telling the story our way – The Cell Block way – where you will get a perspective of the story that the movie did not show, ultimately learning an outcome that you did not expect. Book one of our series, *Paid in Full: Welcome to da Game*, will give you an inside look at a key player in this story, one that is not often talked about – Lulu, the Columbian cocaine kingpin with direct ties to Pablo Escobar, who plugged Azie in with an unlimited amount of top-tier cocaine at dirt-cheap prices that helped boost the trio to neighborhood superstars and certified kingpin status... until greed, betrayal, and murder destroyed everything....

OJ'S LIFE BEHIND BARS, $15.00 & $5 S/H: In 1994, Heisman Trophy winner and NFL superstar OJ Simpson was arrested for the brutal murder of his ex-wife Nicole Brown-Simpson and her friend Ron Goldman. In 1995, after the "trial of the century," he was acquitted of both murders, though most of the world believes he did it. In 2007 OJ was again arrested, but this time in Las Vegas, for armed robbery and kidnapping. On October 3, 2008 he was found guilty sentenced to 33 years and was sent to Lovelock Correctional Facility, in Lovelock, Nevada. There he met inmate-author Vernon Nelson. Vernon was granted a true, insider's perspective into the mind and life of one of the country's most notorious men; one that has never been provided...until now.

BLINDED BY BETRAYAL, $15.00 & $5.00 S/H. Khalil wanted nothing more than to chase his rap dream when he got out of prison. After all, a fellow inmate had connected him with a major record producer that could help him take his career to unimaginable heights, and his girl is in full support of his desire to trade in his gun for a mic. Problem is, Khalil's crew, the notorious Blood Money Squad, awaited him with open arms, unaware of his desire to leave the game alone, and expected him to jump head first into the life of fast money and murder. Will Khalil be able to balance his desire to get out of the game with the expectations of his gang to participate in it? Will he be able to pull away before it's too late? Or, will the streets pull him right back in, ultimately causing his demise? One thing for sure, the streets are loyal to no one, and blood money comes with bloody consequences....

THE MOB, $16.99 & $5 S/H. PaperBoy is a Bay Area boss who has invested blood, sweat, and years into building The Mob – a network of Bay Area Street legends, block bleeders, and underground rappers who collaborate nationwide in the interest of pushing a multi-million-dollar criminal enterprise of sex, drugs, and murder.

Based on actual events, little has been known about PaperBoy, the mastermind behind The Mob, and intricate details of its operation, until now.

Follow this story to learn about some of the Bay Area underworld's most glamorous figures and famous events...

AOB, $15.00 & $5 S/H. Growing up in the Bay Area, Manny Fresh the Best had a front-row seat to some of the coldest players to ever do it. And you already know, A.O.B. is the name of the Game! So, When Manny Fresh slides through Stockton one day and sees Rosa, a stupid-bad Mexican chick with a whole lotta 'talent' behind her walking down the street tryna get some money, he knew immediately what he had to do: Put it In My Pocket!

AOB 2, $15.00 & $5 S/H.

AOB 3, $15.00 & $5 S/H

PIMPOLOGY: THE 7 ISMS OF THE GAME, $15.00 & $5 S/H: It's been said that if you knew better, you'd do better. So, in the spirit of dropping jewels upon the rare few who truly want to know how to win, this collection of exclusive Game has been compiled. And though a lot of so-called players claim to know how the Pimp Game is supposed to go, none have revealed the real. . . Until now!

JAILHOUSE PUBLISHING FOR MONEY, POWER & FAME: $24.99 & $7 S/H: In 2010, after flirting with the idea for two years, Mike Enemigo started writing his first book. In 2014, he officially launched his publishing company, The Cell Block, with the release of five books. Of course, with no mentor(s), how-to guides, or any real resources, he was met with failure after failure as he tried to navigate the treacherous goal of publishing books from his prison cell. However, he was determined to make it. He was determined to figure it out and he refused to quit. In Mike's new book, *Jailhouse Publishing for Money, Power, and Fame,* he breaks down all his jailhouse publishing secrets and strategies, so you can do all he's done, but without the trials and tribulations he's had to go through...

KITTY KAT, ADULT ENTERTAINMENT RESOURCE BOOK, $24.99 & $7.00 S/H: This book is jam packed with hundreds of sexy non nude photos including photo spreads. The book contains the complete info on sexy photo sellers, hot magazines, page turning bookstore, sections on strip clubs, porn stars, alluring models, thought provoking stories and must-see movies.

PRISON LEGAL GUIDE, $24.99 & $7.00 S/H: The laws of the U.S. Judicial system are complex, complicated, and always growing and changing. Many prisoners spend days on end digging through its intricacies. Pile on top of the legal code the rules and regulations of a correctional facility, and you can see how high the deck is being stacked against you. Correct legal information is the key to your survival when you have run afoul of the system (or it is running afoul of you). Whether you are an accomplished jailhouse lawyer helping newbies learn the ropes, an old head fighting bare-knuckle for your rights in the courts, or a hustler just looking to beat the latest write-up – this book has something for you!

PRISON HEALTH HANDBOOK, $19.99 & $7.00 S/H: The *Prison Health Handbook* is your one-stop go-to source for information on how to maintain your best health while inside the American prison system. Filled with information, tips, and secrets from doctors, gurus, and other experts, this book will educate you on such things as proper workout and exercise regimens; yoga benefits for prisoners; how to meditate effectively; pain management tips; sensible dieting solutions; nutritional knowledge; an understanding of various cancers, diabetes, hepatitis, and other diseases all too common in prison; how to effectively deal with mental health issues such as stress, PTSD, anxiety, and depression; a list of things your doctors DON'T want YOU to know; and much, much more!

All books are available on thecellblock.net.

You can also order by sending a money order or institutional check to:

The Cell Block
PO Box 1025
Rancho Cordova, CA 95741

PRISON RIOT RADIO

Industry reps want to hear you!

Are you a rapper? We will upload your freestyles to our website, prisonriotradio.com, FREE for top industry execs to hear!

Pick up the phone and become a star!

We will record you on the phone! All raw freestyles will be recorded FREE. If you need a recording and a beat, the prices are below...

$25 Per Recording

$150 For 8 Recordings

$30 Per Beat

$10 For Cover Art

We accept songs, spoken word, podcasts and interviews! Learn the game and how to get your money!

For more information, to send material, or to set up a phone recording session, email prisonriotradio@gmail.com or jayrene@prisonriotradio@gmail.com.